Software Engineering

Principles, Practices and Modern Technologies

Software Engineering

Principles, Practices and Modern Technologies

Dr. Ramesh Kait

The Readers Paradise
New Delhi - 110002

Software Engineering: Principles, Practices and Modern Technologies

Dr. Ramesh Kait

ISBN - 978-93-5977-416-9

Published by

THE READERS PARADISE

103, 4787/23, Ansari Road, Daryaganj,
New Delhi - 110002
011-23246222, 9654444181, 8700415655
thereadersparadisesales@gmail.com

Price Rs. - 2995.00

Pages - 380 | Paper - 80gsm | Size - 7.5x9.5

Type Seeting : Shri Sai Computers, Delhi

Cover Design : Kamini Bijoria

Printed by : Trident Enterprises, Noida (U.P.)

Preface

In the ever-evolving field of software engineering, mastering both the foundational principles and advanced techniques is essential for success. This book, Mastering Software Engineering, aims to guide you through the essential concepts, tools, and methodologies that every software engineer must understand, while also preparing you for the challenges and opportunities that lie ahead in your career.

The content is divided into five parts, each focusing on a crucial aspect of software engineering. Whether you are just starting your journey or are already an experienced developer, this book is designed to offer both depth and breadth, enabling you to build a comprehensive understanding of the field.

Part 1: Foundations of Software Engineering

The first part sets the stage by establishing the core principles and practices that form the backbone of software engineering. Introduction to Software Engineering outlines the discipline's significance, the distinction between software and hardware, the history of software engineering, and the key challenges developers face in the industry. Software Development Life Cycle (SDLC) explores various methodologies for managing software projects, from the traditional Waterfall model to modern, flexible approaches like Agile, Scrum, and DevOps. Software Engineering Principles emphasizes the best practices for writing high-quality software, focusing on concepts like modularity, reusability, and maintainability, along with principles such as SOLID, DRY, and KISS.

Part 2: Requirements Engineering and Design

This part dives into the processes that bridge the gap between user needs and the final software solution. Requirements Engineering covers the types of software requirements and introduces techniques for gathering and documenting them effectively, including use cases and user stories. Software Architecture and Design addresses key design patterns and architectural approaches, such as monolithic, microservices, and serverless, and emphasizes the importance of choosing the right design paradigms to meet the specific needs of a project.

Part 3: Software Development and Best Practices

In this section, we focus on how to write high-quality code and maintain excellent software development practices. Programming Paradigms and Languages explores the various paradigms of programming, such as procedural, object-oriented, and functional programming, and helps you choose the best programming language for your projects. Coding Standards and Best Practices covers the essentials of clean code, including readability, naming conventions, and documentation, along with the importance of using version control systems like Git. Software Testing and Quality Assurance provides an in-depth look at various testing methodologies, including unit testing, integration testing, and test-driven development, alongside the best practices for ensuring software quality.

Part 4: Advanced Topics in Software Engineering

As software engineering continues to evolve, this part delves into more advanced and emerging areas of the field. Security in Software Engineering covers best practices for writing secure code, dealing with common vulnerabilities, and ensuring data privacy and encryption. Performance Optimization and Scalability addresses strategies for identifying and resolving performance bottlenecks, implementing load balancing and caching, and understanding scaling techniques. Software Engineering for Emerging Technologies examines how emerging fields like artificial intelligence, blockchain, IoT, and quantum computing are reshaping software development and the role of the software engineer.

Part 5: Software Project Management and Career Development

The final part focuses on the organizational and career aspects of being a software engineer. Software Project Management explores how to plan, estimate, and manage projects effectively, with an emphasis on risk management and tools for team collaboration. Ethics and Professionalism in Software Engineering addresses the ethical considerations of software development, the importance of open-source contributions, and diversity and inclusion in tech. Building a Successful Career in Software Engineering offers valuable advice on career growth, including resume building, preparing for technical interviews, and making decisions between freelancing and full-time employment.

Throughout this book, you will be equipped not only with technical knowledge but also with the insight to make informed decisions, overcome challenges, and build a fulfilling career in software engineering. The path to mastering software engineering is a continuous learning journey, and this book is here to be your companion every step of the way.

Author

Contents

Preface

PART–1

FOUNDATIONS OF SOFTWARE ENGINEERING

1. **Introduction to Software Engineering** **3**
   - Definition and Importance
   - Software vs. Hardware
   - Evolution of Software Engineering
   - Key Challenges in Software Development
2. **Software Development Life Cycle (SDLC)** **15**
   - Waterfall Model
   - Agile Methodology
   - Scrum and Kanban
   - DevOps and Continuous Integration/Continuous Deployment (CI/CD)
   - Choosing the Right SDLC Model
3. **Software Engineering Principles** **50**
   - Modularity, Reusability, and Maintainability
   - SOLID Principles
   - DRY (Don't Repeat Yourself) and KISS (Keep It Simple, Stupid)
   - Separation of Concerns

PART–2

REQUIREMENTS ENGINEERING AND DESIGN

4. **Requirements Engineering** **63**
   - Types of Requirements: Functional vs. Non-functional
   - Requirements Gathering Techniques

- Writing Good Software Requirements
- Use Case and User Stories

5. Software Architecture and Design 79
- Architectural Patterns (Monolithic, Microservices, Serverless)
- Design Patterns (Singleton, Factory, Observer, etc.)
- Domain-Driven Design (DDD)
- Model-View-Controller (MVC) and Other Design

PART–3

SOFTWARE DEVELOPMENT AND BEST PRACTICES

6. Programming Paradigms and Languages 113
- Procedural vs. Object-Oriented vs. Functional Programming
- Choosing the Right Language for the Job
- Modern Programming Languages: Python, Java, C++, JavaScript, etc.

7. Coding Standards and Best Practices 132
- Code Readability and Maintainability
- Naming Conventions and Documentation
- Version Control Systems (Git, GitHub, GitLab, Bitbucket)
- Writing Clean Code

8. Software Testing and Quality Assurance 158
- Unit Testing, Integration Testing, System Testing
- Test-Driven Development (TDD)
- Behavior-Driven Development (BDD)
- Automated Testing Tools

PART–4

ADVANCED TOPICS IN SOFTWARE ENGINEERING

9. Security in Software Engineering 193
- Secure Coding Practices
- Common Vulnerabilities (OWASP Top 10)
- Authentication and Authorization
- Data Privacy and Encryption

10. Performance Optimization and Scalability 220
- Performance Bottlenecks and Profiling
- Load Balancing and Caching Strategies

- Horizontal vs. Vertical Scaling
- Cloud-native Application Development

11. Software Engineering for Emerging Technologies **252**
- Artificial Intelligence and Machine Learning in Software Development
- Blockchain and Smart Contracts
- Internet of Things (IoT) Software Engineering
- Quantum Computing and Future Trends

PART–5

SOFTWARE PROJECT MANAGEMENT AND CAREER DEVELOPMENT

12. Software Project Management **287**
- Project Planning and Estimation
- Risk Management in Software Development
- Agile Project Management Tools (JIRA, Trello, etc.)
- Team Collaboration and Communication

13. Ethics and Professionalism in Software Engineering **309**
- Ethical Dilemmas in Software Development
- Open-source and Intellectual Property
- Diversity and Inclusion in Tech

14. Building a Successful Career in Software Engineering **328**
- Resume Building and Technical Interviews
- Contributing to Open-source Projects
- Freelancing vs. Full-Time Jobs
- Continuous Learning and Staying Updated

Appendix **359**
- Case Studies of Successful Software Projects

Bibliography **365**

Index **369**

PART–1

FOUNDATIONS OF SOFTWARE ENGINEERING

The foundations of software engineering provide the essential principles and methodologies that guide the development of reliable, efficient, and maintainable software systems. Software engineering, at its core, is about applying engineering principles to software development. It involves understanding the needs of users, designing solutions, and managing the entire software development process through well-defined stages. Key concepts such as the software development life cycle (SDLC), which includes methodologies like Waterfall and Agile, help structure how projects are planned, executed, and maintained. These methodologies ensure that software is built systematically, meeting quality standards while addressing the complexities of the real world.

Equally important are the fundamental principles of software engineering, which include modularity, reusability, and maintainability. By following these principles, software engineers can create systems that are easier to modify and extend over time. Concepts like the SOLID principles, DRY (Don't Repeat Yourself), and KISS (Keep It Simple, Stupid) guide developers toward writing cleaner, more efficient code. Additionally, the focus on separating concerns allows for a more organized and scalable system architecture. Understanding these foundational elements is critical, as they set the stage for more advanced practices and technologies in software engineering, ensuring that developers are equipped to tackle the challenges they face in creating high-quality, effective software solutions.

1

Introduction to Software Engineering

Software engineering is the discipline of designing, developing, testing, and maintaining software systems. It combines principles from computer science, engineering, and project management to create software that meets user needs and functions efficiently. As a structured approach to software development, software engineering aims to improve both the quality and reliability of software while managing its complexity and scale. Unlike casual coding, software engineering emphasizes systematic planning, rigorous design, and methodical testing to ensure that the final product is robust, scalable, and maintainable.

The importance of software engineering is evident in today's digital world, where software drives everything from mobile apps and web services to enterprise systems and embedded devices. As software becomes more integral to daily life, the demand for skilled engineers who can create high-quality, efficient software has increased. Moreover, the field has evolved significantly over time, from basic programs to complex, distributed systems that must meet stringent performance, security, and user experience requirements. This evolution has brought with it key challenges, such as managing project timelines, balancing cost with functionality, and ensuring that software is adaptable to future changes. By applying well-defined methodologies, such as the Software Development Life Cycle (SDLC), and adhering to core principles like modularity and maintainability, software engineers can mitigate these challenges, producing software that not only works but continues to deliver value in the long term.

Definition and Importance

Software engineering is the disciplined application of engineering principles to the design, development, testing, and maintenance of software systems. It ensures that software is reliable, scalable, and meets user and business requirements through structured processes like the Software Development Life Cycle (SDLC). The importance of software engineering lies in its ability to produce high-quality, efficient, and maintainable software that drives innovation and solves complex problems across industries. By using standardized methodologies, software engineering helps manage project risks, reduce costs, and ensure that software systems are adaptable, secure, and capable of evolving to meet future demands.

Definition: Software engineering is the systematic application of engineering principles to the design, development, testing, and maintenance of software systems. It involves a structured process to ensure that software is reliable, efficient, scalable, and meets user requirements. Software engineering incorporates best practices, methodologies (such as the Software Development Life Cycle), and tools to create high-quality software that is both functional and maintainable. It focuses on solving complex problems by using engineering concepts to manage the entire lifecycle of a software product, from initial planning and design to deployment and continuous improvement. Definitions of software engineering by different authors are as:

1. **By Lan Sommerville (Author of "Software Engineering")**: *"Software engineering is the application of a systematic, disciplined, quantifiable approach to the development, operation, and maintenance of software."*

   Sommerville highlights the importance of a structured, methodical approach in creating software that is both effective and sustainable.

2. **By Roger S. Pressman (Author of "Software Engineering: A Practitioner's Approach")**: *"Software engineering is the application of engineering approaches to software development in order to produce software that is reliable and works efficiently on real machines."*

   Pressman emphasizes the application of engineering techniques to ensure the software is both reliable and efficient in real-world environments.

3. **By Barry Boehm (Author of "Software Engineering Economics")**: *"Software engineering is an engineering discipline that is concerned with all aspects of software production, from the early stages of system specification through to the maintenance of the software after it has gone into use."*

Boehm focuses on the comprehensive nature of software engineering, including all stages from planning to long-term maintenance.

4. **By Winston Royce (Author of "Managing the Development of Large Software Systems")**: *"Software engineering is the process of analyzing user requirements and then designing, building, and testing software to meet those needs."*

   Royce emphasizes the importance of understanding user needs and aligning the development process to meet those needs.

These definitions reflect different facets of software engineering, from systematic methodologies and engineering principles to the emphasis on meeting user needs and ensuring reliability throughout the software lifecycle.

Importance: Software engineering is crucial because it provides the structured methodologies and principles required to design, develop, and maintain reliable, efficient, and scalable software systems. In an increasingly digital world, software engineering ensures that applications and systems meet user needs, perform optimally, and remain secure. It enables innovation by creating technologies that power industries such as healthcare, finance, education, and entertainment. Through practices like testing, debugging, and version control, it enhances software quality, reducing the risk of errors and ensuring functionality. Software engineering also addresses the growing need for collaboration in teams, making it easier to manage complex projects and ensure timely delivery. By focusing on maintainability and long-term sustainability, it ensures that software can evolve with technological advancements and changing user requirements. Furthermore, it ensures that security measures are in place to protect user data and safeguard against cyber threats. Ultimately, software engineering is vital for creating systems that are not only functional and secure but also adaptable, cost-effective, and able to meet the demands of a fast-paced, globalized society. Software engineering is incredibly important for several reasons, especially in today's technology-driven world. Some key reasons why it's essential:

1. **Building Reliable and Scalable Systems:** Software engineering helps in designing systems that are not only reliable but also scalable. This is crucial because businesses and applications need to handle an ever-increasing amount of data and users. Proper software engineering practices ensure systems can grow without breaking down.

2. **Quality and Efficiency:** It ensures the creation of high-quality software that works as expected. Good software engineering practices like testing, debugging, and code reviews ensure that software is efficient, performs well, and is free

of bugs. This saves time and costs in the long run by reducing the need for rework.

3. **Problem-Solving:** Software engineering provides structured approaches to problem-solving. It allows engineers to break down complex issues into manageable components, which leads to better solutions. Whether it's a new product or improving an existing one, software engineering is key to developing solutions that address specific needs.

4. **Innovation and Advancement:** Many of the technologies we take for granted, from smartphones to self-driving cars, rely on software engineering. It drives innovation by creating the tools, applications, and systems that power new technologies and business models, leading to continuous advancements in industries like healthcare, finance, education, and entertainment.

5. **Security:** Software engineering emphasizes creating secure software systems. In an age where cyber threats are prevalent, security cannot be an afterthought. A well-engineered software system ensures that security vulnerabilities are minimized and that user data is protected.

6. **Collaboration and Teamwork:** Software engineering often involves teams of people working together. It promotes collaboration, communication, and version control, ensuring that teams can work efficiently on large and complex projects. This teamwork is essential for managing larger software systems and meeting deadlines.

7. **Cost-effectiveness:** Software engineering practices like requirements gathering, prototyping, and testing help companies develop software that meets user needs without unnecessary costs. By following proper engineering principles, the risk of failure is reduced, and the development process becomes more predictable and efficient.

8. **Meeting User Expectations:** Users expect software to be intuitive, fast, and functional. Software engineering helps create products that meet these expectations, whether it's a web app, mobile app, or enterprise software. By following best practices in design, user experience (UX), and software testing, engineers can create products that are well-received by users.

9. **Long-Term Maintenance and Updates:** Software is rarely static; it requires ongoing updates, bug fixes, and improvements. Software engineering provides strategies for maintaining and updating systems over time, ensuring that

software remains relevant, functional, and secure even as the technology landscape evolves.

10. **Global Impact:** Software engineering isn't just about developing local applications; it has a global impact. The systems we design today touch billions of people worldwide, from healthcare applications that save lives to e-commerce platforms that connect businesses with customers across borders.

Software vs. Hardware

Software and hardware are two fundamental components of any computing system, each playing a distinct and complementary role. Hardware refers to the physical components of a computer, such as the CPU, memory, storage devices, and peripherals like keyboards and monitors. These tangible elements are responsible for executing physical tasks, processing data, and displaying output. On the other hand, software consists of the intangible instructions, programs, and applications that run on hardware. Software includes system software (like operating systems) that manages hardware resources and application software (like word processors or games) that helps users perform specific tasks. While hardware provides the infrastructure for a computer to function, software enables it to perform useful work by providing instructions for the hardware to execute. Software is more flexible and can be easily updated, modified, or replaced without altering the physical components, whereas hardware often requires physical replacement or upgrading for performance improvements. Essentially, hardware and software are interdependent: hardware provides the necessary resources for software to operate, and software drives hardware to perform specific tasks. Both are indispensable for modern computing, with hardware offering the physical capacity and software delivering the intelligence and functionality to make the system useful to users.

Table 1.1

S.No.	Aspect	Software	Hardware
1.	Definition	Intangible code and programs that instruct hardware to perform tasks.	Physical components of a computer system that perform the tasks.
2.	Development	Developed through programming, coding, and design in various languages (e.g., Java, Python).	Developed through engineering processes that involve manufacturing, circuit design, and hardware assembly
3.	Updatability	Can be easily updated, modified, or patched (e.g., software updates).	Requires physical replacement or upgrades (e.g., adding more RAM, changing the hard drive).

4.	Flexibility	More flexible as it can be changed without changing the underlying hardware.	Less flexible, as changes require physical modifications or replacements.
5.	Dependencies	Depends on hardware to execute and perform tasks.	Cannot function without software instructions to control and manage operations.
6.	Maintenance	Regular updates, bug fixes, and patches.	Requires physical repairs or component replacements over time.
7.	Lifecycle	Software can evolve rapidly, with frequent updates and versions.	Hardware changes at a slower pace and involves long-term investment.
8.	Cost	Generally, less expensive to develop and modify (compared to hardware).	High initial costs due to manufacturing and assembly.
9.	Function	Provides instructions and enables functionality (e.g., running applications).	Performs physical operations like processing, storing data, and outputting results.
10.	Examples	Operating systems, applications, databases, web browsers.	CPU, RAM, hard drive, motherboard, monitors, keyboards.

Evolution of Software Engineering

The evolution of software engineering has been shaped by technological advancements, growing system complexity, and the need for more efficient and reliable software development processes. Here's an overview of its evolution:

1. Early Development (1940s–1950s)

- **Pre-Software Engineering Era**: In the early days of computing, there were no established methodologies for software development. Computers were very basic, and software was typically written in machine language or assembly language.

- **Programming by Hand**: Programmers wrote code directly for specific hardware, which was often error-prone and difficult to maintain. The lack of formal practices led to unreliable and inefficient systems.

2. The Birth of Software Engineering (1960s)

- **The Software Crisis**: By the 1960s, software development became more complex with the growth of systems and demand for larger, more reliable applications. This era marked the beginning of the "Software Crisis" a term coined to describe the difficulties in creating software that was reliable, efficient, and easy to maintain.

- **Formalization of Practices**: The need for formal software development practices led to the first software engineering methodologies, including the introduction of structured programming and early software life cycle models.
- **Waterfall Model**: In the late 1960s and early 1970s, the **Waterfall Model** was proposed, focusing on a linear, step-by-step approach to development.

3. Methodologies and Frameworks (1970s–1980s)

- **Structured Programming**: This approach, popularized by figures like Edsger Dijkstra, aimed to improve the clarity, reliability, and efficiency of software code by promoting modularity, top-down design, and the use of control structures.
- **Object-Oriented Programming (OOP)**: In the 1970s, the OOP paradigm was introduced (e.g., Smalltalk and Simula), which emphasized reusability and modularity by organizing software around objects and their interactions. This helped manage increasing complexity and was foundational to many modern languages like Java and C++.
- **Structured Systems Analysis and Design**: Tools and methods such as Data Flow Diagrams (DFD) and Entity-Relationship diagrams emerged to support more structured approaches to software design.

4. Rise of Agile and Iterative Development (1990s–2000s)

- **Agile Manifesto (2001)**: The Agile movement emerged in the late 1990s and early 2000s as a response to the rigid, linear Waterfall method. Agile emphasized collaboration, customer feedback, and the ability to adapt to changes quickly.
- **Scrum, Extreme Programming (XP), and DevOps**: These methodologies focused on small, iterative development cycles, continuous testing, and integration. Agile practices allowed for greater flexibility and rapid delivery of software features.
- **Software Tools**: The use of integrated development environments (IDEs), version control systems, and automated testing tools became mainstream, improving productivity and collaboration among developers.

5. Modern Software Engineering (2010s–Present)

- **Cloud Computing and Microservices**: With the advent of cloud platforms (e.g., AWS, Microsoft Azure, Google Cloud), software engineering practices have evolved to include distributed systems, microservices architecture, and containerization. These technologies allow for scalable, fault-tolerant applications that can be rapidly deployed and maintained.

- **DevOps and Continuous Delivery**: DevOps has become a key practice in modern software engineering, bridging the gap between development and operations. The focus is on continuous integration, continuous delivery (CI/CD), and automating the deployment pipeline to achieve CXfaster releases.

- **AI and Automation**: Software engineering now also integrates artificial intelligence (AI) and machine learning (ML) to optimize various aspects of development, from code generation to testing. Automation tools have further accelerated development cycles.

6. Future Trends

- **Low-Code/No-Code Development**: The rise of platforms that allow for minimal coding is democratizing software creation, enabling people with limited programming experience to build applications.

- **Quantum Computing**: As quantum computing progresses, new paradigms for developing software will emerge, potentially disrupting existing models and practices in software engineering.

- **Ethical and Sustainable Software Engineering**: The growing focus on ethical implications, privacy, and sustainability will shape future practices in software development.

The evolution of software engineering has moved from simple, manual coding to highly structured methodologies, followed by more flexible and iterative models like Agile. Today, it continues to evolve with the integration of cloud technologies, automation, and AI, while future developments promise new paradigms in quantum computing and low-code solutions. As systems grow more complex, the role of software engineering will continue to be pivotal in shaping technology and its impact on society.

Key Challenges in Software Development

Software development faces several key challenges that can impact project success.

Requirement gathering is often the first hurdle, as unclear or changing requirements can lead to misunderstandings and project scope creep. Scope creep occurs when new features are added without proper control, resulting in delayed timelines and budget overruns. Meeting deadlines can be another challenge, especially when unforeseen issues arise, leading to rushed development and potentially lower quality. Ensuring quality assurance and sufficient testing is essential but can be difficult due to time constraints, resulting in undetected bugs or performance problems.

Code quality and maintainability are crucial for long-term success; however, poor coding practices and lack of documentation can create technical debt, making future modifications challenging. Security vulnerabilities pose significant risks, as software applications are prime targets for cyberattacks. Integration with other systems, especially legacy systems, is another hurdle, often requiring extra effort to ensure seamless interoperability.

Team collaboration can be difficult, particularly with distributed teams, while keeping up with rapidly evolving technologies requires constant learning and adaptation. Lastly, managing costs is a recurring issue, as software projects often experience budget overruns due to poor resource estimation. Addressing these challenges requires effective planning, communication, and modern development practices.

Software development is a complex and dynamic process that involves several challenges. Here are some of the key challenges faced in software development:

1. Requirement Gathering and Analysis

- **Miscommunication with stakeholders**: One of the biggest challenges in software development is gathering clear, accurate, and complete requirements from stakeholders. Misunderstandings between developers, users, and clients can lead to the creation of software that doesn't meet user needs.

- **Changing requirements**: In many cases, requirements evolve during development, especially in long projects, making it difficult to keep the software aligned with expectations.

2. Scope Creep

- **Uncontrolled changes**: Scope creep occurs when additional features or functionalities are added to a project without proper control. This can lead to project delays, budget overruns, and misalignment with original goals.

- **Lack of clear boundaries**: Without a well-defined project scope, stakeholders may continuously add new requirements, increasing the complexity of the project.

3. Time Management and Deadlines

- **Tight timelines**: Meeting project deadlines can be challenging, especially when tasks are underestimated or when unexpected issues arise. Delivering quality software on time is often a balancing act.
- **Overwork and burnout**: Developers may experience pressure to work long hours to meet deadlines, leading to burnout and decreased productivity.

4. Quality Assurance and Testing

- **Insufficient testing**: Quality assurance (QA) is crucial, but testing can often be inadequate due to time constraints or limited resources. This can lead to undetected bugs and performance issues.
- **Complexity of testing**: As software becomes more complex, ensuring that all features work as expected in different environments and under different conditions becomes harder.

5. Code Quality and Maintenance

- **Technical debt**: Rushed development or poor coding practices can lead to "technical debt," where shortcuts are taken in the codebase. Over time, this can result in software that is difficult to maintain, scale, or refactor.
- **Lack of documentation**: Insufficient documentation makes it hard for developers to understand, maintain, or modify the code, particularly when team members change.

6. Security Vulnerabilities

- **Cybersecurity threats**: Software applications are increasingly targeted by malicious actors. Addressing security issues in software development is crucial, but security may sometimes be overlooked in the rush to release products.
- **Data privacy**: Ensuring that user data is handled securely and in compliance with regulations like GDPR adds additional complexity to development.

7. Integration with Other Systems

- **Legacy systems**: Integrating new software with older systems (legacy systems) can be challenging due to differences in technology stocks, data formats, and architecture.

- **Interoperability**: Ensuring that different systems can communicate and work together seamlessly is crucial, particularly in enterprise-level applications.

8. Team Collaboration and Communication

- **Distributed teams**: In today's globalized world, many software development teams are spread across different locations, making communication and collaboration difficult. Time zone differences, language barriers, and cultural differences can impact productivity and project success.

- **Conflicting priorities**: Team members or departments may have different priorities, which can lead to delays, confusion, and inefficiency in software development processes.

9. Adapting to Changing Technologies

- **Keeping up with new tools**: The rapid pace of technological change means that developers must constantly learn and adapt to new programming languages, frameworks, and tools. This can be overwhelming and resource-intensive.

- **Obsolescence**: Software developed on outdated technologies or platforms can become obsolete quickly, necessitating frequent updates or full redevelopment.

10. Cost Management

- **Budget overruns**: Poor estimation of resources and time needed to complete a project can lead to unexpected costs. Managing costs while delivering a quality product within budget is a constant challenge.

- **Resource allocation**: Effectively allocating and utilizing resources (e.g., developers, infrastructure) to meet project goals while minimizing waste is a difficult task.

11. User Experience (UX) Design

- **Meeting user expectations**: Designing intuitive, user-friendly interfaces that meet the needs and preferences of users is a significant challenge. Poor UX can lead to low adoption rates and dissatisfaction with the software.

- **Balancing functionality and usability**: Adding features can increase the complexity of an application, potentially making it harder to use. Striking the right balance between functionality and simplicity is a common challenge.

12. Deployment and Maintenance

- **Deployment challenges**: Moving code from development to production environments can cause issues if not properly managed. Deployment tools, automated pipelines, and testing in staging environments are essential to minimize risks.

- **Ongoing maintenance**: After deployment, software often requires continuous updates, patches, and fixes. Managing post-release issues, especially in large-scale systems, can be an ongoing challenge.

In summary, software development faces numerous challenges, from gathering accurate requirements to maintaining code quality and ensuring security. Overcoming these challenges requires effective planning, collaboration, and the use of appropriate tools and methodologies to produce reliable, high-quality software.

******

2

Software Development Life Cycle (SDLC)

A software life cycle model (also termed process model) is a pictorial and diagrammatic representation of the software life cycle. A life cycle model represents all the methods required to make a software product transit through its life cycle stages. It also captures the structure in which these methods are to be undertaken.

In other words, a life cycle model maps the various activities performed on a software product from its inception to retirement. Different life cycle models may plan the necessary development activities to phases in different ways. Thus, no element which life cycle model is followed; the essential activities are contained in all life cycle models though the action may be carried out in distinct orders in different life cycle models. During any life cycle stage, more than one activity may also be carried out.

Fig.1.1 is a graphical representation of the various stages of a typical SDLC. SDLC Cycle represents the process of developing software.

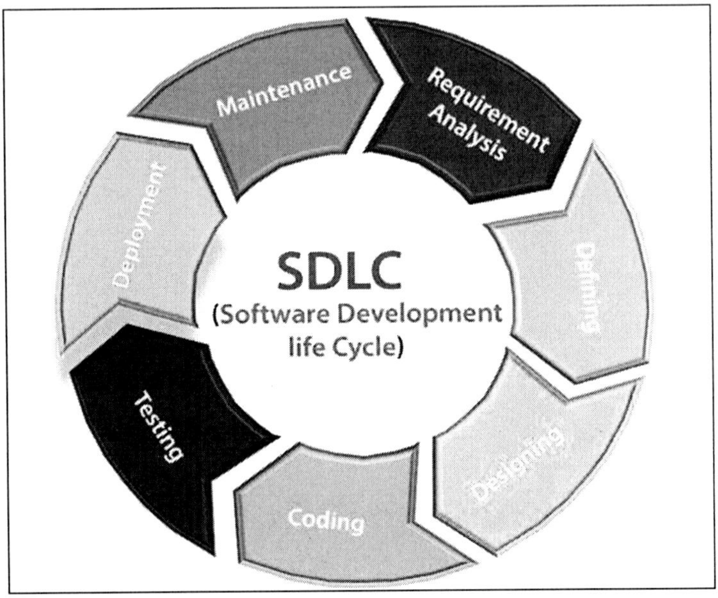

Fig.1.1

SDLC framework includes the following steps:

Stage1: Planning and requirement analysis: Requirement Analysis is the most important and necessary stage in SDLC. The senior members of the team perform it with inputs from all the stakeholders and domain experts or SMEs in the industry. Planning for the quality assurance requirements and identifications of the risks associated with the projects is also done at this stage. Business analyst and Project organizer set up a meeting with the client to gather all the data like what the customer wants to build, who will be the end user, what is the objective of the product. Before creating a product, a core understanding or knowledge of the product is very necessary.

For Example, A client wants to have an application which concerns money transactions. In this method, the requirement has to be precise like what kind of operations will be done, how it will be done, in which currency it will be done, etc. Once the required function is done, an analysis is complete with auditing the feasibility of the growth of a product. In case of any ambiguity, a signal is set up for further discussion. Once the requirement is understood, the SRS (Software Requirement Specification) document is created. The developers should thoroughly follow this document and also should be reviewed by the customer for future reference.

Stage2: Defining Requirements: Once the requirement analysis is done, the next stage is to certainly represent and document the software requirements and get them accepted from the project stakeholders.

This is accomplished through "SRS"- Software Requirement Specification document which contains all the product requirements to be constructed and developed during the project life cycle.

Stage3: Designing the Software: The next phase is about to bring down all the knowledge of requirements, analysis, and design of the software project. This phase is the product of the last two, like inputs from the customer and requirement gathering.

Stage4: Developing the Project: In this phase of SDLC, the actual development begins, and the programming is built. The implementation of design begins concerning writing code. Developers have to follow the coding guidelines described by their management and programming tools like compilers, interpreters, debuggers, etc. are used to develop and implement the code.

Stage5: Testing: After the code is generated, it is tested against the requirements to make sure that the products are solving the needs addressed and gathered during the requirements stage. During this stage, unit testing, integration testing, system testing, acceptance testing are done.

Stage6: Deployment: Once the software is certified, and no bugs or errors are stated, then it is deployed. Then based on the assessment, the software may be released as it is or with suggested enhancement in the object segment. After the software is deployed, then its maintenance begins.

Stage7: Maintenance: Once when the client starts using the developed systems, then the real issues come up and requirements to be solved from time to time.

This procedure where the care is taken for the developed product is known as maintenance.

Need of SDLC: The development team must determine a suitable life cycle model for a particular plan and then observe to it.

Without using an exact life cycle model, the development of a software product would not be in a systematic and disciplined manner. When a team is developing a software product, there must be a clear understanding among team representative about when and what to do. Otherwise, it would point to chaos and project failure. This problem can be defined by using an example. Suppose a software development issue is divided into various parts and the parts are assigned to the team members. From then on, suppose the team representative is allowed the freedom to develop the roles assigned to them in whatever way they like. It is possible that one representative might start writing the code for his part, another might choose to prepare the test documents first, and some other engineer might begin with the design phase of the roles assigned to him. This would be one of the perfect methods for project failure.

A software life cycle model describes entry and exit criteria for each phase. A phase can begin only if its stage-entry criteria have been fulfilled. So, without a software life cycle model, the entry and exit criteria for a stage cannot be recognized. Without software life cycle models, it becomes tough for software project managers to monitor the progress of the project.

SDLC Models in Software Engineering: Software Development life cycle (SDLC) is a spiritual model used in project management that defines the stages include in an information system development project, from an initial feasibility study to the maintenance of the completed application.

There are different software development life cycle models specify and design, which are followed during the software development phase. These models are also called "Software Development Process Models." Each process model follows a series of phase unique to its type to ensure success in the step of software development.

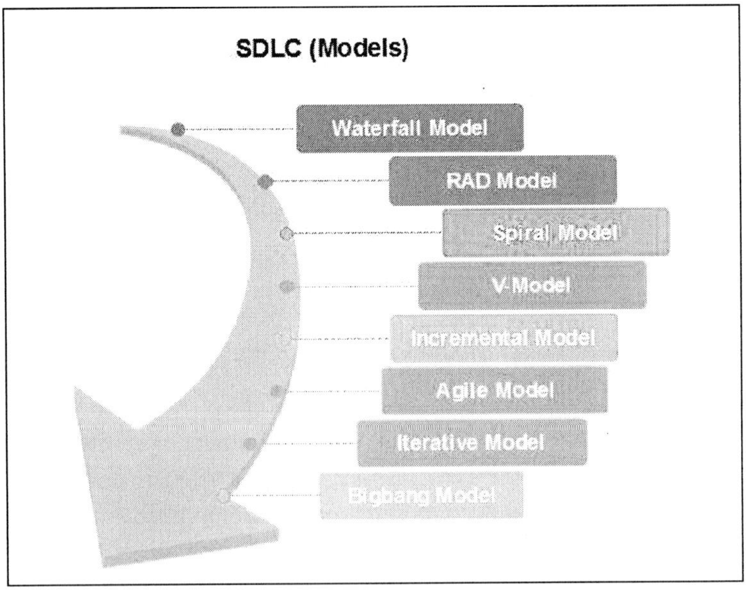

Fig.1.2

The different types of SDLC model are as follow:

1. Waterfall Model: The waterfall is a universally accepted SDLC model. In this method, the whole process of software development is divided into various phases.

The waterfall model is a continuous software development model in which development is seen as flowing steadily downwards (like a waterfall) through the steps of requirements analysis, design, implementation, testing (validation), integration, and maintenance.

Linear ordering of activities has some significant consequences. First, to identify the end of a phase and the beginning of the next, some certification techniques have to be employed at the end of each step. Some verification and validation usually do this mean that will ensure that the output of the stage is consistent with its input (which is the output of the previous step), and that the output of the stage is consistent with the overall requirements of the system.

2. RAD Model: RAD or Rapid Application Development process is an adoption of the waterfall model; it targets developing software in a short period. The RAD model is based on the concept that a better system can be developed in lesser time by using focus groups to gather system requirements.

- Business Modeling
- Data Modeling
- Process Modeling
- Application Generation
- Testing and Turnover

3. Spiral Model: The spiral model is a risk-driven process model. This SDLC model helps the group to adopt elements of one or more process models like a waterfall, incremental, waterfall, etc. The spiral technique is a combination of rapid prototyping and concurrency in design and development activities.

Each cycle in the spiral begins with the identification of objectives for that cycle, the different alternatives that are possible for achieving the goals, and the constraints that exist. This is the first quadrant of the cycle (upper-left quadrant).

The next step in the cycle is to evaluate these different alternatives based on the objectives and constraints. The focus of evaluation in this step is based on the risk perception for the project.

The next step is to develop strategies that solve uncertainties and risks. This step may involve activities such as benchmarking, simulation, and prototyping.

4. V-Model: In this type of SDLC model testing and the development, the step is planned in parallel. So, there are verification phases on the side and the validation phase on the other side. V-Model joins by Coding phase.

5. Incremental Model: The incremental model is not a separate model. It is necessarily a series of waterfall cycles. The requirements are divided into groups at the start of the project. For each group, the SDLC model is followed to develop software. The SDLC process is repeated, with each release adding more functionality until all requirements are met. In this method, each cycle act as the maintenance phase for the previous software release. Modification to the incremental model allows development cycles to overlap. After that subsequent cycle may begin before the previous cycle is complete.

6. Agile Model: Agile methodology is a practice which promotes continues interaction of development and testing during the SDLC process of any project. In the Agile method, the entire project is divided into small incremental builds. All of these builds are provided in iterations, and each iteration lasts from one to three weeks.

Any agile software phase is characterized in a manner that addresses several key assumptions about the bulk of software projects:

- It is difficult to think in advance which software requirements will persist and which will change. It is equally difficult to predict how user priorities will change as the project proceeds.
- For many types of software, design and development are interleaved. That is, both activities should be performed in tandem so that design models are proven as they are created. It is difficult to think about how much design is necessary before construction is used to test the configuration.
- Analysis, design, development, and testing are not as predictable (from a planning point of view) as we might like.

7. Iterative Model: It is a particular implementation of a software development life cycle that focuses on an initial, simplified implementation, which then progressively gains more complexity and a broader feature set until the final system is complete. In short, iterative development is a way of breaking down the software development of a large application into smaller pieces.

8. **Big bang Model:** Big bang model is focusing on all types of resources in software development and coding, with no or very little planning. The requirements are understood and implemented when they come.

This model works best for small projects with smaller size development team which are working together. It is also useful for academic software development projects. It is an ideal model where requirements are either unknown or final release date is not given.

9. **Prototype Model:** The prototyping model starts with the requirements gathering. The developer and the user meet and define the purpose of the software, identify the needs, etc.

Waterfall Model

The Waterfall Model was the first Process Model to be introduced. It is also referred to as a linear-sequential life cycle model. It is very simple to understand and use. In a waterfall model, each phase must be completed before the next phase can begin and there is no overlapping in the phases.

The Waterfall model is the earliest SDLC approach that was used for software development.

The waterfall Model illustrates the software development process in a linear sequential flow. This means that any phase in the development process begins only if the previous phase is complete. In this waterfall model, the phases do not overlap.

Waterfall Model Design: Waterfall approach was first SDLC Model to be used widely in Software Engineering to ensure success of the project. In "The Waterfall" approach, the whole process of software development is divided into separate phases. In this Waterfall model, typically, the outcome of one phase acts as the input for the next phase sequentially.

Fig.1.3 is a representation of the different phases of the Waterfall Model.

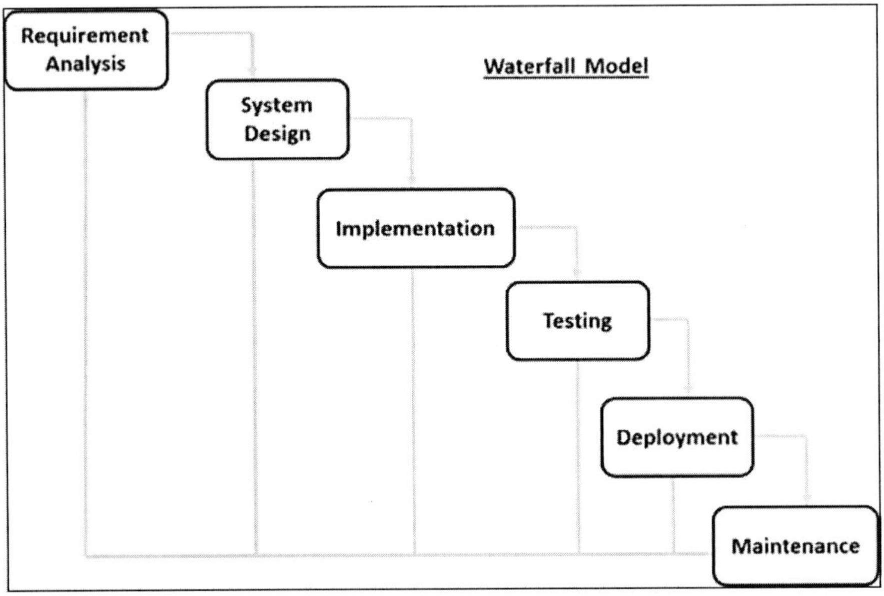

Fig.1.3

The sequential phases in Waterfall model are as:

1. Requirement Gathering and Analysis: All possible requirements of the system to be developed are captured in this phase and documented in a requirement specification document.

The aim of this phase is to understand the exact requirements of the customer and to document them properly. Both the customer and the software developer work together so as to document all the functions, performance, and interfacing requirement of the software. It describes the "what" of the system to be produced and not "how." In this phase, a large document called Software Requirement Specification (SRS) document is created which contained a detailed description of what the system will do in the common language.

2. System Design: The requirement specifications from first phase are studied in this phase and the system design is prepared. This system design helps in specifying hardware and system requirements and helps in defining the overall system architecture.

This phase aims to transform the requirements gathered in the SRS into a suitable form which permits further coding in a programming language. It defines the overall software architecture together with high level and detailed design. All this work is documented as a Software Design Document (SDD).

3. Implementation: With inputs from the system design, the system is first developed in small programs called units, which are integrated in the next phase. Each unit is developed and tested for its functionality, which is referred to as Unit Testing.

During this phase, design is implemented. If the SDD is complete, the implementation or coding phase proceeds smoothly, because all the information needed by software developers is contained in the SDD. During testing, the code is thoroughly examined and modified. Small modules are tested in isolation initially. After that these modules are tested by writing some overhead code to check the interaction between these modules and the flow of intermediate output.

4. Integration and Testing: All the units developed in the implementation phase are integrated into a system after testing of each unit. Post integration the entire system is tested for any faults and failures.

This phase is highly crucial as the quality of the end product is determined by the effectiveness of the testing carried out. The better output will lead to satisfied customers, lower maintenance costs, and accurate results. Unit testing determines the efficiency of individual modules. However, in this phase, the modules are tested for their interactions with each other and with the system.

5. Deployment of System: Once the functional and non-functional testing is done; the product is deployed in the customer environment or released into the market.

6. Maintenance: There are some issues which come up in the client environment. To fix those issues, patches are released. Also to enhance the product some better versions are released. Maintenance is done to deliver these changes in the customer environment. Maintenance is the task performed by every user once the software has been delivered to the customer, installed, and operational.

All these phases are cascaded to each other in which progress is seen as flowing steadily downwards (like a waterfall) through the phases. The next phase is started only after the defined set of goals are achieved for previous phase and it is signed off, so the name "Waterfall Model". In this model, phases do not overlap.

Examples of Waterfall Model: In the olden days, Waterfall model was used to develop enterprise applications like Customer Relationship Management (CRM) systems, Human Resource Management Systems (HRMS), Supply Chain Management Systems, Inventory Management Systems, Point of Sales (POS) systems for Retail chains etc.

Waterfall model was used significantly in the development of software till the year 2000. Even after the Agile manifesto was published in 2001, Waterfall model continued to be used by many organization till the last decade. These days most project follow Agile Methodology, some form of Iterative model or one of the other models depending on their project specific requirement.

In the olden days, applications developed in Waterfall Model like CRM Systems, Supply Chain Management Systems etc would usually take a year or longer to develop. With the evolution of technology, there were cases where large scale enterprise systems were developed over a period of 2 to 3 years but were redundant by the time they were completed. There were several reasons for this.

1. By the time the applications were developed in C, C++ etc, new languages (relatively speaking) like Java, .Net etc would replace them with web-based functionality.

2. Even if the application was developed using a new technology, factors like more competitors entering the market, cheaper alternatives becoming available, better functionality using newer technologies, change in customers requirement etc. increase the risk of developing an application over several years.

However, there are some areas where Waterfall model was continued to be preferred are as:

1. Consider a system where human life is on the line, where a system failure could result in one or more deaths.

2. In some countries, such mishaps could lead to imprisonment for those who are accountable.

3. Consider a system where time and money were secondary considerations and human safety was first.

In such situations, Waterfall model was the preferred approach.

1. Development of Department of Defense (DOD), military and aircraft programs followed Waterfall model in many organizations.

2. This is because of the strict standards and requirements that have to be followed.

3. In such industries, the requirements are known well in advance and contracts are very specific about the deliverable of the project.

4. DOD Agencies typically considered Waterfall model to be compatible with their acquisition process and rigorous oversight process required by the government.

Having said that, even these industries are being disrupted by the use of Iterative model and Agile methodology by organizations like Space X and others. Waterfall model was also used in banking, healthcare, control system for nuclear facilities, space shuttles etc

Advantages:

1. **Clear Structure and Predictability:** The Waterfall model's linear, sequential approach makes it easy to understand and manage, with distinct phases (requirements, design, implementation, testing, deployment).

2. **Easy Management:** The structured nature of the model allows for better project planning, resource allocation, and progress tracking.

3. **Suitable for Small, Well-Defined Projects:** The model is well-suited for projects where requirements are clear and unlikely to change significantly during development.

4. **Thorough Documentation:** The emphasis on documentation in each phase ensures a comprehensive record of the project, aiding in future maintenance and updates.

5. **Cost and Time Estimation:** The sequential nature of the model allows for better estimation of project costs and timelines, as each phase has defined deliverables.

Disadvantages:

1. **Lack of Flexibility:** The Waterfall model's rigid structure makes it difficult to accommodate changes or revisions in requirements once the project is underway.

2. **Late Feedback:** Client feedback is typically sought only after the product is developed, which can lead to costly rework if major issues are discovered late in the process.

3. **Not Suitable for Complex Projects:** The model struggles with complex projects where requirements are likely to evolve or are not well-defined initially.

4. **Testing Delayed:** Testing is often done at the end of the development cycle, which can lead to delays and increased costs if major issues are discovered late in the process.

5. **High Cost of Changes:** Making changes in later stages of the Waterfall model can be very costly, as it may require revisiting earlier phases.

Agile Methodology

The meaning of Agile is swift or versatile." Agile process model" refers to a software development approach based on iterative development. Agile methods break tasks into smaller iterations, or parts do not directly involve long term planning. The project scope and requirements are laid down at the beginning of the development process. Plans regarding the number of iterations, the duration and the scope of each iteration are clearly defined in advance.

Each iteration is considered as a short time "frame" in the Agile process model, which typically lasts from one to four weeks. The division of the entire project into smaller parts helps to minimize the project risk and to reduce the overall project delivery time requirements. Each iteration involves a team working through a full software development life cycle including planning, requirements analysis, design, coding, and testing before a working product is demonstrated to the client.

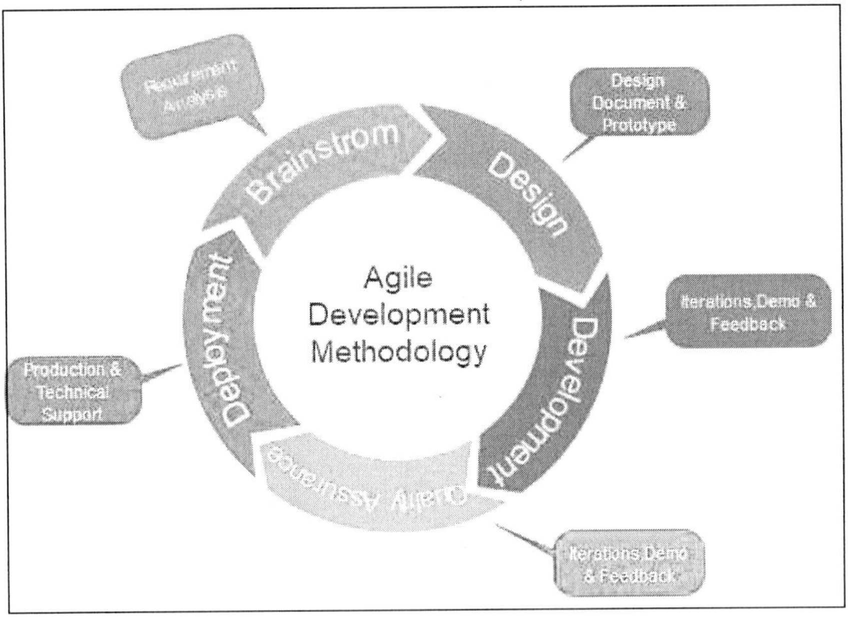

Fig.1.4

Phases of Agile Model: Following are the phases in the Agile model are as follows:

1. **Requirements gathering:** In this phase, you must define the requirements. You should explain business opportunities and plan the time and effort needed to build the project. Based on this information, you can evaluate technical and economic feasibility.

2. **Design the requirements:** When you have identified the project, work with stakeholders to define requirements. You can use the user flow diagram or the high-level UML diagram to show the work of new features and show how it will apply to your existing system.

3. **Construction/ iteration:** When the team defines the requirements, the work begins. Designers and developers start working on their project, which aims to deploy a working product. The product will undergo various stages of improvement, so it includes simple, minimal functionality.

4. **Testing:** In this phase, the Quality Assurance team examines the product's performance and looks for the bug.

5. **Deployment**: In this phase, the team issues a product for the user's work environment.

6. **Feedback:** After releasing the product, the last step is feedback. In this, the team receives feedback about the product and works through the feedback.

Agile Testing Methods: Agile testing is a continuous process integrated throughout the software development lifecycle, emphasizing collaboration, flexibility, and early feedback. It involves various techniques like unit testing, integration testing, functional testing, and regression testing, alongside more agile-specific approaches like Exploratory Testing, BDD (Behavior-Driven Development), and ATDD (Acceptance Test-Driven Development). These methods aim to deliver high-quality software efficiently, aligning with the iterative nature of agile development. Key agile testing methods are as:

1. **Unit Testing:** Focuses on verifying individual components of code to ensure they function correctly.

2. **Integration Testing:** Tests the interaction between different modules or components to ensure they work together seamlessly.

3. **Functional Testing:** Evaluates the software's features and functionalities against specified requirements.

4. **Regression Testing:** Ensures that new code changes haven't introduced any defects in existing functionality.

5. **Acceptance Testing:** Verifies that the software meets the customer's requirements and expectations.

6. **Exploratory Testing:** Testers explore the software freely, without pre-defined test cases, to uncover potential issues.

7. **Behavior-Driven Development (BDD):** Testers work collaboratively with developers and business analysts to define scenarios and expectations, often using examples to guide the development process.

8. **Acceptance Test-Driven Development (ATDD):** Focuses on writing acceptance tests early in the development process, based on customer feedback, to ensure the software meets their needs.

9. **Risk-Based Testing:** Prioritizes testing based on the potential impact and likelihood of defects, focusing on areas with the highest risk.

10. **Test Automation:** Automates repetitive testing tasks to improve efficiency and enable more frequent testing.

Advantages and Disadvantages of the Agile Methodology

Advantages: Agile project management has gained significant popularity due to its numerous advantages. From improved collaboration to better resource utilisation, Agile is designed to help teams deliver high-quality products more efficiently. Some of the key advantages of Agile methodology, which make it a go-to methodology for dynamic, fast-paced projects are:

1. **Enhanced Customer Satisfaction:** Agile's focus on customer involvement and feedback throughout the project life cycle leads to greater customer satisfaction. By working closely with stakeholders, Agile teams ensure that the product is aligned with customer expectations at each stage of development.

   - **Continuous Feedback Loops:** Agile encourages regular customer feedback during each sprint. This allows for real-time adjustments to the product, ensuring it meets evolving customer needs.

   - **Tailored Solutions:** By engaging customers early and often, Agile helps businesses deliver a product that is more in line with what the customer actually wants, rather than relying on assumptions made at the start of the project.

This approach results in higher customer satisfaction, as clients can see tangible progress regularly and have the opportunity to influence the direction of the project.

2. **Flexibility and Adaptability in Project Management:** The Agile model is inherently flexible, enabling teams to pivot and make adjustments when new information or challenges arise. Unlike traditional project management methods, Agile does not lock the project into a rigid plan. This flexibility is a major advantage, especially in fast-changing environments like tech and software development.

    - **Responding to Change:** Agile's iterative nature allows teams to adjust priorities based on feedback or changes in the market. This adaptability ensures that the project remains relevant and on track, even when unforeseen circumstances arise.

    - **Continuous Evolution:** With Agile, teams can revisit and refine the project's goals, features, or scope as needed. This ensures that the project can evolve in alignment with the customer's needs and market conditions.

    In short, Agile allows teams to manage and embrace change, rather than being constrained by it.

3. **Frequent Delivery and Reduced Risk:** Agile encourages frequent delivery of working software, which provides several benefits, including reduced risk and more predictable outcomes.

    - **Incremental Delivery:** By breaking projects into smaller, manageable sprints, Agile teams deliver working versions of the product regularly. This reduces the likelihood of significant project failures and ensures that the team can catch issues early.

    - **Early Problem Detection:** Since each sprint produces a deliverable, problems or risks can be identified early and addressed before they grow into bigger challenges. Regular progress assessments and testing help teams ensure the product meets quality standards.

    - **Reduced Risk of Scope Creep:** Agile's emphasis on continuous review and feedback allows for better control of scope changes. Teams are able to identify when additional features or changes are necessary and whether they fit within the project's goals.

Frequent delivery also allows stakeholders to assess progress regularly and ensure that the project is on track, which minimises the risk of misalignment or delays.

4. **Improved Team Collaboration and Morale:** One of the core principles of Agile is collaboration. Agile promotes close cooperation between team members and stakeholders, which fosters a sense of shared responsibility and camaraderie.

   - **Cross-functional Teams:** Agile encourages collaboration across different roles, bringing together developers, designers, product owners, and stakeholders into one cohesive team. This cross-functional teamwork ensures that different perspectives are integrated into the development process.

   - **Empowerment and Ownership:** Team members are empowered to make decisions and contribute ideas, which fosters a sense of ownership and accountability. This results in higher morale and greater commitment to project success.

   - **Increased Transparency:** Regular stand-ups and sprint reviews ensure that all team members are aware of project progress and challenges. This transparency leads to stronger teamwork and a more supportive work environment.

   Ultimately, Agile promotes a collaborative culture where everyone works together to deliver the best possible outcome, leading to higher team satisfaction and productivity.

5. **Efficient Resource Utilization:** Agile focuses on using resources more efficiently by breaking projects into smaller chunks that require fewer resources at each stage. This results in better planning, budgeting, and overall resource allocation.

   - **Prioritisation of Work:** Agile teams use tools like the product backlog to prioritise the most important tasks. This ensures that the team works on high-value activities first, using resources where they can have the greatest impact.

   - **Optimising Effort:** The focus on small, incremental tasks allows teams to allocate resources more effectively, ensuring that effort is spread evenly and work is completed in manageable phases.

- **Minimising Wastage:** Because Agile allows for quick adjustments based on feedback, teams can avoid spending unnecessary time and resources on features that are not required, helping to reduce waste.

This more efficient use of resources helps teams stay within budget and deliver projects on time.

6. **Emphasis on Technical Excellence:** Agile places a strong emphasis on technical excellence and encourages teams to continually improve their skills and practices. This focus on quality results in better products that meet the required standards.

   - **Code Quality:** Agile teams are committed to maintaining high standards of coding quality. Regular testing and integration during each sprint ensure that the software is reliable, robust, and scalable.

   - **Continuous Improvement:** Teams use retrospectives to reflect on each sprint, identifying areas for improvement. This allows them to refine processes, improve technical skills, and reduce defects over time.

   - **Focus on Simplicity:** Agile prioritises simplicity in design and development. By keeping things simple, teams can avoid unnecessary complexity and deliver more effective solutions.

   By continually focusing on technical excellence, Agile helps teams produce high-quality products that meet both customer needs and industry standards.

7. **Reduced Overhead and Bureaucracy:** Traditional project management often involves heavy documentation, complex planning processes, and hierarchical structures. In contrast, Agile reduces overhead and bureaucracy, streamlining the development process.

   - **Lean Processes:** Agile minimises unnecessary paperwork and administrative tasks. Instead of focusing on detailed documentation, Agile teams prioritise delivering value and producing working software.

   - **Empowered Teams:** Agile encourages decentralised decision-making, giving teams the autonomy to make decisions without needing approval from multiple layers of management. This reduces the need for constant oversight and accelerates decision-making.

- **Efficient Communication:** Agile promotes direct and open communication between team members and stakeholders, reducing the need for formal meetings or reports. This fosters an environment where issues can be addressed quickly and effectively.

By cutting down on bureaucracy, Agile makes it easier for teams to focus on the most important task delivering high-quality products that meet customer expectations.

Disadvantages: While the Agile model offers numerous advantages, it also presents several challenges and drawbacks. The flexibility and adaptability that make Agile effective in many scenarios can also lead to complications when not properly managed. Some of the significant disadvantages of Agile methodology, which teams and organisations should be aware of when deciding whether Agile is the right fit for their projects are as:

1. **Lack of Predictability in Project Outcomes:** One of the most commonly cited disadvantages of Agile development methodologies is the lack of predictability in terms of project timelines, budget, and scope.

    - **Uncertain Timelines:** Agile's iterative process means that the completion of a project is often difficult to predict in advance. While teams plan for each sprint, the overall timeline may shift based on customer feedback, evolving requirements, or unforeseen challenges.

    - **Budget Variability:** Agile does not provide a clear-cut budget from the start. Since requirements can change, and the project's direction may evolve over time, the total cost of the project can fluctuate, making it difficult for businesses to set a fixed budget.

    - **Scope Creep:** As new requirements are added in response to ongoing customer feedback, there is always the risk that the scope of the project will expand beyond initial expectations, potentially affecting both timelines and resources.

    In projects that require a high degree of predictability or fixed deadlines, Agile's fluidity can become a significant disadvantage.

2. **Limited Documentation Practices:** In contrast to traditional project management approaches, Agile places less emphasis on extensive documentation. While Agile encourages working software over comprehensive documentation, this can sometimes lead to difficulties in maintaining a clear project record.

- **Lack of Formal Documentation:** Agile relies on frequent communication and collaboration, but the lack of detailed documentation can create challenges in tracking decisions, changes, and project requirements, especially for new team members or for compliance purposes.

- **Knowledge Transfer:** In large or long-term projects, team turnover or changes can result in loss of vital project knowledge if there is insufficient documentation. Without well-documented processes, it can be difficult for new team members to get up to speed quickly.

- **Challenges with Compliance:** For industries with strict regulatory requirements (e.g., healthcare or finance), the minimal documentation may not meet industry standards, potentially leading to compliance risks.

While Agile's lighter documentation can make development more efficient, it may also create gaps in information, which could affect the project's transparency and accountability.

3. **Increased Demands on Team Resources:** Agile's focus on continuous iteration and frequent feedback puts a high demand on team resources. The pace and collaboration required can strain the team, especially in smaller organisations or teams that lack sufficient staffing.

- **Intense Workload:** Agile's rapid sprint cycles and emphasis on constant communication can lead to burnout, especially if the team is small or lacks the right resources. The need to constantly adjust, plan, and review can be exhausting over time.

- **Resource Overload:** In certain projects, especially those with evolving requirements, team members may find themselves juggling multiple tasks or constantly revising work. This can lead to inefficient allocation of resources and slower progress, particularly if the workload is not properly managed.

- **Need for Versatility:** Agile teams are typically required to be cross-functional, meaning team members often wear multiple hats. This can stretch individual capacity and may not always play to the strengths of all team members.

Thus, Agile can sometimes lead to resource depletion and overburdened teams if not managed carefully.

4. **Risk of Fragmented Output:** Due to the iterative nature of Agile and the focus on delivering small, incremental pieces of work, there is a risk of fragmented output. The end result may sometimes feel like a collection of parts rather than a cohesive product.

   - **Disjointed Features:** As Agile prioritises frequent delivery over overall consistency, different iterations might result in features that don't integrate seamlessly. This can be especially problematic in larger projects where various teams may work on different features without full coordination.

   - **Quality Control Issues:** Without an overarching vision, the product can become fragmented in terms of design, usability, and overall flow. Frequent changes can also lead to inconsistent quality across different parts of the product.

   - **Integration Challenges:** As components are developed in parallel across multiple sprints, integrating these elements into a unified final product can become complex, especially if early work was not sufficiently aligned with later iterations.

   While Agile aims to build a product incrementally, there is a risk that the output may lack cohesion if not carefully managed.

5. **Absence of a Definitive Project End:** Another significant disadvantage of Agile is that projects do not have a clearly defined end date or milestone.

   - **No Fixed Completion Date:** In Agile, the project continues evolving based on feedback and adjustments, making it difficult to pinpoint when the project is truly "finished." This open-ended nature can create confusion for stakeholders, particularly those who expect a fixed timeline.

   - **Continuous Improvements:** Agile focuses on delivering value continuously, which means that even when a product is technically "complete," there may still be room for improvements or new features. This can create a never-ending cycle of work, with no clear endpoint.

   - **Stakeholder Expectations:** The absence of a final deadline can lead to frustration from clients or stakeholders who may expect a finished product by a specific date. Agile's flexibility can sometimes conflict with external pressures to deliver something tangible and complete.

This lack of a definitive project end can make it challenging to manage client expectations and project closure.

6. **Difficulties in Measuring Overall Progress:** Agile's focus on iterative development means that measuring overall progress can be challenging, especially if there are no clear, predefined goals.

   - **Difficulty in Tracking Milestones:** Since Agile focuses on delivering incremental pieces of work, it's harder to gauge overall progress towards the final product. Traditional project management often relies on tracking major milestones, but Agile's fluid nature makes it more difficult to define and monitor these milestones effectively.

   - **Lack of Quantitative Metrics:** While Agile teams track individual sprints and deliverables, measuring success or progress on a broader scale can be elusive. Metrics such as velocity or burn-down charts may not provide a clear view of how much work is left or if the project is truly on track.

   - **Changing Priorities:** Agile's responsiveness to changing customer needs means that priorities can shift during the project. This dynamic nature makes it harder to define success or establish clear benchmarks of progress.

   This can be particularly challenging for teams that need to provide stakeholders with measurable indicators of success.

7. **Heavy Dependence on Customer Engagement:** Agile projects rely heavily on continuous customer feedback and engagement, which can become a disadvantage in certain contexts.

   - **Customer Availability:** Agile requires constant communication with the customer or end-user. If the customer is unavailable, lacks clarity, or provides inconsistent feedback, it can hinder the project's progress and lead to misunderstandings or misaligned expectations.

   - **Stakeholder Confusion:** In some cases, customers may have evolving or shifting priorities, making it difficult for the development team to remain focused. Frequent changes in direction can lead to confusion or dissatisfaction with the progress of the project.

   - **Overburdening the Customer:** The need for regular feedback can also be burdensome for customers, especially if they are not well-versed in

Agile processes. This can lead to frustration or disengagement, which may affect the project's success.

Thus, the heavy dependence on customer participation can lead to delays or misalignment, particularly when customers are not fully committed or available for ongoing feedback.

8. **Scaling Challenges in Large Projects:** Agile is often seen as a great fit for small to medium-sized projects, but it can face scaling challenges when applied to larger, more complex initiatives.

   - **Coordination Across Multiple Teams:** As projects grow in size, managing multiple Agile teams can become difficult. The risk of fragmented work increases as different teams tackle different parts of the project, making it challenging to maintain cohesion and consistency across the product.

   - **Increased Complexity:** Large projects require careful coordination, especially when different components depend on each other. Agile's flexibility may make it difficult to synchronise work across teams or ensure all teams are following the same processes and principles.

   - **Tooling and Infrastructure:** Scaling Agile often requires specialised tools and infrastructure to manage and track multiple teams' work. Without these tools, large projects can become unmanageable, and communication breakdowns may occur.

   As Agile methods struggle to scale effectively in larger environments, organisations may face significant challenges in ensuring that large projects stay on track.

Scrum and Kanban

Scrum and Kanban are two popular Agile frameworks used to improve project management, collaboration, and product delivery in both software and non-software environments.

Scrum: Scrum is an Agile framework used to develop and deliver complex products through short, time-boxed iterations called Sprints, typically lasting 2–4 weeks. It emphasizes collaboration, flexibility, and continuous improvement. In Scrum, work is organized from a Product Backlog, a prioritized list of features and tasks managed by the Product Owner.

The Scrum Team consisting of the Product Owner, Scrum Master, and Development Team holds a Sprint Planning meeting to select tasks for the upcoming sprint. The team meets daily in a short Daily Stand-up to synchronize efforts and discuss progress or obstacles. At the end of each sprint, the team presents the completed work in a Sprint Review and reflects on performance in a Sprint Retrospective to identify improvements. Scrum encourages the delivery of a potentially shippable product increment after every sprint, ensuring fast feedback and adaptability to change. It promotes transparency, accountability, and customer involvement, making it especially useful for projects with evolving requirements. Scrum's structure, combined with frequent inspections and adjustments, allows teams to respond quickly to challenges, continuously enhance product quality, and deliver value more efficiently. It's widely used in software development but is also applicable to various other industries. The key principles of Scrum are as:

1. **Control Over the Empirical Process:** In Scrum, the empirical process is based on observation of hard evidence and experimentation rather than theory. There are three main ideas to empirical process control: transparency, inspection, and adaptation.

2. **Self-organization:** As the Scrum process relies on many individuals, self-organization is essential. Everyone involved is empowered to work independently, and the self-organization principle allows for greater buy-in among all parties, while making it easier to assess individual contributions.

3. **Collaboration:** Scrum is a collaborative process, as evidenced by the many roles involved (more on that below). This principle also focuses on three dimensions of collaboration: awareness, articulation, and appropriation.

4. **Value-based Prioritization:** This principle involves organizing and prioritizing tasks based on their value and how they need to be completed.

5. **Time-boxing:** In Scrum, tasks are completed in "sprints," with specific lengths of time assigned to each one. Other elements, including "sprint planning" and daily meetings, are also given specific start and stop times. This time-boxing ensures that all involved know how much time is allocated to each step, with the goal of eliminating wasted time and delays.

6. **Iterative Development:** This final principle speaks to the understanding that a project may need to be refined multiple times during the development process. Iterative development allows the team to make adjustments and manage change easier.

Three Pillar of Scrum: The three pillars of Scrum are Transparency, Inspection, and Adaptation. These pillars are essential for Scrum's empirical process control, ensuring that progress is based on observation and experience rather than pre-determined plans.

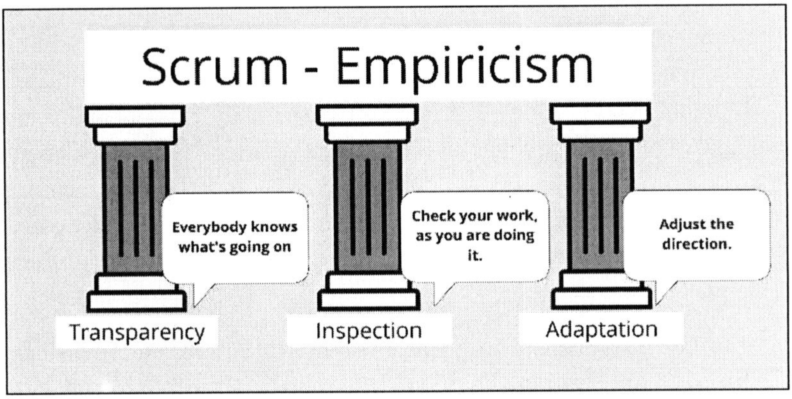

Fig.1.5

1. **Transparency:** Ensures that all aspects of the work are visible to both the team and stakeholders. This promotes open communication and allows for better understanding and alignment.

2. **Inspection:** Involves regularly evaluating the team's progress and the product being developed. This can be done through activities like daily stand-ups, sprint reviews, and sprint retrospectives.

3. **Adaptation:** Means making changes based on the inspection findings. This involves adapting the product, processes, or practices to better meet the needs of the customer and the team.

Kanban: Kanban is a visual project management method used to enhance workflow efficiency. It focuses on visualizing work, limiting work in progress (WIP), and managing flow to improve team productivity and reduce bottlenecks. Key principles include visualizing the workflow, limiting WIP, focusing on flow, and continuously improving the process. The four principles of Kanban are:

1. **Start with what you do now:** Kanban recognizes the value of your existing processes and practices. At the start of any project, change management professionals will conduct a discovery phase to review and understand your current process. Kanban's goal is to build on this process and improve it instead of introducing a whole new set of rules out of the bat.

This allows you to thoroughly review your workflow, roles, responsibilities, titles, communications, and more. Thus, maximizing efficiencies and cost savings as well as focusing on where improvements need to be made.

2. **Agree to pursue incremental, evolutionary change:** The concept of continuous improvement is critical to Kanban and is a quality it shares with Agile and Scrum methodologies. Delivering change in small, steady increments is also shared by these project management approaches. Doing so helps minimize disruption and make the change process more manageable.

   Significant changes are more challenging to implement and likely to meet internal resistance. Senior management may be concerned about costs, while project teams may feel that changes to working practices may impede their productivity. Kanban recognizes this, emphasizing small, continuous, incremental change instead.

3. **Respect the current process, roles, responsibilities, titles:** Being respectful helps reinforce the idea that Kanban will not be overly disruptive or completely change established operating models. This is particularly important if those models are effective. This approach positions Kanban as a compromising and collaborative means of improving legacy processes without fundamentally disrupting an organization's operations. This whole approach helps to gain support for Kanban in an environment where various teams are attached to established practices. It is beneficial in larger organizations where change is slower, and there are more people to convince.

4. **Encourage acts of leadership at all levels in your organization**As part of Kanban's emphasis on collaboration, anyone can take ownership of and address an issue. With the transparency Kanban provides, any team member should be able to take action and justify it with solid data to back them up. This encouraging culture helps to empower team members to take the lead, take risks, and grow professionally and personally.

Differences Between Scrum and Kanban: Scrum and Kanban are both Agile frameworks, but they differ in their approach to managing work. Scrum uses fixed-length sprints (time-boxed iterations) and has defined roles and meetings, while Kanban focuses on continuous flow and is more flexible with roles and meetings.

Fig.1.2

S.No.	Feature	Scrum	Kanban
1.	Timeboxing	Works in fixed-length sprints (e.g., 2-4 weeks).	No timeboxes; work flows continuously.
2.	Planning	Detailed sprint planning at the start of each sprint.	Just-in-time planning; work is pulled into the workflow as needed.
3.	Work Board	Scrum board resets after each sprint; focuses on the tasks planned for the sprint.	Kanban board is continuous; focuses on visualizing the state of work items and their progress through the workflow.
4.	Roles	Defined roles: Scrum Master, Product Owner, Development Team.	No mandatory roles; can include Service Delivery Manager and Service Request Manager for workflow support.
5.	Commitment	Commitment is made to a specific sprint goal; changes are not made during a sprint.	Commitment based on capacity; work is pulled in based on available capacity.
6.	Meetings	Mandatory meetings: Sprint Planning, Daily Stand-up, Sprint Review, Sprint Retrospective.	No mandatory meetings; meetings are flexible and depend on team needs; may include daily stand-ups, and service-level meetings.
7.	Cadence	More structured framework with fixed-length iterations (sprints).	More flexible; allows for continuous delivery and adaptation.
8.	Change Philosophy	A Scrum team is not allowed to make any changes during an active sprint.	Change can happen at any time; teams can adapt to changing needs as they work on tasks.

DevOps and Continuous Integration/Continuous Deployment (CI/CD)

DevOps and Continuous Integration/Continuous Deployment (CI/CD) are modern software development practices aimed at improving the speed, quality, and reliability of software delivery.

DevOps: DevOps is a combination of the terms "Development" and "Operations." It represents a cultural and professional movement that focuses on unifying software development (Dev) and IT operations (Ops) teams to improve collaboration, increase efficiency, and accelerate software delivery.

In traditional software development models, development and operations teams worked separately. Developers would build and test code, then hand it off to operations for deployment and maintenance. This often led to miscommunication, delays, and software failures due to differing goals and disconnected workflows. DevOps aims to eliminate these silos by promoting a collaborative culture and using automation tools to integrate development, testing, deployment, and monitoring processes. The result is a more streamlined and efficient software delivery pipeline, with quicker feedback loops and improved product quality. The principles of DevOps are as:

1. **Automation of the software development lifecycle:** This includes automating testing, builds, releases, the provisioning of development environments, and other manual tasks that can slow down or introduce human error into the software delivery process.
2. **Collaboration and communication:** A good DevOps team has automation, but a great DevOps team also has effective collaboration and communication.
3. **Continuous improvement and minimization of waste:** From automating repetitive tasks to watching performance metrics for ways to reduce release times or mean-time-to-recovery, high performing DevOps teams are regularly looking for areas that could be improved.
4. **Hyperfocus on user needs with short feedback loops:** Through automation, improved communication and collaboration, and continuous improvement, DevOps teams can take a moment and focus on what real users really want, and how to give it to them.

By adopting these principles, organizations can improve code quality, achieve a faster time to market, and engage in better application planning.

Phases of DevOps: The key phases of DevOps, often represented as an infinite loop to show the continuous and integrated nature of the process:

1. **Plan:** Define requirements, goals, and timelines. Involves collaboration between stakeholders and teams to outline features and updates. Tools: Jira, Trello, Azure Boards.

2. **Develop:** Developers write code based on planned features. Version control systems track changes. Tools: Git, GitHub, GitLab, Bitbucket.
3. **Build:** Code is compiled, dependencies are resolved, and builds are generated automatically. Tools: Maven, Gradle, Jenkins.
4. **Test:** Automated and manual tests are conducted to ensure code quality and functionality. Tools: Selenium, JUnit, TestNG.
5. **Release:** The tested build is prepared for deployment. It may be staged for further testing or approved for production. Tools: Jenkins, GitLab CI/CD, Spinnaker.
6. **Deploy:** Code is deployed to production or staging environments. This can be done manually or automatically (CD). Tools: Kubernetes, Docker, Ansible, Terraform.
7. **Operate:** The application is now live and serving users. Operations teams monitor system performance and ensure uptime. Tools: Kubernetes, Docker Swarm, Nagios.
8. **Monitor:** Continuous monitoring of application performance, usage, and issues. Feedback is collected to improve future releases. Tools: Prometheus, Grafana, ELK Stack, New Relic.

Continuous Integration (CI): Continuous Integration (CI) is a software development practice where developers frequently integrate their code into a shared repository usually multiple times a day. Each integration is verified through an automated build process that includes compiling the code and running a suite of automated tests. This approach allows teams to identify and fix bugs quickly, improves software quality, and reduces the time required to deliver updates. The main goal of CI is to prevent integration problems often referred to as "merge conflicts" or "integration hell" by ensuring that new code changes work well with the existing codebase. By automating the build and test process, developers receive immediate feedback on their changes, making it easier to detect errors early and keep the codebase in a deployable state at all times.

CI is typically implemented using tools like Jenkins, GitHub Actions, GitLab CI/CD, or CircleCI, which automate the process of building, testing, and sometimes even deploying applications. It encourages smaller, more frequent code commits, leading to smoother collaboration among team members and faster development cycles. Best practices for CI include writing thorough automated tests, keeping the build process fast, and addressing failed builds immediately. When combined with practices like Continuous Delivery (CD) or

Continuous Deployment, CI becomes a foundational part of modern DevOps workflows, enabling teams to deliver reliable software quickly and efficiently.

1. **Frequent Merging:** Developers are encouraged to merge their code changes into the main branch of the shared repository frequently, often multiple times a day.

2. **Automated Builds and Tests:** After each merge, automated processes build the software and run various tests (e.g., unit tests, integration tests) to ensure the new code works as expected and doesn't introduce any regressions.

3. **Early Bug Detection:** By identifying and resolving integration problems early, CI helps to prevent large integration headaches and reduces the cost of fixing bugs later in the development process.

4. **Improved Collaboration:** CI promotes a collaborative environment where developers can easily share and integrate their work without fear of causing major conflicts.

5. **Faster Feedback:** Automated builds and tests provide developers with quick feedback on the status of their code, enabling them to make necessary changes more efficiently.

Working of Continuous Integration: The working of continuous integration is as:

1. **Code Commit:** A developer writes code and commits it to a shared version control system like Git (e.g., GitHub, GitLab, Bitbucket).

2. **Trigger Build:** Every time code is committed, it triggers an automated process, often called a CI pipeline. This is typically managed by a CI server or tool (e.g., Jenkins, GitHub Actions, CircleCI, Travis CI, GitLab CI).

3. **Build the Application:** The CI system pulls the latest code and builds the software. This might involve compiling code, packaging applications, or setting up environments.

4. **Run Automated Tests:** Tests are run to ensure the code works correctly. These include:

   - **Unit tests** (test individual pieces of logic)

   - **Integration tests** (check how components work together)

   - **End-to-end tests** (simulate real user scenarios)

If any test fails, the build is marked as broken, and the team is alerted.

5. **Feedback Loop:** Results are reported back to the developer quickly, often within minutes. If the build fails, the developer fixes the issue and recommits. If it passes, the change is now integrated and ready for further stages like deployment.

6. **Artifacts and Deployment (Optional):** Some CI pipelines go further by generating build artifacts (e.g., packaged applications) or automatically deploying to staging environments.

Advantages of Continuous Integration (CI)

1. **Early Bug Detection**: CI ensures that code is tested immediately after it's committed, making it easier to identify and fix bugs early in the development process.

2. **Improved Code Quality**: Automated testing and frequent integration promote cleaner, more maintainable code and reduce the risk of introducing errors.

3. **Faster Feedback**: Developers get quick feedback on their changes, which helps them correct issues right away instead of days or weeks later.

4. **Reduced Integration Problems**: By integrating code frequently, teams avoid the dreaded "merge hell" and minimize conflicts between developers' work.

5. **Better Collaboration**: Since everyone works on the same main branch and integrates changes regularly, teamwork becomes smoother and more coordinated.

6. **Automation of Routine Tasks**: CI automates builds and tests, saving developers time and reducing manual errors.

7. **Improved Project Transparency**: With centralized CI dashboards and logs, the team always knows the current state of the project and the health of the codebase.

Disadvantages of Continuous Integration (CI)

1. **Initial Setup Effort**: Setting up CI tools, configuring test environments, and writing automated tests can require significant initial time and effort.

2. **Requires Strong Test Coverage**: CI is only as effective as the tests it runs. Without a solid suite of automated tests, CI can't provide meaningful feedback.

3. **Maintenance Overhead**: Test scripts, build configurations, and pipelines need to be maintained alongside the application code, which can increase workload.

4. **False Positives or Flaky Tests**: Inconsistent test results can lead to failed builds, even when the code is fine. This can erode confidence in the CI system.

5. **Slower Builds with Large Projects**: As projects grow, CI builds can take longer, potentially slowing down the development workflow if not optimized.

6. **Learning Curve**: Developers unfamiliar with CI tools and workflows may need time to adapt, especially in teams transitioning from manual processes.

7. **Tooling and Infrastructure Costs**: Hosting your own CI server or using premium CI services may add to project costs, especially for larger teams or complex pipelines.

Continuous Deployment (CD): Continuous Deployment (CD) is a software development practice where every change that passes automated testing is automatically released into production without manual intervention. It builds upon Continuous Integration (CI), which ensures that code is regularly merged and tested. In Continuous Deployment, the pipeline doesn't stop at testing once the code passes all tests, it's automatically deployed to live environments. This means new features, bug fixes, and improvements can reach users quickly and frequently. The goal of CD is to streamline the delivery process, reduce human error, and maintain a consistent, repeatable deployment workflow that can scale with the needs of the business.

To successfully implement Continuous Deployment, a high level of automation and test coverage is essential. The deployment pipeline must include robust unit tests, integration tests, and end-to-end tests to ensure that only high-quality, stable code reaches production. Tools like GitLab CI/CD, GitHub Actions, CircleCI, and AWS CodePipeline are commonly used to automate the deployment process. Continuous Deployment enables faster innovation, reduces time-to-market, and allows teams to respond to customer feedback more rapidly. It requires a cultural shift toward trust in automated processes, strong monitoring, and often the use of techniques like feature flags and blue-green deployments to minimize risk during releases. When done correctly, Continuous Deployment empowers teams to deliver software with speed, confidence, and reliability. Phases of Continuous Development:

1. **Continuous Integration (CI):** Developers frequently merge code changes into a shared repository. Automated builds and tests are then run on these changes to identify integration issues early.

2. **Continuous Testing:** Automated tests are executed throughout the development lifecycle to ensure code quality and functionality.

3. **Continuous Delivery (CD):** This phase prepares the software for release, automating the build, testing, and deployment processes. It ensures that the code is ready to be deployed to production.

4. **Continuous Deployment (CD):** This is the final step where the software is automatically deployed to production after passing the testing and delivery stages.

Advantages of Continuous Delivery/Deployment (CD)

1. **Faster Time-to-Market**: CD allows teams to release new features, bug fixes, and improvements to users quickly and frequently.

2. **Reduced Manual Effort**: Automation eliminates repetitive manual tasks involved in deployment, reducing human error and freeing up developer time.

3. **Higher Release Confidence**: With automated testing and deployment pipelines, teams gain confidence that the code is production-ready at all times.

4. **Quick Feedback Loops**: Continuous delivery enables fast feedback from real users, allowing teams to make data-driven decisions and iterate faster.

5. **Improved Product Quality**: Frequent, smaller releases reduce the chances of large-scale bugs and make it easier to isolate and fix problems.

6. **Better Customer Satisfaction**: Users get access to new features and fixes more quickly, improving their overall experience and engagement.

7. **Scalability and Consistency**: Automated deployments ensure consistent behavior across different environments (staging, production, etc.), helping teams scale efficiently.

Disadvantages of Continuous Delivery/Deployment (CD)

1. **High Setup and Maintenance Effort**: Creating and maintaining robust deployment pipelines, test environments, and automation scripts can be time-consuming and complex.

2. **Strong Test Automation is Essential**: Without reliable and comprehensive automated testing, there's a risk of deploying broken or unstable code.

3. **Cultural Resistance:** Shifting to CD often requires a significant cultural change within teams and organizations, which may face resistance.

4. **Increased Monitoring Needs**: With frequent releases, teams must invest in strong monitoring and alerting systems to detect and respond to issues in production.

5. **Security Concerns**: Automated deployment can introduce vulnerabilities if proper security checks and controls aren't part of the pipeline.

6. **Potential for Releasing Bugs Faster**: If tests miss critical issues, CD can push faulty code into production quickly, affecting users before manual review can catch it.

7. **Complex Rollback Strategies Needed**: Automated deployments require well-planned rollback or feature flag systems in case of failure, adding extra complexity.

Differences Between DevOps, Continuous Integration (CI), and Continuous Deployment (CD): The differences between DevOps, Continuous Integration (CI), and Continuous Delivery/Deployment (CD) is as in table 1.3.

Table 1.3

S.No.	Aspects	DevOps	Continuous Integration	Continuous Deployment
1	Definition	A culture and set of practices to unify Dev and Ops teams.	Practice of frequently integrating code and running automated tests.	Automating the release of code to staging or production environments.
2	Focus Area	Collaboration, automation, and monitoring across SDLC.	Code integration and testing.	Deployment and delivery pipeline.
3	Goal	Deliver software faster and more reliably through team collaboration.	Detect integration errors early.	Deliver updates to users quickly and safely.
4	Scope	Broad (includes CI, CD, monitoring, infrastructure, etc.).	Narrow (focuses on code integration and build verification).	Developers, testers, operations, deployment tools.
5	Involves	Culture, tools, processes, teams (Dev + Ops).	Developers, version control, CI tools.	Developers, testers, operations, deployment tools.

Choosing the Right SDLC Model

Choosing the right Software Development Life Cycle (SDLC) model depends on various factors, including project scope, complexity, risk, budget, timeline, and client involvement. For projects with clear requirements, limited changes, and a need for predictable timelines, the Waterfall model is suitable. For projects requiring flexibility and adaptability to evolving requirements, Agile and Iterative models are more appropriate. Some factors to consider are as:

1. **Project Scope and Complexity:** Larger, more complex projects might benefit from models like Spiral or Agile, which allow for iterative development and risk management.
2. **Flexibility and Adaptability:** If requirements are likely to change or the project needs to adapt to new information, models like Agile, Iterative, or Spiral are good choices.
3. **Budget and Resource Availability:** Some models, like Waterfall, may be simpler to manage initially, but others, like Agile, might require more resources and expertise for training.
4. **Risk Management:** Projects with high-risk factors or uncertainties might benefit from models like Spiral, which actively addresses risk throughout the development process.
5. **Project Timeline:** If you need a predictable timeline, Waterfall might be a good choice. For projects where flexibility is more important than a fixed timeline, Agile is preferable.
6. **Client Involvement:** If you need strong client collaboration and feedback throughout the project, Agile, Prototype, or Iterative models are more appropriate.
7. **Industry Requirements:** Certain industries might have specific requirements for SDLC models (e.g., government contracts often prefer Waterfall).

Choosing the Right Model: The ways to choose the right model is as:

1. **Analyze Requirements:** Understand the project scope, timeline, and client needs.
2. **Evaluate Risks:** Assess potential risks and uncertainties.

3. **Consider Team Expertise:** Ensure the chosen model aligns with the team's skills and experience.

4. **Determine Client Involvement:** Factor in the desired level of client engagement.

5. **Prioritize Flexibility:** Choose a model that allows for adaptation to changes.

By carefully considering these factors and the characteristics of different SDLC models, you can select the most appropriate approach for your project.

******

3

Software Engineering Principles

Software engineering principles are foundational guidelines that help developers design, build, and maintain high-quality software in a systematic, efficient, and scalable way. These principles ensure that software is reliable, maintainable, and meets the needs of users and businesses. Whether you're working on a small application or a complex enterprise system, following these principles improves code quality, reduces bugs, and enhances team productivity.

1. **Abstraction:** Abstraction means focusing on essential features while hiding unnecessary details. In software design, this allows developers to manage complexity by working at a higher level, such as designing class structures without worrying about internal implementation details. This principle improves clarity and promotes code reuse.

2. **Modularity:** Modularity involves breaking a system into smaller, independent modules or components that can be developed and tested separately. Each module performs a specific function, and modules interact with each other through well-defined interfaces. Modularity improves maintainability, scalability, and debugging.

3. **Encapsulation:** Encapsulation is the bundling of data and methods that operate on that data within a single unit, typically a class. It also restricts direct access to some of an object's components, which helps prevent unintended interference.

Encapsulation protects internal object states and ensures better control over data.

4. **Separation of Concerns (SoC):** SoC means dividing a program into distinct sections, each responsible for a specific aspect or functionality. This leads to cleaner, more organized code and allows different parts of the system to be developed or modified independently. For example, separating business logic from UI code makes it easier to maintain and test.

5. **DRY (Don't Repeat Yourself):** The DRY principle encourages developers to avoid duplicating code. Instead, common logic should be abstracted into reusable functions or modules. This reduces the chance of errors and makes code easier to maintain, as changes only need to be made in one place.

6. **KISS (Keep It Simple, Stupid):** This principal advocates for simplicity in design and code. Simple solutions are easier to understand, debug, and maintain. Avoiding unnecessary complexity makes software more robust and reduces the likelihood of bugs.

7. **YAGNI (You Aren't Gonna Need It):** YAGNI reminds developers not to implement features until they are actually needed. Premature optimization or adding unnecessary functionality can lead to wasted time and increased code complexity. Focus on current requirements, not anticipated ones.

8. **High Cohesion and Low Coupling:** Cohesion refers to how closely related the responsibilities of a single module are. High cohesion means that a module does one thing well. Coupling refers to the degree of dependency between modules. Low coupling is ideal, as it means modules can be changed without impacting others. Together, high cohesion and low coupling lead to flexible, maintainable systems.

9. **Open/Closed Principle:** A system should be open for extension but closed for modification. This means new functionality can be added without changing existing code, typically achieved using interfaces or inheritance.

Modularity, Reusability, and Maintainability

Modularity in SDLC: Modularity refers to the practice of dividing a software system into separate, independent units or modules, each responsible for a specific functionality. In the context of the SDLC:

1. During the Design Phase, modularity helps in breaking down the system architecture into manageable components.

2. It simplifies development, as each module can be built, tested, and debugged independently.

3. Modularity improves parallel development, allowing teams to work on different modules simultaneously.

4. It enhances code readability and makes it easier to identify and fix bugs in a specific part of the system without affecting the entire application.

Reusability in SDLC: Reusability means the ability to use existing software components or code in new applications with little or no modification. In the SDLC:

1. In the Requirement Analysis and Design stages, identifying reusable components helps reduce development time and cost.

2. During Implementation, using reusable libraries, modules, or APIs ensures consistency and speeds up coding.

3. It leads to higher productivity, reduces duplication of effort, and promotes standardization across multiple projects.

4. Reusable code is often well-tested and reliable, reducing the chances of introducing bugs into new systems.

Maintainability in SDLC: Maintainability is the ease with which a software system can be updated to correct faults, improve performance, or adapt to a changed environment. Throughout the SDLC:

1. In the Design Phase, maintainability is influenced by following good software engineering principles like modularity, clear documentation, and consistent naming conventions.

2. Maintainable software is easier to test and debug, especially during the Testing and Maintenance phases.

3. It lowers the long-term cost of the system, as developers can make changes with minimal risk of introducing errors.

4. High maintainability ensures the system can evolve with business needs and technology trends, extending its useful life.

SOLID Principles

The SOLID principles are a set of five object-oriented design guidelines Single Responsibility, Open/Closed, Liskov Substitution, Interface Segregation, and Dependency Inversion that aim to improve software quality. Integrating these principles into each phase of the Software Development Life Cycle (SDLC) leads to robust, scalable, and maintainable software systems.

1. **Single Responsibility Principle (SRP):** During the design and development phases, SRP encourages breaking down a system into smaller, focused components. Each class or module should have only one reason to change, meaning it should handle only one job. For example, a UserService should manage user logic, while EmailService handles email sending. This separation simplifies testing and maintenance in the testing and maintenance phases, as changes in one part of the system are less likely to affect others.

2. **Open/Closed Principle (OCP):** This principle is most relevant during the design and development stages. A system should be open for extension (new features can be added) but closed for modification (existing code doesn't need to change). For example, adding a new payment method shouldn't require altering existing payment logic just extend the functionality via interfaces or abstract classes. This approach reduces bugs and regression issues during testing and makes it easier to scale or enhance features during maintenance.

3. **Liskov Substitution Principle (LSP):** LSP supports the implementation and testing phases by ensuring that subclasses can replace base classes without breaking the system. For example, if a class Bird has a method fly(), a subclass Penguin shouldn't override it in a way that contradicts expectations (since penguins can't fly). Violating LSP can lead to unexpected behavior and bugs. Ensuring this consistency makes unit and integration testing more reliable and simplifies future enhancements.

4. **Interface Segregation Principle (ISP):** During requirement analysis and design, ISP helps in creating focused, role-specific interfaces rather than forcing classes to implement large, unnecessary interfaces. This leads to a cleaner architecture. For instance, instead of having one IMachine interface with print(), scan(), and fax(), create separate interfaces like IPrinter, IScanner, and IFax. This promotes loose coupling and is especially helpful during development and maintenance, as updates to one functionality won't affect unrelated modules.

5. **Dependency Inversion Principle (DIP):** DIP is critical in the design, development, and testing phases. It promotes depending on abstractions (e.g., interfaces) rather than concrete implementations. This allows different parts of the application to work independently and makes the code more testable through dependency injection. For example, a class should rely on an ILogger interface rather than a concrete FileLogger. This abstraction allows flexibility and easier substitution during testing (e.g., with mock objects) and reduces coupling for future enhancements.

DRY (Don't Repeat Yourself) and KISS (Keep It Simple, Stupid)

The DRY (Don't Repeat Yourself) principle is a core software engineering concept that emphasizes reducing duplication in code. It was first introduced in the book The Pragmatic Programmer by Andy Hunt and Dave Thomas. The idea is simple: every piece of knowledge or logic in a system should exist in a single, unambiguous place. When developers repeat logic, it increases the risk of errors and inconsistency. For example, if the same validation logic appears in multiple files and a change is needed, a developer must remember to update it everywhere. If even one instance is missed, it can introduce bugs. By writing reusable functions, using modules, and adhering to clean architecture patterns, teams can eliminate redundancy and make software easier to maintain and scale. In the context of the Software Development Life Cycle (SDLC), DRY plays an essential role in the design, development, and maintenance phases. During development, avoiding code duplication results in cleaner and shorter code that is easier to read and debug. In the testing phase, fewer duplicated logic paths mean fewer test cases and reduced effort. Over the long term, DRY supports better maintainability, as updates to business logic, design patterns, or error handling can be done in one place without worrying about inconsistencies. It also encourages modularity and abstraction, which are crucial for building flexible and scalable systems. In summary, DRY helps developers write smarter, cleaner code and significantly improves collaboration and long-term project sustainability.

KISS (Keep It Simple, Stupid): The KISS (Keep It Simple, Stupid) principal advocates for simplicity in software design and development. It emphasizes that systems work best when they are kept simple rather than made complex unnecessarily. Originally coined by the U.S. Navy in the 1960s, the principle has become a cornerstone of effective software engineering. The core idea is that developers should avoid overengineering solutions or introducing complexity that doesn't solve an immediate problem. Simple code is easier to read, understand, test, and maintain. For example, choosing a straightforward if-else statement over an abstract, complex pattern when it isn't needed can often save time and reduce bugs. KISS reminds developers to build for clarity and functionality first, rather than cleverness.

In the SDLC, KISS is particularly important during the design and implementation phases. It helps teams focus on delivering features that meet the current requirements without bloating the codebase with "future-proofing" that may never be used. Simpler code also makes onboarding new developers easier and speeds up debugging during the testing phase. During maintenance, software that follows KISS is much easier to update or refactor. While simplicity doesn't mean lack of functionality, it means delivering that functionality in the cleanest, most direct way possible. When combined with principles like DRY, KISS fosters the development of robust, understandable, and adaptable systems. In essence, KISS is about making code as simple as it can be but no simpler so that it remains powerful yet manageable.

Separation of Concerns

Separation of Concerns (SoC) is a fundamental software engineering principle that emphasizes organizing code in such a way that different parts of a program handle different, clearly defined tasks or "concerns." A *concern* refers to a specific piece of functionality or behavior in a software system such as user interface handling, data processing, business logic, or database access. By separating these concerns, developers can write cleaner, more manageable code that is easier to maintain, extend, and debug.

The principle of SoC plays a critical role across the Software Development Life Cycle (SDLC), particularly in the design, development, and maintenance phases. During the design phase, software architects structure the system so that different modules or layers are responsible for specific functionalities. A common example is the three-tier architecture: the presentation layer (user interface), the business logic layer (application functionality), and the data access layer (communication with databases). By separating these layers, changes in one part of the application (e.g., updating the UI) don't affect others (e.g., data storage logic), reducing the risk of unintended side effects.

In the development phase, SoC makes the codebase more modular and organized. Developers can work on individual components independently, allowing for better collaboration and parallel development. It also simplifies unit testing and debugging since each component has a clear, isolated responsibility. For instance, if there's an error in how data is displayed to the user, developers can focus on the UI code without having to sift through the entire business logic or data access code.

SoC is also invaluable during the maintenance phase of the SDLC. As software evolves to accommodate new requirements, updates are easier to apply when concerns are well-separated. Modifying one aspect of the application is less likely to break others, which improves overall stability and reduces the cost and effort of maintenance. This also enhances reusability, as individual components can often be reused across different projects or modules if they're designed with clear boundaries.

Frameworks and patterns like Model-View-Controller (MVC), Service-Oriented Architecture (SOA), and microservices are built around the principle of Separation of Concerns. In MVC, for example, the Model manages data and business logic, the View handles UI rendering, and the Controller manages user input. This separation allows front-end and back-end developers to work independently while maintaining a cohesive system structure.

In conclusion, Separation of Concerns is not just a best practice but a foundational approach that brings structure and clarity to software systems. It supports better code organization, simplifies testing and debugging, enhances maintainability, and allows for greater flexibility and scalability. Whether you are building a small app or a complex enterprise system, applying SoC across the SDLC will lead to cleaner, more reliable, and more adaptable software.

SUMMARY OF FOUNDATIONS OF SOFTWARE ENGINEERING

Software engineering is the disciplined application of engineering principles to the development, operation, and maintenance of software systems. It is essential due to the growing reliance on software in all sectors, emphasizing structured processes to ensure quality, efficiency, and reliability. Unlike hardware, software is intangible and constantly evolving, posing unique challenges, such as managing complexity, changing requirements, and ensuring maintainability. The Software Development Life Cycle (SDLC) guides the process through various models, including the traditional Waterfall model and modern approaches like Agile, Scrum, Kanban, and DevOps, each suitable for different project needs. Agile encourages adaptability and customer collaboration, while DevOps integrates development and operations with practices like Continuous Integration and Continuous Deployment (CI/CD) to streamline delivery. Core engineering principles such as modularity, reusability, and maintainability are vital for building scalable systems. Key design philosophies like SOLID principles promote good object-oriented design, while DRY (Don't Repeat Yourself) and KISS (Keep It Simple, Stupid) encourage efficient and understandable code. Separation of Concerns further supports organized system design by dividing functionality into distinct components. Choosing the right methodologies and adhering to these principles ensures software that is robust, scalable, and easy to maintain. Overall, the foundation of software engineering lies in balancing technical excellence with effective project management to meet user needs within constraints.

1. Introduction to Software Engineering

Software engineering is the systematic application of engineering principles to the development, design, testing, deployment, and maintenance of software systems. It aims to produce high-quality, reliable, and efficient software that meets user requirements while staying within budget and time constraints. As software becomes integral to nearly every aspect of modern life healthcare, finance, transportation, communication its complexity and scale have grown, making structured development practices essential. Unlike hardware, which is physical and relatively stable, software is intangible and constantly evolving, requiring continuous updates and improvements. The field emerged in response to the "software crisis" of the mid-20th century, when many projects failed due to poor planning and execution. Today, software engineering emphasizes teamwork, documentation, modularity, and maintainability to manage complexity and change effectively. It not only improves product quality but also ensures that software systems are scalable, secure, and adaptable to future needs.

- **Definition and Importance:** Software engineering is the application of engineering principles to the design, development, testing, deployment, and maintenance of software. Its main goal is to produce high-quality, reliable, efficient, and maintainable software systems that meet user requirements within budget and time constraints. Unlike ad-hoc programming, software engineering emphasizes structured methodologies, documentation, and standard practices to reduce errors, improve performance, and ensure scalability.

  The importance of software engineering has grown exponentially due to the increasing reliance on software in every aspect of life from communication and transportation to healthcare and finance. Well-engineered software can boost productivity, enhance security, reduce costs, and provide a competitive edge.

- **Software vs. Hardware:** Software refers to a set of instructions that tell a computer how to perform specific tasks. It is intangible and evolves over time through updates, patches, or complete rewrites. Hardware, on the other hand, includes the physical components of a computer system such as CPUs, RAM, and hard drives.

  While hardware follows predictable patterns of wear and technological obsolescence, software requires continuous updates to fix bugs, add features, and adapt to new environments. The flexibility and complexity of software make its engineering more nuanced and challenging than hardware design.

- **Evolution of Software Engineering:** In the early days of computing (1950s-60s), software was written by hardware engineers with little focus on structure or maintainability. This led to the "software crisis," where projects ran over budget, were late, or failed altogether.

  To address this, software engineering emerged in the 1970s with the introduction of formal methodologies, structured programming, and better project management practices. Over the years, new paradigms such as object-oriented programming, Agile development, and DevOps have transformed the field to make software more adaptive, scalable, and user-focused.

- **Key Challenges in Software Development:** Despite advances, software development faces persistent challenges:

  - **Changing Requirements:** Clients often alter their needs mid-development, impacting timelines and design.
  - **Complexity:** Large systems are difficult to design, test, and maintain.
  - **Quality Assurance:** Ensuring bug-free, secure, and efficient code is challenging.
  - **Time and Cost Constraints:** Balancing quality with budget and delivery deadlines.
  - **Team Collaboration:** Effective communication among diverse teams is vital but hard to manage.

2. Software Development Life Cycle (SDLC)

The SDLC is a structured process that guides software development from concept to deployment and maintenance. It ensures systematic and efficient project execution.

- **Waterfall Model:** The Waterfall model is a linear, sequential approach consisting of distinct phases: requirements, design, implementation, testing, deployment, and maintenance. Each phase must be completed before the next begins.

- **Agile Methodology:** Agile promotes iterative development, customer collaboration, and adaptability to change. Work is divided into small increments (called iterations or sprints) with continuous feedback and testing.

- **Scrum and Kanban:** Scrum is an Agile framework with defined roles (Product Owner, Scrum Master, Team) and events (Sprint Planning, Daily Stand-up, Sprint Review, and Retrospective). Work is broken into 2–4-week sprints. Kanban focuses on visualizing work in progress using boards and limiting work items to improve flow and efficiency. Both aim to improve team communication and productivity by promoting transparency and adaptability.

- **DevOps and CI/CD:** DevOps bridges development and operations, emphasizing automation, continuous feedback, and faster delivery. Core practices include Continuous Integration (CI) developers merge code frequently, and automated tests validate the code. Continuous Deployment (CD) automatically deploying tested code to production. This reduces human error, accelerates releases, and improves collaboration between teams.

- **Choosing the Right SDLC Model:** The choice of SDLC model depends on factors like project size, complexity, team expertise, timeline, and client flexibility. Waterfall may suit fixed-scope, well-documented projects, while Agile or DevOps fits fast-paced, evolving environments.

3. Software Engineering Principles

Effective software design follows time-tested principles to improve readability, maintainability, and scalability.

- **Modularity, Reusability, and Maintainability**

  - **Modularity:** Breaking down a system into manageable, independent components (modules) that can be developed and tested separately.

  - **Reusability:** Writing code that can be reused across projects or systems, saving time and ensuring consistency.

  - **Maintainability:** Ensuring the code is easy to understand, modify, and extend over time.

These principles reduce complexity and improve long-term software health.

- **SOLID Principles:** Introduced by Robert C. Martin (Uncle Bob), these five principles guide object-oriented design:

  - **Single Responsibility Principle (SRP):** A class should have only one reason to change.

- **Open/Closed Principle (OCP):** Software entities should be open for extension but closed for modification.
- **Liskov Substitution Principle (LSP):** Subclasses should be substitutable for their base classes.
- **Interface Segregation Principle (ISP):** Clients should not be forced to depend on interfaces they do not use.
- **Dependency Inversion Principle (DIP):** High-level modules should not depend on low-level modules; both should depend on abstractions.

Applying SOLID leads to more flexible and robust codebases.

- **DRY and KISS:** DRY (Don't Repeat Yourself) avoid duplicating code; centralize logic to a single location. This prevents inconsistencies and simplifies updates. KISS (Keep It Simple, Stupid) design systems to be as simple as possible. Overcomplicating leads to errors and makes maintenance harder. Together, these encourage clarity and efficiency in development.
- **Separation of Concerns:** This principle emphasizes dividing software into distinct sections, each handling a separate concern (e.g., UI, business logic, data access). By isolating responsibilities, code becomes easier to manage, test, and debug. For example, using MVC (Model-View-Controller) architecture separates data models, user interface, and control logic.

******

PART–2

REQUIREMENTS ENGINEERING AND DESIGN

Requirements engineering and design are foundational phases in software development that ensure the final product meets user needs and performs effectively. Requirements engineering involves systematically gathering, analyzing, documenting, validating, and managing the needs and expectations of stakeholders. It starts with eliciting requirements through interviews, surveys, and observation, followed by analyzing and refining them for clarity, consistency, and feasibility. These are categorized into functional requirements, which define specific system behaviors, and non-functional requirements, which describe quality attributes such as performance, security, and usability. Once validated, the requirements are documented in a Software Requirements Specification (SRS), serving as a blueprint for development. The design phase translates these requirements into a structured technical solution, starting with high-level architectural design, which outlines the system's overall structure, components, and data flow. This is followed by low-level design, detailing module-level logic, algorithms, and data structures. Good design emphasizes principles like modularity, reusability, scalability, and maintainability. Together, requirements engineering and design establish a clear, shared understanding of system goals and create a roadmap for efficient and effective software development.

4

Requirements Engineering

Requirements engineering in software engineering is a critical and initial phase of project development, essential for successful systems. It serves as a bridge between stakeholders' aspirations and software possibilities, shaping project scope, schedule, and outcomes. This process involves understanding user needs, defining system functionalities, and managing constraints to gather, document, analyze, and validate requisites systematically. Collaboration among stakeholders is crucial, and detailed documentation ensures that developers understand the project's essence.

Effective requirements engineering demands iterative refinement and validation, creating accurate and achievable project goals, while also preventing scope changes and project failures. It is an ongoing process throughout the software development lifecycle, where revisiting and refining requirements are key to the success of the software project.

Requirement Engineering Process: Requirement Engineering is a fundamental process in software development that focuses on understanding, documenting, validating, and managing the needs and constraints of stakeholders to ensure the successful development of a software system.

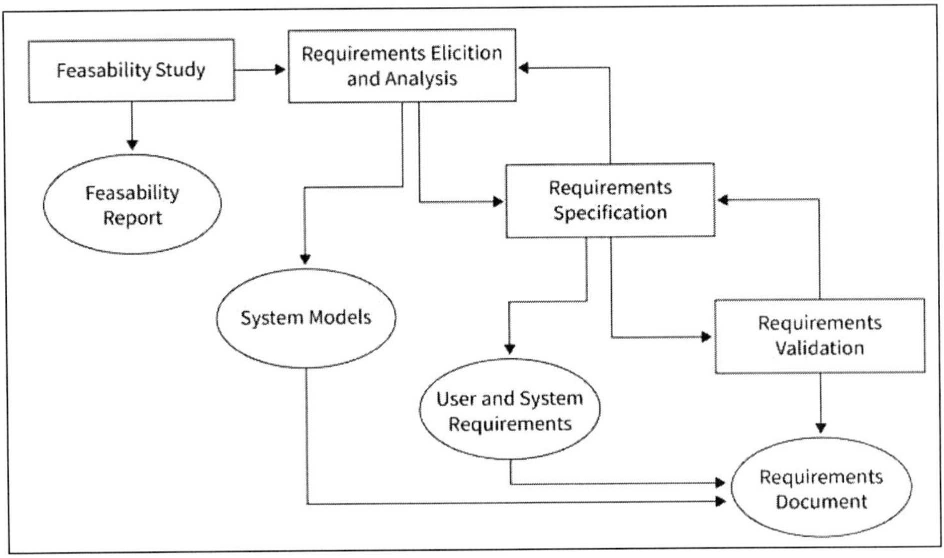

Fig.2.1

The process typically consists of several steps to ensure that the final software product meets the needs and expectations of the users and stakeholders.

1. **Feasibility Study:** This is the initial phase of the requirement engineering process. It involves evaluating the feasibility of the proposed software project. The main objective is to determine whether the project is technically, economically, and operationally viable. During this phase, the following aspects are considered:

   - **Technical Feasibility:** Can the proposed system be developed with the available technology and resources?
   - **Economic Feasibility:** Is the project economically viable in terms of cost and benefits?
   - **Operational Feasibility:** Will the system work effectively within the existing organizational structure and processes?

2. **Requirement Elicitation and Analysis:** This phase involves gathering and analyzing requirements from stakeholders, including users, customers, and domain experts. The goal is to understand the needs of the system and translate them into specific software requirements. This process involves several techniques, such as:

- **Interviews:** Direct communication with stakeholders to gather information.
- **Surveys:** Distributing questionnaires to collect opinions and preferences.
- **Workshops:** Group sessions to brainstorm and gather requirements collaboratively.
- **Observation:** Actively observing users to understand their workflow and needs.
- **Prototyping:** Building a preliminary version of the software to elicit feedback.

Once requirements are gathered, they are analyzed for consistency, completeness, and feasibility. Conflicts and ambiguities are resolved, and the requirements are organized into different categories based on their characteristics (e.g., functional, non-functional).

3. **Software Requirement Specification:** In this phase, the gathered and analyzed requirements are documented formally. The Software Requirement Specification (SRS) document is created, which serves as a blueprint for the development process. The SRS includes the following components:

    - **Functional Requirements:** Descriptions of what the system should do in terms of specific functions and features.
    - **Non-functional Requirements:** Constraints and qualities the system must possess (e.g., performance, security).
    - **User Interfaces:** Descriptions of how users will interact with the system.
    - **Data Requirements:** Details about the data the system will store, process, and manage.

4. **Software Requirement Validation:** This step involves validating the documented requirements to ensure they accurately represent the stakeholders' needs and expectations. The aim is to identify and rectify any errors or misunderstandings before development begins. Techniques used for requirement validation include:

    - **Reviews:** Expert reviews and walkthroughs to identify issues in the SRS.

- **Prototyping:** Building a working model of the software to validate requirements.
- **Simulation:** Simulating the software's behavior to test its alignment with requirements.

5. **Software Requirement Management:** Requirement management is an ongoing process that involves maintaining and tracking changes to requirements throughout the software development lifecycle. It includes activities such as:
   - **Version Control:** Managing different versions of the requirements document.
   - **Change Control:** Managing and documenting changes to requirements and their impact.
   - **Traceability:** Establishing links between requirements and design, implementation, and testing.
   - **Prioritization:** Assigning priorities to requirements to guide development efforts.
   - **Communication:** Ensuring stakeholders are informed about changes and updates to requirements.

Types of Requirements: Functional vs. Non-functional

In software engineering, requirements define what a system should do and how it should perform. They are broadly classified into three main types: functional requirements, non-functional requirements, and domain requirements. Each type addresses different aspects of the software system and contributes to building a complete and reliable solution.

Functional Requirements: Functional requirements define the specific behaviors, functions, and features that a software system must perform to fulfill user needs and business objectives. They describe what the system should do, focusing on how it responds to inputs, processes data, and generates outputs. These requirements are essential because they form the core functionality of the software and directly influence system design, implementation, and testing.

Functional requirements are typically expressed through use cases, user stories, or system specifications. They detail interactions between users and the system and outline processes the software must support. Examples include user registration, login/logout, data entry and validation, processing transactions, generating reports, sending notifications, or integrating with other systems.

These requirements help developers understand how the system should behave in different scenarios and guide testers in verifying whether the system functions as intended. They should be clear, complete, consistent, and testable to avoid ambiguity and reduce the risk of project failure.

For example, in an online banking system, functional requirements might include allowing users to check account balances, transfer funds, and receive transaction alerts. Each of these features represents a functional requirement that must be accurately captured and implemented.

Overall, functional requirements form the backbone of a software project. Without them, the development team cannot build a system that meets user expectations. Therefore, gathering, analyzing, and documenting functional requirements carefully is critical to delivering successful and reliable software solutions.

Key aspects of functional requirements:

1. **User-centric:** Functional requirements are often expressed from the user's perspective, focusing on how they will interact with the software and what they expect the system to do in response.

2. **System behavior:** They specify how the system should behave under specific conditions, including inputs, processes, and outputs.

3. **Development guidance:** Functional requirements provide developers with a clear understanding of what features and functionalities need to be implemented to meet the system's goals.

4. **Foundation for design:** They form the basis for software design and implementation, ensuring that the system delivers the intended functionality.

Non-functional: A non-functional Requirement (NFR) defines the quality attributes, performance standards, and constraints of a system, focusing on how a system operates rather than what it does. Unlike functional requirements that describe specific behaviors or functions of a system (such as user authentication or data entry), NFRs ensure that these functions are performed in a way that meets user expectations and system constraints. They set the benchmark for aspects like performance, scalability, security, usability, maintainability, and reliability. For instance, an NFR might state that a system should load within two seconds under normal load or that it should be available 99.9% of the time during a calendar year. These requirements are crucial for determining the overall user experience and long-term sustainability of a product. NFRs often influence design decisions, system architecture, and testing strategies, playing a key role in ensuring that the end product is not only functional but also efficient, secure, and robust.

While NFRs may not be as visible as functional requirements in the user interface, they are equally critical for a system's success. Poorly defined or overlooked non-functional requirements can lead to performance bottlenecks, security vulnerabilities, or user dissatisfaction. For example, in a healthcare application, it's not enough for the system to simply store patient data—it must do so securely and in compliance with regulatory standards like HIPAA. Similarly, a mobile app must be not only feature-rich but also lightweight and responsive across different devices. NFRs also help in defining service level agreements (SLAs), guide software testing strategies (such as load or stress testing), and support decision-making during development and deployment. Therefore, identifying and clearly specifying non-functional requirements early in the project lifecycle is essential to building high-quality, reliable systems that align with both business goals and user needs. Importance of non-functional requirements are as:

1. **User Experience:** NFRs directly impact the user experience, ensuring that the system is not only functional but also enjoyable and efficient to use.

2. **System Quality:** NFRs contribute to the overall quality of the system, making it reliable, stable, and robust.

3. **Business Needs:** NFRs often align with business needs, ensuring that the system meets specific performance and security requirements.

4. **Architectural Decisions:** NFRs are essential inputs for architectural decisions, guiding the design and development of the system.

5. **Testing and Validation:** NFRs provide criteria for testing and validating the system, ensuring that it meets the defined quality standards.

Differences Between Functional and Non-functional Requirement: The differences between functional and non-functional requirement are shown in fig.2.1.

Table 2.1

S.No.	Aspect	Functional Requirement	Non-Functional Requirement
1	Definition	Describes *what* the system should do.	Describes *how* the system should behave.
2	Focus	Focuses on specific functionalities or features.	Focuses on performance, usability, security, etc.
3	Example	The system shall allow users to log in.	The system shall respond to login requests within 2 seconds
4	Testing	Verified through functional testing (e.g., unit, integration).	Verified through performance, load, or security testing.
5	User Interaction	Directly visible to the end-user.	Often indirectly experienced by the user.
6	Documentation Format	Typically written as use cases or user stories.	Written as quality attributes, constraints, or metrics.
7	Importance in Design	Drives the system's behavior and logic.	Shapes system architecture and user experience.

Requirements Gathering Techniques

Requirements gathering is a critical phase in the software development lifecycle. It involves identifying and documenting the needs and expectations of stakeholders for a new or modified product. The success of any project largely depends on how accurately and comprehensively the requirements are gathered and analyzed. A poorly executed requirements gathering process can lead to project delays, budget overruns, and systems that fail to meet stakeholder expectations. To ensure clarity, completeness, and accuracy, various techniques are employed during this phase. Some of the most commonly used requirements gathering techniques:

1. **Interviews:** Interviews are one of the most commonly used and effective requirements gathering techniques, involving direct, face-to-face or virtual conversations with stakeholders to understand their needs, expectations, and goals for a system. They can be structured (with a predefined set of questions), semi-structured (a mix of planned and open-ended questions), or unstructured (free-flowing and informal). This technique allows analysts to dive deep into specific topics, ask follow-up questions, and gain insights that might not emerge through other methods. Interviews are especially useful when dealing with

subject matter experts or end-users who can provide detailed insights into current processes, pain points, and desired improvements. However, to be successful, interviews must be well-planned, with clear objectives and relevant questions. The interviewer must also have good communication skills to build rapport and encourage openness. One key advantage is the ability to clarify ambiguous points in real time. However, this method can be time-consuming, and the quality of results depends heavily on the interviewer's skills and the interviewee's willingness to share information. In larger projects, conducting multiple interviews with different stakeholders ensures a comprehensive understanding of requirements from various perspectives. Proper documentation of interview findings is crucial to avoid misunderstandings later in the development process. Additionally, analysts often record interviews (with permission) to ensure no details are lost and to support further analysis. Overall, interviews are a foundational technique for eliciting clear and detailed requirements directly from those who will use or be impacted by the system.

2. **Questionnaires and Surveys:** Questionnaires and surveys are structured techniques used to gather information from a large number of stakeholders efficiently. They are particularly effective when input is needed from geographically dispersed users or when time and resources are limited. Surveys consist of a set of questions either open-ended (qualitative) or close-ended (quantitative) designed to gather specific information about users' expectations, preferences, and current challenges. This technique allows for standardized data collection, making it easier to analyze trends and identify common needs. Questionnaires are also beneficial when anonymity is important, as users may be more honest about their concerns or dissatisfaction if they do not have to identify themselves. However, the quality of information gathered depends largely on the design of the questionnaire. Poorly worded, ambiguous, or leading questions can result in inaccurate or misleading responses. Therefore, crafting clear, concise, and unbiased questions is essential. Pilot testing the questionnaire with a small group before full distribution can help identify any issues. One limitation of this method is the lack of real-time interaction, which means there's no opportunity to ask follow-up questions or clarify unclear answers. Despite this, questionnaires remain an excellent tool for gathering high-level input from many stakeholders, prioritizing features, or validating ideas collected through other methods like interviews or workshops. They are especially useful in the early stages of a project to gauge overall user sentiment and expectations. When analyzed effectively, survey results can provide valuable insights that

support informed decision-making and better align the final product with user needs.

3. **Observation:** Observation, also known as job shadowing, is a highly effective requirements gathering technique that involves watching users interact with current systems or perform their daily tasks within their natural work environment. This method is particularly useful for understanding real-world workflows, identifying inefficiencies, and capturing non-verbal cues and unspoken needs that might not be expressed during interviews or surveys. Observation can be either passive where the analyst simply watches without interfering or active, where the observer may ask questions during the process. The main strength of this technique lies in its ability to reveal the "actual" process rather than the "perceived" one, as users often omit or forget key steps when describing their tasks verbally. Observation is especially valuable in uncovering hidden requirements, workarounds, and informal processes that are critical to the functioning of a system but may not be documented. However, it is time-consuming and may not be feasible for large user bases. Additionally, the Hawthorne Effect where people alter their behavior because they know they're being observed can skew results. To reduce this effect, observers should remain as unobtrusive as possible. Notes, photographs (if permitted), and task recordings are often used to document findings. Observation is ideal for systems that are operational and where understanding user behavior in context is essential. Combining this technique with interviews or prototyping can provide a more holistic understanding of user needs and system requirements, making it a valuable tool for business analysts and UX designers alike.

4. **Workshops:** Workshops are collaborative and interactive sessions where stakeholders and development team members come together to discuss, define, and refine system requirements. This technique is highly effective for gathering input from multiple perspectives in a short amount of time and for resolving conflicting requirements early in the project. Workshops often involve structured activities such as brainstorming, prioritization exercises, and process modeling, and may be facilitated by a business analyst or project manager. One specialized form of workshop is the Joint Application Development (JAD) session, where users and developers jointly define system requirements in an intensive, structured workshop format. Workshops encourage active participation, promote shared understanding among stakeholders, and foster consensus on key issues. This method is particularly useful for complex projects that involve multiple departments or when there are communication gaps between technical

and non-technical participants. A well-planned workshop can quickly produce a large volume of high-quality requirements, while also building stakeholder ownership and trust. However, workshops require careful planning, skilled facilitation, and the availability of key participants, which can be challenging to coordinate. To be effective, workshops should have clear goals, a structured agenda, and defined roles for participants. The use of visual aids like whiteboards, sticky notes, flowcharts, or mind maps can enhance discussion and help participants articulate ideas more clearly. Post-workshop documentation is essential to capture agreements and action points. Overall, workshops are a dynamic and productive way to engage stakeholders and collaboratively define system requirements in a time-efficient manner.

Writing Good Software Requirements

Writing good software requirements is one of the most essential tasks in the software development lifecycle. Whether you're building a mobile app, an enterprise solution, or a web-based system, the quality of your requirements determines the clarity of the development process, the efficiency of testing, and ultimately, the satisfaction of end users. Poorly written requirements can lead to misunderstandings, scope creep, missed deadlines, and costly rework. In contrast, well-written software requirements serve as a reliable blueprint, guiding the design, development, testing, and deployment of a successful product.

Best Practices for Writing Good Requirements

1. **Understand the Business Context:** Before you begin writing requirements, it is crucial to understand the problem the software is intended to solve. Meet with stakeholders, study existing systems, analyze business processes, and gather domain knowledge. Understanding the "why" behind a requirement is just as important as knowing "what" needs to be built.

2. **Engage Stakeholders Early and Often:** Include key stakeholders such as end-users, product owners, subject matter experts, and sponsors in the requirements-gathering process. Their feedback will help ensure the requirements reflect real-world needs and reduce the risk of rework later.

3. **Use Simple, Concise Language:** Avoid jargon, overly technical terms, or complex sentences. Use clear and direct language that is understandable to both technical and non-technical readers. For example, instead of saying "The application shall initialize the authentication mechanism," simply write "The system shall allow users to log in using a username and password."

4. **Use the Correct Format and Templates:** Organize your requirements using consistent templates or structured formats such as the IEEE Software Requirements Specification (SRS) format. Common sections include:

   - Introduction and scope
   - Functional requirements
   - Non-functional requirements
   - Assumptions and constraints
   - Use cases or user stories
   - Acceptance criteria

Structured formatting ensures all areas are covered and makes the document easier to read and review.

5. **Incorporate Use Cases and User Stories:** Use cases and user stories provide context and help visualize user interactions with the system. A use case describes a sequence of actions that a system performs in response to a user's input. A user story, popular in agile methodologies, describes the need from the user's perspective. For example: "As a registered user, I want to reset my password so I can regain access to my account."

6. **Avoid Vague Words:** Words like "fast," "user-friendly," "secure," or "efficient" are subjective and open to interpretation. Instead, quantify these attributes. For example, replace "The system should be fast" with "The system shall respond to user inputs within 2 seconds under normal load conditions."

7. **Review and Validate Regularly:** Requirements should not be written once and forgotten. Schedule regular reviews with stakeholders and the development team to confirm that the requirements are still valid and feasible. This also helps catch gaps or inconsistencies early.

8. **Use Diagrams and Visual Aids:** Complement textual requirements with diagrams such as flowcharts, wireframes, data models, or user interface mockups. Visuals enhance understanding, especially for complex systems, and can reduce misinterpretations.

Common Mistakes to Avoid: Some common mistakes used to avoid while writing good software writing are as follows:

1. **Writing design into requirements**: Focus on what the system should do, not how it should do it. Avoid prescribing specific implementation details unless absolutely necessary.
2. **Overloading one requirement**: Each requirement should describe one functionality. Compound requirements are harder to test and maintain.
3. **Neglecting edge cases and error handling**: Requirements should also define what happens in abnormal or failure conditions.
4. **Ignoring non-functional requirements**: Many teams focus only on functional features and overlook performance, security, or compliance needs.
5. **Failing to prioritize**: Without prioritization, developers might work on low-impact features while critical needs are delayed.

Tools to Support Requirement Writing: Modern tools can help manage and organize software requirements effectively:

- **JIRA** (for agile teams using user stories and epics)
- **Confluence** (for collaborative documentation)
- **Microsoft Word or Excel** (for traditional requirement specifications)
- **DOORS** or **Helix RM** (for large enterprise systems requiring traceability and audit logs)
- **Lucidchart, Draw.io** (for diagrams and process flows)

These tools allow version control, collaboration, traceability, and integration with development and testing workflows.

Importance of Good Requirements: Writing good software requirements is not just a documentation exercise; it's an investment in the project's success. Clear, comprehensive, and validated requirements:

1. Reduce ambiguity and miscommunication
2. Align team members on goals and scope
3. Serve as a baseline for development, testing, and validation
4. Help manage changes more effectively
5. Improve customer satisfaction by delivering what was actually needed

Projects with well-defined requirements have a higher chance of staying on budget, meeting deadlines, and delivering a product that adds value.

Good software requirements are the foundation of successful software projects. They bridge the gap between what users want and what developers build. By following best practices such as using clear language, prioritizing requirements, involving stakeholders, and validating frequently you ensure that your requirements document becomes a reliable guide for the entire development lifecycle. Ultimately, the time and effort invested in writing good requirements pay off by reducing misunderstandings, enhancing product quality, and increasing customer satisfaction. Whether you're working in agile, waterfall, or a hybrid model, mastering the skill of writing good requirements is crucial for every analyst, developer, and project manager.

Use Case and User Stories

In the world of software development, understanding user needs and how they interact with a system is critical to building effective and user-friendly applications. Two of the most widely used techniques for capturing these requirements are Use Cases and User Stories. While both are focused on describing interactions between users and systems, they differ in format, detail, and their role in the software development process. This document explores both concepts in depth, comparing their structure, purpose, and usage to help teams determine when and how to use them effectively.

Use case: A Use Case is a detailed description of how a user interacts with a system to achieve a specific goal. It outlines the steps taken by the user (referred to as the "actor") and how the system responds to those actions. Use cases are commonly used in traditional and object-oriented software development methodologies and serve as a foundational tool for capturing functional requirements. They help bridge the gap between stakeholders, developers, and testers by providing a clear narrative of system behavior from the user's point of view. A typical use case includes components such as a title, actors, preconditions (what must be true before the use case starts), the main flow (or basic flow), alternate or exception flows (how the system should behave in less common situations), and postconditions (what is true after the use case is completed). For example, in a "User Login" use case, the actor is a registered user, and the system steps might include verifying credentials and granting access to a user dashboard. This structure helps ensure that all scenarios are considered during design and development.

Use cases are especially useful when developing complex systems with multiple user roles and interactions. They provide a visual and textual roadmap that helps teams understand how various parts of the system function in relation to each other. Use cases can be complemented with UML (Unified Modeling Language) diagrams for better visualization of relationships between actors and system functionalities. Unlike user stories, which are brief and agile-focused, use cases are comprehensive and typically used in detailed documentation, especially in industries that require thorough system analysis and traceability (e.g., healthcare, finance, government). Well-written use cases enable developers to build features accurately, testers to derive meaningful test cases, and stakeholders to validate that user goals are being met. Ultimately, use cases play a crucial role in ensuring that systems are designed to meet real user needs while considering both normal operations and exceptional situations. Key Components of a use case are as:

1. **Title**: A brief name describing the interaction.
2. **Actor(s)**: The user or external system interacting with the system.
3. **Preconditions**: Conditions that must be true before the use case can start.
4. **Main Flow (Basic Flow)**: The typical sequence of steps from start to finish.
5. **Alternative Flows**: Variations on the main flow due to exceptions or different paths.
6. **Postconditions**: The state of the system after the use case is completed.
7. **Assumptions and Notes**: Additional context or clarifications.

Advantages of Use Cases: Some advantages of use cases are as follows:

1. **Comprehensive Coverage:** Use cases provide an in-depth look at all possible user interactions with the system, including edge cases and alternate paths.
2. **Improved Communication:** They serve as a detailed reference for developers, testers, and business analysts.
3. **Support for Complex Systems:** Ideal for systems where the interaction logic is complex and multi-step.
4. **Basis for Test Cases:** Testers can derive functional test cases directly from use case flows.

However, use cases can become too detailed or time-consuming for fast-moving Agile teams.

User Stories: User Stories are short, simple descriptions of a feature or functionality told from the perspective of the user who desires it. They are a fundamental part of Agile methodologies like Scrum and Kanban, focusing on delivering small, incremental pieces of functionality that provide value to the end-user. The basic format of a user story is often written as: "As a [type of user], I want [an action or feature], so that [I can achieve a goal or benefit]." This format keeps the focus on user needs, making it clear what the system must do, why it is important, and for whom it is intended. For example, "As a registered user, I want to reset my password so that I can regain access to my account" clearly communicates the user's desire and the expected outcome. User stories are intentionally brief and non-technical, allowing all stakeholders, including business owners, developers, and testers, to quickly understand the requirement. They also provide the flexibility to adapt as requirements evolve over time.

One of the main strengths of user stories is their focus on delivering value quickly and iteratively. They are typically small enough to be completed within a single sprint in Agile development, which encourages fast feedback from stakeholders and frequent delivery of working software. This helps ensure that the system is constantly evolving in line with user needs, rather than being built in isolation over months or years. Additionally, user stories are often accompanied by acceptance criteria, which specify the conditions under which a story is considered "done." These criteria help guide developers and testers, ensuring the functionality meets the agreed-upon standards. One challenge with user stories is their lack of detailed information; for more complex features, additional documentation like diagrams, wireframes, or expanded stories may be needed. However, the simplicity and focus on user goals make user stories an excellent tool for creating clear, actionable, and testable requirements that keep teams focused on delivering the most valuable features first.

Advantages of User Stories: Some advantages of user stories are as follows:

1. **Simplicity and Clarity:** User stories are written in plain language, making them easy for all stakeholders to understand.

2. **Customer-Centric:** Keeps the focus on user value and encourages constant feedback and adaptation.

3. **Supports Iterative Development:** Perfect for delivering small, incremental features that can be tested and validated quickly.

4. **Easy to Prioritize:** Because stories are small and modular, teams can easily prioritize and shift tasks based on business needs.

The trade-off is that user stories may lack the depth needed to fully understand complex workflows unless supplemented with additional artifacts like story maps or flow diagrams.

Differences Between Use Cases and User Stories: The differences between use case and user stories are listed in table 2.2.

Table 2.2

S.No.	Aspect	Use Case	User Stories
1	Purpose	Describes detailed interactions between users and the system, including alternate paths.	Describes a simple, high-level user need and its intended benefit.
2	Structure	Structured with components like title, actors, preconditions, main flow, alternative flows, and postconditions.	Follows a simple format: "As a [user], I want [action], so that [benefit]."
3	Scope	Covers comprehensive, end-to-end processes, often involving multiple user roles and system behaviors.	Covers a single functionality or feature with a clear user goal.
4	Usage	Often used in traditional software development or detailed documentation (e.g., waterfall).	Common in Agile development methodologies (e.g., Scrum, Kanban) for iterative, incremental delivery.
5	Focus	Focuses on system functionality and behavior from the user's perspective.	Focuses on delivering user value and ensuring the system meets user needs.
6	Format	Formal, with a comprehensive narrative and potentially accompanying diagrams (e.g., UML).	Informal, with a user-centric statement, often written on index cards or in simple text.
7	Flexibility	Less flexible, typically follows a detailed process, and requires significant updates for changes.	Highly flexible, can be easily adapted, refined, and split for iterative work.
8	Associated Artifacts	Often includes visual aids like use case diagrams, activity diagrams, or flowcharts.	Often includes acceptance criteria, estimates, and may involve additional clarification artifacts (e.g., mockups).
9	Examples	"User logs into the system, enters credentials, system verifies credentials, and grants access."	"As a user, I want to reset my password so I can regain access to my account."

5

Software Architecture and Design

Software architecture and design are fundamental aspects of software engineering that focus on structuring systems to ensure scalability, maintainability, and performance. Software architecture refers to the high-level structure of a system, defining its components, their relationships, and how they interact, often represented through architectural patterns such as client-server, microservices, or layered architecture. It provides a blueprint that guides development and aligns technical solutions with business goals. Software design, on the other hand, deals with the lower-level implementation details, focusing on the logic and structure within components, using design principles like SOLID and design patterns such as MVC, Singleton, or Factory. Together, architecture and design address both the macro and micro aspects of a system, ensuring that it is robust, efficient, and adaptable to change. Key quality attributes like reliability, security, usability, and performance are directly influenced by architectural decisions. Good software architecture also considers trade-offs, addressing concerns like cost, time, and technical constraints. Communication among stakeholders including developers, architects, business analysts, and clients is crucial during the architecture and design phases to ensure the system meets both functional and non-functional requirements. Additionally, architectural documentation and modeling tools such as UML or C4 diagrams help visualize the system's structure and foster better understanding among team members. As systems grow in complexity, a well-defined architecture becomes even more critical for managing dependencies, enabling reuse, and supporting continuous integration and delivery. Ultimately, effective software architecture and design are essential for building high-quality software systems that can evolve with changing requirements and technologies.

Software architecture design is the process of defining the high-level structure and organization of a software system, including its components, interactions, and principles. It involves making fundamental structural choices that impact the system's long-term maintainability, scalability, and performance. A well-designed architecture serves as a blueprint for the development project, guiding the implementation and evolution of the software.

Key Aspects of Software Architecture Design: Component identification and definition: Identifying the core modules or components of the system and defining their responsibilities and interfaces.

Relationship definition, establishing how components interact with each other, including data flow, communication protocols, and dependencies.

1. **Non-functional Requirements:** Considering factors like performance, security, scalability, and reliability when designing the architecture.
2. **Choosing an Appropriate Architectural Pattern:** Selecting a suitable architectural style (e.g., microservices, MVC, layered architecture) based on the system's needs and constraints.
3. **Documentation and Communication:** Creating clear documentation and communicating the architecture to stakeholders and developers.

Software Design: Software design provides a design plan that describes the elements of a system, how they fit, and work together to fulfill the requirement of the system. The objectives of having a design plan are as follows:

1. To negotiate system requirements, and to set expectations with customers, marketing, and management personnel.
2. Act as a blueprint during the development process.
3. Guide the implementation tasks, including detailed design, coding, integration, and testing.

It comes before the detailed design, coding, integration, and testing and after the domain analysis, requirements analysis, and risk analysis.

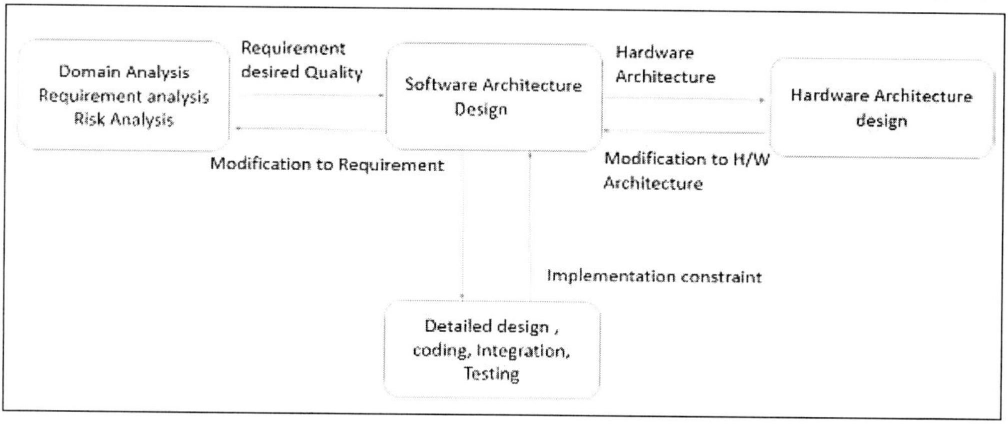

Fig.2.2

Goals of Architecture: The primary goal of the architecture is to identify requirements that affect the structure of the application. A well-laid architecture reduces the business risks associated with building a technical solution and builds a bridge between business and technical requirements.

Some of the other goals are as follows:

1. Expose the structure of the system, but hide its implementation details.
2. Realize all the use-cases and scenarios.
3. Try to address the requirements of various stakeholders.
4. Handle both functional and quality requirements.
5. Reduce the goal of ownership and improve the organizations market position.
6. Improve quality and functionality offered by the system.
7. Improve external confidence in either the organization or system.

Benefits of Good Software Architecture Design:

1. **Improved Maintainability:** A well-structured architecture makes it easier to understand, modify, and extend the software.
2. **Enhanced Scalability:** The architecture can be designed to handle increasing loads and demands.
3. **Better Performance:** Optimized component interactions and data flow can lead to improved performance.

4. **Reduced Development Costs:** A clear architecture can streamline the development process and reduce the risk of rework.

5. **Increased Adaptability:** A flexible architecture can adapt to changing requirements and business needs.

Tools and Techniques for Software Architecture Design:

1. **Diagramming Tools:** Tools like Lucidchart and Miro help visualize the architecture and communicate it to stakeholders.

2. **Design Patterns:** Utilizing established design patterns (e.g., Model-View-Controller) can help create reusable and robust solutions.

3. **Code Analysis Tools:** Tools that analyze the codebase and identify potential design flaws or issues.

4. **Architecture Documentation Tools:** Tools for creating and managing architecture documentation.

In essence, software architecture design is a critical phase in the software development lifecycle that ensures the system's quality, scalability, and long-term viability.

Architectural Patterns (Monolithic, Microservices, Serverless)

Architectural patterns are standardized solutions to common design problems in software architecture, guiding the structure and organization of systems to ensure scalability, maintainability, and efficiency. Among the most widely used patterns are Monolithic, Microservices, and Serverless architectures. A Monolithic architecture organizes an application as a single, unified unit where all functionalities are interconnected and deployed together. This pattern is simple to develop, test, and deploy initially but can become difficult to scale and maintain as the codebase grows. In contrast, a Microservices architecture divides the application into small, independent services, each responsible for a specific business capability. These services communicate over lightweight protocols like HTTP or messaging queues and can be developed, deployed, and scaled independently, enabling greater flexibility, fault isolation, and continuous delivery. However, it introduces challenges in managing service coordination, data consistency, and system complexity. Serverless architecture, built on cloud platforms such as AWS Lambda or Azure Functions, abstracts server management entirely, allowing developers to focus solely on writing code that responds to events. It offers automatic scaling, reduced operational overhead, and cost-efficiency for applications with unpredictable or infrequent workloads. Nevertheless, serverless systems may suffer from issues like cold starts, vendor lock-in, and limited execution time. Selecting the appropriate architectural pattern depends on factors such as application complexity, scalability requirements, team size, and deployment strategy. In many real-world scenarios, organizations adopt a hybrid approach, leveraging the strengths of multiple architectural patterns to meet both technical and business objectives effectively while ensuring system reliability and performance.

Monolithic Architecture: A Monolithic architecture is a traditional model of software design where an entire application is built as a single, cohesive unit. All components, such as the user interface, business logic, and data access layer, are interconnected and operate within a single codebase and runtime environment. This approach is often simpler to develop and test initially, especially for smaller teams or applications with straightforward requirements. Developers can run the entire application on a local machine, making debugging and version control easier. Additionally, deployment is straightforward since only one package or file is released to a server. Frameworks like Spring Boot for Java or ASP.NET for C# are often used to create monolithic applications efficiently.

However, monolithic applications come with limitations, especially as the system grows in size and complexity. Since all components are tightly coupled, a small change in one module may require rebuilding and redeploying the entire application. This increases the risk of introducing bugs and makes the deployment process time-consuming. Scaling is also less flexible, as the whole application must scale together even if only one part of it is under heavy load. Over time, the codebase can become unwieldy, leading to what's often called a "big ball of mud" a tangled, difficult-to-maintain system. Despite these challenges, monolithic architecture remains a viable choice for smaller projects or startups where speed of development and simplicity outweigh scalability and flexibility concerns. It can also serve as a stepping stone before transitioning to more modular patterns like microservices. Key characteristics of monolithic architecture:

1. **Single Codebase:** All application components are integrated into a single, unified codebase.

2. **Tightly Coupled:** Components are interconnected and rely on each other, meaning changes in one area can affect others.

3. **Self-Contained:** Monolithic applications are designed to function independently, minimizing reliance on external systems.

4. **Simple Development and Deployment:** The unified nature of the codebase simplifies development and deployment processes.

5. **Scalability Challenges:** Scaling a monolithic application requires scaling the entire application, which can be less efficient than scaling individual components.

6. **Maintenance Complexity:** As the application grows, maintaining a monolithic codebase can become complex and time-consuming.

Microservices Architecture: Microservices architecture is a modern design approach that structures an application as a collection of small, loosely coupled services, each responsible for a specific business function. These services communicate via lightweight protocols such as HTTP/REST or messaging queues and are typically deployed independently. Each microservice is self-contained and can be developed, deployed, and scaled separately, often by small, autonomous teams. This promotes better modularity, code reuse, and continuous delivery. Microservices are language-agnostic, meaning different services can be written in different programming languages or use different data storage technologies, depending on what best suits the specific task. Organizations like Netflix and Amazon have successfully adopted this architecture to handle large-scale, distributed systems with rapid feature releases.

However, implementing microservices comes with its own set of challenges. The distributed nature of the system adds complexity in terms of network communication, service discovery, fault tolerance, and data consistency. Developers must manage inter-service communication, which may involve retries, load balancing, and fallback mechanisms. Monitoring and debugging become more difficult, requiring sophisticated tools for observability like centralized logging, tracing, and health checks. Additionally, deployment and configuration management are more complex and usually require containerization (e.g., Docker) and orchestration tools like Kubernetes. Despite these hurdles, microservices offer immense benefits for large, evolving applications with high demands for scalability, flexibility, and resilience. They align well with agile development and DevOps practices, allowing teams to iterate quickly and deploy updates to specific parts of the application without affecting the entire system. Key design principles are as under:

1. **Decentralized Data Management:** Each service typically manages its own data, promoting autonomy and reducing dependencies.

2. **Independent Deployment:** Services can be deployed, updated, and scaled independently without impacting other parts of the application.

3. **Well-defined APIs:** Services communicate with each other through clearly defined APIs, ensuring loose coupling and enabling independent evolution.

4. **Bounded Contexts:** Each service typically handles a specific business capability within a defined boundary (bounded context).

5. **Polyglot Programming:** Services can be implemented in different programming languages and technologies, offering flexibility.

6. **Service Discovery:** Mechanisms like service registries help services find and connect with each other.

7. **Fault Tolerance:** Design patterns like circuit breakers and asynchronous messaging enhance resilience and fault tolerance.

8. **Observability:** Tools and patterns for monitoring, tracing, and logging help in understanding and troubleshooting the distributed system.

9. **API Gateways:** A central entry point for managing API traffic, security, and routing.

10. **Database per Service:** Each service manages its own database, promoting autonomy and reducing dependencies.

Serverless Architecture: Serverless architecture is a cloud-native design pattern where application logic is executed in stateless compute containers, often referred to as "functions," that are triggered by events and fully managed by a cloud provider. Services like AWS Lambda, Azure Functions, and Google Cloud Functions allow developers to run code without provisioning or managing servers. This model abstracts the infrastructure layer, automatically handling scaling, fault tolerance, and resource allocation. As a result, developers can focus entirely on business logic and innovation instead of operations. Serverless is ideal for use cases like APIs, real-time file processing, chatbots, or scheduled tasks. One of its most appealing features is the cost model you only pay for the compute time you actually use, making it highly cost-efficient for variable or low-traffic workloads.

Despite its advantages, serverless architecture has some trade-offs. Functions are typically short-lived and stateless, requiring external services (like databases or object storage) to maintain state. Cold starts, which are delays that occur when a function is triggered after a period of inactivity, can affect performance in latency-sensitive applications. There's also a risk of vendor lock-in, as applications become tightly coupled with a specific cloud provider's ecosystem and APIs. Furthermore, testing and debugging can be more complex due to the distributed and event-driven nature of serverless environments. While it may not be suitable for every scenario, particularly for long-running or complex workflows, serverless architecture is an excellent fit for lightweight, modular, and highly scalable applications. It supports rapid development cycles and is increasingly adopted in modern, agile-driven software teams. Key aspects of serverless architecture design are as under:

1. **Event-driven:** Applications are designed to respond to specific events, triggering the execution of code.

2. **Pay-per-use:** You only pay for the computing time your functions use.
3. **Infrastructure Abstraction:** Cloud providers manage the servers, allowing developers to focus on code.
4. **Scalability:** Cloud providers can automatically scale resources up or down based on demand.
5. **Function focus:** Serverless architectures often involve breaking down applications into smaller, independent functions.
6. **API Gateway:** An API gateway acts as a central entry point for requests, routing them to appropriate serverless functions.
7. **Common Patterns:** Popular patterns include API Gateway & Lambda, fan-out pattern, messaging pattern, and function focus.
8. **Observability and Monitoring:** It's crucial to have tools for monitoring the health, performance, and errors of your serverless applications.
9. **Testing:** Thorough testing, including integration tests, is essential to ensure the reliability and performance of your serverless functions.
10. **Cost Optimization:** Careful design choices and resource utilization can help optimize costs.
11. **Security:** Addressing security concerns is crucial, including proper authentication, authorization, and encryption.
12. **Hybrid Approaches:** Serverless can be combined with traditional microservices or other architectures to achieve a balance between scalability and cost-effectiveness.

Benefits of Serverless Architecture:

1. **Reduced Costs:** Pay-per-use model reduces infrastructure costs.
2. **Increased Scalability:** Automatic scaling ensures applications can handle fluctuating demand.
3. **Faster Development:** Focus on code rather than infrastructure frees up development time.
4. **Improved Efficiency:** Serverless can optimize resource utilization and reduce overhead.

5. **Simplified Operations:** Cloud providers manage infrastructure, reducing operational burden.

Challenges of Serverless Architecture:

1. **Cold Starts:** Functions can experience a delay when first invoked.
2. **Debugging and Tracing:** Debugging serverless applications can be more challenging than traditional applications.
3. **Complexity in Large Applications:** Managing complex applications with many serverless functions can require careful design and orchestration.
4. **Vendor Lock-in:** Choosing a specific serverless platform can create vendor lock-in.
5. **Data consistency:** Ensuring data consistency across different serverless functions can be a challenge.
6. **Complexity in error handling:** Handling errors across multiple functions and services can be more complex than in traditional architectures.
7. **Security concerns:** Security configurations need to be carefully managed to protect against various threats.

In essence, serverless architecture offers a powerful approach to building and deploying applications, but it also requires careful consideration of its design, implementation, and challenges to achieve its full potential.

Differences Between Monolithic, Microservices and Serverless: The main differences between Monolithic, Microservices and Serverless are listed in table 2.3.

Table 2.3

S.No.	Aspect	Monolithic	Microservices	Serverless
1	Structure	Single unified codebase	Multiple independent services	Functions triggered by events
2	Deployment	One unit deployed together	Each service deployed independently	Each function deployed separately
3	Scalability	Scales as a whole application	Scales individual services	Auto-scales per function based on demand
4	Development Speed	Faster for small teams and projects	Faster for large teams with modular	Very fast for small, event-driven features
5	Complexity	Simpler initially, increases with size	Complex due to service interactions	Complex in orchestration and debugging
6	Maintenance	Harder as the codebase grows	Easier with proper service boundaries	Easier but depends on function design and cloud provider tools
7	Technology Stack	Typically, a single tech stack	Different stacks for different services possible	Depends on cloud provider's supported runtimes
8	Cost Efficiency	Costly to scale, pays for always-on infrastructure	Cost depends on resource use and service count	Pay-per-use, very cost-efficient for irregular workloads
9	Fault Isolation	Low – one bug can crash the entire app	High – failure in one service doesn't affect	High – isolated functions reduce impact of failure
10	Use Cases	Small to medium apps, quick MVPs	Large, complex, and distributed systems	Event-driven apps, APIs, automation, real-time processing
11	Cold Start Issues	None	Rare, depends on service type	Yes – cold starts can affect performance
12	Vendor Lock-in	Low – platform agnostic	Moderate – depends on deployment tools	High – tightly coupled to cloud providers
13	Example Technologies	Spring Boot, Django, Ruby on Rails	Docker, Kubernetes, REST, gRPC	AWS Lambda, Azure Functions, Google Cloud Functions

Design Patterns (Singleton, Factory, Observer, etc.)

Design patterns are proven solutions to common software design problems that improve code readability, reusability, and scalability. They provide templates for how to structure and organize classes and objects in object-oriented programming. Among the most widely used are creational, structural, and behavioral patterns. Creational patterns like the Singleton, Factory, and Builder focus on object creation mechanisms, making systems more flexible in deciding which objects to create. For example, the Singleton ensures only one instance of a class exists, commonly used in logging or configuration. The Factory pattern abstracts the instantiation process, allowing code to create objects without knowing the exact class being instantiated. Structural patterns such as Adapter, Decorator, and Facade deal with class and object composition, helping ensure components work together seamlessly. The Adapter allows incompatible interfaces to work together, while the Decorator adds responsibilities to objects dynamically. Behavioral patterns like Observer, Strategy, and Command focus on communication between objects. The Observer pattern enables a subject to notify multiple observers about state changes, useful in event-driven systems. The Strategy pattern defines a family of algorithms and allows them to be interchangeable at runtime, promoting flexibility. Design patterns are not code templates but conceptual solutions, often implemented differently depending on the language or context. They help developers write more maintainable and modular code by encapsulating best practices and reducing complexity in software architecture.

Singleton Pattern: The singleton pattern is a software design pattern that ensures a class has only one instance and provides a global point of access to it. It's used when you need to restrict the creation of an object to a single instance and make it readily accessible throughout the application.

The Singleton pattern ensures that a class has only one instance and provides a global point of access to that instance. This is useful in scenarios where exactly one object is needed to coordinate actions across a system such as configuration managers, logging services, or thread pools. The Singleton pattern restricts the instantiation of a class to a single object by making the constructor private and exposing a static method (usually getInstance()) to return the same object every time. This pattern also prevents cloning, serialization, or reflection-based instantiation that could result in more than one instance.

While the Singleton is simple to implement, it comes with trade-offs. It introduces global state into an application, which can make testing and debugging more challenging. Since the Singleton object is shared across the application, it can become a bottleneck or lead to unexpected behaviors in multi-threaded environments unless it's implemented with thread-safety mechanisms. Lazy initialization can be used to delay the creation of the instance until it's actually needed, which conserves resources. In languages like Java and C#, modern Singleton implementations often use double-checked locking or static initializers to ensure both laziness and thread safety. Though sometimes overused, when applied correctly, the Singleton pattern can provide a clean, centralized way to manage shared resources.

Key Characteristics:

1. **Single Instance:** Only one object of the class can exist.
2. **Global Access:** The single instance can be accessed from anywhere within the application.
3. **Lazy Initialization:** The instance is typically created only when it's first requested.
4. **Thread-Safe:** Implementations often ensure that the instance creation is thread-safe, preventing multiple instances from being created in concurrent environments.

When to use the Singleton Pattern:

1. **Managing shared resources:** For example, a single database connection or a configuration manager.
2. **Logging:** When you need a single instance of a logger to manage all log operations.
3. **Caching:** For a single cache instance to store and retrieve data.
4. **Thread pools:** When you need a single thread pool instance.

Example in Java:

```
public class Singleton {
  private static Singleton instance;
  private Singleton() {
  }
  public static Singleton getInstance() {
    if (instance == null) {
      instance = new Singleton();
    }
    return instance;
  }
```

}

Benefits:

1. **Controlled access to a resource:** Ensures only one instance of a class is used, preventing resource conflicts.

2. **Reduced memory overhead:** By limiting instantiation, the memory footprint of the application is reduced.

3. **Simplified resource management:** Provides a central point of access for managing shared resources.

Drawbacks:

1. **Violation of single responsibility principle:** The singleton class often has multiple responsibilities (managing its own instantiation and providing access).

2. **Can make testing difficult:** Singletons can make unit testing challenging because they can be difficult to mock or replace.

3. **Can lead to tightly coupled code:** Classes that depend on a singleton become tightly coupled to it, making it harder to refactor or maintain.

Factory Pattern: The Factory Pattern is a creational design pattern that encapsulates the creation of objects, providing a way to create objects without specifying the exact classes of objects that will be created. It essentially hides the instantiation logic, making the code more flexible and easier to maintain. This pattern is particularly useful when you have multiple similar object types and want to create one of them based on a given input.

The Factory pattern is a creational design pattern used to create objects without specifying the exact class of object that will be created. Instead of instantiating classes directly with the new keyword, the pattern delegates object creation to a factory method. This decouples the client code from the actual object creation logic, promoting flexibility and scalability. For example, a shape drawing application might use a ShapeFactory class that returns different types of shapes like Circle, Square, or Triangle based on input. The client doesn't need to know the concrete class it's using, just the interface or abstract class that all shapes implement.

This design pattern is particularly useful when the exact type of object is determined by dynamic input or configuration. It allows for easy addition of new product types without changing existing client code, following the Open/Closed Principle. There are several variations, including the Simple Factory (not technically a design pattern but often used),

Factory Method, and Abstract Factory. The Factory Method allows subclasses to decide which class to instantiate, while the Abstract Factory provides an interface to create families of related objects. However, using factories can sometimes lead to code that's harder to trace, especially if overused or poorly documented. Still, the pattern is extremely powerful in systems requiring high flexibility, extensibility, and modularity, especially when combined with dependency injection and interfaces.

Benefits:

1. **Decoupling:** The client code is decoupled from the specific implementation classes of the objects.

2. **Flexibility:** Adding new object types is easier, as you only need to add a new factory class.

3. **Maintainability:** The object creation logic is centralized in the factory, making it easier to manage and modify.

4. **Abstraction:** The client code works with abstract types, not concrete implementations.

Example: Imagine you're building a game and have different character types (e.g., Warrior, Wizard, Rogue). Instead of having the game class directly create each character, you can use a CharacterFactory. The game class can ask the factory for a specific character type, and the factory will return the appropriate character object.

Variations of the Factory Pattern:

1. **Factory Method:** A more basic form where a class defines a method for creating objects, and subclasses can override this method to create different types of objects.

2. **Abstract Factory:** A more complex form that creates families of related objects.

3. **Simple Factory:** A simple, non-abstract factory.

In essence, the Factory Pattern provides a cleaner, more organized, and more flexible way to create objects in object-oriented programming.

Observer Pattern: The Observer pattern is a behavioral design pattern where one object, the subject, maintains a list of dependent objects called observers. When the subject's state changes, it automatically notifies all observers, allowing them to react to the change. This pattern facilitates a one-to-many dependency and promotes loose coupling between the subject and its observers.

The Observer pattern is a behavioral design pattern in which an object, known as the subject, maintains a list of its dependents, called observers, and automatically notifies them of any state changes. This pattern is widely used to implement distributed event-handling systems, where multiple components need to respond to changes in one central object. For example, in a GUI application, buttons (subjects) can notify listeners (observers) when they are clicked. Similarly, in a stock market app, multiple modules might observe a stock ticker and get updates when prices change.

The core benefit of the Observer pattern is that it promotes loose coupling between components. The subject doesn't need to know anything about the observers it only knows that they implement a common interface. This makes the system easier to extend and maintain, as observers can be added or removed at runtime without altering the subject. The pattern follows the Publish-Subscribe model, where subjects publish events and observers subscribe to them. However, challenges arise in ensuring that updates are timely and do not cause performance bottlenecks. Also, care must be taken to avoid memory leaks caused by lingering observer references. Modern implementations may use event buses or reactive programming libraries (like RxJS or Java's Flow API) to streamline observer management. The Observer pattern is essential in UI frameworks, real-time systems, and anywhere that requires decoupled, event-driven behavior. Key Components:

1. **Subject (Observable):** This object holds the state and manages a list of observers. It provides methods for registering, unregistering, and notifying observers about state changes.

2. **Observer:** These are the objects that are interested in the state of the subject. They subscribe to the subject to receive notifications when the subject's state changes.

Working of Observer Pattern:

1. **Subscription:** Observers register themselves with the subject to receive notifications.

2. **Notification:** When the subject's state changes, it iterates through its list of observers and calls a specific method on each observer to inform them about the change.

3. **Response:** Observers then react to the notification by updating their internal state or performing other actions based on the change in the subject's state.

Benefits:

1. **Loose Coupling:** The subject and observers are not tightly coupled, making the code more flexible and maintainable.

2. **Flexibility:** The observer pattern allows for easy addition or removal of observers without affecting the subject or other observers.

3. **Reusability:** The same subject can be used with different types of observers.

Use Cases:

1. **Event-Driven Systems:** Handling user interface events, network events, or other asynchronous events.

2. **GUI Programming:** Updating user interface elements when the underlying model changes.

3. **Notification Systems:** Sending notifications to users about changes in data or application status.

Example:

Imagine a weather station that measures temperature, humidity, and pressure. The weather station (the subject) can notify multiple clients (observers) about changes in these readings. Each client can then display the current weather conditions on their own screen.

In essence, the Observer pattern provides a way to create a dynamic and flexible communication mechanism between objects, allowing for a clear separation of concerns and a more maintainable codebase.

Difference Between Singleton, Factory, Observer: The difference between Strategy, Factory, Observer is listed in table 2.4.

Table 2.4

S.No.	Aspect	Singleton	Factory	Observer
1	Purpose	Ensure a class has only one instance	Create objects without specifying class name	Notify multiple objects about state changes
2	Pattern Type	Creational	Creational	Behavioral
3	Core Concept	Single global instance	Object creation logic centralized	Publisher-Subscriber mechanism
4	Usage Scenario	Logging, config settings, DB connection	When object creation is complex or dynamic	Event handling, UI listeners, real-time updates
5	Main Participants	Class with private constructor & instance	Factory method or class	Subject and Observers
6	Example in Real World	Logger, Configuration manager	ShapeFactory, GUI components factory	News feed subscribers, UI events
7	Object Creation	Controlled, only once	Abstracted and delegated	Not relevant (not about creation)
8	Communication Direction	One object, globally accessible	Factory → Product	Subject → Observers
9	Decoupling Level	Low (global state)	Medium (decouples instantiation from usage)	High (One object, globally accessible don't need to know subject internals)
10	Drawbacks	Global state, hard to test/mock	Can lead to too many subclasses	Can be hard to debug, risk of memory leaks

Domain-Driven Design (DDD)

Domain-Driven Design (DDD) is a software development approach focused on modeling software to match the real-world business domain it's meant to serve. Introduced by Eric Evans in his book Domain-Driven Design: Tackling Complexity in the Heart of Software, DDD aims to align the software structure and language with the core business concepts and logic, improving communication, maintainability, and long-term success of complex systems.

At its heart, DDD emphasizes the importance of the domain the sphere of knowledge and activity around which the application logic revolves. It encourages close collaboration between domain experts and developers to build a shared understanding of the problem space. This shared understanding is expressed through a Ubiquitous Language, a common vocabulary developed by the team and used consistently in both code and conversation. This helps avoid miscommunication and ensures that software artifacts accurately reflect the business requirements.

DDD divides the application into layers, with each layer having a clear responsibility, these layers are shown in fig.2.3.

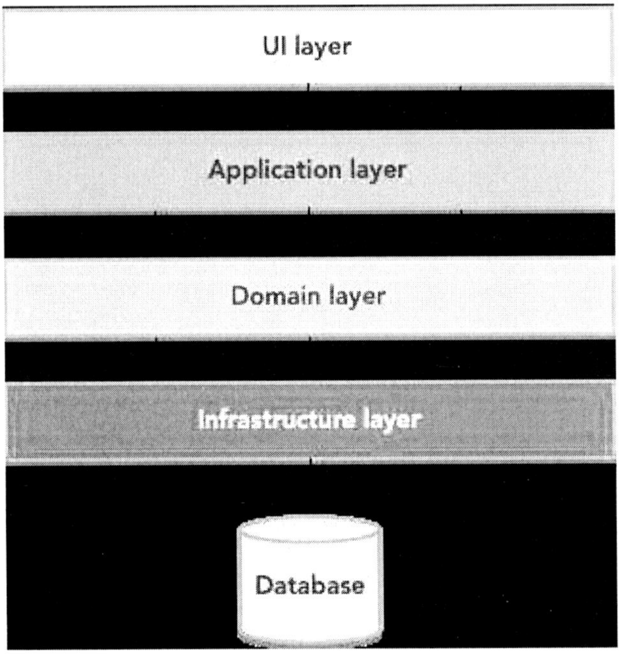

Fig.2.3

The main layers include:

1. **User Interface (UI) Layer:** This layer provides the user interface, allowing users to interact with the application. It receives requests from the user and passes them to the Application Layer, displaying the results back to the user.

2. **Application Layer:** This layer acts as an intermediary between the UI and the Domain Layer. It orchestrates the execution of use cases, coordinating interactions with the Domain Layer to fulfill application-specific tasks.

3. **Domain Layer:** This layer is the heart of DDD, containing the core business logic, entities, and value objects. It models the domain's concepts and rules, ensuring the software accurately reflects the business's needs.

4. **Infrastructure Layer:** This layer handles the technical aspects of the application, such as database interactions, messaging queues, and other external

dependencies. It provides the necessary infrastructure for the higher layers to function without worrying about the underlying details.

A central concept in DDD is the Bounded Context, which defines a boundary within which a particular domain model is valid. Large systems often span multiple domains, and different parts of the system may use the same terms with different meanings. By isolating models within bounded contexts, DDD helps reduce ambiguity and allows each context to evolve independently. Communication between contexts is handled through well-defined interfaces and translation mechanisms.

DDD Tools: Strategic Domain-Driven Design (DDD) focuses on the high-level, architectural design of software systems, aiming to align software with the business domain. It involves identifying core and generic subdomains, establishing boundaries with Bounded Contexts, and defining relationships between them through Context Mapping. A key aspect is the use of a Ubiquitous Language to facilitate communication between domain experts and developers.

a more detailed breakdown:

1. **Identifying Core and Generic Subdomains:** In Domain-Driven Design (DDD), identifying Core and Generic Subdomains is a key strategic design activity that helps prioritize development efforts and allocate resources effectively. The Core Subdomain represents the heart of the business—the area that provides a competitive advantage and where the most complex and valuable domain logic resides. It's where innovation happens and where the business differentiates itself, so it requires the most attention, expertise, and custom development. On the other hand, Generic Subdomains are necessary to support the system but are not specific to the business domain; they are standard, reusable, and often solved with off-the-shelf solutions or libraries (e.g., authentication, logging, messaging systems). Identifying these subdomains involves close collaboration with domain experts to understand which parts of the system truly drive business value and which are more infrastructural or commoditized. By clearly distinguishing these, teams can focus custom development efforts on the core while leveraging existing tools or services for the generic parts, leading to more efficient and strategic software design.

   - **Core Subdomains:** These represent the unique, competitive advantages of a business and form the heart of the application.

- **Generic Subdomains:** These are standard, widely applicable functionalities that are not unique to the business, like a shopping cart in an e-commerce site.

2. **Defining Bounded Contexts:** In Domain-Driven Design (DDD), a Bounded Context defines a clear boundary within which a specific domain model is defined and applicable. It establishes the limits of a model's meaning, language, and behavior, ensuring that terms, rules, and logic remain consistent and unambiguous within that scope. Bounded Contexts are crucial when dealing with large or complex systems where different parts of the business may use the same terminology differently. For example, the word "Order" might mean one thing in a sales context and something entirely different in logistics. By defining bounded contexts, teams can develop and evolve each model independently without confusion or unintended side effects. Communication between bounded contexts happens through well-defined interfaces, such as APIs, events, or anti-corruption layers, which translate and adapt models across boundaries. This approach improves modularity, scalability, and team autonomy, as each context can be managed by a separate team using the most appropriate tools, architecture, or even programming language. Ultimately, bounded contexts help ensure that the software remains aligned with the business and evolves cleanly as requirements change or grow over time.

   Bounded contexts are conceptual boundaries that define where a particular domain model is applicable. They help manage complexity by creating separate domains for different parts of the system.

   Each Bounded Context has its own Ubiquitous Language, a shared language used by both domain experts and developers within that context.

3. **Context Mapping:** Context Mapping is a strategic design technique in Domain-Driven Design (DDD) used to visualize and manage the relationships between multiple Bounded Contexts within a system or organization. Since large systems often consist of various subsystems, each with its own model and language, context mapping helps teams understand how these contexts interact, collaborate, and depend on each other. It identifies integration points and defines patterns of communication, such as Shared Kernel, Customer/Supplier, Conformist, Anti-Corruption Layer, and others. These patterns clarify the nature of relationships whether they are cooperative, dependent, or defensive allowing for better coordination and autonomy among teams. For example, a team using a Conformist pattern accepts and conforms to another team's model,

while an Anti-Corruption Layer acts as a protective translation layer between incompatible models. Context maps not only make architectural boundaries explicit but also help in aligning organizational structure with system design, following Conway's Law. They are especially valuable in distributed systems, such as microservices architectures, where misunderstanding between contexts can lead to integration issues and system fragility. By clearly mapping contexts and their interactions, teams can make more informed decisions about integration strategies, boundaries, and responsibilities, ultimately leading to more maintainable and scalable systems.

Context mapping tool visualizes the relationships and dependencies between different Bounded Contexts, helping to understand how they interact and how to manage those interactions.

Context mapping helps determine the relationships between bounded contexts, such as customer/supplier, shared kernel, and anti-corruption layers.

4. **Ubiquitous Language:** In Domain-Driven Design (DDD), Ubiquitous Language is a shared, common language developed and used consistently by both technical and non-technical team members to describe the domain, including its entities, behaviors, processes, and rules. This language evolves out of collaboration between developers and domain experts and is embedded in the code, tests, documentation, and daily conversations. The goal of ubiquitous language is to eliminate misunderstandings and ambiguity by ensuring that everyone engineers, business stakeholders, and analysts speaks the same language when discussing the system. For example, terms like "Invoice," "Shipment," or "Customer" should have a single, agreed-upon meaning within a particular bounded context. When the same word has different meanings in different parts of the system, those meanings are isolated within separate bounded contexts to avoid confusion. Ubiquitous language enhances communication, strengthens the connection between the code and the business, and reduces the cognitive load when navigating complex systems. It ensures that the software truly reflects the domain it serves, and that changes in business requirements can be clearly translated into code updates. Ultimately, it fosters alignment, clarity, and agility across cross-functional teams, making the development process more efficient and resilient to change.

   Ubiquitous language shared language between domain experts and developers ensures everyone understands the terms and concepts used in the domain model.

It helps bridge the gap between the business domain and the software implementation.

Tools and Techniques: The tools and techniques are as under:

1. **Domain Storytelling:** Using stories to uncover knowledge from domain experts and stakeholders.
2. **EventStorming:** A collaborative workshop to model the domain by focusing on events and their consequences.
3. **Mind Maps:** Visual tools for brainstorming and organizing ideas about the domain.
4. **UML Diagrams:** A standardized graphical language for modeling software systems.
5. **Flow Charts:** Visual representations of processes and workflows within the domain.
6. **Swimlane Diagrams:** Visual representations of processes and workflows across different teams or roles.

DDD is especially valuable in complex domains where business rules are central to success. However, it can be overkill for simple applications. It works best when teams are willing to invest in continuous collaboration, thoughtful modeling, and disciplined architecture.

In modern practice, DDD often pairs well with other paradigms like microservices, event-driven architecture, and CQRS (Command Query Responsibility Segregation), where each microservice aligns with a bounded context.

In summary, Domain-Driven Design is not just a way to write code it's a way to think about software. By focusing on the domain, building shared understanding, and applying strategic modeling patterns, DDD enables teams to build software that truly reflects the business it serves.

Model-View-Controller (MVC) and Other Design

MVC (Model-View-Controller) is an architectural design pattern that encourages improved application organization through a separation of concerns. It divides an interactive application into three components i.e., model, View and Controller. It enforces the isolation of business data (Models) from user interfaces (Views), with a third component (Controllers) traditionally managing logic, user-input and coordinating both the models and views. The goal of MVC is to help structure the separate the concerns of an application into three parts:

1. **Model**: The Model represents the application's data and business logic. It is responsible for retrieving data from the database, processing it, and updating the View accordingly. The Model is independent of the user interface and does not depend on the View or Controller. It encapsulates the core functionality and rules of the application.

2. **View**: The View is responsible for rendering the user interface and displaying data to the user. It observes the Model and updates the display whenever the Model changes. The View is passive and does not contain business logic; its primary role is to present information to the user in a format that is easy to understand.

3. **Controller**: The Controller acts as an intermediary between the Model and the View. It receives user input from the View, processes it (often updating the Model), and returns the display output to the View. The Controller interprets user actions, such as button clicks or form submissions, and determines the appropriate response.

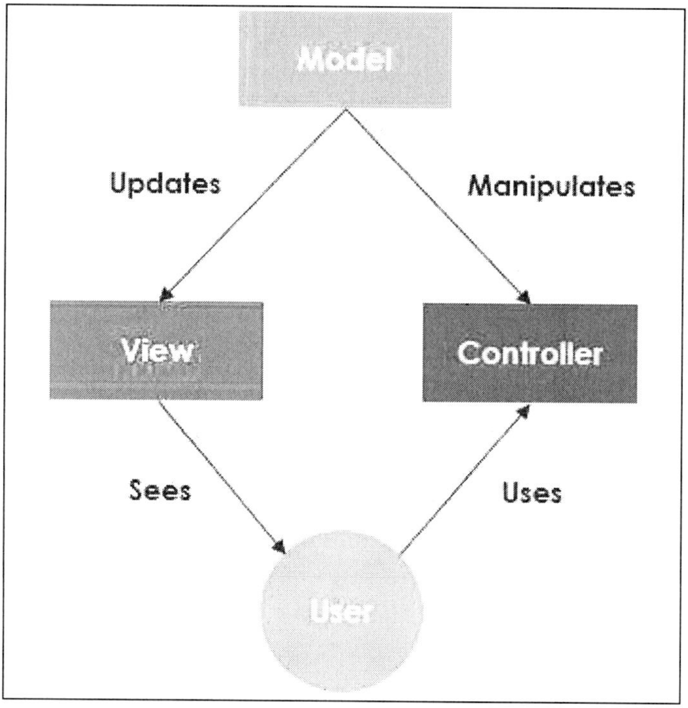

Fig.2.4

The Purpose of MVC Framework: As mentioned above, MVC software framework helps us to separate the different aspects of the application (input logic, business logic, and GUI), while providing a loose coupling between these elements. Thus, the information (most reusable) logic belongs in the model, the GUI belongs in the view. Input logic belongs in the controller. This separation helps you manage complexity when you build an application because it enables you to focus on one aspect of the implementation at a time. MVC Framework is a good idea for a number of reasons, including:

1. **Simultaneous Development:** Because MVC decouples the various components of an application, developers are able to work in parallel on different components without affecting or blocking one another.

2. **Reusability:** The same (or similar) view for one application can be refactored for another application with different data because the view is simply handling how the data is being displayed to the user.

3. **Improved Scalability:** If your application begins experiencing performance issues because database access is slow, you can upgrade the hardware running the database without other components being affected

4. **Low Coupling:** The very nature of the MVC framework is such that there is low coupling among models, views or controllers.

5. **Better Extendibility:** As the components have a low dependency on each other, making changes to one (to fix bugs or change functionality) does not affect another

Other Design Paradigms

In addition to MVC, several other design paradigms are commonly used in software development to address various architectural challenges:

1. **Model-View-ViewModel (MVVM)**: MVVM is an architectural pattern that facilitates the separation of concerns in applications, particularly those with rich user interfaces. It introduces the ViewModel component, which acts as a mediator between the View and the Model. The ViewModel retrieves data from the Model and exposes it in a format that is easy for the View to display. MVVM is particularly popular in applications that use data-binding frameworks, as it allows for a more declarative approach to UI development.

2. **Model-View-Presenter (MVP)**: MVP is a derivative of the MVC pattern that emphasizes a more active role for the Presenter. In MVP, the Presenter

handles all the presentation logic and updates the View directly. The View is responsible for displaying data and forwarding user interactions to the Presenter. MVP is often used in applications where the View needs to be more passive and delegate most of the logic to the Presenter.

3. **Layered Architecture**: Layered architecture divides an application into distinct layers, each with a specific responsibility. Common layers include the presentation layer (handling user interactions), the business logic layer (processing data), and the data access layer (interacting with databases). This approach promotes separation of concerns and makes the application easier to maintain and scale.

4. **Event-Driven Architecture (EDA)**: EDA is an architectural paradigm where the flow of the program is determined by events. Components communicate by producing and consuming events, allowing for a decoupled and asynchronous system. EDA is particularly useful in systems that require high scalability and responsiveness, such as real-time applications.

5. **Microservices Architecture**: Microservices architecture structures an application as a collection of loosely coupled services, each responsible for a specific business function. Each service is independently deployable and communicates with other services through well-defined APIs. This approach enhances scalability and flexibility but introduces challenges related to service coordination and data consistency.

6. **Client-Server Architecture**: In client-server architecture, the system is divided into two main components: the client, which requests services, and the server, which provides them. This model is foundational to many networked applications, including web and mobile apps. It allows for centralized data management and resource sharing.

7. **Peer-to-Peer (P2P) Architecture**: In P2P architecture, each node (peer) in the network can act as both a client and a server, sharing resources and services directly with other peers. This decentralized approach is commonly used in file-sharing systems and blockchain technologies.

8. **Service-Oriented Architecture (SOA)**: SOA is an architectural pattern where software components (services) are designed to provide specific business functionalities. These services communicate over a network, often using standardized protocols such as HTTP or SOAP. SOA promotes reusability and

flexibility but requires careful management of service interactions and data consistency.

Each of these design paradigms offers unique advantages and is suited to different types of applications and organizational needs. Selecting the appropriate paradigm depends on factors such as the application's complexity, scalability requirements, and the development team's expertise.

Develop Use Case Scenario Using MVC Sequence Diagrams: You can use stereotypes for the lifeline in the MVC sequence diagram to make visually clear what type of objects you are using in the MVC. An MVC Sequence diagram has interface objects, controller objects and entity objects:

1. Entities are objects representing system data: Customer, Product, Transaction, Cart, etc.

2. Boundaries are objects that interface with system actors: UserInterface, DataBaseGateway, ServerProxy, etc.

3. Controls are objects that mediate between boundaries and entities. A controller object often correspond to use cases scenario and often represented by a sequence diagram.

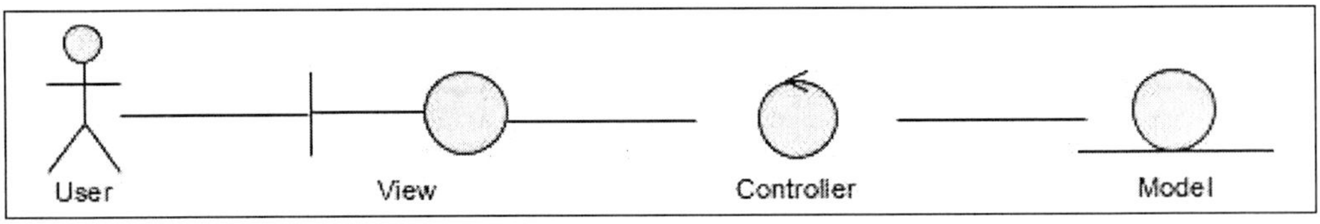

Fig.2.5

And here is the simplistic and hypothetical sequence diagram for MVC. What you see in this diagram, a web-user initiated a query and an event is generated that is handled by the controller and gets information that is needed from the model, validates the information and passes back the result set to the view.

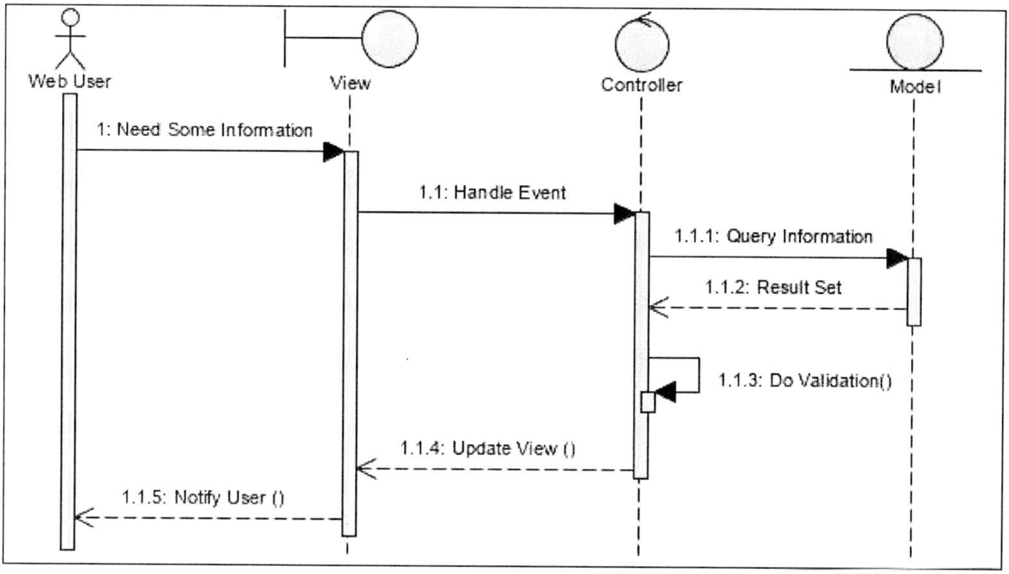

Fig.2.6

Example MVC Sequence Diagram: Suppose an application that let you search for persons. The UI must have a text field where the user can enter a search string and it might have a button to start the search. Finally, it must have an area where the search results are displayed. In our case, it is implemented with a list component.

The "Search for Persons" use case Scenario is:

1. The user enters a search string in the text field
2. The user clicks the search button.
3. The search result is displayed in the result list.

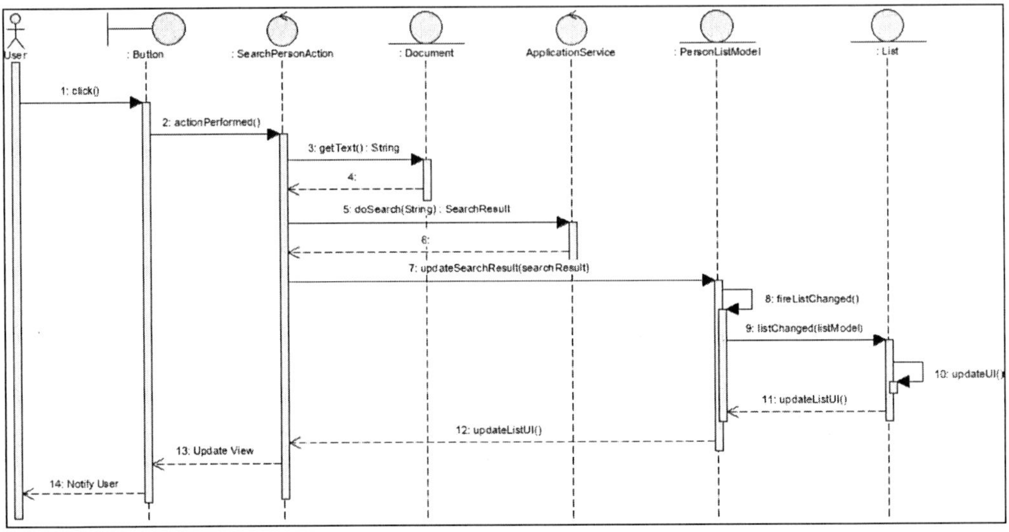

Fig.2.7

The sequence fig.2.6 shows how the user's button click moves through the application until the result gets finally displayed in the list component.

SUMMARY OF REQUIREMENTS ENGINEERING AND DESIGN

Requirements Engineering is the process of identifying, analyzing, documenting, and validating what a software system should do. It involves both functional requirements (specific features and behaviors) and non-functional requirements (performance, security, usability, etc.). Techniques such as interviews, surveys, workshops, and observation help gather accurate requirements. Good requirements are clear, testable, and aligned with user needs. Tools like use cases and user stories help express requirements in user-focused terms.

Software Design involves planning how to build the system based on the requirements. It includes selecting architectural patterns like monolithic, microservices, or serverless, and applying design patterns such as Singleton, Factory, and Observer for solving recurring problems. Domain-Driven Design (DDD) helps model complex business domains, while patterns like MVC (Model-View-Controller) and MVVM structure application components clearly.

Together, requirements engineering and design ensure that software is both useful and maintainable, aligning technology with business goals.

4. Requirements Engineering

Requirements Engineering is the process of defining, documenting, and maintaining the requirements for a software system. It involves understanding what users need (functional requirements) and how the system should perform (non-functional requirements such as performance, security, and usability). Key activities include requirements elicitation through interviews, surveys, and observation, followed by analysis, specification, validation, and management. Clear, testable, and prioritized requirements serve as the foundation for successful software development. Tools like use cases and user stories help bridge communication between stakeholders and developers, ensuring the final product meets business goals and user expectations effectively.

- **Types of Requirements: Functional vs. Non-functional:** In software development, requirements are categorized into two primary types: functional and non-functional. Functional requirements define the specific behaviors, features, or functions of a system. They describe what the system should do, such as processing transactions, managing user accounts, or generating reports. Non-functional requirements, on the other hand, specify the quality attributes, system performance, or constraints under which the system must operate. These include aspects like scalability, security, usability, and reliability. While functional requirements focus on the system's capabilities, non-functional requirements address how well the system performs its functions.

- **Requirements Gathering Techniques:** Effective requirements gathering is crucial for the success of any software project. Several techniques are employed to collect comprehensive and accurate requirements:

  - **Interviews:** Engaging with stakeholders through structured or unstructured interviews to understand their needs and expectations.

  - **Surveys and Questionnaires:** Distributing standardized forms to a larger audience to gather quantitative data on user preferences and requirements.

  - **Workshops:** Collaborative sessions where stakeholders and developers discuss and define requirements in real-time.

  - **Observation:** Analyzing users' interactions with existing systems to identify pain points and areas for improvement.

  - **Document Analysis:** Reviewing existing documentation, such as business process models or legacy system specifications, to extract relevant requirements.

- **Writing Good Software Requirements:** Well-crafted software requirements are clear, concise, and unambiguous. To write effective requirements, use simple and precise language, avoid technical jargon that may confuse non-technical stakeholders, ensure each requirement is testable and measurable, clearly define the scope and boundaries of the system and prioritize requirements based on business value and feasibility.

- **Use Cases and User Stories:** Use cases and user stories are tools used to capture functional requirements:

    - **Use Cases:** Detailed descriptions of how users interact with a system to achieve specific goals. They outline the steps involved, alternative flows, and exceptions.

    - **User Stories:** Short, informal descriptions of a feature told from the perspective of the end-user. They follow the format: "As a [type of user], I want [an action] so that [a benefit]."

5. Software Architecture and Design

Software Architecture and Design involves creating the structural blueprint of a software system, ensuring it meets both technical and business requirements. Architecture defines the system's high-level components and their interactions, often using patterns like monolithic, microservices, or serverless based on scalability and deployment needs. Design focuses on lower-level details, applying reusable design patterns such as Singleton, Factory, and Observer to solve common problems. Approaches like Domain-Driven Design (DDD) and Model-View-Controller (MVC) help structure code around business logic and user interface concerns. Together, architecture and design ensure the system is robust, maintainable, and aligned with user needs.

- **Architectural Patterns:** Software architecture defines the high-level structure of a system. Several architectural patterns guide this structure:

    - **Monolithic Architecture:** A traditional model where all components of the system are integrated into a single, unified codebase. While simpler to develop initially, monolithic systems can become challenging to scale and maintain as they grow.

    - **Microservices Architecture:** In this approach, the system is divided into small, independent services, each responsible for a specific business function. Microservices communicate over well-defined APIs and can be developed, deployed, and scaled independently, offering flexibility and resilience.

- **Serverless Architecture:** This model abstracts infrastructure management by allowing developers to focus on writing code. The cloud provider automatically manages the execution of functions in response to events, scaling resources as needed, which can lead to cost savings and simplified operations.

- **Design Patterns:** Design patterns are proven solutions to common software design problems. Some widely used patterns include:

  - **Singleton Pattern:** Ensures a class has only one instance and provides a global point of access to it. This is useful for managing shared resources like configuration settings or logging mechanisms.

  - **Factory Pattern:** Defines an interface for creating objects but allows subclasses to alter the type of objects that will be created. It promotes loose coupling by decoupling object creation from its usage.

  - **Observer Pattern:** Establishes a one-to-many dependency between objects, where a change in one object (the subject) automatically updates all dependent objects (observers). This is commonly used in event-driven systems to maintain consistency across components.

- **Domain-Driven Design (DDD):** DDD is an approach to software development that emphasizes collaboration between technical and domain experts to create a shared understanding of the domain. Key concepts in DDD include, Bounded Contexts, this define explicit boundaries within which a particular domain model is valid. This helps in managing complexity by isolating different parts of the system.

  Ubiquitous Language this is a common vocabulary used by both developers and domain experts to ensure clear communication and understanding. Entities and Value Objects entities have a distinct identity that runs through time and different states, while value objects are immutable and defined only by their attributes.

- **Model-View-Controller (MVC):** Model-view controller is a design pattern that separates an application into three interconnected components, Model this represents the data and business logic next is View this displays the data to the user and last is Controller this handles user input and updates the model and view accordingly. This separation allows for modularization, making the application easier to manage and scale.

- **Other design paradigms include:**

  Model-View-View Model (MVVM): An evolution of MVC, MVVM introduces the ViewModel, which acts as an intermediary between the View and Model, facilitating data binding and separation of concerns.

  - **Model-View-Presenter (MVP):** Similar to MVC, but in MVP, the Presenter handles all the presentation logic and updates the View directly, making the View more passive.
  - **Event-Driven Architecture (EDA):** In EDA, the system is designed around the production, detection, and reaction to events, allowing for asynchronous communication and improved scalability.
  - **Microservices Architecture:** As previously discussed, this approach structures an application as a collection of loosely coupled services, each responsible for a specific business function.
  - **Service-Oriented Architecture (SOA):** SOA is an architectural pattern where an application is designed as a collection of loosely coupled, reusable services that communicate with each other over a network. Each service in an SOA performs a specific business function or operation and can be accessed by other services or external clients.

In summary, requirements engineering and software design are foundational aspects of software development. By thoroughly gathering and analyzing requirements, and by applying appropriate architectural and design patterns, developers can create systems that are robust, scalable, and aligned with user needs and business goals.

******

PART–3

SOFTWARE DEVELOPMENT AND BEST PRACTICES

Software development is a structured process of designing, coding, testing, and maintaining applications or systems. It begins with understanding user requirements and continues through to delivering a functional product that solves real-world problems. Modern development often follows methodologies like Agile or DevOps, which emphasize collaboration, adaptability, and continuous improvement. Agile promotes iterative development and constant feedback, while DevOps bridges the gap between development and operations to ensure smoother, faster deployments. Both aim to reduce time to market and improve software quality by integrating processes and encouraging communication across teams.

Best practices in software development are essential for building reliable, maintainable, and efficient software. These include writing clean, modular code; following consistent coding standards; using version control systems like Git; and conducting regular code reviews. Automated testing and continuous integration (CI) ensure that changes do not break existing functionality, while documentation helps current and future developers understand the system. Security and scalability considerations must be addressed early to avoid costly fixes later. Ultimately, adopting best practices not only improves code quality but also enhances team collaboration and project success.

6

Programming Paradigms and Languages

Programming paradigms are fundamental styles or approaches to writing and organizing code, each offering different ways to solve problems. The most common paradigms include procedural, object-oriented, functional, and declarative programming. Procedural programming, like in C, focuses on step-by-step instructions and procedures. Object-oriented programming (OOP), used in languages like Java and Python, organizes code into objects and classes, promoting reuse and modularity. Functional programming, seen in languages like Haskell and parts of JavaScript, treats computation as the evaluation of mathematical functions and avoids changing state. Declarative programming, including SQL, emphasizes what the program should accomplish rather than how.

Programming languages are the tools developers use to implement these paradigms, and many modern languages support multiple paradigms. For instance, Python supports procedural, object-oriented, and functional programming, making it versatile for various applications. JavaScript, primarily used for web development, also supports multiple paradigms and is known for its event-driven nature. Java and C++ are widely used for enterprise and systems development due to their strong OOP features. Rust and Go are gaining popularity for system-level programming because of their performance and safety. The choice of paradigm and language often depends on the project requirements, team expertise, and the problem domain. Understanding multiple paradigms and languages enables developers to choose the best tools for any given task, leading to more effective and maintainable software.

Procedural vs. Object-Oriented vs. Functional Programming

Procedural, Object-Oriented, and Functional Programming are three core programming paradigms, each with its own approach to structuring and solving problems in software development. Procedural programming focuses on a step-by-step sequence of instructions using functions and control structures like loops and conditionals. It emphasizes procedures or routines and is commonly used in languages like C. Object-Oriented Programming (OOP), used in languages like Java and Python, organizes code into objects that contain both data and behavior. It is based on principles like encapsulation, inheritance, and polymorphism, making it ideal for building complex, modular, and reusable software systems. In contrast, Functional programming emphasizes the use of pure functions, immutability, and avoiding shared state or side effects. It treats computation as the evaluation of mathematical functions and is often seen in languages like Haskell and Scala, or in functional aspects of JavaScript and Python. While procedural programming is linear and task-focused, OOP models real-world entities, and functional programming promotes clean, predictable code especially useful in concurrent or data-heavy applications. Many modern languages blend these paradigms, allowing developers to choose the best approach based on the problem they're solving.

Procedural Language: Procedural Language is also known as 3GL which means third generation language. It is a type of programming language that follows a procedure; set of commands or guidelines that must be followed for smooth execution of the program. It works on step-by-step basis. It requires the user to tell not only What to do but also How to do it. Its basic idea is to have a program specify the sequence of steps that implements a particular algorithm. Hence, Procedural languages are based on algorithms.

In these developers use variables, loops, and functions to create a program performing a specific task which does calculations and displays a desired output.

It follows a top-down approach. It is carried out in a fixed sequence with a start and end point. The entire program is divided into functions and its main focus is on functions only. The program's code executes linearly with logical steps. In this, the code is written first and executed with some conditions. The procedure calls to decide the conditions.

There are no data-hiding features in procedural language. It is command command-driven language. It is operated by means of commands keyed in by the user or issued by the program. In procedural language, both iterative and recursive calls are used. It works through the state of the machine. It returns only restricted data types and allowed values. It is highly efficient despite the fact the size of the program is quite large and is not suitable for critical applications with complex code. It takes a lot of time but it needs very less memory.

In procedural language, no access specifiers are used. For eg: In structure all the members are public.

Features of Procedural Programming Language

1. **Local Variables:** A local variable is a variable that is limited to a specific part of a program and is announced locally in the procedural language, local on the specific function, as the only place to access it.

2. **Global Variables: A** global variable is a variable that is declared outside a function and is able to be accessed by any function of the program. It is also known as the opposite of the local variable.

3. **Modularity:** The practice of splitting a program into modules or functions so that each function is devoted to a certain task is referred to as modularity.

4. **Pre-Defined Functions:** Pre-defined functions are the amplification of functions which are already defined by the user and don't need the programmer to define them again. A built-in function is already defined in the system libraries, so it is also called a library function.

5. **Parameter Passing:** Parameter passing is a mechanism that allows the transfer of data between different functions of the program. The parameters are passed between the called and the calling function, thus allowing data exchange.

Types of Procedural Language: The types of procedural language are as:

1. **FORTRAN:** FORTRAN is a short form of FORmula TRANslation. It is an application in critical engineering calculations and high-performance computing.

2. **C:** It is a middle-level language. It is basically designed to write System software and requires advanced programming skills to read and write the desired code.

3. **BASIC:** BASIC is the short form of Beginner All Purpose Symbolic Instruction Code. It is a high-level programming language that is simple to use.

4. **Pascal:** Pascal is easy to learn. It produces transparent, efficient and reliable programs.

5. **ALGOL:** ALGOL stands for Algorithmic Language. It is mostly used for scientific calculations.

6. **COBOL:** COBOL stands for COmmon Business Oriented Language. It is easy to read, write and understand. It is basically designed for Business Applications.

7. **Java:** Java is a platform independent language. It generates a machine code from source code with the help of Just In Time compiler.

Example:

```
#include <stdio.h>

void foo(){

        printf("Arbitrary step 2");

        printf("Arbitrary step 3");

}

int main()

 {

        printf("Arbitrary step 1");

         foo();

        printf("Arbitrary step 4");

        int my_var = 3;

        if(my_var > 0){

        printf("Complete ✅ ");

  } else {

        printf("Error ❌ ") } return 0;

  }
```

Object-Oriented Programming: Object-Oriented Programming (OOP) is a programming paradigm that organizes software design around objects, which are instances of classes that encapsulate both data (attributes) and behavior (methods). It aims to model real-world entities and interactions in a more intuitive and modular way, making complex software systems easier to develop, maintain, and scale. The core principles of OOP include encapsulation, inheritance, polymorphism, and abstraction. Encapsulation ensures that the internal state of an object is hidden and only accessible through well-defined interfaces, enhancing security and reducing code complexity. Inheritance allows one class to inherit properties and behaviors from another, promoting code reuse and minimizing redundancy.

Polymorphism enables the same operation to behave differently on different classes, allowing for more flexible and dynamic code. Abstraction hides unnecessary implementation details and shows only the essential features of an object, simplifying how users interact with complex systems. OOP is especially useful in large-scale applications where managing multiple components and relationships is critical. For example, in a banking system, objects like Account, Customer, and Transaction can interact in well-defined ways, each handling its own responsibilities. Languages such as Java, Python, C++, and C# are commonly used for object-oriented programming. By encouraging modularity, reusability, and organized code structure, OOP supports better collaboration among developers, easier debugging and testing, and more scalable software development.

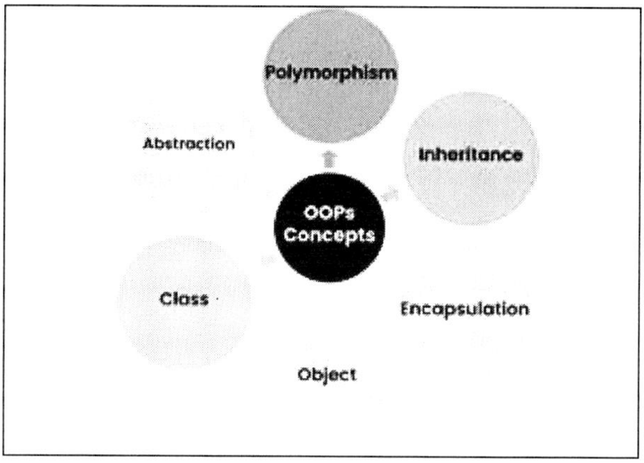

Fig.3.1

1. **Class:** In object-oriented programming, a class is a blueprint from which individual objects are created (or, we can say a class is a data type of an object type). In Java, everything is related to classes and objects. Each class has its methods and attributes that can be accessed and manipulated through the objects.

```
class Dog {
    constructor(name, birthday) {
        this.name = name;
        this.birthday = birthday;
    }
```

```
//Declare private variables
 _attendance = 0;
 getAge() {
       //Getter
       return this.calcAge();
   }
calcAge() {
     //calculate age using today's date and birthday
     Retur n Date.now() - this.birthday; } bark() { return console.log("Woof!");
   }
    updateAttendance() {
         //add a day to the dog's attendance days at the petsitters
          this._attendance++;
   }
}
```

2. **Object**: In object-oriented programming, an object is an entity that has two characteristics (states and behavior). Some of the real-world objects are book, mobile, table, computer, etc. An object is a variable of the type class, it is a basic component of an object-oriented programming system. A class has the methods and data members (attributes), these methods and data members are accessed through an object. Thus, an object is an instance of a class.

```
//instantiate a new object of the Dog class, and individual dog named Rufus
const rufus = new Dog("Rufus", "2/1/2017");
```

3. **Inheritance:** In object-oriented programming, inheritance is a process by which we can reuse the functionalities of existing classes to new classes. In the concept of inheritance, there are two terms base (parent) class and derived (child) class. When a class is inherited from another class (base class), it (derived class) obtains all the properties and behaviors of the base class.

4. **Polymorphism:** The term "polymorphism" means "many forms". In object-oriented programming, polymorphism is useful when you want to create multiple forms with the same name of a single entity. To implement polymorphism in Java, we use two concepts method overloading and method overriding.

   The method overloading is performed in the same class where we have multiple methods with the same name but different parameters, whereas, the method overriding is performed by using the inheritance where we can have multiple methods with the same name in parent and child classes.

5. **Abstraction:** In object-oriented programming, an abstraction is a technique of hiding internal details and showing functionalities. The abstract classes and interfaces are used to achieve abstraction in Java.

   The real-world example of an abstraction is a Car, the internal details such as the engine, process of starting a car, process of shifting gears, etc. are hidden from the user, and features such as the start button, gears, display, break, etc are given to the user. When we perform any action on these features, the internal process works.

6. **Encapsulation:** In an object-oriented approach, encapsulation is a process of binding the data members (attributes) and methods together. The encapsulation restricts direct access to important data. The best example of the encapsulation concept is making a class where the data members are private and methods are public to access through an object. In this case, only methods can access those private data.

Functional Programming: Functional programming (FP) is a programming paradigm that treats computation as the evaluation of mathematical functions and avoids changing state or mutable data. It emphasizes pure functions, which always produce the same output given the same input and have no side effects, making programs more predictable and easier to debug. This approach promotes writing small, reusable, and composable functions that can be combined to perform complex operations.

A key feature of functional programming is immutability, meaning that once a variable is assigned a value, it cannot be changed. Instead of modifying data, new data structures are created when transformations are needed. This reduces bugs related to shared state or unexpected side effects, which is especially valuable in concurrent or parallel programming environments.

Functional programming also supports higher-order functions, which are functions that can take other functions as arguments or return them as results. This allows for powerful abstractions and flexible code reuse. Recursion often replaces traditional loops in FP, as it aligns better with the concept of immutable state.

Languages like Haskell, Scala, Erlang, and Lisp are designed specifically for functional programming, but many modern languages like JavaScript, Python, and Java also support functional features. Functional programming is especially well-suited for data processing, mathematical computations, and applications that require high reliability and maintainability. By avoiding side effects and focusing on pure functions, FP helps developers write cleaner, more testable, and more scalable code, leading to more robust and error-resistant software systems.

A list of some of these programming languages:

1. **Haskell:** Made specifically for functional programming, Haskell is a statically typed programming language. It compiles code faster, is memory safe, efficient, and easier to read.

2. **Python:** Although python supports functional programming, however, it was designed to prioritize object-oriented programming first.

3. **Erlang:** Although it is not popularly used like Haskell, Erlang is best suited for concurrent systems. Messaging apps like WhatsApp and Discord make use of Erlang because of its scalability.

4. **JavaScript:** Similar to Python, JavaScript isn't specifically designed for functional programming. However, functional programming features like lambda expressions and attributes are supported making JavaScript a top used language among multi-paradigm languages.

5. **Clojure:** Clojure is a functional programming language that provides tools to avoid mutable states. Although it supports both mutable and immutable data types, it is less strict than other languages.

6. **Scala:** Supporting both functional and object-oriented programming, Scala was designed to address the shortcomings of Java. It also comes with a built-in static typed system similar to Haskell.

Table 3.1

S.No.	Aspect	Procedural Programming	Object-Oriented Programming (OOP)	Functional Programming
1	Programming Style	Linear, step-by-step instructions	Based on objects and classes	Based on mathematical functions
2	Main Building Block	Procedures / Functions	Objects (instances of classes)	Pure Functions
3	Focus	What to do (tasks)	Who is doing what (objects & behavior)	What to solve (declarations, expressions
4	Data and Behavior	Separate	Encapsulated together in objects	Data is immutable, behavior via functions
5	State Management	Uses and modifies global/local variables	State is managed within objects	Avoids shared state, uses immutable data
6	Code Reusability	Through functions	Through inheritance, polymorphism, and encapsulation	Through higher-order and reusable functions
7	Control Flow	Uses loops and conditionals	Uses methods, messages between objects	Uses recursion and function composition
8	Modularity	Via functions and procedures	Via classes and objects	Via small pure functions
9	Ease of Testing	Moderate, may depend on state	Can be complex due to inter-object interactions	Easier, due to stateless and pure functions
10	Use Case	Suitable for simple, linear applications	Best for large, complex systems with many entities	Ideal for tasks requiring immutability & stateless logic
11	Examples of Languages	C, Pascal, BASIC	Java, C++, Python (OOP style)	Haskell, Lisp, Scala, F#, Elixir

Choosing the Right Language for the Job

When selecting a language for a job, consider your desired career path, the specific role's requirements, and the industry's demands. For example, if you're aiming for web development, JavaScript, Python, or Ruby might be good choices, while data science roles might favor Python. Additionally, exploring job postings and industry trends can help identify in-demand languages.

1. **Understanding Your Career Goals:** Understanding your career goals is essential for making informed decisions about your education, skills, and job

opportunities. It involves identifying what you're passionate about, the type of work environment you thrive in, and the kind of impact you want to make. Whether you're drawn to creative design, data analysis, software development, or leadership roles, having clear goals helps you stay focused and motivated. It also allows you to choose the right tools, technologies, and experiences to build your career path. Setting short-term and long-term goals ensures you grow steadily and adapt to the ever-evolving demands of the tech industry.

- **Web Development:** JavaScript, Python, Ruby are popular.
- **Mobile App Development:** Java (Android), Kotlin (Android), Swift (iOS).
- **Data Science/AI:** Python.
- **Game Development:** C++, C#.
- **Backend Application Development:** Java, Python, C#, Kotlin, GoLang.
- **System Programming:** C, C++.

2. **Researching Job Market Needs:** Researching job market needs is crucial for aligning your skills with current industry demands. It involves analyzing job postings, industry trends, and emerging technologies to identify which roles are in high demand and what qualifications employers seek. This research helps you focus on learning relevant skills, certifications, and tools that increase your employability. Platforms like LinkedIn, Glassdoor, and industry reports can provide insights into salary expectations, in-demand programming languages, and regional job availability. Staying informed about market needs not only improves your chances of getting hired but also ensures your career path remains adaptable and future-proof in a competitive field.

   - **Check Job Boards:** Look at job postings on platforms like Indeed, LinkedIn, and others.
   - **Identify Industry Trends:** Research industry reports and articles to see which languages are most sought after.

3. **Experimenting and Learning:** Experimenting and learning are vital parts of career growth, especially in the tech industry where change is constant. Trying out different tools, languages, and projects helps you discover what you enjoy and where your strengths lie. Whether it's building a personal website,

contributing to open-source, or taking online courses, hands-on experience deepens your understanding and boosts your confidence. Mistakes and challenges are part of the learning process, pushing you to grow and adapt. Continuous learning keeps your skills sharp and relevant, while experimentation fuels creativity and innovation, helping you stay competitive and passionate about your chosen career path.

- **Try Multiple Languages:** Don't just pick one; experiment with different languages to see which one aligns with your preferences and career goals.
- **Start with Easier Languages:** If you're new to programming, consider starting with languages like Python or JavaScript, which have easier learning curves.

4. **Factors to Consider:** When choosing a career path or a programming language, several important factors should be considered. These include your personal interests, long-term career goals, and the type of work you enjoy. Market demand, salary potential, and job availability in your region or preferred industry also play key roles. Additionally, think about the learning curve, available resources, and community support for the language or field you're entering. Consider whether you prefer working in a team or independently, and whether you want to specialize or stay versatile. Balancing passion with practicality helps ensure both job satisfaction and career sustainability in the long run.

- **Job Prospects:** Some languages have a higher demand than others, especially in specific fields.
- **Learning Curve:** Some languages are easier to learn than others.
- **Salary Potential:** Certain languages may offer higher average salaries, particularly in specialized areas.
- **Industry Trends:** Stay informed about which languages are most in demand in your target industry.

5. **Examples of Languages and Their Use Cases:** Different programming languages serve different purposes based on their strengths and use cases.

JavaScript: Web development (front-end and back-end with Node.js).

- **Python:** Data science, machine learning, web development.

- **Java:** Enterprise applications, Android development.
- **C++:** Game development, system programming, high-performance applications.
- **C#:** Game development (Unity), .NET framework applications.
- **Go:** Cloud computing, backend development.
- **Ruby:** Web development (Rails framework), back-end.
- **PHP:** Web development (backend).

By carefully considering these factors and aligning your choices with your goals, you can make an informed decision about the best language for your job search.

Modern Programming Languages: Python, Java, C++, JavaScript, etc.

Modern programming languages are designed to meet the evolving demands of today's tech industry, offering a balance of performance, scalability, and developer productivity. Python stands out for its readability and versatility, making it a top choice for data science, machine learning, automation, and web development. JavaScript is essential for web development, powering dynamic frontend interfaces and full-stack solutions using frameworks like React and Node.js. Java, known for its portability and stability, remains a staple in enterprise environments and Android app development. C++, with its high-performance capabilities, is widely used in system software, game engines, and embedded systems.

Emerging languages like Rust and Go are also gaining traction. Rust offers memory safety and high performance, making it ideal for system-level programming without the common pitfalls of C/C++. Go, developed by Google, is praised for its simplicity and concurrency support, making it a popular choice for backend services and cloud infrastructure. The growing demand for cross-platform apps has also pushed languages like Dart (with Flutter) into the spotlight. Choosing the right language depends on your project requirements, career goals, and preferred development domain, whether it's web, mobile, AI, or systems programming. Staying updated with modern languages ensures long-term relevance and flexibility.

Python: Python is a high-level, interpreted, general-purpose programming language known for its simplicity, readability, and versatility. It was created by Guido van Rossum and first released in 1991. One of Python's main goals is to make code easy to write and understand, which is why it emphasizes clear syntax and indentation rather than complex syntax rules.

Python supports multiple programming paradigms, including procedural, object-oriented, and functional programming. It is dynamically typed, meaning variable types are determined at runtime, and it uses automatic memory management, which simplifies development.

Python is an interpreted language, which means the code is executed line-by-line, making it easier to debug and suitable for scripting, automation, and rapid application development. It is also cross-platform, meaning it can run on different operating systems like Windows, macOS, and Linux without requiring code changes.

One of the key strengths of Python is its extensive standard library and the large collection of third-party packages available through PyPI (Python Package Index). These packages cover everything from web development (e.g., Django, Flask) and data analysis (e.g., Pandas, NumPy) to machine learning (e.g., TensorFlow, scikit-learn), game development (e.g., Pygame), and automation (e.g., Selenium, PyAutoGUI). Python is widely used in various fields:

1. **Web Development:** Frameworks like Django and Flask allow developers to build robust web applications quickly.
2. **Data Science and Machine Learning**: Libraries such as NumPy, Pandas, Matplotlib, scikit-learn, and TensorFlow make Python the leading language in this domain.
3. **Scripting and Automation:** Python is often used for automating repetitive tasks, such as file handling, web scraping, and testing.
4. **Software Development:** Python can be used to build desktop applications, games, and backend services.
5. **Education:** Because of its readability and simplicity, Python is often the first language taught in computer science courses.

Python's popularity has grown rapidly due to its community support, open-source nature, and ease of integration with other technologies. It supports embedding into C/C++ programs and provides bindings to languages like Java via Jython.

Python 2 and Python 3 were two major versions for a long time. However, Python 2 reached its end of life in 2020, and Python 3 is now the standard. Python 3 introduced several improvements, including better Unicode support, new syntax features, and performance enhancements.

Python programs typically have the .py file extension and can be run using the Python interpreter. Tools like Jupyter Notebook make it easier to write and test Python code interactively, especially in data science and research.

In conclusion, Python's clean syntax, strong ecosystem, and wide applicability make it one of the most powerful and popular programming languages in the world today. Whether you're building web apps, analyzing data, training machine learning models, or automating tasks, Python is a reliable and beginner-friendly choice.

Java: Java is a high-level, object-oriented, class-based programming language designed to have as few implementation dependencies as possible. It was developed by James Gosling at Sun Microsystems and released in 1995. Java's key principle is "write once, run anywhere" (WORA), meaning code written in Java can run on any platform that has a Java Virtual Machine (JVM), without needing to be recompiled.

Java is both a programming language and a platform. The Java Platform includes the Java Development Kit (JDK), Java Runtime Environment (JRE), and the JVM. When you write Java code, it's compiled into bytecode, which the JVM interprets or compiles just-in-time (JIT) to native machine code for execution. This architecture makes Java platform-independent at the source and binary levels.

Java is known for its strong object-oriented programming (OOP) foundation. Everything in Java is based around classes and objects, which encourages modular, reusable, and maintainable code. Java supports core OOP principles like encapsulation, inheritance, polymorphism, and abstraction.

Some of Java's key features include:

1. **Simple and Readable Syntax**: Java's syntax is clean and resembles C++, but it removes complex features like operator overloading and multiple inheritance.
2. **Platform Independence:** Java code runs on any OS with a JVM.
3. **Robust and Secure**: Java provides strong memory management, exception handling, and a security model with sandboxing.
4. **Multithreaded**: Java allows concurrent execution of two or more threads, making it suitable for applications that require multitasking.
5. **Automatic Garbage Collection:** Java automatically handles memory management, reducing the chance of memory leaks.
6. **Rich API and Libraries:** Java has a vast standard library that supports data structures, networking, I/O, utilities, XML parsing, and more.

Java is used in a wide range of domains:

1. **Enterprise Applications:** Java is widely used in large-scale enterprise systems with frameworks like Spring and Hibernate.
2. **Web Development:** Java supports server-side development with technologies like JSP, Servlets, and frameworks like Spring Boot.
3. **Mobile Applications**: Java is the primary language for Android app development.
4. **Desktop GUI Applications:** Java provides libraries like AWT, Swing, and JavaFX for building desktop applications.
5. **Scientific Applications:** Due to its portability and robustness, Java is used in scientific computing environments as well.

Java has a strong and active developer community. The language continues to evolve with regular updates. Modern versions, such as Java 17 (LTS) and Java 21, have introduced features like enhanced switch expressions, records, sealed classes, and improved performance.

Java is also widely taught in computer science courses due to its balance between simplicity and real-world capability. Tools like Eclipse, IntelliJ IDEA, and NetBeans provide powerful development environments for building, testing, and debugging Java applications.

In conclusion, Java remains one of the most widely used and versatile programming languages in the world. Its platform independence, robust architecture, and strong community support make it a preferred choice for everything from enterprise systems to mobile apps and cloud-based solutions.

C++: C++ is a powerful, high-performance, general-purpose programming language that supports both procedural and object-oriented programming. It was developed by Bjarne Stroustrup at Bell Labs in the early 1980s as an extension of the C language, adding object-oriented features while retaining C's speed and low-level capabilities. C++ is widely used for system/software development, game engines, real-time simulations, desktop applications, and embedded systems.

C++ is a compiled language, meaning the source code is translated into machine code by a compiler before execution, resulting in faster runtime performance. It allows direct manipulation of hardware through pointers and memory management, giving developers fine control over system resources, which is crucial in performance-critical applications.

One of C++'s core strengths is its support for object-oriented programming (OOP). It introduces key OOP concepts such as:

1. **Classes and Objects:** For encapsulating data and behavior.
2. **Inheritance:** Allows a class to derive properties from another class.
3. **Polymorphism:** Enables a function or method to behave differently based on the context.
4. **Encapsulation:** Protects data from unauthorized access by bundling it within objects.
5. **Abstraction:** Hides complexity and shows only relevant data.

C++ also supports function overloading, operator overloading, templates, and exception handling, giving it great flexibility and expressive power. Templates, in particular, enable generic programming, allowing functions and classes to operate with any data type.

C++ programs are structured in files with .cpp extensions, and header files (.h or .hpp) are used to declare functions and classes. The Standard Template Library (STL) is one of C++'s most powerful features. It provides pre-written classes and functions for commonly used data structures (like vectors, stacks, queues, and maps) and algorithms (like sort, search, and transform), enabling developers to write efficient and reusable code.

C++ is often used in:

1. **Operating Systems:** Many components of operating systems like Windows, macOS, and Linux are written in C++.
2. **Game Development:** Game engines like Unreal Engine use C++ for performance-intensive operations.
3. **Embedded Systems:** Its low-level capabilities make C++ ideal for writing firmware and real-time software.
4. **Finance and Trading:** Used in building high-frequency trading platforms due to its speed.
5. **Desktop Applications:** Applications like Photoshop and web browsers (e.g., Chrome) are built using C++.

Though powerful, C++ also has a steeper learning curve compared to languages like Python. Developers must manage memory manually using pointers, new, and delete, which increases the risk of bugs like memory leaks or segmentation faults. However, modern C++ (from C++11 onward) has introduced features like smart pointers, auto keyword, lambda expressions, move semantics, and multithreading support, making it more robust, expressive, and easier to use.

In conclusion, C++ remains one of the most important programming languages in software development. Its combination of speed, flexibility, and control makes it ideal for applications where performance and efficiency are critical. Mastery of C++ also provides a strong foundation for understanding how software interacts with hardware and for learning other programming languages.

JavaScript: JavaScript is a high-level, interpreted programming language primarily known for enabling interactive web development. Created by Brendan Eich in 1995 while working at Netscape, JavaScript was initially designed to add dynamic behavior to web pages. Today, it is a core technology of the web alongside HTML and CSS.

JavaScript is lightweight, event-driven, and multi-paradigm, supporting object-oriented, imperative, and functional programming styles. Unlike languages like Java or C++, JavaScript is dynamically typed and runs directly in the web browser, making it ideal for client-side scripting. Modern JavaScript can also be used on the server side, thanks to platforms like Node.js.

At its core, JavaScript allows developers to make web pages more dynamic and interactive. Tasks such as form validation, interactive maps, animations, and real-time updates (like chat apps) are all made possible using JavaScript. It interacts with the Document Object Model (DOM) to manipulate HTML and CSS, allowing developers to change the structure, style, and content of a webpage on the fly.

JavaScript follows an event-driven model, meaning it responds to user actions like clicks, keypresses, and mouse movements. It uses a single-threaded model with an event loop, enabling non-blocking asynchronous programming via callbacks, promises, and async/await.

JavaScript has evolved significantly since its early days. Modern JavaScript is standardized under ECMAScript (ES), with ES6 (ECMAScript 2015) introducing major features like:

1. let and const for block-scoped variables
2. Arrow functions
3. Template literals
4. Destructuring
5. Classes and modules
6. Promises

7. Default parameters
8. Spread and rest operators

JavaScript is object-based, meaning everything is either an object or behaves like one. It supports prototypal inheritance, which differs from classical inheritance in languages like Java or C++. Objects in JavaScript can inherit properties directly from other objects.

The JavaScript ecosystem is vast, with numerous frameworks and libraries that make development faster and more efficient. Popular tools include:

1. **Frontend frameworks:** React.js, Angular, Vue.js
2. **Backend:** Node.js with Express.js
3. **Testing tools:** Jest, Mocha
4. **Package management:** npm (Node Package Manager), Yarn
5. **Build tools:** Webpack, Babel, Vite

JavaScript is not limited to browsers anymore. With Node.js, you can build server-side applications, command-line tools, REST APIs, and even use JavaScript for IoT and desktop apps (via Electron).

Security in JavaScript is crucial, especially in web applications. Common vulnerabilities include Cross-Site Scripting (XSS) and Cross-Site Request Forgery (CSRF), which require developers to follow best practices and use proper frameworks to mitigate risks.

In conclusion, JavaScript is one of the most widely-used and versatile programming languages in the world. It powers most modern web applications and continues to grow in capability and popularity, thanks to its flexibility, ease of use, and a massive open-source community. Whether you're building a simple webpage or a full-stack application, JavaScript is an essential tool for any developer.

Differences Between Python, Java, C++, JavaScript: The differences between Python, Java, C++, JavaScript is listed in table 3.2.

Table 3.2

S.No.	Feature	Python	Java	C++	JavaScript
1	Type	Interpreted, high-level	Compiled to bytecode, high-level	Compiled, mid-to-low level	Interpreted, high-level
2	Paradigm	Multi-paradigm	Object-oriented	Procedural & object-oriented	Multi-paradigm (event-driven, functional)
3	Syntax	Simple, readable	Verbose	Complex (similar to C)	Light, web-friendly syntax
4	Execution	Interpreter (CPython)	JVM (Java Virtual Machine)	Compiled to machine code	Browser (client-side) or Node.js (server)
5	Use Cases	Data science, AI, scripting, web dev	Enterprise apps, Android, web backend	System programming, game dev, embedded	Web dev (frontend/backend), UI/UX
6	Performance	Slower than C++/Java	Faster than Python, slower than C++	Very fast, close to hardware	Fast in browser, not as fast as C++
7	Memory Management	Automatic (Garbage Collection)	Automatic (Garbage Collection)	Manual (with destructors)	Automatic (Garbage Collection)
8	Learning Curve	Easy for beginners	Moderate	Steeper learning curve	Easy to moderate
9	Object-Oriented	Yes (multi-paradigm)	Yes (pure OOP)	Yes (also procedural)	Yes (prototype-based)
10	Concurrency	Threading with GIL limitations	Strong multithreading	Complex (manual threading)	Event-driven (async, promises)
11	Typical File Extension	.py	.java	.cpp / .h	.js

******

7

Coding Standards and Best Practices

Coding standards and best practices ensure code is clean, consistent, and maintainable. They include proper naming, formatting, commenting, and error handling. Following these guidelines improves readability, reduces bugs, and enhances teamwork. Tools like linters and formatters help enforce standards, leading to higher quality, scalable, and more efficient software development.

Coding Standards: Coding standards are a set of rules and best practices that guide how code should be written, formatted, and organized to ensure clarity, consistency, and maintainability. These standards cover aspects such as naming conventions, indentation, code structure, commenting, and error handling. By following consistent naming patterns like camelCase, PascalCase, or snake_case, developers make code easier to read and understand. Proper indentation, spacing, and organization help highlight the logical flow of a program, while meaningful comments and documentation explain complex logic and enhance collaboration. Coding standards also promote the use of reusable code, reduce bugs, and improve software quality. They are especially vital in team environments where multiple developers contribute to the same project. Tools like linters and formatters enforce these rules automatically, and most programming languages have community-accepted guidelines, such as PEP8 for Python or the Airbnb Style Guide for JavaScript. Adhering to coding standards not only results in cleaner code but also saves time during debugging, testing, and code reviews. Ultimately, good coding standards lead to more efficient development processes and scalable, maintainable software systems.

Importance of Coding Standards

1. **Improves Readability:** Consistent code style makes it easier for developers to read and understand code quickly.
2. **Enhances Maintainability:** Clean and standardized code is easier to debug, update, and extend over time.
3. **Promotes Team Collaboration:** When everyone follows the same rules, working on shared codebases becomes smoother and more efficient.
4. **Reduces Errors and Bugs:** Standards encourage writing structured, well-tested code that helps avoid common mistakes.
5. **Speeds Up Onboarding:** New developers can get up to speed faster when the code follows familiar and documented conventions.
6. **Supports Automation Tools:** Linters, formatters, and code analyzers work best when code adheres to a consistent style.
7. **Improves Code Review Process:** Reviewers can focus on logic and functionality instead of nitpicking formatting issues.
8. **Boosts Reusability:** Well-written and standardized code can be easily reused across projects.
9. Ensures Scalability: As projects grow, standardized code helps maintain structure and prevent technical debt.
10. **Reflects Professionalism:** Following standards shows discipline and care, improving the overall quality of the software.

Common Coding Standards: The common coding standards are as:

1. **Naming Conventions:** Naming conventions ensure consistent, clear, and meaningful identifiers in code. Use camelCase for variables, PascalCase for classes, and UPPER_CASE for constants. Use meaningful and descriptive names for variables, functions, and classes. Follow consistent casing:
    - camelCase for variables/functions (e.g., totalAmount)
    - PascalCase for classes (e.g., UserProfile)
    - UPPER_CASE for constants (e.g., MAX_LIMIT)

- snake_case for Python functions and variables (e.g., calculate_total)

2. **Indentation and Formatting:** Indentation and formatting improve readability. Use consistent spaces (2–4) for indentation, avoid mixing tabs and spaces, and keep line length under 80–120 characters.

   - Use consistent indentation (usually 2 or 4 spaces).
   - Do not mix tabs and spaces.
   - Keep line length within 80–120 characters.
   - Add proper spacing around operators and after commas.

3. **Code Structure:** Code structure ensures clarity and maintainability. Follow the Single Responsibility Principle, keep functions concise, group related code logically, and avoid unnecessary complexity or duplication.

   - Follow the Single Responsibility Principle – one function/class does one thing.
   - Keep functions short and focused.
   - Group related code logically (e.g., utility functions, related classes).

4. **Comments and Documentation:** Comments and documentation clarify code intent. Write meaningful comments explaining *why* something is done, not *what*. Use docstrings for functions/classes to describe inputs and outputs.

   - Use comments to explain *why* something is done, not *what*.
   - Write docstrings or method headers with input/output details.
   - Keep comments concise and up to date.

5. **Error Handling:** Error handling involves using try-catch or try-except blocks to manage exceptions. Provide meaningful error messages, avoid empty catches, and handle errors appropriately for robust code.

   - Handle exceptions using try-except or try-catch blocks.
   - Avoid empty catch blocks.
   - Always provide meaningful error messages.

6. **Code Reusability:** Code reusability promotes writing modular, efficient code. Avoid duplication by creating reusable functions, classes, and modules, following the DRY principle (Don't Repeat Yourself).

   - Avoid code duplication (DRY principle).
   - Use functions, modules, or classes for reusable logic.
   - Use constants instead of hardcoded values.

7. **Version Control Standards:** Version control standards include clear commit messages, logical commit units, and consistent branch naming conventions. Use Git to track changes and collaborate effectively on projects.

   - Write clear and meaningful commit messages.
   - Follow branch naming conventions (feature/login-page, bugfix/header-alignment).
   - Commit small, logical units of work.

8. **Security Practices:** Security practices involve validating and sanitizing inputs, avoiding hardcoded sensitive data, and using secure coding patterns for authentication, encryption, and safe data handling to prevent vulnerabilities.

   - Validate and sanitize all user inputs.
   - Avoid hardcoding sensitive information like API keys.
   - Use secure coding patterns for authentication and data handling.

9. **Language-Specific Standards:** Language-specific standards ensure consistency and best practices within a language. Follow official guidelines, like PEP 8 for Python or Java conventions, to maintain clean, efficient code.

   - **Python:** Follow PEP 8
   - **Java:** Follow Oracle's Java Code Conventions
   - **JavaScript:** Use ESLint or Airbnb JS Style Guide
   - **C++:** Refer to Google C++ Style Guide or ISO C++ Guidelines

10. **Tool Support:** Tool support includes using linters, formatters, and IDE extensions to enforce coding standards. Tools like ESLint, Prettier, and PyLint automate style checks and improve code quality.

- Use linters (e.g., pylint, ESLint) for enforcing style rules.
- Use code formatters (e.g., Black, Prettier) for auto-formatting.

Best Practices: Best practices in software development refer to a set of standardized techniques, methods, and conventions that lead to cleaner, more efficient, and maintainable code. These practices not only improve the quality of the software but also streamline collaboration between team members, ensure scalability, and reduce technical debt. Below are some key best practices that every developer should aim to follows:

1. **Write Readable and Maintainable Code:** Readable code is critical for future maintenance and collaboration. To achieve this:
   - **Naming Conventions:** Choose meaningful and descriptive names for variables, functions, and classes. Follow language-specific conventions such as camelCase for JavaScript and Python functions, or PascalCase for classes in most languages.
   - **Consistent Formatting:** Maintain consistent indentation (2–4 spaces, no tabs) and line length (80–120 characters) to enhance code readability. Use blank lines to separate logical blocks of code.
   - **Commenting and Documentation:** Document complex or non-obvious code with clear comments explaining the *why* behind a solution, not just the *what*. In addition, use docstrings or annotations to describe the input, output, and purpose of functions, classes, or methods.
2. **Use Version Control Systems (VCS):** Version control systems, such as Git, are essential for tracking changes, collaborating, and ensuring code integrity.
   - **Commit Often:** Make small, logical commits with meaningful messages. Each commit should represent a single unit of work and describe what was changed and why.
   - **Branching and Merging:** Use branches for new features, bug fixes, or experiments. Merge frequently to keep the main branch up-to-date and avoid large, complicated merge conflicts.
   - **Use Pull Requests:** When working in teams, pull requests allow others to review and discuss changes before merging them into the main codebase.
3. **Follow the DRY Principle:** The Don't Repeat Yourself (DRY) principle encourages code reuse, which enhances maintainability.

- **Avoid Duplication:** Instead of repeating logic, encapsulate it in functions, methods, or classes. This makes your code more modular and easier to update.
- **Abstract Common Logic:** Identify patterns in your code and refactor them into reusable components or helper functions. This also reduces the potential for errors and inconsistencies.

4. **Write Automated Tests:** Testing is essential for ensuring that your software behaves as expected and preventing future bugs.
   - **Unit Testing:** Write unit tests for small units of functionality, such as individual functions or methods. Use testing frameworks like JUnit (Java), PyTest (Python), or Mocha (JavaScript).
   - **Integration Testing:** Write tests that check how different components of your software work together.
   - **Continuous Integration (CI):** Automate the testing process using CI tools to run tests on each commit. This helps catch issues early and ensures a high-quality codebase.
5. **Optimize for Performance:** Performance should be considered early in the development process, but only optimize when necessary.
   - **Avoid Premature Optimization:** Focus on clarity and functionality first. Only optimize when a performance issue becomes evident or after profiling indicates a bottleneck.
   - **Profile and Test:** Use profiling tools to identify performance bottlenecks. Test different approaches to solving performance problems and choose the one that offers the best trade-off between speed and readability.
6. **Secure Coding Practices:** Security should be embedded in every stage of the development process to safeguard your software against malicious attacks.
   - **Input Validation:** Always validate and sanitize user inputs to prevent injection attacks, such as SQL injection or cross-site scripting (XSS).
   - **Use HTTPS:** Always use HTTPS to secure data transmitted over the internet. Never transmit sensitive data in plain text.

- **Follow Security Best Practices:** Use libraries that follow security standards, avoid hardcoding sensitive information like passwords and API keys, and regularly patch vulnerabilities.

7. **Document and Maintain Codebase:** Clear, concise documentation and code maintenance are essential for long-term project success.

   - **Write Clear Documentation:** Provide sufficient documentation for your codebase, including setup instructions, architectural decisions, and usage guides. This is essential for onboarding new developers and ensuring that others can understand and contribute to your project.

   - **Regular Refactoring:** Over time, software can become messy as new features are added. Refactor your code regularly to improve its structure, remove obsolete code, and maintain performance.

8. **Prioritize Collaboration and Communication:** Effective communication is vital, especially in team-based projects.

   - **Code Reviews:** Conduct regular code reviews to catch errors, share knowledge, and maintain code quality. Provide constructive feedback and encourage others to contribute ideas.

   - **Collaborative Development:** Use tools like Slack, Jira, or Trello to track tasks and communicate with team members. Keep the communication channels open to ensure that everyone is aligned on project goals.

9. **Keep Learning and Stay Updated:** Software development is an ever-evolving field, and staying updated with new technologies, tools, and methodologies is key to staying competitive.

   - **Continuous Learning:** Engage with the development community, attend workshops, read blogs, and try out new technologies or languages to expand your knowledge and skillset.

   - **Code Reviews and Pair Programming:** Learn from peers during code reviews and consider adopting pair programming to share knowledge and improve coding practices.

Adhering to best practices is essential for building reliable, scalable, and maintainable software. By writing clean code, using version control, testing rigorously, optimizing performance, and ensuring security, developers can create high-quality software that meets both user and business needs. Moreover, maintaining good documentation, fostering collaboration, and continuously learning will ensure that the software development process remains efficient and effective. Following these best practices not only improves the software but also enhances the overall developer experience, leading to better collaboration, faster delivery, and fewer issues down the road.

Code Readability and Maintainability

Code readability and maintainability are essential for understanding, updating, and scaling software efficiently. Readable code uses clear naming, consistent formatting, and concise comments. Maintainable code is modular, well-documented, and easy to test or refactor. Together, they improve collaboration, reduce bugs, and ensure long-term software quality and project sustainability.

Code Readability: Code readability refers to how easily a developer can understand the structure, logic, and purpose of a codebase. It's one of the most important qualities of high-quality software. Readable code allows developers whether teammates, new hires, or even the original author revisiting the code after months to quickly grasp what the code does and how it does it, without wasting time deciphering complex or poorly written logic.

Readable code should have clear and meaningful names for variables, functions, and classes. Descriptive naming eliminates the need for unnecessary comments and helps convey intent directly through code. Proper indentation and spacing, as well as consistent formatting, also improve readability by visually separating different parts of the code and indicating control flow.

Comments play a supporting role in readability. They should be used to explain *why* something is done, not what is being done (which should be clear from the code itself). Additionally, keeping code modular and organized breaking it into small, focused functions or classes makes it easier to understand and test individual parts.

Readable code also adheres to language-specific conventions, such as PEP 8 for Python or the JavaScript Airbnb Style Guide. Using linters and formatters helps maintain consistency automatically.

Ultimately, readable code is not just about writing for machines; it's about writing for people. It reduces confusion, improves collaboration, speeds up development, and makes onboarding and code reviews significantly smoother.

Code Maintainability: Code maintainability is the ease with which a software system can be modified to correct faults, improve performance, or adapt to a changed environment.

Maintainable code is vital for the long-term success and scalability of a software project. As software evolves, developers often need to update features, fix bugs, or refactor old logic. If the code isn't maintainable, these changes become time-consuming, error-prone, and frustrating.

Maintainable code typically follows the Single Responsibility Principle, where each module, class, or function does one specific task. This modular approach allows developers to isolate and change functionality without affecting unrelated parts of the system. Separation of concerns is key keeping business logic, user interface, and data access layers distinct makes the codebase easier to navigate and modify.

Good maintainability also means the code is well-documented and well-tested. Documentation should explain the system architecture and any complex logic. Unit and integration tests ensure that future changes don't break existing functionality, giving developers confidence when refactoring or adding features.

Avoiding code duplication, following consistent naming and formatting standards, and removing dead or obsolete code are also part of writing maintainable code. Tools like version control systems, linters, and static analysers help enforce these practices and catch issues early.

In short, maintainable code ensures that a project remains flexible and adaptable over time. It saves time, reduces bugs, supports team collaboration, and helps organizations evolve their software to meet changing needs without starting from scratch.

Python Naming Conventions: Python, known for its simplicity and readability, places a strong emphasis on writing clean and maintainable code. One of the key aspects contributing to this readability is adhering to Python Naming Conventions. In this article, we'll delve into the specifics of Python Naming Conventions, covering modules, functions, global and local variables, classes, and exceptions. Each section will be accompanied by runnable code examples to illustrate the principles in action.

What is Naming Conventions in Python?

Naming conventions in Python refer to rules and guidelines for naming variables, functions, classes, and other entities in your code. Adhering to these conventions ensures consistency, readability, and better collaboration among developers. The Naming Conventions in Python which are follows.

1. **Modules:** Modules in Python are files containing Python definitions and statements. When naming a module, use lowercase letters and underscores,

making it descriptive but concise. Let's create a module named math_operations.py. In this example, code defines two functions: add_numbers that returns the sum of two input values, and subtract_numbers that returns the difference between two input values. To demonstrate, if you call add_numbers(5, 3) it will return 8, and if you call subtract_numbers(5, 3) it will return 2.

```
def add_numbers(a, b):
result = a + b
print(f"The sum is: {result}")
return result
def subtract_numbers(a, b):
result = a - b
print(f"The difference is: {result}")
return result
# Example usage:
add_result = add_numbers(5, 3)
subtract_result = subtract_numbers(5, 3)
```

Output: The sum is: 8

The difference is: 2

2. **Variable:** Globals variable should be in uppercase with underscores separating words, while locals variable should follow the same convention as functions. Demonstrating consistency in naming conventions enhances code readability and maintainability, contributing to a more robust and organized codebase. In below, code defines a global variable GLOBAL_VARIABLE with a value of 10. Inside the example_function, a local variable local_variable is assigned a value of 5, and the sum of the global and local variables is printed.

```
GLOBAL_VARIABLE = 10

def example_function():
```

```
local_variable = 5
print(GLOBAL_VARIABLE + local_variable)

# Call the function to print the result
example_function()
```

Output: 15

3. **Classes:** Classes in Python names should follow the CapWords (or CamelCase) convention. This means that the first letter of each word in the class name should be capitalized, and there should be no underscores between words. This convention helps improve code readability and consistency in programming projects.

   In this example, the class "Car" has an initializer method (__init__) that sets the make and model attributes of an instance. The "display_info" method prints the car's make and model.

```
class Car:
def __init__(self, make, model):
self.make = make
self.model = model

def display_info(self):
print(f"{self.make} {self.model}")
```

4. **Exceptions:** Exception in Python names should end with "Error," following the CapWords convention. it is advisable to choose meaningful names that reflect the nature of the exception, providing clarity to developers who may encounter the error. In this example, below code creates an instance of CustomError with a specific error message and then raises that exception within a try block. The except block catches the CustomError exception and prints a message.

```
class CustomError(Exception):
def __init__(self, message):
```

```
super().__init__(message)

# Creating an instance of CustomError

custom_exception = CustomError("This is a custom error message")

# Catching and handling the exception

try:

raise custom_exception

except CustomError as ce:

print(f"Caught a custom exception: {ce}")
```

Output: Caught a custom exception: This is a custom error message

Importance of Naming Conventions: The importance of Naming Conventions in Python is following.

1. Naming conventions enhance code readability, making it easier for developers to understand the purpose and functionality of variables, functions, classes, and other code elements.

2. Consistent naming conventions contribute to code maintainability. When developers follow a standardized naming pattern, it becomes more straightforward for others to update, debug, or extend the code.

3. Naming conventions are especially important in collaborative coding environments. When multiple developers work on a project, adhering to a common naming style ensures a cohesive and unified codebase.

4. Well-chosen names can help prevent errors. A descriptive name that accurately reflects the purpose of a variable or function reduces the likelihood of misunderstandings or unintentional misuse.

In conclusion, by emphasizing readability, supporting collaborative development, aiding error prevention, and enabling seamless tool integration, these conventions serve as a guiding principle for Python developers. Consistent and meaningful naming not only enhances individual understanding but also fosters a unified and coherent coding environment. Embracing these conventions ensures that Python code remains robust, accessible, and adaptable, ultimately promoting best practices in software development.

Documentation: Documentation in software development is the process of creating written text, guides, or comments that explain how code works, how to use it, and why certain decisions were made. It's an essential part of building reliable, understandable, and maintainable software.

Good documentation serves developers, testers, users, and future maintainers by providing clarity on the functionality, structure, and usage of code. It reduces the learning curve for new team members, speeds up debugging, and ensures continuity when projects are handed off.

There are several types of documentation:

1. **Inline Comments:** Placed directly in code to explain complex or non-obvious logic.
2. **Docstrings/Function Documentation:** Brief descriptions of what a function, class, or module does, including its inputs, outputs, and possible exceptions.
3. **Project Documentation:** Files like README.md, installation guides, or setup instructions that describe the purpose of the project, how to run it, and how to contribute.
4. **API Documentation:** Guides for developers who use your software or library, explaining available functions, endpoints, parameters, and examples.

Effective documentation is clear and concise, well-structured, consistently formatted and regularly updated.

Tools like Javadoc, Sphinx, Doxygen, and Swagger can generate documentation automatically from structured code comments.

Documentation is a vital communication tool. It enhances collaboration, improves productivity, and makes software easier to understand, use, and maintain whether for teammates, end-users, or even your future self.

Version Control Systems (Git, GitHub, GitLab, Bitbucket)

Version Control Systems (VCS) are essential tools in modern software development that help manage changes to source code over time. They allow multiple developers to work collaboratively on the same project without overwriting each other's work. The most popular VCS is Git, a distributed system that enables every developer to have a full copy of the codebase and its history. With Git, developers can create branches, make commits, merge code, and revert changes when necessary. This structure not only ensures a robust workflow but also improves code quality and development speed.

Platforms like GitHub, GitLab, and Bitbucket build on Git by offering cloud-based repositories and additional collaboration features. GitHub is widely used for both open-source and private projects and supports tools like GitHub Actions for CI/CD automation. GitLab offers a full DevOps lifecycle solution, including built-in CI/CD pipelines and issue tracking. Bitbucket, integrated with Atlassian tools like Jira, is ideal for Agile development teams. All these platforms support pull requests (or merge requests), making it easier to review code before merging. Overall, version control systems provide a reliable way to track progress, manage code changes, and facilitate teamwork in software development.

Git: Git is a powerful, open-source distributed version control system created by Linus Torvalds in 2005 to manage the Linux kernel's development. It allows developers to track changes in their source code, collaborate with others, and manage multiple versions of their codebase efficiently. Unlike centralized systems, Git provides each user with a full copy of the repository, including its entire history, enabling offline work, faster performance, and data redundancy. One of Git's key strengths is its branching and merging capabilities, which allow developers to create separate branches for features or bug fixes and then merge them seamlessly into the main project. Git also uses a staging area where changes can be reviewed before committing, offering granular control over what gets added to the codebase. All data in Git is secured through SHA-1 hashing, ensuring data integrity and tracking every change with precision. It supports a wide range of workflows, such as Gitflow or trunk-based development, and integrates seamlessly with platforms like GitHub, GitLab, and Bitbucket for cloud-based collaboration and CI/CD automation. Git commands like clone, commit, merge, push, and pull are central to daily operations, and its efficiency makes it ideal for both small personal projects and large enterprise systems. Ultimately, Git empowers developers to build, test, and deploy software collaboratively, with full visibility and control over every line of code. Core Features of Git

1. **Distributed Architecture:** Each developer has the complete project repository, including its full history, on their local machine. This enables offline work, faster operations, and better data backup.

2. **Branching and Merging:** Git allows developers to create lightweight branches quickly. Each branch can represent a feature, fix, or experiment. Git's merging capabilities are powerful, allowing developers to bring changes from one branch into another with minimal conflict.

3. **Staging Area (Index):** Git introduces a unique concept called the staging area, where you can prepare and review changes before committing them. This provides flexibility and control over what gets included in each commit.

4. **Speed and Efficiency:** Most operations in Git are performed locally, making them extremely fast. Operations like viewing history, switching branches, and committing changes don't require network access.

5. **Data Integrity:** Every file and commit in Git are checksummed using a SHA-1 hash, ensuring data is not corrupted or altered without detection. This built-in integrity protects the codebase over time.

Common Git Commands: A list of common Git commands that are used frequently in day-to-day software development:

1. **git init:** Initializes a new Git repository in the current directory. Example:

```
git init
```

2. **git clone:** Creates a local copy of a remote Git repository. Example:

```
git clone <repository-url>
```

3. **git status:** Displays the current state of the working directory and staging area, including changes to be committed, changes not staged, and untracked files. Example:

```
git status
```

4. **git add:** Stages changes (add them to the staging area) before committing. Example:

```
git add <file-name>     # Add a specific file
git add                 # Add all changes in the current directory
```

5. **git commit:** Records changes made to the repository. Commits changes from the staging area into the repository history. Example:

```
git commit -m "Commit message"    # Commit with a message
```

6. **git log:** Shows the commit history, displaying a list of commits made to the repository. Example:

```
git log
```

7. **git diff:** Displays the differences between the working directory and the staging area or between commits. Example:

   git diff # Show differences in the working directory

   git diff <commit1> <commit2> # Show differences between two commits

8. **git branch:** Lists, creates, or deletes branches. Example:

   git branch # List all branches

   git branch <branch-name> # Create a new branch

   git branch -d <branch-name> # Delete a branch

9. **git checkout:** Switches branches or restores files from a specific commit. Example:

   git checkout <branch-name> # Switch to another branch

   git checkout <file-name> # Restore a specific file

10. **git merge:** Merges the changes from one branch into another (usually the current branch). Example:

    git merge <branch-name>

11. **git pull:** Fetches changes from a remote repository and automatically merges them into the local branch. Example:

    git pull <remote> <branch> # Pull from a specific remote and branch

12. **git push:** Sends committed changes to a remote repository. Example:

    git push <remote> <branch-name> # Push changes to a specific branch on remote

13. **git remote:** Manages remote repositories (add, remove, or view remotes). Example:

    git remote add <name> <url> # Add a new remote repository

    git remote -v # View the current remotes

14. **git reset:** Unstages files, or rewinds the commit history to a previous state. Example:

    git reset <file-name> # Unstage a file

git reset —hard <commit-id> # Reset the repository to a specific commit

15. **git fetch:** Retrieves changes from a remote repository without automatically merging them. Example:

    git fetch <remote> # Fetch changes from a remote repository

16. **git stash:** Temporarily saves changes that are not yet ready to be committed. Useful for when you need to switch branches without committing. Example:

    git stash # Save changes to the stash

    git stash pop # Apply the most recent stash

    git stash list # List all stashed changes

17. **git tag:** Creates a tag (a named reference to a specific commit), often used for marking release points. Example:

    git tag <tag-name> # Create a tag

    git tag -a <tag-name> -m "Message" # Annotated tag with a message

18. **git clean**: Removes untracked files and directories from the working directory. Example:

    git clean -fd # Remove untracked files and directories

These are some of the most common Git commands used for version control. They help developers manage the source code, collaborate with others, and keep track of changes efficiently.

GitHub: GitHub is a cloud-based platform that uses Git for version control, enabling developers to collaborate, manage code repositories, and track changes efficiently. Launched in 2008 and acquired by Microsoft in 2018, GitHub has become the world's largest host of source code, supporting millions of developers and projects globally. It offers powerful features like pull requests for code review, issues and discussions for project tracking, and GitHub Actions for automating workflows such as testing and deployment. GitHub also supports Markdown-based documentation, project boards, and security tools like Dependabot for managing vulnerabilities. Developers can host both public and private repositories, making GitHub ideal for open-source collaboration and enterprise development alike. It integrates seamlessly with tools like VS Code, Slack, and CI/CD platforms. GitHub also offers features like Pages for hosting static websites and Codespaces for cloud-based development environments. Its intuitive web interface, robust API, and large developer community make it an essential platform for modern software development, fostering collaboration, transparency, and code quality across teams of any size. Key Features of GitHub are as follows:

1. **Repositories**: GitHub repositories host your project files, including code, documentation, and configuration files. Each repository can be public (open to everyone) or private (accessible only to selected collaborators).

2. **Pull Requests (PRs)**: A pull request is a way to propose changes to a codebase. Developers can review, comment, and suggest improvements before merging changes. This promotes collaboration and ensures code quality.

3. **Issues and Discussions**: GitHub provides a built-in issue tracker for reporting bugs, suggesting features, or organizing tasks. Discussions allow broader team communication beyond just code problems.

4. **GitHub Actions**: This is GitHub's integrated CI/CD (Continuous Integration and Continuous **Deployment)** feature. It allows developers to automate workflows—like running tests, building code, or deploying software right from the repository.

5. **Project Boards**: GitHub includes kanban-style boards for managing tasks and tracking development progress, similar to tools like Trello or Jira.

6. **GitHub Pages**: Developers can host static websites (documentation, portfolios, blogs) directly from their repositories using GitHub Pages.

7. **Security and Code Scanning**: GitHub provides tools like Dependabot to alert developers of vulnerabilities in dependencies. Code scanning can automatically check for security issues in pull requests.

8. **Codespaces**: GitHub Codespaces is a cloud-based development environment that allows you to write, run, and debug code directly in your browser or in Visual Studio Code, without setting up a local machine.

Why Developers Use GitHub: Developers use GitHub for efficient collaboration, version control, and project management. It supports code reviews, automates workflows with GitHub Actions, and integrates with popular tools. GitHub enhances open-source contribution, offers cloud access, and ensures security with features like Dependabot, making it a powerful platform for modern software development.

1. **Collaboration:** GitHub makes it easy for multiple developers to work on the same project simultaneously. Features like pull requests, code review, and inline commenting streamline teamwork and feedback.

2. **Version Control:** Built on Git, GitHub tracks every change made to a project. Developers can roll back to earlier versions, compare changes, and manage code history effectively.

3. **Open-source Contribution:** GitHub hosts millions of open-source repositories. Developers can contribute to global projects, learn from others' code, and build portfolios that demonstrate real-world contributions.

4. **Project Management Tools:** With issues, labels, milestones, and project boards, GitHub helps developers plan and track work efficiently, similar to tools like Trello or Jira.

5. **Automation and CI/CD:** GitHub Actions lets developers automate testing, deployment, and other workflows directly from their codebase, improving productivity and consistency.

6. **Documentation Support:** GitHub supports Markdown for creating clear and attractive README files, , and documentation that's easy to maintain alongside the code.

7. **Security and Dependency Management:** Features like Dependabot alerts and code scanning help identify and fix vulnerabilities automatically, improving code safety.

8. **Cloud-Based and Accessible:** Being cloud-hosted, GitHub allows developers to access and manage their code from anywhere, on any device.

9. **Integration:** GitHub integrates seamlessly with tools like VS Code, Slack, Jira, Docker, and Azure, supporting a complete development pipeline.

10. **Community and Visibility:** GitHub has a vast, active community. Developers use it to share projects, gain followers, and build reputations that can lead to job opportunities or collaborations.

GitLab: GitLab is a powerful, all-in-one DevOps platform that allows teams to collaboratively plan, build, test, deploy, and monitor software within a single application. It integrates every stage of the software development lifecycle (SDLC), providing tools for version control, CI/CD (Continuous Integration and Continuous Deployment), project management, security testing, and performance monitoring. Originally launched as an open-source Git repository manager, GitLab has evolved into a comprehensive DevOps solution that supports everything from code hosting and collaboration to automated delivery and infrastructure as code.

One of GitLab's core strengths lies in its ability to streamline workflows by eliminating the need for multiple tools. Traditionally, software development teams would use separate applications for source code management, CI/CD, issue tracking, security testing, and deployment. With GitLab, all of these tools are integrated into a single platform, reducing complexity, improving visibility, and enabling faster delivery cycles. This is especially valuable in today's fast-paced development environments where agility and speed are critical.

GitLab supports Git for version control and includes features like merge requests, code review, and branching strategies that enhance collaboration among developers. Its CI/CD pipelines allow for the automation of building, testing, and deploying code, which minimizes human error and accelerates time-to-market. Developers can define pipelines using a .gitlab-ci.yml file, customizing stages and jobs according to their project's needs. GitLab also includes built-in Docker container support, Kubernetes integration, and tools for infrastructure management using IaC (Infrastructure as Code) principles.

Security is a key focus of GitLab, with features designed to "shift left" and integrate security earlier in the development process. It offers built-in security testing capabilities such as Static Application Security Testing (SAST), Dynamic Application Security Testing (DAST), container scanning, license compliance, and dependency scanning. These tools help developers identify and fix vulnerabilities before code reaches production, significantly reducing security risks.

In addition to development and security, GitLab offers robust project and product management tools. Teams can manage work through issues, epics, milestones, and kanban-style boards. Agile methodologies are well supported with burndown charts, velocity tracking, and customizable workflows that fit various team structures. GitLab's flexibility allows organizations to adapt the platform to their unique development styles and operational requirements.

GitLab is available in both self-managed and cloud-hosted versions, giving teams the freedom to deploy the platform in the environment that best suits their needs. Its open-core model means the core functionality is free and open-source, while advanced features are available through premium and ultimate paid tiers. GitLab's strong community, active development, and transparent roadmap contribute to its popularity and rapid innovation.

Overall, GitLab is more than just a Git repository it's a full DevOps lifecycle platform that helps organizations build better software, faster and more securely. By centralizing tools and processes, promoting collaboration, and automating routine tasks, GitLab empowers teams to focus on what matters most: delivering high-quality applications to users.

The key features of GitLab are as follows:

1. **Git Repository Management**: Host and manage code using Git with support for branching, merging, and version history.
2. **Merge Requests (MRs)**: Collaborate with team members through code reviews, approvals, and threaded discussions.
3. **Web IDE**: Edit code directly from the browser without switching to a local editor.
4. **CI/CD Pipelines**: Automate building, testing, and deploying applications with powerful and customizable pipelines.
5. **Auto DevOps**: Automatically configure CI/CD pipelines with best practices.
6. **Issue Tracking**: Manage tasks, bugs, and features with built-in issue tracking.
7. **Project Management**: Use boards, epics, milestones, and roadmaps to plan and track work.
8. **Security Testing**: Built-in SAST, DAST, container scanning, and secret detection for secure development.
9. **License Compliance**: Detect and manage open-source licenses in your dependencies.
10. **Environment Management**: Manage multiple deployment environments (e.g., dev, staging, production).
11. **Review Apps**: Preview changes in a live environment before merging.
12. **Feature Flags**: Gradually roll out features and control their visibility.
13. **Monitoring & Analytics**: Access performance metrics, pipeline analytics, and value stream tracking.
14. **Wiki & Documentation**: Maintain internal or public-facing documentation within projects.
15. **Integration & APIs**: Integrate with popular tools like Slack, Jira, and Jenkins, and use REST or GraphQL APIs.

16. **Custom Runners**: Run CI/CD jobs on your own infrastructure.

17. **Access Control**: Define user roles and permissions for better security.

18. **Single Sign-On (SSO)**: Authenticate users via OAuth, SAML, or LDAP.

19. **Audit Logs**: Track activity and ensure compliance with audit-ready logs.

Bitbucket: Bitbucket is a web-based Git repository management tool developed by Atlassian, designed to support collaborative software development. It allows teams to host, manage, and version control their code repositories using Git or Mercurial (although Mercurial support was phased out in 2020). Bitbucket is integrated tightly with other Atlassian products like Jira, Trello, and Confluence, offering seamless workflow integration for development teams. The platform provides tools for branch management, code reviews through pull requests, and issue tracking, helping teams collaborate more effectively. Bitbucket also includes built-in CI/CD capabilities with Bitbucket Pipelines, enabling automated testing and deployment of code directly from the repository.

In addition to core Git functionality, Bitbucket emphasizes security, offering features like branch permissions, IP whitelisting, and two-step verification. It supports both public and private repositories, allowing organizations to control access to their code. Bitbucket integrates with third-party tools and services, including Slack and Bamboo, further enhancing team collaboration. With its scalability, Bitbucket caters to both small teams and large enterprises, making it a versatile tool for managing complex projects. Through its cloud-based offering and on-premise solution (Bitbucket Server), Bitbucket ensures flexibility and high availability for teams around the world, helping them stay productive and secure. The features of Bitbucket in a concise, pointwise format:

1. **Git & Mercurial Repository Hosting**: Supports Git and previously supported Mercurial for version control.

2. **Public & Private Repositories**: Host both public and private repositories with customizable access settings.

3. **Branch Permissions**: Set permissions on specific branches to control who can push or merge changes.

4. **Pull Requests**: Enable code collaboration with pull requests, inline comments, and code reviews.

5. **Bitbucket Pipelines (CI/CD)**: Integrated Continuous Integration/Continuous Deployment to automate testing, builds, and deployments directly from repositories.

6. **Gitflow Workflow Support**: Easy branching strategies for managing features, releases, and hotfixes.
7. **Seamless Integration with Atlassian Products**: Integrates with Jira, Trello, and Confluence for better project management and tracking.
8. **IP Whitelisting**: Restrict repository access to specific IP addresses for added security.
9. **Two-Factor Authentication (2FA)**: Adds an extra layer of security to accounts and repositories.
10. **Code Search & History**: Search code across repositories and access detailed commit history.
11. **Notifications**: Integrates with Slack and other tools for real-time notifications and updates.
12. **Access Control**: Role-based access management to control user permissions on repositories a Git Repository Hosting & CI/CD nd projects.
13. **API Access**: Robust REST API for custom integrations and automation.
14. **On-Premise (Bitbucket Server)**: Available as both cloud-based (Bitbucket Cloud) and on-premise (Bitbucket Server) solutions.
15. **Scalability**: Suitable for small teams to large enterprises with scalable repository and user management.
16. **Custom Workflows**: Customizable workflow integrations and extensions for enhanced team productivity.

Differences Between Git, GitHub, GitLab, Bitbucket: The differences between Git, GitHub, GitLab, Bitbucket is listed in table 3.3.

Table 3.3

S.No.	Features	Git	GitHub	GitLab	Bitbucket
1	Type	Version Control System	Cloud-based Git Repository Hosting	Complete DevOps Platform	Git Repository Hosting & CI/CD
2	Primary Function	Track changes in source code	Host Git repositories, collaboration	End-to-end DevOps lifecycle (CI/CD, Issue Tracking, etc.)	Git repository hosting, CI/CD, Collaboration
3	Repository Support	Local Git repositories	Git repositories	Git repositories	Git and Mercurial repositories
4	Collaboration	Command-line based (locally)	Pull Requests, Issues, Discussions	Merge Requests, Issues, Boards	Pull Requests, Issues, Comments
5	CI/CD	No built-in CI/CD	GitHub Actions for CI/CD	Integrated CI/CD (GitLab Pipelines)	Bitbucket Pipelines for CI/CD
6	Project Management	No built-in project management	Issues, Projects, Wikis	Issue Tracking, Milestones, Boards	Issue Tracking, Boards, Pipelines
7	Security	Depends on configuration	Two-factor Authentication, Security Policies	Built-in security tools (SAST, DAST, etc.)	Two-factor Authentication, IP whitelisting
8	Integration with Tools	None (works with many third-party tools)	Integrates with many third-party apps	Integrates with various tools, Jira, Kubernetes	Integrates with Slack, Jira, Bamboo
9	Repository Visibility	Local repositories	Public and private repositories	Public and private repositories	Public and private repositories
10	Pricing	Free (open-source)	Free for public, Paid for private	Free (open-source), Paid plans available	Free for small teams, Paid plans available
11	Hosting	Self-hosted (local or cloud)	Cloud-based (GitHub.com)	Self-hosted (GitLab Server), Cloud-based (GitLab.com)	Cloud-based (Bitbucket.org), Self-hosted (Bitbucket Server)
12	Interface	Command-line tool	Web interface, CLI, Desktop apps	Web interface, CLI, API	Web interface, CLI, Desktop apps
13	Ownership	Open-source, independent	Owned by Microsoft	Independent, open-core model	Owned by Atlassian

Writing Clean Code

Writing clean code is an essential skill for any Python developer. Clean code is not just code that works; it's code that is easy to read, understand, maintain, and extend. Python, known for its simplicity and readability, encourages clean coding practices, but it still requires thoughtful design and discipline from the developer. Some key principles and best practices for writing clean Python code are as:

1. **Follow PEP 8 – Python's Style Guide:** PEP 8 is the official style guide for Python. It outlines conventions for indentation, line length, spacing, naming, and more. Adhering to PEP 8 helps ensure consistency and readability. For example, use 4 spaces per indentation level, limit lines to 79 characters, and add blank lines between functions and classes. Tools like black, flake8, and pylint can automate style checks and formatting.

2. **Use Meaningful Names:** Variable and function names should clearly describe their purpose. Avoid single-letter names except for counters or iterators in loops. A function like def calculate_total_price(cart): is far more informative than def calc(tp):. Good naming makes code self-documenting and reduces the need for excessive comments.

3. **Keep Functions Small and Focused:** A clean function should do one thing and do it well. If a function is trying to load data, filter it, and send an email all in one go, it becomes hard to understand and test. Instead, break complex tasks into smaller, well-named functions. This also encourages code reuse and makes unit testing easier.

4. **Avoid Code Duplication:** Repeating the same logic in multiple places makes code harder to maintain. Follow the DRY (Don't Repeat Yourself) principle by creating reusable functions or classes. If a piece of logic is used more than once, extract it into a function.

5. **Use List Comprehensions Wisely:** List comprehensions are a Pythonic way to write cleaner and more concise loops. For example, [x**2 for x in range(10)] is more readable than using a for loop with .append(). However, avoid overly complex or nested comprehensions, as they can hurt readability.

6. **Write Docstrings and Comments:** Well-written docstrings explain what a function or class does, its parameters, and its return value. Inline comments should explain why something is done, not what is done that should already be clear from the code itself.

7. **Use Pythonic Idioms:** Python offers expressive features like unpacking, context managers (with), and built-in functions (enumerate, zip, any, all). These help you write code that is both concise and expressive.

8. **Organize Code with Modules and Packages:** Structure your project logically. Keep related code together and separate concerns across modules and packages. For example, separate business logic, database access, and utility functions into different files.

9. **Refactor and Test Regularly:** Clean code evolves through iteration. Regularly refactor code as you better understand the problem. Pair this with automated tests using unittest or pytest to ensure changes don't break existing functionality.

******

8

Software Testing and Quality Assurance

Software Testing and Quality Assurance (QA) are critical components of the software development lifecycle (SDLC). They ensure that the software meets specified requirements, functions correctly, and delivers a reliable, user-friendly experience. Although often used interchangeably, testing and QA have distinct purposes testing is primarily about identifying bugs, while quality assurance focuses on preventing defects and improving the development process.

Software Testing: Software testing is the process of evaluating and verifying that a software application or system functions as intended, ensuring that it meets the specified requirements, performs reliably, and remains free from defects. This process involves executing the software to identify bugs or errors and determining whether it behaves as expected under different conditions. Testing can be done at various stages of software development, ranging from unit testing (testing individual components) to system testing (evaluating the entire system) and user acceptance testing (ensuring it meets user needs). Different testing methods, such as manual and automated testing, are employed to check aspects like functionality, performance, security, and usability. By simulating various user interactions and environmental factors, testers aim to uncover potential vulnerabilities, edge cases, and areas for improvement. The ultimate goal is to deliver a high-quality product that meets the user's needs while minimizing the risk of failure or malfunction. Software testing is crucial for reducing maintenance costs, improving user satisfaction, and increasing the reliability of software, making it an essential part of the software development life cycle.

Type of Software testing: We have various types of testing available in the market, which are used to test the application or the software.

With the help of fig.3.2, we can easily understand the type of software testing.

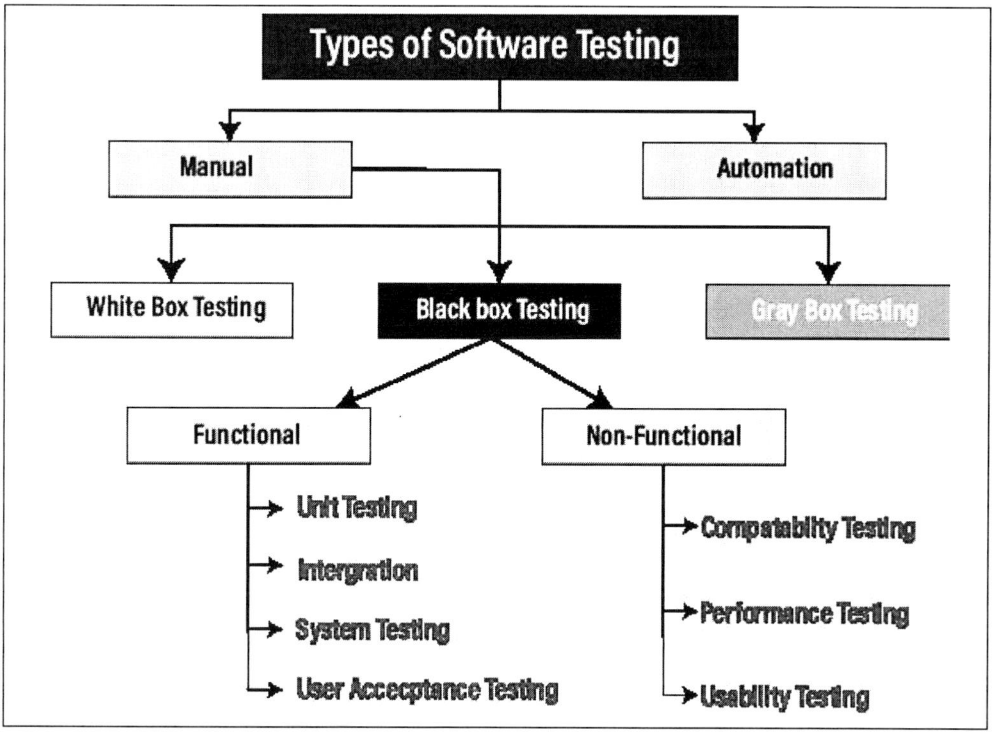

Fig.3.2

Testing can either be done manually or using an automated testing tool:

1. **Manual Testing:** The process of checking the functionality of an application as per the customer needs without taking any help of automation tools is known as manual testing. While performing the manual testing on any application, we do not need any specific knowledge of any testing tool, rather than have a proper understanding of the product so we can easily prepare the test document. Manual testing can be further divided into three types of testing, which are as follows:

   - White box testing
   - Black box testing

- Gray box testing

2. **Automation Testing:** Automation testing is a process of converting any manual test cases into the test scripts with the help of automation tools, or any programming language is known as automation testing. With the help of automation testing, we can enhance the speed of our test execution because here, we do not require any human efforts. We need to write a test script and execute those scripts.

Benefits of Software Testing: The benefits of software testing are as follows:

1. **Reduced Development Costs:** Identifying bugs early in the development process is less expensive to fix than later on.

2. **Improved Software Quality:** Thorough testing ensures the software meets the expected standards and requirements.

3. **Increased User Satisfaction:** A well-tested product is more likely to be reliable, user-friendly, and meet user needs.

4. **Enhanced Project Success:** Effective testing minimizes risks related to software quality, security, and performance, contributing to project success.

Unit Testing, Integration Testing, System Testing

Unit testing, integration testing, and system testing are key levels of software testing that ensure application reliability. Unit testing focuses on testing individual components or functions in isolation to confirm they work as intended. It's typically done by developers and helps catch bugs early in development. Integration testing comes next, verifying that multiple components or systems interact correctly when combined. This level checks data flow and communication between modules, ensuring that integrated parts work together as expected. Finally, system testing evaluates the complete and fully integrated application in its entirety. It tests the system against the defined requirements to ensure it meets functional and performance expectations. System testing is often performed by QA teams and includes various test types such as usability, security, and performance testing. Together, these testing levels help build robust software by detecting issues at every stage, from individual units to full system behavior, before release.

Unit Testing: Unit Testing is a software testing technique in which individual units or components of a software application are tested in isolation. These units are the smallest pieces of code, typically functions or methods, ensuring they perform as expected. Unit testing helps identify bugs early in the development cycle, enhance code quality, and reduce the cost of fixing issues later. It is an essential part of Test-Driven Development (TDD), promoting reliable code.

Unit testing is the process of testing the smallest parts of your code, like it is a method in which we verify the code's correctness by running one by one. It's a key part of software development that improves code quality by testing each unit in isolation.

You write unit tests for these code units and run them automatically every time you make changes. If a test fails, it helps you quickly find and fix the issue. Unit testing promotes modular code, ensures better test coverage, and saves time by allowing developers to focus more on coding than manual testing.

Unit Test: A unit test is a small piece of code that checks if a specific function or method in is an application works correctly. It will work as the function inputs and verifying the outputs. These tests check that the code work as expected based on the logic the developer intended.

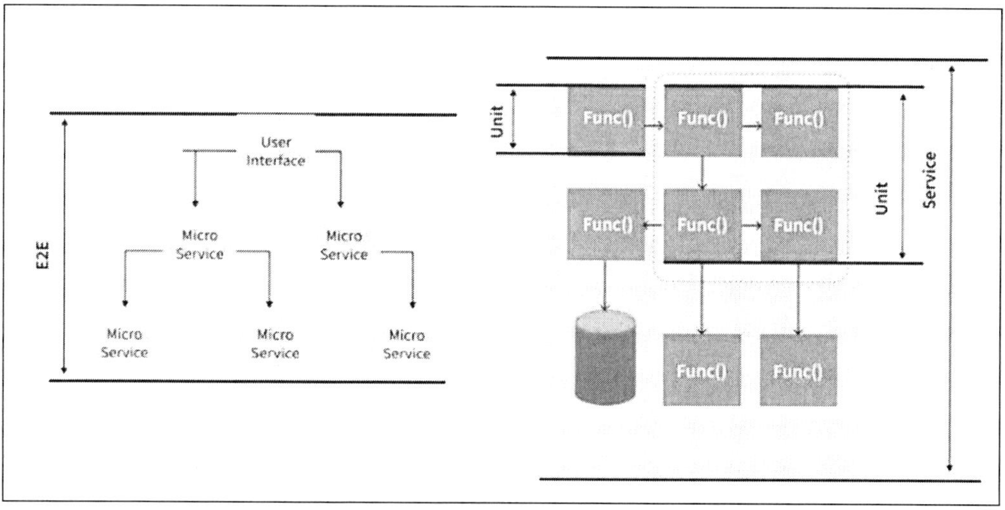

Fig.3.3

In these multiple tests are written for a single function to cover different possible scenarios and these are called test cases. While it is ideal to cover all expected behaviors, it is not always necessary to test every scenario.

Unit tests should run one by one, it means that they do not depend on other system parts like databases or networks. Instead, data stubs can be used to simulate these dependencies. Writing unit tests is easiest for simple, self-contained code blocks There are two types of Unit testing methods:

1. **Manual Unit Testing:** Manual Testing is like checking each part of a project by hand, without using any special tools. People, like developers, do each step of the testing themselves. But manual unit testing isn't used much because there are better ways to do it and it has some problems:

    - It costs more because workers have to be paid for the time they spend testing, especially if they're not permanent staff.
    - It takes a lot of time because tests have to be done every time the code changes.
    - It is hard to find and fix problems because it is tricky to test each part separately.
    - Developers often do manual testing themselves to see if their code works correctly.

2. **Automated Unit Testing:** Automation Unit Testing is a way of checking if software works correctly without needing lots of human effort. We use special tools made by people to run these tests automatically. These are part of the process of building the software. Here's how it works:

    - Developers write a small piece of code to test a function in the software. This code is like a little experiment to see if everything works as it should.
    - Before the software is finished and sent out to users, these test codes are taken out. They're only there to make sure everything is working properly during development.
    - Automated testing can help us check each part of the software on its own. This helps us find out if one part depends too much on another. It's like putting each piece of a puzzle under a magnifying glass to see if they fit together just right.
    - We usually use special tools or frameworks to do this testing automatically. These tools can tell us if any of our code doesn't pass the tests we set up.
    - The tests we write should be really small and focus on one specific thing at a time. They should also run on the computer's memory and not need internet connection.

    So, automated unit testing is like having a helper that checks our work as we build software, making sure everything is in its right place and works as expected.

Example: The example of the java with unit test cases with the proper unit test code:

```
public class Calculator {

   // Method to add two numbers
   public int add(int a, int b) {
       return a + b;
   }

   // Method to subtract two numbers
   public int subtract(int a, int b) {
       return a - b;
   }
}
```

Create the TestNG Test Class

```
package com.example.tests;

import org.testng.Assert;
import org.testng.annotations.BeforeMethod;
import org.testng.annotations.Test;

public class CalculatorTest {

   private Calculator calculator;

   // This method runs before each test method
   @BeforeMethod
   public void setUp() {
       calculator = new Calculator();
   }
```

```
    // Test for the 'add' method
    @Test
    public void testAdd() {
        int result = calculator.add(5, 3);
        // Assert that the result of 5 + 3 is 8
        Assert.assertEquals(result, 8, "Addition result is incorrect");
    }

    // Test for the 'subtract' method
    @Test
    public void testSubtract() {
        int result = calculator.subtract(5, 3);
        // Assert that the result of 5 - 3 is 2
        Assert.assertEquals(result, 2, "Subtraction result is incorrect");
    }
}
```

Output:

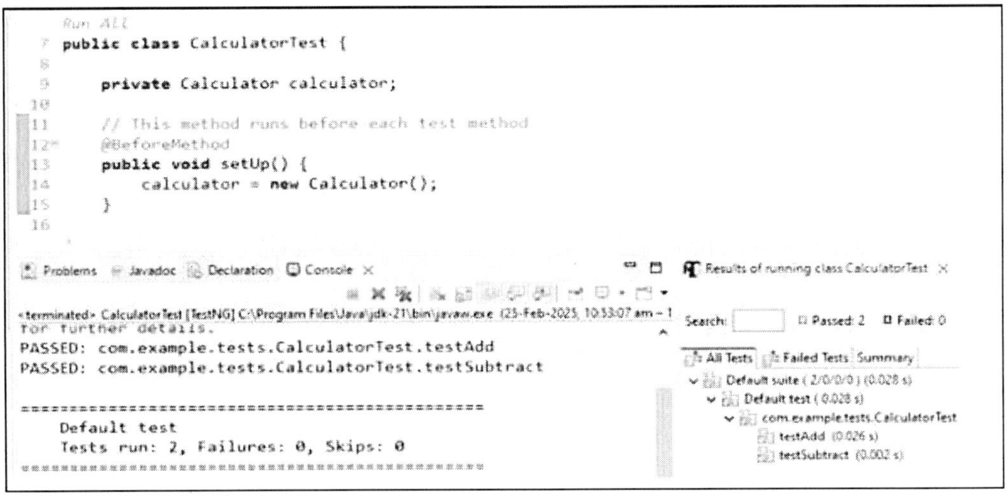

Unit Testing Techniques: There are 3 types of Unit Testing Techniques. They are follows:

1. **Black Box Testing:** This testing technique is used in covering the unit tests for input, user interface, and output parts.
2. **White Box Testing:** This technique is used in testing the functional behavior of the system by giving the input and checking the functionality output including the internal design structure and code of the modules.
3. **Gray Box Testing:** This technique is used in executing the relevant test cases, test methods, and test functions, and analyzing the code performance for the modules.

Benefits of unit Testing: The Unit testing benefits which used in the software development with many ways:

1. **Early Detection of Issues:** Unit testing allows developers to detect and fix issues early in the development process before they become larger and more difficult to fix.
2. **Improved Code Quality:** Unit testing helps to ensure that each unit of code works as intended and meets the requirements, improving the overall quality of the software.
3. **Increased Confidence:** Unit testing provides developers with confidence in their code, as they can validate that each unit of the software is functioning as expected.
4. **Faster Development:** Unit testing enables developers to work faster and more efficiently, as they can validate changes to the code without having to wait for the full system to be tested.
5. **Better Documentation:** Unit testing provides clear and concise documentation of the code and its behavior, making it easier for other developers to understand and maintain the software.
6. **Facilitation of Refactoring:** Unit testing enables developers to safely make changes to the code, as they can validate that their changes do not break existing functionality.
7. **Reduced Time and Cost:** Unit testing can reduce the time and cost required for later testing, as it helps to identify and fix issues early in the development process.

Disadvantages of Unit Testing: The disadvantages of unit testing are as follows:

1. **Time and Effort:** Unit testing requires a significant investment of time and effort to create and maintain the test cases, especially for complex systems.

2. **Dependence on Developers:** The success of unit testing depends on the developers, who must write clear, concise, and comprehensive test cases to validate the code.

3. **Difficulty in Testing Complex Units:** Unit testing can be challenging when dealing with complex units, as it can be difficult to isolate and test individual units in isolation from the rest of the system.

4. **Difficulty in Testing Interactions:** Unit testing may not be sufficient for testing interactions between units, as it only focuses on individual units.

5. **Difficulty in Testing User Interfaces:** Unit testing may not be suitable for testing user interfaces, as it typically focuses on the functionality of individual units.

6. **Over-reliance on Automation:** Over-reliance on automated unit tests can lead to a false sense of security, as automated tests may not uncover all possible issues or bugs.

7. **Maintenance Overhead:** Unit testing requires ongoing maintenance and updates, as the code and test cases must be kept up-to-date with changes to the software.

Integration Testing: Integration testing is the process of testing the interface between two software units or modules. It focuses on determining the correctness of the interface. The purpose of integration testing is to expose faults in the interaction between integrated units. Once all the modules have been unit-tested, integration testing is performed.

Integration testing is a software testing technique that focuses on verifying the interactions and data exchange between different components or modules of a software application. The goal of integration testing is to identify any problems or bugs that arise when different components are combined and interact with each other. Integration testing is typically performed after unit testing and before system testing. It helps to identify and resolve integration issues early in the development cycle, reducing the risk of more severe and costly problems later on. Integration testing is one of the basic types of software testing and there are many other basic and advance software testing

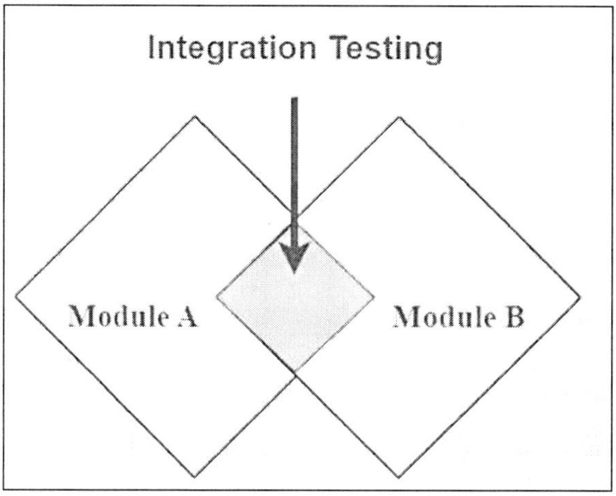

Fig.3.4

1. Integration testing can be done by picking module by module. This can be done so that there should be a proper sequence to be followed.

2. And also, if you don't want to miss out on any integration scenarios then you have to follow the proper sequence.

3. Exposing the defects is the major focus of the integration testing and the time of interaction between the integrated units.

Why is Integration Testing Important?

Integration testing is important because it verifies that individual software modules or components work together correctly as a whole system. This ensures that the integrated software functions as intended and helps identify any compatibility or communication issues between different parts of the system. By detecting and resolving integration problems early, integration testing contributes to the overall reliability, performance, and quality of the software product.

Integration Test Approaches: There are four types of integration testing approaches. Those approaches are the following:

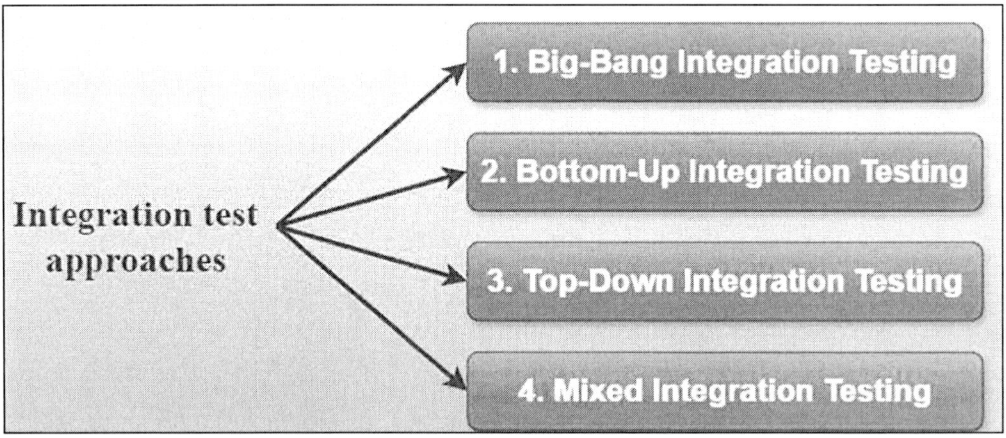

Fig.3.5

1. **Big-Bang Integration Testing:** It is the simplest integration testing approach, where all the modules are combined and the functionality is verified after the completion of individual module testing. In simple words, all the modules of the system are simply put together and tested. This approach is practicable only for very small systems. If an error is found during the integration testing, it is very difficult to localize the error as the error may potentially belong to any of the modules being integrated. So, debugging errors reported during Big Bang integration testing is very expensive to fix. Big-bang integration testing is a software testing approach in which all components or modules of a software application are combined and tested at once. This approach is typically used when the software components have a low degree of interdependence or when there are constraints in the development environment that prevent testing individual components. The goal of big-bang integration testing is to verify the overall functionality of the system and to identify any integration problems that arise when the components are combined. While big-bang integration testing can be useful in some situations, it can also be a high-risk approach, as the complexity of the system and the number of interactions between components can make it difficult to identify and diagnose problems.

2. **Bottom-Up Integration Testing:** In bottom-up testing, each module at lower levels is tested with higher modules until all modules are tested. The primary purpose of this integration testing is that each subsystem tests the interfaces among various modules making up the subsystem. This integration testing uses test drivers to drive and pass appropriate data to the lower-level modules.

3. **Top-Down Integration Testing:** Top-down integration testing technique is used in order to simulate the behaviour of the lower-level modules that are not yet integrated. In this integration testing, testing takes place from top to bottom. First, high-level modules are tested and then low-level modules and finally integrating the low-level modules to a high level to ensure the system is working as intended.

4. **Mixed Integration Testing:** A mixed integration testing is also called sandwiched integration testing. A mixed integration testing follows a combination of top down and bottom-up testing approaches. In top-down approach, testing can start only after the top-level module have been coded and unit tested. In bottom-up approach, testing can start only after the bottom level modules are ready. This sandwich or mixed approach overcomes this shortcoming of the top-down and bottom-up approaches. It is also called the hybrid integration testing. also, stubs and drivers are used in mixed integration testing.

Applications of Integration Testing

1. **Identify the components:** Identify the individual components of your application that need to be integrated. This could include the frontend, backend, database, and any third-party services.

2. **Create a test plan:** Develop a test plan that outlines the scenarios and test cases that need to be executed to validate the integration points between the different components. This could include testing data flow, communication protocols, and error handling.

3. **Set up test environment:** Set up a test environment that mirrors the production environment as closely as possible. This will help ensure that the results of your integration tests are accurate and reliable.

4. **Execute the tests:** Execute the tests outlined in your test plan, starting with the most critical and complex scenarios. Be sure to log any defects or issues that you encounter during testing.

5. **Analyze the results:** Analyze the results of your integration tests to identify any defects or issues that need to be addressed. This may involve working with developers to fix bugs or make changes to the application architecture.

6. **Repeat testing:** Once defects have been fixed, repeat the integration testing process to ensure that the changes have been successful and that the application still works as expected.

System Testing: System Testing is a type of software testing that is performed on a completely integrated system to evaluate the compliance of the system with the corresponding requirements. In system testing, integration testing passed components are taken as input.

1. The goal of integration testing is to detect any irregularity between the units that are integrated. System testing detects defects within both the integrated units and the whole system. The result of system testing is the observed behavior of a component or a system when it is tested.

2. System Testing is carried out on the whole system in the context of either system requirement specifications or functional requirement specifications or the context of both. System testing tests the design and behavior of the system and also the expectations of the customer.

3. It is performed to test the system beyond the bounds mentioned in the software requirements specification (SRS). System Testing is performed by a testing team that is independent of the development team and helps to test the quality of the system impartial.

4. It has both functional and non-functional testing. System Testing is a black-box testing. System Testing is performed after the integration testing and before the acceptance testing.

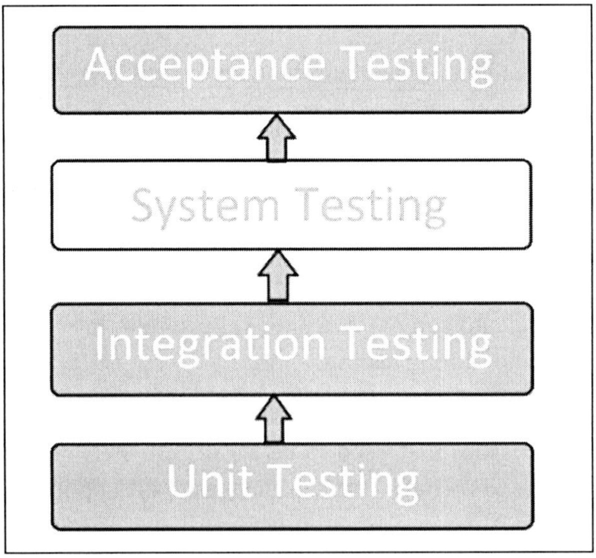

Fig.3.6

System Testing Process: The process of system testing is shown in fig.3.6. System testing is performed in the following steps:

1. **Setup Test Environment:** Create testing environment for the better-quality testing.
2. **Generate Test Case:** Generate test case for the testing process.
3. **Generate Test Data:** Generate the data that is to be tested.

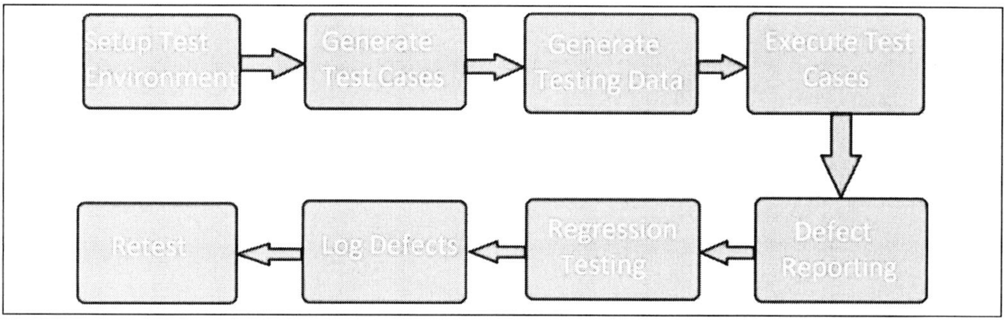

Fig.3.7

4. **Execute Test Case:** After the generation of the test case and the test data, test cases are executed.
5. **Defect Reporting:** Defects in the system are detected.
6. **Regression Testing:** It is carried out to test the side effects of the testing process.
7. **Log Defects:** Defects are fixed in this step.
8. **Retest:** If the test is not successful then again test is performed.

Advantages of System Testing

1. In System Testing The testers do not require more knowledge of programming to carry out this testing.
2. It will test the entire product or software so that we will easily detect the errors or defects which cannot be identified during the unit testing and integration testing.
3. The testing environment is similar to that of the real time production or business environment.

4. It checks the entire functionality of the system with different test scripts and also it covers the technical and business requirements of clients.
5. After this testing, the product will almost cover all the possible bugs or errors and hence the development team will confidently go ahead with acceptance testing
6. Verifies the overall functionality of the system.
7. Detects and identifies system-level problems early in the development cycle.
8. Helps to validate the requirements and ensure the system meets the user needs.
9. Improves system reliability and quality.
10. Facilitates collaboration and communication between development and testing teams.
11. Enhances the overall performance of the system.
12. Increases user confidence and reduces risks.
13. Facilitates early detection and resolution of bugs and defects.
14. Supports the identification of system-level dependencies and inter-module interactions.
15. Improves the system's maintainability and scalability.

Disadvantages of System Testing

1. System Testing is time consuming process than another testing techniques since it checks the entire product or software.
2. The cost for the testing will be high since it covers the testing of entire software.
3. It needs good debugging tool otherwise the hidden errors will not be found.
4. Can be time-consuming and expensive.
5. Requires adequate resources and infrastructure.
6. Can be complex and challenging, especially for large and complex systems.
7. Dependent on the quality of requirements and design documents.
8. Limited visibility into the internal workings of the system.

9. Can be impacted by external factors like hardware and network configurations.
10. Requires proper planning, coordination, and execution.
11. Can be impacted by changes made during development.
12. Requires specialized skills and expertise.
13. May require multiple test cycles to achieve desired results.

Best Practices for System Testing: To make system testing effective, follow these best practices:

1. **Clear Test Plan and Requirements:** Make sure you have a well-defined test plan and clear requirements. This ensures all parts of the system are covered and tested correctly.
2. **Test Early and Often:** Start testing as soon as possible in the development process and continue testing regularly. Finding and fixing issues early helps save time and money.
3. **Use Automation for Repetitive Tests:** Automate tests that you run repeatedly, like regression or performance tests. This saves time and allows you to focus on more complex testing.
4. **Create Realistic Test Scenarios:** Design test cases based on how users will actually use the system. This includes testing for edge cases, unusual inputs, and potential system failures.
5. **Collaborate with Developers:** Work closely with developers throughout the testing process. They can help identify problems faster and provide insights into how the system functions.

Differences Between Unit Testing, Integration Testing, System Testing: The differences between Unit Testing, Integration Testing, System Testing are listed in table 3.4.

Table 3.4

S.No.	Aspect	Unit Testing	Integration Testing	System Testing
1	Definition	Tests individual units or components in isolation.	Tests interactions between integrated units/modules.	Tests the entire system as a whole against requirements.
2	Scope	Narrow scope (one function, method, or class).	Moderate scope (interaction between multiple components).	Broad scope (entire system with all integrated parts).
3	Performed By	Developers.	Developers/QA.	QA (Quality Assurance) team.
4	Focus	Validates correctness of individual units.	Ensures correct interaction and data flow between components.	Validates the system's compliance with requirements.
5	Execution Time	Fast (as it tests small code units).	Moderate (due to interaction complexity).	Slow (involves testing the whole system).
6	Nature of Tests	Functional (focuses on logic of a single unit).	Functional and behavioral (focuses on communication between units).	Functional, non-functional (performance, security, etc.).
7	Test Environment	Isolated (mock objects/stubs may be used).	Partially integrated (real components, but not full system).	Real or near-real environment with full system integration.
8	Purpose	Detect bugs in specific code units early.	Ensure components interact correctly in real scenarios.	Ensure the system meets business and technical requirements.

Test-Driven Development (TDD)

Test Driven Development (TDD) is a software development methodology that emphasizes writing tests before writing the actual code. It ensures that code is always tested and functional, reducing bugs and improving code quality. In TDD, developers write small, focused tests that define the desired functionality, then write the minimum code necessary to pass these tests, and finally, refactor the code to improve structure and performance. This cyclic process helps in creating reliable, maintainable, and efficient software. By following TDD, teams can enhance code reliability, accelerate development cycles, and maintain high standards of software quality

Test-driven development (TDD) is a method of coding in which you first write a test and it fails, then write the code to pass the test of development, and clean up the code. This process recycled for one new feature or change. In other methods in which you write either all the code or all the tests first, TDD will combine and write tests and code together into one.

Test-Driven Development (TDD) is a method in software development where the focus is on writing tests before writing the actual code for a feature. This approach uses short development cycles that repeat to ensure quality and correctness.

Process of Test-Driven Development (TDD): It is the process in which test cases are written before the code that validates those cases. It depends on the repetition of a concise development cycle. Test-driven Development is a technique in which automated Unit tests are used to drive the design and free decoupling of dependencies.

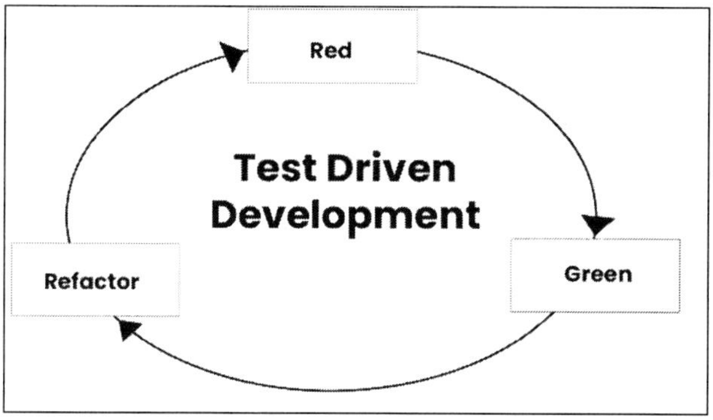

Fig.3.8

The following sequence of steps is generally followed:

1. Run all the test cases and make sure that the new test case fails.
2. **Red:** Create a test case and make it fail, Run the test cases
3. **Green:** Make the test case pass by any means.
4. **Refactor:** Change the code to remove duplicate/redundancy. Refactor code is done to remove duplication of code.
5. Repeat the above-mentioned steps again and again

Write a complete test case describing the function. To make the test cases the developer must understand the features and requirements using user stories and use cases.

Advantages of Test-Driven Development (TDD):

1. **Improved Code Quality:** Since tests are written before code, developers are forced to think about the design and behavior of the code upfront, leading to cleaner and more maintainable code.

2. **Early Bug Detection:** Bugs are identified immediately after each small increment of code is written, allowing for early detection and reducing the cost of fixing issues later in the development cycle.

3. **Refactoring with Confidence:** TDD encourages continuous refactoring, as developers can rely on the suite of tests to ensure that no functionality is broken during changes or improvements.

4. **Better Documentation:** The tests themselves act as a form of documentation, explaining the expected behavior of code. This makes it easier for new developers to understand the system.

5. **Reduced Debugging Time:** Since tests are run frequently and issues are caught immediately, the time spent debugging is minimized, leading to quicker development cycles.

6. **Improved Design:** TDD leads to modular, well-structured code because developers typically write small units of code with clear interfaces to pass tests, promoting better design practices.

7. **Support for Continuous Integration:** With a robust test suite, it's easier to integrate code continuously into the main codebase, ensuring that new changes do not break existing functionality.

Disadvantages of Test-Driven Development (TDD):

1. **Initial Learning Curve:** Developers unfamiliar with TDD may face a learning curve, especially in writing meaningful tests before implementing functionality.

2. **Slower Initial Development:** Writing tests before code may slow down the initial development process because it requires additional time for writing tests and considering design upfront.

3. **Overhead in Test Maintenance:** As the codebase grows, maintaining the test suite can become cumbersome. Tests must be updated with every change to ensure they remain accurate and relevant.

4. **Limited Testing Scope:** TDD mainly focuses on unit tests, which may not be sufficient for testing the entire system, such as integration or end-to-end scenarios. Additional testing levels are still needed.

5. **Risk of Overfitting:** If developers focus too much on passing tests, they might design code to fit the test cases rather than fulfilling the broader functional requirements, leading to a less flexible solution.

6. **Test-Driven Design Can Lead to Over-Specification:** Writing tests before the implementation might lead to over-specifying the requirements in the tests, limiting flexibility during development or causing unnecessary complexity.

7. **Difficult for Legacy Systems:** In legacy systems, implementing TDD may be difficult because the codebase is already established, and adding tests for existing code can be time-consuming and may require significant refactoring.

8. **Requires Discipline:** TDD requires developers to strictly adhere to the cycle of writing a test, then writing the code to pass it. Without discipline, developers may skip tests, leading to incomplete coverage and missed bugs.

Behavior-Driven Development (BDD)

Behavior-driven development (BDD) is an agile software development methodology that prioritizes collaboration among developers, testers, and non-technical stakeholders to ensure customer-centric outcomes. In BDD, requirements are defined in terms of desired behaviors and user stories, enabling clearer communication and a focus on delivering business value.

Behavioral Driven Development (BDD) refers to an Agile software development process that is derived from the TDD (Test Driven Development) methodology. BDD is considered a test to illustrate the behavior of the system. It encourages the use of conversation and concrete examples in simple language for everyone involved in the development to bring better clarity to the behavior of the system. In this development, techniques define various ways to develop a feature based on the system's behavior, and the techniques are combined from Test Driven Development (TDD) and Domain Driven Development (DDD).

Behavioral Driven Development is a good approach in Automated Testing as it is more focused on the behavior of the system rather than the implementation of the code. BDD is facilitated through natural language to express the behavior of the system and the expected outcomes from the system. In BDD all parties are involved like a customer, developer, tester, and stakeholder for a collaborated conversation and illustration of the system's behavior.

BDD Process: In Behavior-Driven Development (BDD), teams collaborate closely and explore to characters in a play. The business team acts as the playwright, crafting the script (requirements) based on what they desire users to experience. The development team plays the role of actors, bringing the script to life by implementing the software. Meanwhile, the QA team serves as the director, overseeing the actors' performances and ensuring the play unfolds as planned.

The script in BDD is written using a language called Gherkin, which employs simple phrases like "Given," "When," and "Then" to outline the expected behavior of the software. For instance, a scenario might be described as "Given a user is logged in, When they click on the 'logout' button, Then they should be logged out and redirected to the login page." These scripts are subsequently translated into automated tests that verify if the software behaves as anticipated.

What makes BDD effective is its ability to align everyone involved in the project, ensuring they comprehend and agree on the final outcome. This shared understanding reduces miscommunication and discrepancies, leading to a higher likelihood of project success.

BDD Best Practices: When using Behavior-Driven Development (BDD), it's important to follow some key practices to make the most out of it:

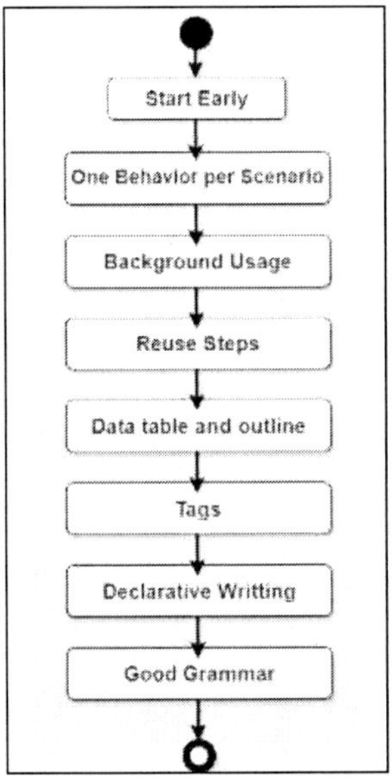

Fig.3.9

1. **Start Early**: Begin writing your test scenarios early to define software behavior and foresee potential issues. It's like planning your trip before you hit the road, saving time and reducing problems later.

2. **One Behavior per Scenario**: Keep each scenario focused on one behavior. Just like cooking one dish at a time ensures perfection, this makes scenarios easier to understand and maintain.

3. **Background Usage**: If certain steps are repeated in every scenario, put them in the Background section for clarity and efficiency.

4. **Reuse Steps**: Save time by reusing step definitions frequently used in different scenarios.

5. **Data Tables and Outlines**: When dealing with large data sets, use Data Tables and Scenario Outlines for clarity and organization.

6. **Tags**: Use tags to organize and run specific groups of scenarios, similar to labeling food containers in the fridge for easy access.

7. **Declarative Writing**: Write scenarios in a way that mirrors how a user would describe them, avoiding overly technical language.

8. **Good Grammar**: Ensure scenarios are well-written with correct grammar and spelling to avoid confusion and maximize understanding.

Advantages of BDD: Behavior-Driven Development (BDD) offers several advantages follows:

1. **Enhanced Collaboration**: BDD promotes collaboration among business stakeholders, developers, and testers by using a common language to describe requirements. This fosters better understanding and alignment among team members.

2. **Clearer Requirements**: Writing scenarios in plain language using Gherkin syntax helps clarify requirements and expectations. This reduces ambiguity and ensures that everyone has a shared understanding of the desired behavior.

3. **Focus on User Behavior**: BDD emphasizes the behavior of the system from the user's perspective. By focusing on user stories and scenarios, BDD ensures that development efforts are aligned with user needs and priorities.

4. **Early Issue Detection**: BDD encourages writing tests before implementation, allowing teams to identify potential issues early in the development process. This leads to faster feedback loops and reduces the cost of fixing defects later on.

5. **Automated Testing**: BDD scenarios can be automated using tools like Cucumber or SpecFlow. Automated tests provide fast and reliable feedback on the application's behavior, enabling teams to detect regressions quickly and ensure ongoing quality.

6. **Improved Documentation**: BDD scenarios serve as executable documentation for the system's behavior. This documentation remains up-to-date as tests are regularly executed, providing a living specification of the software.

7. **Better Code Quality**: BDD encourages writing testable and modular code that adheres to the behavior described in the scenarios. This leads to better-designed software with fewer defects and easier maintenance.

Disadvantages of BDD: Behavior-Driven Development (BDD) offers several Disadvantages follows:

1. **Initial Learning Curve:** Adopting BDD requires teams to learn new frameworks, tools, and methodologies, which can initially slow down the development process as team members familiarize themselves with the new approach.

2. **Time-Consuming Process:** Writing feature files, defining scenarios, and maintaining step definitions can be time-consuming, especially for large and complex projects, leading to potential delays in delivery.

3. Dependency on Stakeholder Involvement: BDD relies heavily on collaboration between stakeholders, including business analysts, developers, testers, and product owners. Lack of active participation from stakeholders can hinder the effectiveness of BDD.

4. **Difficulty in Complex Scenarios:** BDD excels in capturing behavior for straightforward scenarios but may struggle to handle highly complex scenarios or edge cases, leading to ambiguity or inefficiencies in test automation.

5. **Maintenance Overhead:** As the project evolves, maintaining and updating existing feature files and step definitions to reflect changes in requirements or functionality can become challenging and resource-intensive.

6. **Potential Over-Engineering:** Without proper guidance and oversight, teams may over-engineer their BDD tests, adding unnecessary complexity and reducing maintainability in the long run.

7. **Tooling Limitations:** The effectiveness of BDD heavily depends on the availability and suitability of supporting tools and frameworks. Limited tooling options or compatibility issues with existing systems can hinder adoption and implementation.

Automated Testing Tools

Automated testing tools are essential for improving the efficiency, accuracy, and speed of the software testing process. These tools help execute tests automatically, compare actual outcomes with expected results, and report discrepancies, reducing the manual effort involved in testing.

Here are some popular automated testing tools, categorized by their primary function:

1. **Unit Testing Tools:** Unit testing tools are essential for validating individual components or functions of a program. Popular tools include JUnit for Java, NUnit for .NET, pytest for Python, and RSpec for Ruby. These tools help automate test execution, detect bugs early, and ensure code quality through efficient, isolated tests.

    - **JUnit (Java):** A widely used testing framework for Java applications. It allows developers to write and run repeatable tests.
    - **NUnit (.NET):** Similar to JUnit but designed for .NET applications. It provides annotations to organize and run tests.
    - **pytest (Python):** A powerful testing framework for Python that supports simple unit tests to complex functional testing.
    - **JUnit5 (Java):** An updated version of JUnit with more features, such as nested tests and parameterized tests.

2. **Functional Testing Tools**: Functional testing tools automate the verification of software functionality against expected behavior. Popular tools include Selenium for web applications, Cypress for end-to-end testing, TestComplete for cross-platform testing, and Katalon Studio for UI testing. These tools ensure that applications perform correctly under various conditions and user interactions.

- **Selenium**: A popular tool for automating web applications. It supports multiple browsers and programming languages like Java, Python, and C#. Selenium WebDriver allows developers to write scripts to control a web browser and perform functional testing.
- **Cypress**: A fast and reliable testing framework for web applications that focuses on developer experience. It runs directly in the browser, providing real-time feedback during tests.
- **TestComplete**: A comprehensive test automation tool that supports functional testing for desktop, mobile, and web applications. It includes AI-powered visual recognition for UI elements.

3. **Performance Testing Tools:** Performance testing tools evaluate how well software performs under various load conditions. Key tools include Apache JMeter for load testing, LoadRunner for simulating virtual users, and Gatling for high-performance testing. These tools help identify bottlenecks, optimize system performance, and ensure scalability and reliability under heavy traffic.

   - **Apache JMeter**: An open-source tool designed for load testing and performance measurement. It is used to test the performance of applications under various load conditions.
   - **LoadRunner** (Micro Focus): A performance testing tool used to simulate virtual users and measure the system's performance under load.
   - **Gatling**: An open-source load testing tool primarily used for testing the performance of web applications. It is based on Scala and offers high scalability for heavy traffic simulations.

4. **API Testing Tools:** API testing tools automate the validation of APIs to ensure they function correctly. Popular tools include Postman for testing RESTful APIs, SoapUI for SOAP and REST APIs, and Rest Assured for Java-based API testing. These tools verify API responses, error handling, security, and integration with other systems.

   - **Postman**: A popular tool for testing RESTful APIs. It allows users to send HTTP requests, inspect responses, and automate tests for APIs.
   - **SoapUI**: A widely-used tool for testing SOAP and REST APIs. It provides features for functional, security, and load testing of APIs.

- **Rest Assured** (Java): A Java library that simplifies the testing of REST APIs. It allows for easy creation and verification of HTTP requests and responses.

5. **Continuous Integration (CI) Tools**: Continuous Integration (CI) tools automate the process of integrating code changes into a shared repository, ensuring early detection of errors. Key tools include Jenkins for automating builds and tests, GitLab CI for integrated DevOps workflows, and Travis CI for seamless integration with GitHub, enhancing development efficiency.

   - **Jenkins**: A widely used open-source CI/CD tool that helps automate the testing, building, and deployment of software. Jenkins integrates well with various automated testing tools like Selenium and JUnit.
   - **GitLab CI**: A robust tool built into GitLab for continuous integration and delivery, which supports test automation workflows.
   - **Travis CI**: A cloud-based CI tool that integrates with GitHub and allows automated testing on different platforms.

6. **Mobile Testing Tools:** Mobile testing tools automate testing for mobile applications across various platforms. Popular tools include Appium for cross-platform testing on Android and iOS, Espresso for Android UI testing, and XCUITest for iOS applications. These tools ensure functionality, performance, and usability on different devices and operating systems.

   - **Appium**: An open-source tool for automating mobile applications on both Android and iOS. It allows tests to be written in multiple programming languages like Java, Python, and JavaScript.
   - **Robot Framework**: An open-source automation framework used for acceptance testing and robotic process automation (RPA). It works with mobile apps and web applications.
   - **Espresso** (Android) / **XCUITest** (iOS): Native testing frameworks provided by Google (Espresso) and Apple (XCUITest) for automating functional tests for mobile applications.

7. **Visual Testing Tools:** Visual testing tools automate the detection of visual discrepancies in web and mobile applications. Popular tools include Percy for visual regression testing in CI/CD pipelines, Applitools Eyes powered by AI

for cross-browser visual validation, and Testim for UI testing, ensuring consistent and error-free visual presentation.

- **Percy**: An automated visual testing platform that integrates with CI/CD workflows and compares visual changes in applications across different environments and browsers.
- **Applitools Eyes**: A visual testing and monitoring tool that uses AI to ensure the visual consistency of web and mobile applications across different browsers and devices.
- **Testim**: Uses AI to automate UI tests, enabling teams to run visual regression tests across various browsers.

8. **Security Testing Tools:** Security testing tools help identify vulnerabilities and ensure the protection of applications. Popular tools include OWASP ZAP for penetration testing, Burp Suite for web application security testing, and Fortify for static and dynamic analysis. These tools help detect security flaws and strengthen applications against potential threats.

- **OWASP ZAP (Zed Attack Proxy)**: An open-source tool used for penetration testing and finding security vulnerabilities in web applications.
- **Burp Suite**: A popular tool for web application security testing that helps identify vulnerabilities through manual and automated methods.
- **Fortify**: A comprehensive security testing suite that scans applications for vulnerabilities and offers insights into security risks.

9. **Behavior-Driven Testing Tools:** Behavior-Driven Testing Tools focus on testing software behavior in collaboration with stakeholders. Cucumber enables writing tests in Gherkin syntax for readability, SpecFlow works for .NET applications, and Behat is used in PHP projects. These tools support collaboration and help ensure that software meets expected behaviors as defined by users and developers.

- **Cucumber**: A tool that supports behavior-driven development (BDD). It allows teams to write tests in plain language (Gherkin syntax), making it accessible to both technical and non-technical stakeholders.
- **SpecFlow** (C#): A BDD testing framework for .NET, which allows tests to be written in Gherkin syntax similar to Cucumber.

- **Behat** (PHP): A BDD tool for PHP applications, often used for acceptance testing with the Gherkin language.

10. **Regression Testing Tools:** Regression Testing Tools automate the process of re-running tests to ensure new code changes don't negatively impact existing functionality. Popular tools include Selenium for web automation, QTP (UFT) for functional and regression testing, and TestComplete for cross-platform testing. These tools enhance the reliability of continuous development cycles.

    - **QTP (QuickTest Professional)**: An automated functional testing tool for regression testing, commonly used for web and desktop applications. It is now called Micro Focus UFT.

    - **Selenium Grid**: A tool for running Selenium tests in parallel across multiple machines and browsers, making regression testing faster and more efficient.

SUMMARY OF SOFTWARE DEVELOPMENT AND BEST PRACTICES

Software development is a complex process that involves the creation, design, testing, and maintenance of software applications. Best practices in software development are fundamental principles and techniques that lead to high-quality, efficient, and reliable software. These best practices touch on various aspects of development, including programming paradigms, coding standards, software testing, and quality assurance.

6. Programming Paradigms and Languages

Programming paradigms define how software is structured and written, influencing maintainability, scalability, and efficiency. Procedural programming organizes code into sequences of instructions and function calls, suitable for simple, linear tasks but less effective for large-scale systems (e.g., C and Pascal). Object-oriented programming (OOP) organizes code into objects that combine data and methods, promoting modularity and reusability, making it ideal for complex, large applications (e.g., Java, C++, Python). Functional programming treats computation as the evaluation of functions, emphasizing immutability and avoiding side effects, which is useful for concurrent and mathematical problems (e.g., Haskell, Scala, Elixir). While each paradigm has its strengths, modern programming languages like Python, JavaScript, and C++ blend multiple paradigms, allowing developers to choose the most effective approach for specific tasks. The choice of programming language depends on project requirements, the problem domain, and the developer's familiarity with the language's features.

- **Procedural vs. Object-Oriented vs. Functional Programming:** Programming paradigms are approaches to programming that dictate how software developers structure and write code. The three most common paradigms are procedural programming, object-oriented programming (OOP), and functional programming.

- ➢ **Procedural Programming**: This paradigm organizes the program as a set of instructions or functions that operate on data. It is based on a step-by-step procedure where functions or procedures are called sequentially to achieve a goal. Languages like C and Pascal are examples of procedural programming languages. Procedural programming emphasizes on the flow of control and data across the program, making it simpler to understand for small to medium applications but often harder to scale for larger, more complex applications.

- ➢ **Object-Oriented Programming (OOP)**: OOP is a paradigm based on the concept of "objects," which are instances of "classes." These objects contain both data (attributes) and methods (functions) that operate on that data. OOP facilitates code reuse, modularity, and maintainability, as it focuses on encapsulation, inheritance, and polymorphism. Popular languages such as **Java**, C++, Python, and C# support OOP principles. OOP is preferred for large-scale applications because of its scalability and ability to manage complex systems through abstraction and modularity.

- ➢ **Functional Programming**: Functional programming treats computation as the evaluation of mathematical functions and avoids changing state or mutable data. It emphasizes immutability, first-class functions, and higher-order functions. Haskell, Scala, and F# are examples of functional programming languages, though functional concepts are present in languages like JavaScript and Python. Functional programming encourages pure functions, which can enhance program reliability and scalability by minimizing side effects and making code easier to reason about.

- **Choosing the Right Language for the Job:** Selecting the right programming language for a specific task depends on multiple factors, including the problem domain, performance requirements, developer expertise, and ecosystem support. Each language excels in different areas:

  - ➢ **Python**: Known for its simplicity and readability, Python is widely used in fields like data science, web development (with frameworks like Django and Flask), and artificial intelligence (AI) and machine learning (ML). It is a dynamically typed language, making it quick to write but requiring careful management of runtime errors.

- **Java**: A statically typed, object-oriented language, Java is widely used for building large-scale, enterprise-level applications. Its "write once, run anywhere" philosophy makes it a solid choice for cross-platform applications. Java is commonly used in Android app development, web development, and financial services.

- **C++**: Known for its performance and control over system resources, C++ is commonly used in system programming, game development, and applications that require high performance, such as real-time simulations. While it is powerful, it comes with the complexity of managing memory manually.

- **JavaScript**: As the primary language for web development, JavaScript is essential for building interactive web applications. With frameworks like React, Angular, and Node.js, it has grown beyond the browser to also handle server-side applications, making it a versatile language for full-stack development.

- **Modern Programming Languages:** The rise of modern programming languages has introduced features and paradigms that improve productivity and maintainability. These languages combine aspects of procedural, object-oriented, and functional programming to offer flexibility and efficiency. Python, JavaScript, Go, Swift, and Rust are some of the modern languages that have gained popularity due to their ease of use, performance, and community support. The choice of language often depends on the specific application requirements, existing ecosystem, and developer proficiency.

7. Coding Standards and Best Practices

Coding standards and best practices ensure code is readable, maintainable, and efficient. Key principles include consistent naming conventions for variables, functions, and classes to improve clarity and avoid confusion. Code readability is enhanced through proper indentation, modularization, and commenting, making it easier for others to understand and modify the code. Version control systems like Git allow developers to track changes, collaborate, and maintain code history. Writing clean code follows principles like DRY (Don't Repeat Yourself) and KISS (Keep It Simple, Stupid), ensuring code is simple, efficient, and easy to extend while reducing potential errors.

- **Code Readability and Maintainability:** Writing code that is readable and maintainable is essential for long-term project success. Readable code helps developers quickly understand, modify, and debug the codebase. It should be easy to follow, even for someone unfamiliar with the project. Key aspects of maintainable code include clear and descriptive variable names, proper indentation, consistent formatting, and modularization of functions.

- **Naming Conventions and Documentation:** Naming conventions and documentation are crucial for maintaining clarity and consistency throughout the codebase. Clear and descriptive names for variables, functions, classes, and modules help developers understand their purpose. Common naming conventions include camelCase for variables and functions, PascalCase for classes, and UPPER_SNAKE_CASE for constants. Documentation, especially inline comments and external documentation, helps explain the reasoning behind the code, edge cases, and complex logic, making it easier for future developers to modify or extend the application.

- **Version Control Systems (Git, GitHub, GitLab, Bitbucket):** Version control systems (VCS) are tools that help track changes to source code over time, allowing multiple developers to collaborate effectively. Git is the most widely used VCS, providing features like branching, merging, and version tracking. Platforms like GitHub, GitLab, and Bitbucket offer additional features, including issue tracking, code review, and continuous integration (CI) pipelines, enhancing team collaboration and project management. Version control ensures that the development process is organized and transparent, enabling easy rollback and auditing of changes.

- **Writing Clean Code:** Clean code refers to code that is simple, readable, and easy to maintain. It follows principles such as DRY (Don't Repeat Yourself), which encourages code reuse, and KISS (Keep It Simple, Stupid), which advocates for simplicity in logic and design. Writing clean code also involves avoiding unnecessary complexity, following consistent naming conventions, using comments appropriately, and refactoring code when necessary to improve clarity and structure.

8. Software Testing and Quality Assurance

- **Unit Testing, Integration Testing, System Testing:** Software testing is an essential practice in ensuring that applications function as expected and are free of defects. There are several levels of testing, each focusing on different aspects of the application:

- **Unit Testing**: Unit tests focus on verifying the functionality of individual components or units of the application, such as functions or methods. These tests are typically automated and help detect bugs early in development. Frameworks like JUnit (Java), pytest (Python), and NUnit (.NET) are commonly used for unit testing.

- **Integration Testing**: Integration tests verify the interactions between different modules or systems within an application. They ensure that data flows correctly between components and that the system behaves as expected when components are combined. Tools like Postman (for API testing) and Selenium (for UI interaction) can be used for integration testing.

- **System Testing**: System testing involves testing the entire system as a whole to ensure that it meets the specified requirements. This includes functional, performance, and security testing. Tools like TestComplete and Jenkins can be used to perform automated system tests.

- **Test-Driven Development (TDD):** Test-Driven Development (TDD) is a software development methodology in which tests are written before the actual code. In TDD, developers write a test, run it to see it fail, write the code to pass the test, and then refactor the code. This cycle promotes writing modular, testable, and maintainable code. TDD ensures that the application's behavior aligns with requirements and prevents regression during future development.

- **Behavior-Driven Development (BDD):** Behavior-Driven Development (BDD) is an extension of TDD that focuses on the behavior of the application from the perspective of its users. It uses natural language constructs to define test cases, making it easier for non-technical stakeholders to understand. BDD frameworks like Cucumber and SpecFlow allow teams to write tests in plain English, ensuring collaboration between developers, testers, and business analysts.

- **Automated Testing Tools:** Automated testing tools enhance the efficiency and speed of testing. They allow tests to be executed automatically, reducing human intervention and the risk of errors. Tools like Selenium, Jenkins, and JUnit support automated unit, integration, and system testing. Automated tests can be integrated into continuous integration (CI) pipelines, ensuring rapid feedback and high-quality software delivery.

******

PART–4

ADVANCED TOPICS IN SOFTWARE ENGINEERING

Advanced topics in software engineering encompass a variety of specialized areas that push the boundaries of traditional software development. These topics include microservices architecture, which focuses on building scalable and independently deployable services, promoting agility and resilience in large systems. Another key area is DevOps, emphasizing the integration of development and operations to automate workflows and improve software delivery pipelines. Machine learning and AI integration within software engineering explores how algorithms can optimize performance, adapt to new data, and enhance user experiences. Additionally, cloud-native development leverages cloud computing platforms to create applications that are flexible, scalable, and highly available. Concurrency and parallelism play a critical role in optimizing performance in multi-threaded environments, and the efficient use of resources is a major challenge in modern applications. Agile and Scrum methodologies continue to evolve, with an emphasis on improving collaboration, flexibility, and iterative progress, while software testing and quality assurance advancements focus on automated testing frameworks, continuous integration, and ensuring high standards of code reliability. Security engineering, addressing vulnerabilities and implementing secure coding practices, is also critical as cyber threats become increasingly sophisticated. Finally, Blockchain technology in software engineering has gained attention for its applications in decentralized systems, digital currencies, and secure data transactions. These advanced topics collectively shape the future of software development, pushing the industry toward more efficient, secure, and adaptive systems.

9

Security in Software Engineering

Security in software engineering is a critical aspect that ensures the protection of software systems, their users, and their data from malicious attacks and unauthorized access. As software becomes increasingly integrated into every facet of daily life, ensuring its security has become paramount. One of the fundamental aspects of security in software engineering is secure software design, which involves identifying and mitigating potential vulnerabilities early in the development lifecycle. This process includes applying secure coding practices—such as input validation, output encoding, and proper error handling—to prevent common threats like SQL injection, cross-site scripting (XSS), and buffer overflows. Additionally, developers must follow security principles like least privilege (minimizing access to data and resources) and defense in depth (implementing multiple layers of security) to protect the software at various levels. Effective threat modeling allows engineers to anticipate and evaluate potential attack vectors, ensuring that security is integrated from the beginning of the development process rather than being treated as an afterthought. Moreover, encryption plays a vital role in securing data both in transit and at rest, ensuring that even if data is intercepted or compromised, it remains unreadable without the proper decryption key.

In addition to secure development practices, software testing and auditing are essential components of maintaining security. Regular security testing, including penetration testing and vulnerability scanning, helps identify weaknesses that could be exploited by attackers. Static and dynamic analysis tools can automatically detect flaws in code and runtime behavior, ensuring that vulnerabilities are addressed before deployment. Another critical aspect of security is incident response planning—having a structured process in place for responding to security breaches when they occur. This includes monitoring systems for unusual activity, conducting thorough forensic investigations, and implementing patch management to fix vulnerabilities post-deployment. Software updates are also crucial, as they address newly discovered security issues, and failure to apply timely updates can leave systems exposed. Additionally, user authentication and access control mechanisms such as multi-factor authentication (MFA) and role-based access control (RBAC) are essential in protecting against unauthorized access. In today's interconnected world, where cloud-based services and third-party libraries are commonly used, it is essential to ensure that these external dependencies are secure and up to date, as they can introduce additional risks. Ultimately, security in software engineering is an ongoing commitment to safeguarding software from the ever-evolving landscape of threats, requiring continuous learning, adaptation, and vigilance from engineers. The key aspects of software security in engineering are as under:

1. **Secure Design:** Designing software with security in mind from the outset, considering potential vulnerabilities and implementing appropriate controls.

2. **Secure Coding:** Following secure coding standards and practices to prevent vulnerabilities from being introduced into the code.

3. **Threat Modeling:** Identifying potential threats to the system and developing strategies to mitigate them.

4. **Security Testing:** Evaluating the security posture of the software through various testing techniques, such as static analysis, dynamic analysis, and penetration testing.

5. **Vulnerability Management:** Tracking and addressing identified vulnerabilities throughout the software's lifecycle.

6. **Authentication and Authorization:** Implementing robust mechanisms to verify the identity of users and control their access to system resources.

7. **Encryption:** Protecting sensitive data at rest and in transit using cryptographic techniques.

8. **Input Validation and Output Encoding:** Preventing attacks by sanitizing user input and properly encoding output to prevent malicious code injection.

9. **Secure Configuration:** Ensuring that the software and its environment are configured securely, minimizing attack surfaces.

10. **Security Awareness and Training:** Educating developers and other stakeholders about security best practices and potential risks.

Software Development Life Cycle (SDLC): Software development life cycle (SDLC) is a structured process that is used to design, develop, and test good-quality software. SDLC, or software development life cycle, is a methodology that defines the entire procedure of software development step-by-step. The goal of the SDLC life cycle model is to deliver high-quality, maintainable software that meets the user's requirements. SDLC in software engineering models outlines the plan for each stage so that each stage of the software development model can perform its task efficiently to deliver the software at a low cost within a given time frame that meets user's requirements. SDLC is a process followed for software building within a software organization. SDLC consists of a precise plan that describes how to develop, maintain, replace, and enhance specific software. The life cycle defines a method for improving the quality of software and the all-around development process.

Stages of the Software Development Life Cycle: SDLC specifies the task(s) to be performed at various stages by a software engineer or developer. It ensures that the end product is able to meet the customer's expectations and fits within the overall budget. Hence, it's vital for a software developer to have prior knowledge of this software development process.

Stage 1 Planning & Requirement Analysis	**Stage 2** Defining Requirements	**Stage 3** Design	**Stage 4** Development	**Stage 5** Testing	**Stage 6** Deployment & Maintenace
Planning	Defining	Design	Development	System Testing	Deployment and Maintenace
Define Project Scope	Functional Requirement	HLD	Coding Standard	Manual Testing	Release Planning
Set Objectives and Goals	Technical Requirement	LLD	Scalable Code	Automated Testing	Deployment Automation
Resource Planning	Requirement Reviews & Approved		Version Control		Maintenance
			Code Review		Feedback

Fig.4.1

SDLC is a collection of these six stages, and the stages of SDLC are as follows:

Stage 1: Planning and Requirement Analysis: Planning is a crucial step in everything, just as in software development. In this same stage, requirement analysis is also performed by the developers of the organization. This is attained from customer inputs, and sales department/market surveys.

The information from this analysis forms the building blocks of a basic project. The quality of the project is a result of planning. Thus, in this stage, the basic project is designed with all the available information.

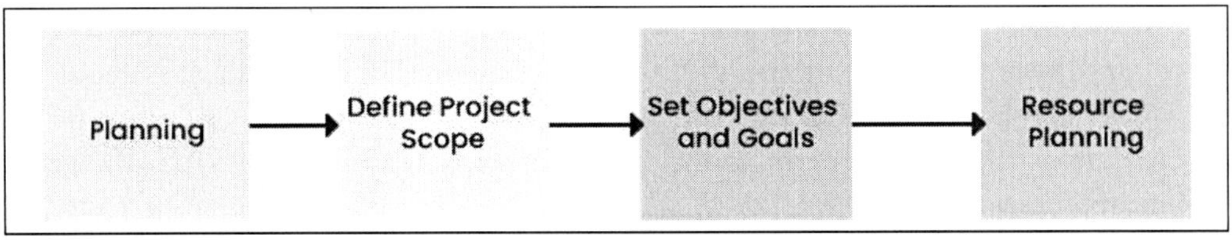

Fig.4.2

Planning and Requirement Analysis, is crucial for setting the foundation of the project. In this phase, the goal is to gather and understand the detailed requirements of the software from stakeholders, which includes clients, end-users, and other relevant parties. This involves identifying both functional requirements (what the system must do) and non-functional requirements (such as performance, security, and scalability). The team also evaluates constraints like budget, timeline, and resource availability to ensure the project's feasibility. A thorough analysis of the project's risks, including technical challenges and external dependencies, is conducted to anticipate potential obstacles. The Software Requirements Specification (SRS) document is created, capturing all these details and acting as a formal reference for the development team. This document becomes a key deliverable that aligns stakeholders' expectations and guides decision-making in subsequent stages. Additionally, in this phase, a high-level project plan is developed, including milestones, deliverables, and timelines, ensuring the project stays on track. Effective planning and requirement analysis help to avoid misunderstandings, reduce scope creep, and provide clarity for the next phases of the SDLC, ultimately contributing to the project's success.

Stage 2: Defining Requirements: In this stage, all the requirements for the target software are specified. These requirements get approval from customers, market analysts, and stakeholders.

This is fulfilled by utilizing SRS (Software Requirement Specification). This is a sort of document that specifies all those things that need to be defined and created during the entire project cycle.

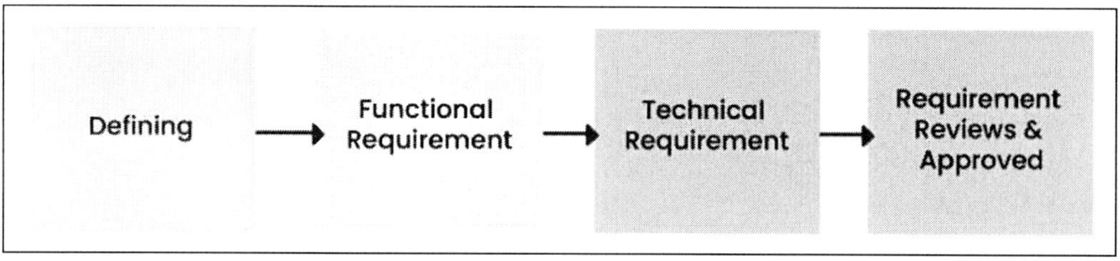

Fig.4.3

Defining requirements, focuses on translating the high-level goals established in the planning phase into clear, detailed, and actionable specifications. This phase involves a deeper dive into understanding both functional and non-functional requirements. Functional requirements describe the system's behaviors and features such as user interactions, data processing, and specific tasks the software should perform. Non-functional requirements, on the other hand, outline the system's performance criteria, security standards, scalability, and reliability expectations. During this stage, the development team works closely with stakeholders to validate and refine these requirements, ensuring they align with the project's objectives and constraints.

A critical outcome of this phase is the creation of the Software Requirements Specification (SRS) document, which serves as a comprehensive reference guide for both the development and testing teams. The SRS helps prevent scope creep by clearly defining what is and isn't included in the project, acting as a contract between stakeholders and developers. Additionally, the requirements are prioritized based on factors like business value, user need, and technical complexity. Once the requirements are fully defined and approved by stakeholders, the project can move forward with a clear and agreed-upon roadmap, setting the stage for design and implementation.

Stage 3: Designing Architecture: SRS is a reference for software designers to come up with the best architecture for the software. Hence, with the requirements defined in SRS, multiple designs for the product architecture are present in the Design Document Specification (DDS).

This DDS is assessed by market analysts and stakeholders. After evaluating all the possible factors, the most practical and logical design is chosen for development.

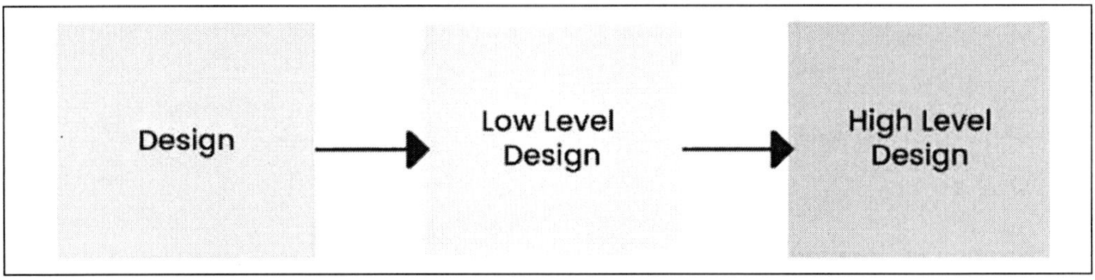

Fig.4.4

Designing architecture, is where the foundation for the system's structure is laid. In this phase, the development team defines the high-level architecture and technical framework that will guide the entire project. The goal is to ensure that the software is scalable, maintainable, and secure while meeting the requirements outlined in the previous stages. The design process begins with creating a blueprint of the system, which includes the selection of software architectures, such as client-server, microservices, or monolithic, based on the project's needs.

Key elements of this phase include designing the system's data architecture, network architecture, and user interface (UI) design. The team also decides on the technologies, frameworks, and tools that will be used, as well as defining how various components will interact with each other. This includes database design, API structures, and integration points.

The output of the design phase is typically a System Design Document that provides detailed specifications for the architecture, components, interfaces, and data flow. Additionally, prototypes or mockups may be developed for user interfaces to ensure alignment with stakeholder expectations. By the end of this stage, the project should have a solid technical foundation and a roadmap for development and testing, minimizing risks during the implementation phase.

Stage 4: Developing Product: At this stage, the fundamental development of the product starts. For this, developers use a specific programming code as per the design in the DDS. Hence, it is important for the coders to follow the protocols set by the association. Conventional programming tools like compilers, interpreters, debuggers, etc. are also put into use at this stage. Some popular languages like C/C++, Python, Java, etc. are put into use as per the software regulations.

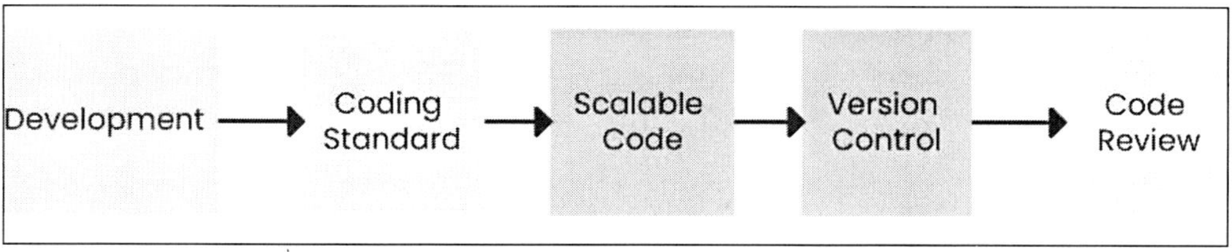

Fig.4.5

Developing the Product, is where the actual coding and software creation begin. During this phase, the design specifications from the previous stage are translated into executable software. Developers write code based on the detailed requirements and architecture outlined in earlier stages, ensuring that each feature functions according to the predefined specifications. This phase involves implementing both the backend (server-side) and frontend (client-side) components, databases, APIs, and integrations, using the appropriate programming languages, frameworks, and tools selected during the design phase.

Development typically proceeds in iterations or sprints, especially in Agile methodologies, allowing teams to regularly review progress, make adjustments, and incorporate feedback from stakeholders. Version control systems (such as Git) are used to manage code changes and ensure collaboration between team members. Additionally, developers follow coding standards and best practices to maintain code quality, readability, and security.

Throughout the development phase, ongoing communication with project managers and stakeholders ensures alignment with business goals and user needs. Automated testing tools may also be used to catch early bugs or issues during development. By the end of this phase, a fully functional prototype or the initial version of the product is ready for integration testing, marking the transition to the next stage in the SDLC.

Stage 5: Product Testing and Integration: After the development of the product, testing of the software is necessary to ensure its smooth execution. Although, minimal testing is conducted at every stage of SDLC. Therefore, at this stage, all the probable flaws are tracked, fixed, and retested. This ensures that the product confronts the quality requirements of SRS.

Documentation, Training, and Support: Software documentation is an essential part of the software development life cycle. A well-written document acts as a tool and means to information repository necessary to know about software processes, functions, and maintenance. Documentation also provides information about how to use the product. Training in an attempt to improve the current or future employee performance by increasing an employee's ability to work through learning, usually by changing his attitude and developing his skills and understanding.

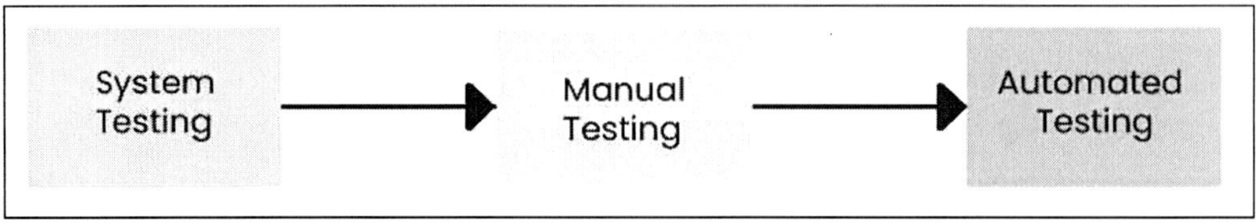

Fig.4.6

Product Testing and Integration, is crucial for ensuring the quality, reliability, and functionality of the software. In this phase, the product undergoes rigorous testing to identify and fix defects or issues before it is released to users. Different types of testing are performed, such as unit testing, where individual components are tested in isolation, and integration testing, where the interactions between components or systems are verified to ensure they work together as expected. System testing is performed to validate the complete functionality, while acceptance testing ensures the product meets business requirements and stakeholder expectations.

The testing phase also includes performance testing to assess the software's speed, scalability, and resource consumption under various conditions, and security testing to identify vulnerabilities that could be exploited by malicious actors. Automated testing tools may be used to speed up the process, ensuring consistent results across multiple test cycles.

During integration, the product is gradually combined with other systems, databases, or services it needs to interact with. The integration process verifies that data flows correctly between systems and those external dependencies, like third-party APIs, work seamlessly. Any issues discovered during testing are addressed, and the product is refined to ensure its stable and ready for deployment.

Stage 6: Deployment and Maintenance of Products: After detailed testing, the conclusive product is released in phases as per the organization's strategy. Then it is tested in a real industrial environment. It is important to ensure its smooth performance. If it performs well, the organization sends out the product as a whole. After retrieving beneficial feedback, the company releases it as it is or with auxiliary improvements to make it further helpful for the customers. However, this alone is not enough. Therefore, along with the deployment, the product's supervision.

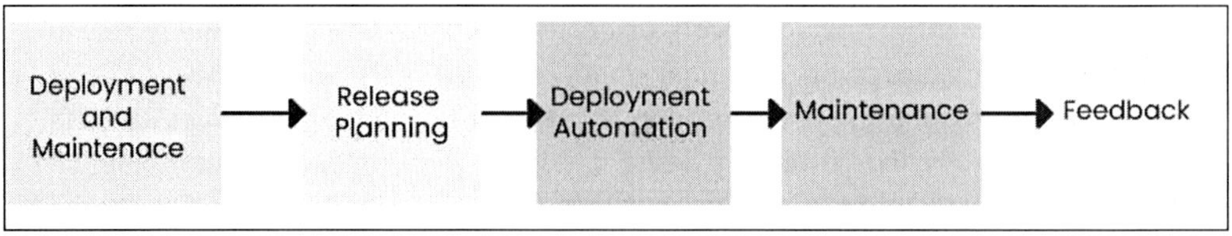

Fig.4.7

Deployment and Maintenance, is the final phase before the software is released to end users and continues to evolve post-launch. Deployment involves transferring the product from a development environment to a live production environment where users can access it. This phase can be done in stages, starting with a beta release for limited users or a pilot deployment to ensure stability. The deployment process also includes configuring the necessary infrastructure, setting up databases, and ensuring the software integrates properly with other systems.

Once deployed, maintenance becomes an ongoing process to ensure the software continues to perform well over time. This includes fixing bugs, addressing user feedback, and updating the software to meet changing business needs or technological advancements. It is common for updates to be released regularly to enhance features, improve performance, and address security vulnerabilities. This phase also involves monitoring the software's performance to detect potential issues early, conducting periodic security audits, and ensuring the system remains compliant with any new regulations.

In Agile or iterative development models, the deployment and maintenance phase may overlap with further development cycles, ensuring that the software evolves continuously and remains aligned with user needs and expectations.

The Role of Security in the SDLC: Security considerations should be integrated into every phase of the SDLC, from initial planning and design to coding, testing, deployment, and maintenance. This proactive approach minimizes the risk of introducing vulnerabilities and reduces the cost of fixing security flaws later in the development process. In essence, software security in engineering is a multifaceted discipline that aims to create secure, reliable, and resilient software applications. By incorporating security best practices throughout the SDLC, software developers can protect their applications and their users from a wide range of cyber threats.

Secure Coding Practices

Secure coding practices are essential to creating resilient and secure applications, protecting them from vulnerabilities and cyber threats. They involve principles like validating and sanitizing user input to prevent injection attacks, implementing robust authentication and authorization mechanisms to safeguard access, and adhering to the principle of least privilege, granting only the necessary permissions to limit potential exploitation. Using trusted, updated libraries and frameworks ensures the application remains shielded against known vulnerabilities. Encryption is critical for securing sensitive data, whether it is stored or transmitted, while adopting secure defaults ensures a baseline level of security. Comprehensive threat modeling and code review during development identify and mitigate vulnerabilities early. Secure APIs with authentication, rate-limiting, and proper error handling prevent misuse, while static and dynamic analysis tools assist in identifying flaws in the code during development and runtime. Automated testing, especially penetration testing, helps simulate attacks to expose potential weaknesses. Logging and monitoring systems are vital for detecting and responding to suspicious activities in real time. A proactive approach to security is incomplete without investing in developer training and fostering a culture of security awareness within the organization. By integrating these practices into the software development lifecycle, engineers can create applications that not only meet functional requirements but are also fortified against evolving security challenges, ensuring user trust and compliance with data protection regulations. These strategies collectively uphold the integrity, confidentiality, and availability of software systems in a dynamic threat landscape. Core principles are as under:

1. **Input Validation**: Ensure all user input is properly sanitized and validated to prevent injection attacks (e.g., SQL injection). Input validation ensures that user inputs are properly checked and sanitized to prevent malicious data from causing harm. Techniques include enforcing constraints such as format, type, and length, as well as using whitelists to allow only expected inputs. Validation protects against attacks like SQL injection and cross-site scripting (XSS) by neutralizing harmful characters. Additionally, encoding input when rendering on web pages mitigates the risk of executing malicious scripts. This practice is fundamental for safeguarding application integrity.

2. **Authentication & Authorization**: Implement robust mechanisms for verifying user identity and access control. Use multi-factor authentication where possible. Authentication ensures users are who they claim to be, using methods like passwords, tokens, or multi-factor authentication. Authorization governs access to resources based on user roles and permissions, adhering to the principle of least privilege. These practices prevent unauthorized access to sensitive data and functionalities. Implementing logging helps track attempts and detect suspicious activities, reinforcing system security.

3. **Least Privilege**: Grant minimal access or permissions needed for functionality, reducing the risk of misuse or exploitation. The principle of least privilege limits access rights and permissions to the minimum required for a task. For instance, a user needing read access should not be granted write access. This reduces the scope of potential misuse or damage from compromised accounts or vulnerabilities. Regularly auditing permissions and revoking unnecessary access are key steps in applying least privilege effectively across applications and systems.

4. **Code Review**: Regularly review code to identify vulnerabilities and enforce best practices. Code reviews involve a systematic examination of code by peers to identify security flaws, bugs, and adherence to best practices. They provide an opportunity to spot overlooked vulnerabilities, improve maintainability, and ensure compliance with secure coding standards. Automated tools can complement manual reviews, but human scrutiny remains essential for nuanced analysis.

5. **Secure Dependencies**: Use trusted libraries and frameworks, and keep them updated to patch known security flaws. Third-party libraries and frameworks should be carefully vetted for security risks before use. Regular updates and patching are crucial to mitigate vulnerabilities as they are discovered. Tools like software composition analysis (SCA) help detect outdated or insecure dependencies. Avoid using untrusted sources and ensure licenses are valid to maintain the integrity of the software.

Best Practices

1. **Use Encryption**: Encrypt sensitive data both in transit and at rest to prevent unauthorized access. Encryption is vital for protecting sensitive data from unauthorized access or breaches. It ensures that even if data is intercepted, it remains unreadable to attackers. Use strong encryption algorithms such as AES for data at rest and TLS for data in transit. Avoid hardcoding encryption keys in the code; instead, store them securely in specialized environments like Hardware Security Modules (HSMs). Always encrypt sensitive user information, such as passwords, using hashing algorithms like bcrypt. Regularly update cryptographic libraries to address vulnerabilities in outdated protocols. Employ key rotation strategies to periodically change encryption keys, reducing exposure to compromised keys. By implementing encryption throughout the system, organizations enhance confidentiality and maintain user trust.

2. **Apply Secure Defaults**: Configure systems to be secure by default rather than relying on optional security settings. Secure defaults ensure systems are configured securely from the outset. Avoid leaving systems or applications exposed with default settings that can be exploited. For example, disable unnecessary features, enforce strong password policies, and restrict permissions to essential access only. Ensure error messages do not reveal sensitive information that could help attackers. Security settings should require explicit changes for weaker configurations rather than allowing insecure defaults.

Automating secure configurations during deployment can prevent human errors and ensure consistent adherence to security policies across all environments.

3. **Secure APIs**: Design APIs with authentication, rate-limiting, and proper error handling to prevent exploitation. APIs are often targets for exploitation, so designing them securely is crucial. Implement authentication protocols like OAuth or API keys to ensure only authorized users can access them. Rate-limiting prevents abuse through excessive requests, reducing the risk of denial-of-service attacks. Ensure error messages are generic and do not expose system details. Input validation and output encoding protect APIs from injection attacks, while encryption secures data exchanges. Conduct regular API security testing to identify vulnerabilities. By adhering to these practices, APIs become reliable gateways for communication while minimizing risks.

4. **Threat Modeling**: Assess risks and identify potential attack vectors early in the development cycle. Threat modeling is a proactive approach to identifying and mitigating security risks during the software development lifecycle. Start by identifying assets, potential attack vectors, and vulnerabilities. Assess the likelihood and impact of each threat to prioritize remediation efforts. Use structured methodologies such as STRIDE (Spoofing, Tampering, Repudiation, Information Disclosure, Denial of Service, Elevation of Privileges) or PASTA (Process for Attack Simulation and Threat Analysis). Engage all stakeholders, including developers, testers, and security experts, to ensure comprehensive risk assessment. Regularly update threat models as software evolves to address emerging threats. This practice enhances overall security awareness and provides actionable insights for safeguarding applications.

Common Vulnerabilities (OWASP Top 10)

The OWASP Top 10 identifies common vulnerabilities in web applications. It includes areas like Broken Access Control, Cryptographic Failures, Injection, and Insecure Design. The list is regularly updated to reflect emerging threats. The OWASP Top 10 is a widely recognized list of the most critical web application security risks. The list serves as a guide for developers, security professionals, and organizations as they prioritize their efforts in identifying and mitigating critical web application security risks.

The presence of a risk on the OWASP Top 10 list does not necessarily indicate its prevalence or severity in all web applications, and the Top Ten is not ranked in a specific order or by priority.

The OWASP Top 10 web application security risks for 2021 are:

1. **Broken Access Controls:** This vulnerability results when insufficient enforcement of access controls and authorization allow attackers to access unauthorized functionality or data. This may be due to insecure direct object references (IDORs), which can arise when an application fails to validate or authorize user input that is used as a direct reference to an internal object. It may also occur due to missing function level access controls, when the application only validates access controls at the initial authentication or authorization stage but does not consistently enforce those controls throughout the application's functions or operations. A web application firewall (WAF) can help protect against these attacks by monitoring and enforcing access controls to prevent unauthorized access to sensitive objects or resources.

2. **Cryptographic Failures:** This risk occurs due to inadequate protection of sensitive data during transit and at rest. Cryptographic failures can lead to data breaches, unauthorized access to confidential information, and non-compliance with data privacy regulations, such as the EU General Data Protection Regulation (GDPR), and financial standards like PCI Data Security Standards (PCI DSS). These failures can result from insecure cryptographic storage, storing data in plain text, or insecure key management. The risk can also derive from information leakage, which can originate from weak key or random number generation or from flaws in cryptographic protocols.

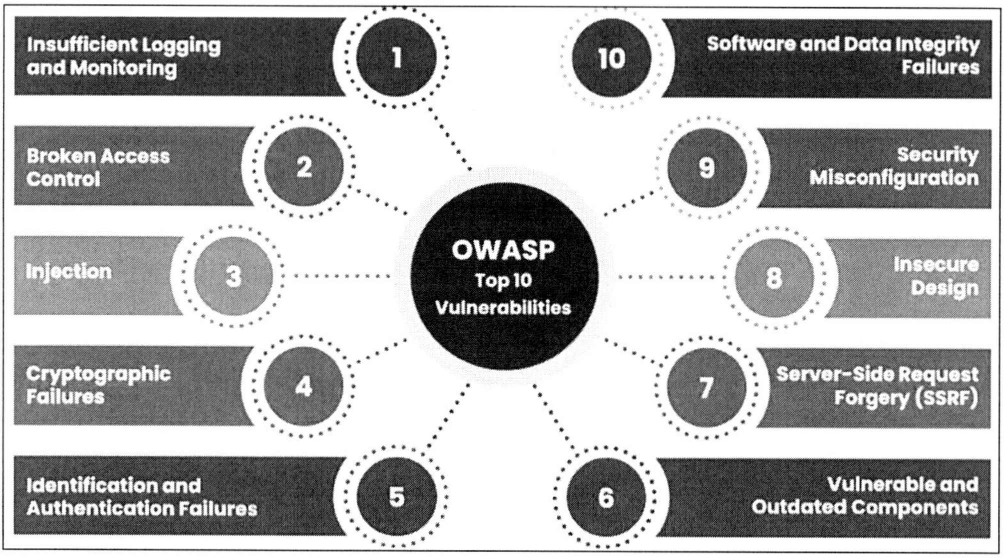

Fig.4.8

3. **Injection Attacks:** Injection flaws occur when attackers insert untrusted or hostile data into command or query languages, or when user-supplied data is not validated, filtered, or sanitized by the application, leading to unintended execution of malicious commands. This risk category spans NoSQL, OS command, LDAP, and SQL injection attacks, and also includes Cross-Site Scripting (XSS), in which attackers inject malicious client-side scripts, such as JavaScript, into web pages viewed by other users. This can result in the theft of sensitive information, such as login credentials, personal data, or session cookies. A WAF can help detect and block malicious code injection attempts by inspecting and filtering incoming requests, including reflected (non-persistent), stored (persistent), and document object module- (DOM-) based XSS, preventing them from reaching the application.

4. **Insecure Design:** This is a broad category representing different weaknesses, expressed as missing or ineffective security controls and architectural flaws. These flaws can occur when an application is designed to rely on processes that are inherently insecure, or when needed security controls to defend against specific attacks are not implemented. These risks can be lessened through increased use of threat modeling, secure design patterns, and reference architectures.

5. **Security Misconfigurations:** A lack of security hardening in web application frameworks, platforms, servers, or security controls can lead to unauthorized access, exposure of sensitive information, or other security vulnerabilities. Risks due to security misconfigurations can also result from improperly configured permissions on cloud services or the installation or enablement of unnecessary features such as unused ports, services, accounts, or privileges. Misconfiguration for both web apps and APIs is a significant risk because major cloud providers have varying default security postures and architecture is increasingly becoming decentralized and distributed across a multi-cloud fabric.

6. **Vulnerable and Outdated Components:** Using outdated, unpatched, or vulnerable components, such as libraries, frameworks, or plugins can expose applications to known security flaws, increasing the risk of exploitation. These risks can result from unsupported or out-of-date software, including the operating system (OS), web/application server, database management system (DBMS), applications, APIs, and all components, runtime environments, and libraries. These threats are particularly dangerous when organizations do not have timely, risk-based measures in place for fixing or upgrading a system's underlying

platform, frameworks, and dependencies, leaving the system open to days or weeks of unnecessary exposure to known risks. Complex software supply chains and automation via CI/CD pipelines increase the risk of introducing vulnerable software into the IT stack. A WAF can serve as a critical stopgap to guard against vulnerability exploitation.

7. **Identification & Authentication Failures:** Weaknesses in authentication, identity, and session management can allow attackers to compromise user accounts, passwords, session tokens, or to exploit insecure session handling. Failures in these areas can permit automated attacks such as credential stuffing. Password-related vulnerabilities are the most common source of these risks, as many people reuse passwords or use default, weak, or well-known passwords. Session management issues can also lead to authentication-related attacks, particularly if user sessions or authentication tokens aren't properly invalidated during logout or a period of inactivity. Attacks that bypass authentication controls are an increasing risk for both web apps and APIs, as detailed in the OWASP Top 10, API Security Top 10, and Automated Threats projects.

8. **Software and Data Integrity Failures:** These vulnerabilities result from application code and infrastructure that fail to protect against integrity violations of data and software. This can result when an application relies upon plugins, libraries, or modules from untrusted sources, repositories, and CDNs. It can also occur during software updates, sensitive data modifications, and CI/CD pipeline changes that are not validated. Attackers can potentially upload their own updates to be distributed and run on all installations. Insecure deserialization, where an application takes untrusted serialized data and consumes that data without ensuring that it is valid, is also a part of this risk category, allowing for attacks such as remote code execution (RCE) and privilege escalation.

9. **Security Logging and Monitoring Failures:** Inadequate logging and monitoring can hinder timely detection and response to security incidents, making it difficult to identify and mitigate attacks or unauthorized activities. This can mean that auditable events, such as logins, failed logins, and high-value transactions are not identified or logged, and that applications do not detect active attacks in real-time.

10. **Server-side Request Forgery (SSRF):** These vulnerabilities occur when an application does not validate or sanitize a URL input by a user before pulling data from a remote resource. Attackers can use these flaws to force applications

to access malicious web destinations even if protected by a firewall or other defense. These attacks can also result if the targeted resource has trust relationships with other systems, such as a cloud metadata service or backend APIs, allowing an attacker to make requests to those trusted services and extract sensitive information or perform unauthorized actions. To help mitigate SSRF, design systems for least privilege access and use a WAF to explicitly define the uniform resource identifier (URI) parameters in your security policy and allow/disallow hosts that can access them.

Authentication and Authorization

Authentication and authorization are crucial for securing systems and data. Authentication verifies user identity using methods like passwords, tokens, or multi-factor authentication, ensuring users are who they claim to be. Authorization, on the other hand, controls access to resources based on user roles or attributes, enforcing the principle of least privilege. Together, these mechanisms protect sensitive information by preventing unauthorized access or actions. Implementing strong credentials, secure session handling, role-based access control (RBAC), and periodic audits ensures reliability. Regular logging and monitoring help detect anomalies, while encryption safeguards credentials and permissions, building a robust foundation for modern security practices.

Authentication: Authentication is the process of verifying the identity of users, ensuring that they are who they claim to be before granting access to systems or resources. Robust authentication mechanisms are crucial for maintaining the security of applications and preventing unauthorized access. Common methods include passwords, biometric verification, tokens, and multi-factor authentication (MFA). Passwords should be strong, unique, and stored securely using hashing algorithms like bcrypt. Biometric authentication, such as fingerprint or facial recognition, provides a higher level of assurance by relying on physical traits that are difficult to replicate. Token-based authentication, including JSON Web Tokens (JWT) and OAuth, ensures secure access and session management by exchanging digitally signed credentials. MFA adds an extra layer of security by requiring users to verify their identity through multiple factors, such as something they know (password), something they have (a physical token or smartphone), or something they are (biometric data). Secure coding practices in authentication include protecting credentials during transmission using encryption (e.g., TLS) and implementing measures to prevent brute force attacks, such as account lockouts and rate-limiting. Additionally, applications should provide secure recovery mechanisms for forgotten credentials without exposing sensitive information. Regular audits of authentication mechanisms and staying updated with emerging technologies are essential to mitigate risks such as credential theft, phishing, or identity spoofing.

Some ways to authenticate one's identity are listed here:

1. Usernames or passwords can be used to establish one's identity, thus gaining access to the system.
2. OTPs are another way to get access to the system for a single transaction
3. Apps that generate security codes via the third party, thus enabling access for the user
4. Biometrics such as an eye scan or fingerprints can be used to gain access

Some systems may require successful verification via multiple factors.

Authorization: Authorization ensures that authenticated users have access only to the resources and actions they are permitted to use, based on their roles or privileges. It plays a critical role in enforcing the principle of least privilege, which limits access rights to the minimum necessary for users to perform their tasks. Role-based access control (RBAC) and attribute-based access control (ABAC) are common models for implementing authorization. RBAC assigns permissions based on predefined roles (e.g., administrator, user, guest), while ABAC determines access based on attributes such as user identity, time, or device type. Authorization policies must be strictly enforced at every layer of the application, from front-end interfaces to backend services, ensuring that users cannot bypass restrictions or elevate privileges. Secure APIs should validate access tokens and permissions for each request, and sensitive endpoints should require explicit authorization checks. Misconfigurations in authorization can lead to critical vulnerabilities, such as broken access control, where attackers exploit flaws to gain unauthorized privileges. Logging and monitoring access-related activities are vital for detecting anomalies and responding to security incidents. Implementing tools like identity and access management (IAM) systems helps simplify and centralize the management of user permissions. Regular review of access control policies and periodic audits are crucial to ensure that authorization mechanisms remain aligned with organizational policies and evolving security needs. By combining robust authentication with well-designed authorization strategies, organizations can build a secure foundation for protecting sensitive data and systems while fostering trust among users.

Authorization often follows authentication and is listed as various types which are as under:

1. Single-factor authentication uses only a username and password, thus enabling the user to access the system quite easily.

2. Two-level security asks for a two-step verification, thus authenticating the user to access the system. For this process, along with the username and password, some unique information including security questions, like first school name and such details, need to be answered. Or the user identity can also be verified with OTP.

3. An advanced level secure authorization calls for multiple level security from varied independent categories. These are also utilised more by financial institutions, banks or law enforcement agencies, thus eliminating the need for data exposure to a 3rd party or hackers.

Differences Between Authentication and Authorization: The differences between authentication and authorization are listed in table 4.1.

Table 4.1

S.No.	Aspect	Authentication	Authorization
1	Purpose	Confirm user identity in a system.	Determine what resources a user can access.
2	Software Component	Implemented in login modules (e.g., OAuth, JWT).	Managed in access control modules (e.g., RBAC, ACL).
3	Development Focus	Focuses on user identity verification logic.	Focuses on resource access control logic.
4	Timing in Request Flow	Happens at the beginning of user interaction.	Happens after identity is verified.
5	Technologies Used	LDAP, OAuth, SAML, JWT, biometric APIs.	Role-based Access Control (RBAC), ABAC, policy engines.
6	Data Handled	Handles credentials like username/password.	Handles access rules, roles, permissions.
7	Security Risk	Risk of identity theft or spoofing.	Risk of privilege escalation or unauthorized access.
8	Testing Focus	Unit and integration testing for login functionality.	Authorization tests to ensure correct access policies.

Data Privacy and Encryption

Data privacy and encryption are fundamental pillars of modern cybersecurity, ensuring that sensitive information is protected from unauthorized access and misuse. Data privacy refers to the proper handling, processing, storage, and usage of personal or confidential data, aligning with legal regulations such as GDPR, HIPAA, or CCPA. It emphasizes user consent, transparency, and control over personal information. Encryption, on the other hand, is a technical mechanism that transforms readable data into unreadable code using cryptographic algorithms, ensuring that even if data is intercepted, it cannot be understood without the decryption key. It is widely used in securing communication channels (like HTTPS), data at rest (on hard drives or databases), and data in transit (during transfer over networks). Encryption supports data privacy by providing a secure layer that protects data confidentiality and integrity. Together, these concepts help organizations maintain user trust, comply with data protection laws, and mitigate risks of data breaches and cyberattacks. As digital ecosystems expand, the integration of strong encryption protocols and robust privacy policies is essential for safeguarding critical information in both personal and enterprise environments.

Data Privacy: Data privacy refers to the design and implementation of systems that ensure the secure and ethical handling of users' personal data. With the increasing reliance on software applications to collect, store, and process information, engineers play a critical role in embedding privacy safeguards directly into the architecture of digital systems. This is often achieved through privacy-by-design a development approach where privacy considerations are integrated from the initial stages of system design rather than being added as an afterthought.

Key principles of data privacy in software engineering include data minimization (collecting only the necessary data), secure data storage, user consent management, data encryption, and access control mechanisms. Developers are expected to implement secure coding practices, protect against vulnerabilities like SQL injection or cross-site scripting (XSS), and use protocols like HTTPS to secure data in transit. Furthermore, software engineers must ensure compliance with data protection regulations such as GDPR, CCPA, or HIPAA, depending on the nature and location of the application.

Tools such as pseudonymization, anonymization, and audit logging are commonly used to protect user identities and track data usage. Engineers also need to consider user rights, such as the ability to access, correct, or delete personal data, which must be supported through application features.

Ultimately, data privacy in software engineering is not just a technical challenge but also an ethical responsibility. Engineers must balance functionality with privacy to build trustworthy systems that protect users in an increasingly connected digital environment. Key aspects of data privacy in software engineering are as:

1. **Privacy by Design:** Integrating privacy considerations from the initial stages of software development, rather than as an afterthought.

2. **Data Minimization:** Collecting only the necessary data to perform a specific function and minimizing data retention.

3. **Secure Data Storage and Transmission:** Using encryption, tokenization, and other security measures to protect data at rest and in transit.

4. **Access Controls:** Limiting who can access specific data based on their roles and responsibilities.

5. **Data Subject Rights:** Providing users with the ability to access, rectify, and erase their data, as well as opt-out of certain data collection practices.

6. **Transparency and Consent:** Being open about how data is collected, used, and shared, and obtaining explicit consent from users before collecting or using their data.

7. **Data Breach Prevention and Response:** Having robust procedures in place to prevent data breaches and quickly respond to any incidents that do occur.

8. **Compliance with Regulations:** Adhering to relevant data privacy laws and regulations, such as GDPR, CCPA, and others.

9. **Data Privacy Engineering:** A specialized discipline within software engineering focused on building privacy-preserving systems and features.

Integrating Data Privacy into the Software Development Lifecycle: Incorporating data privacy into the software development lifecycle (SDLC) involves several key practices:

1. **Privacy Impact Assessments (PIAs)**: Conducting PIAs during the planning phase helps identify potential privacy risks and implement mitigation strategies.

2. **Secure Coding Practices**: Developers should follow secure coding guidelines to prevent vulnerabilities that could compromise data privacy.

3. **Regular Audits and Monitoring**: Continuous monitoring and periodic audits ensure that privacy measures remain effective and compliant with evolving regulations.

4. **User Education and Control**: Providing users with tools to manage their privacy settings and educating them about their rights enhances transparency and trust.

Challenges in Data Privacy: Data privacy is a critical concern in software engineering, especially as organizations collect, store, and process vast amounts of personal data. While there are established frameworks and best practices to help developers secure this data, several challenges persist in maintaining data privacy within software systems. These challenges arise due to the increasing complexity of modern technologies, the evolving regulatory landscape, and the diverse threats to data security. Below are some of the most significant challenges faced by software engineers in the realm of data privacy:

1. **Compliance with Evolving Regulations:** Data protection laws, such as the General Data Protection Regulation (GDPR) in the EU and the California Consumer Privacy Act (CCPA) in the U.S., are frequently updated. Each region may have different rules regarding data collection, usage, and sharing. For software developers, staying compliant with these laws requires continuous monitoring of regulatory changes and adapting systems to meet these evolving requirements. Ensuring that software complies with global regulations, especially for international companies, can be a complex task.

2. **Data Breaches and Cybersecurity Threats:** One of the most pressing concerns for software engineers is preventing data breaches. As cyberattacks grow more sophisticated, software applications are increasingly targeted. Hackers use various methods, such as SQL injection, phishing attacks, or ransomware, to access personal data. If a breach occurs, it can lead to identity theft, financial losses, and damage to the reputation of the organization. Engineers must design software systems with robust security measures, such as encryption, multi-factor authentication (MFA), and regular vulnerability assessments, to mitigate this risk.

3. **Third-Party Integrations and Supply Chain Risks:** Modern software systems often rely on third-party libraries, APIs, and services. While these integrations provide enhanced functionality, they also introduce potential data privacy risks. If third-party services do not follow the same stringent data privacy practices, they may expose user data to unauthorized parties. For instance, a third-party service provider might not adequately encrypt or secure data or could use the data for purposes that contradict user consent. Ensuring that third-party vendors are compliant with data privacy standards requires thorough vetting and ongoing monitoring.

4. **Data Minimization:** One of the fundamental principles of data privacy is data minimization only collecting and processing the data necessary for a given purpose. However, software engineers often face pressure to gather more data than needed, either to enhance features, personalize user experiences, or for analytics purposes. The challenge lies in balancing data utility with privacy concerns. Collecting excessive or unnecessary data increases the risk of misuse and makes compliance with privacy regulations more difficult. Developers need to carefully assess the data requirements of their systems and adhere to the principle of collecting only what is absolutely necessary.

5. **User Consent Management:** Obtaining and managing user consent is another significant challenge in software engineering. In many jurisdictions, users must explicitly agree to the collection, use, and sharing of their personal data. However, ensuring that users fully understand what they are consenting to can be difficult, especially when privacy policies are long and complex. Software engineers must design clear, intuitive consent mechanisms that allow users to make informed decisions. This includes opt-in options, the ability to easily withdraw consent, and ensuring that consent is recorded and auditable.

6. **Data Storage and Retention:** How and where personal data is stored is a crucial aspect of data privacy. Data needs to be securely stored and retained only for as long as necessary to fulfill its intended purpose. However, in some cases, organizations may store personal data indefinitely for analytics or other business purposes. This creates challenges for software engineers in determining the proper data retention policies and ensuring that data is securely deleted when no longer needed. Additionally, storing data in multiple locations, such as on cloud servers, can complicate the management and enforcement of privacy standards across systems.

7. **Anonymization and Pseudonymization:** Techniques like anonymization and pseudonymization are essential for protecting user privacy. Anonymization involves removing any identifying information from data, making it impossible to trace it back to the individual. Pseudonymization, on the other hand, replaces identifiable information with pseudonyms, but the data can still be re-identified under certain conditions. While these methods can help protect privacy, they come with their own challenges. Achieving true anonymization, especially in complex datasets, is difficult, and improper implementation of pseudonymization can still leave data vulnerable to re-identification.

8. **Data Localization:** Data localization refers to the practice of storing and processing data within the borders of specific countries or regions to comply with local laws and regulations. For software engineers working on applications with global users, ensuring compliance with data localization requirements can be challenging. It may require deploying servers in multiple geographic locations or adhering to different storage policies based on the user's region. This can increase infrastructure costs and complexity, especially when trying to meet the data privacy standards of multiple countries simultaneously.

9. **Balancing Usability and Privacy:** Developers often face the challenge of balancing usability with privacy. Many software features that enhance user experience, such as personalized recommendations or targeted advertising, require the collection of vast amounts of personal data. However, from a privacy perspective, this could pose a risk if not implemented correctly. Software engineers must find ways to design applications that respect user privacy while still offering useful and engaging features. This often involves implementing opt-out options, anonymizing data, and giving users control over what data they share.

10. **Emerging Technologies and Data Privacy:** Emerging technologies such as artificial intelligence (AI), machine learning (ML), and big data analytics often require processing large datasets, including personal information. While these technologies can deliver significant benefits, they also present new challenges in terms of data privacy. AI systems, for example, may unintentionally reveal sensitive information through their algorithms or predictions. Additionally, the more data these systems process, the more difficult it becomes to ensure compliance with privacy regulations. Engineers must account for these risks when designing and implementing AI-driven systems, ensuring that user data is processed responsibly.

Encryption: Encryption is the process of converting readable information (plaintext) into an unreadable format (ciphertext) to protect it from unauthorized access. It is a method of preserving data confidentiality by transforming it into ciphertext, which can only be decoded using a unique decryption key produced at the time of the encryption or before it. The conversion of plaintext into ciphertext is known as encryption. By using encryption keys and mathematical algorithms, the data is scrambled so that anyone intercepting it without the proper key cannot understand the contents.

When the intended recipient receives the encrypted data, they use the matching decryption key to return it to its original, readable form. This approach ensures that sensitive information such as personal details, financial data, or confidential communications remains secure as it travels over networks or is stored on devices. Key objective of encryption data are as follows:

1. **Confidentiality:** Encryption ensures that only authorized parties can get access to data and recognize the information.

2. **Data Integrity:** Encryption can also provide data integrity by making sure that the encrypted data remains unchanged during transmission. Any unauthorized changes to the encrypted information will render it undecipherable or will fail integrity checks.

3. **Authentication:** Encryption may be used as part of authentication mechanisms to verify the identification of the communication party.

4. **Non-Repudiation:** Through encryption, events can make sure that they cannot deny their involvement in growing or sending a selected piece of data.

Types of Data Encryption: There are multiple encryption techniques, each of which have been developed with various security requirements in mind, the types are as follows:

1. Symmetric Key Encryption: There are a few strategies used in cryptography algorithms. For encryption and decryption processes, some algorithms employ a unique key. In such operations, the unique key must be secured since the system or person who knows the key has complete authentication to decode the message for reading. This approach is known as "symmetric encryption" in the field of network encryption.

Symmetric Key Encryption is a cryptographic technique where the same key is used for both the encryption and decryption processes. It involves converting plaintext (readable data) into ciphertext (unreadable data) using a shared secret key and a specific encryption algorithm. The main goal of symmetric key encryption is to ensure that only authorized parties with the secret key can access the original data.

The process of symmetric encryption works as follows: the sender encrypts the data using a secret key, and the receiver decrypts it with the same key. This makes symmetric encryption faster and more efficient than asymmetric encryption, especially when handling large amounts of data. Common symmetric encryption algorithms include AES (Advanced Encryption Standard), DES (Data Encryption Standard), and Blowfish. AES is widely used due to its strong security and performance efficiency. However, the major challenge with symmetric encryption is the secure exchange and management of the key. If an unauthorized party intercepts the key, they can decrypt the data. To address this, asymmetric encryption is often used for secure key exchange. Overall, symmetric key encryption is essential in modern cybersecurity, protecting data in transit (e.g., SSL/TLS encryption) and data at rest (e.g., file and disk encryption).

Working on Symmetric Encryption: These operations are performed to share the message securely over the network using the symmetric encryption technique.

- **Key Generation:** This is the first step in the symmetric encryption technique in which the private key needs to be chosen and must be securely communicated/ transferred over the network for the further use.

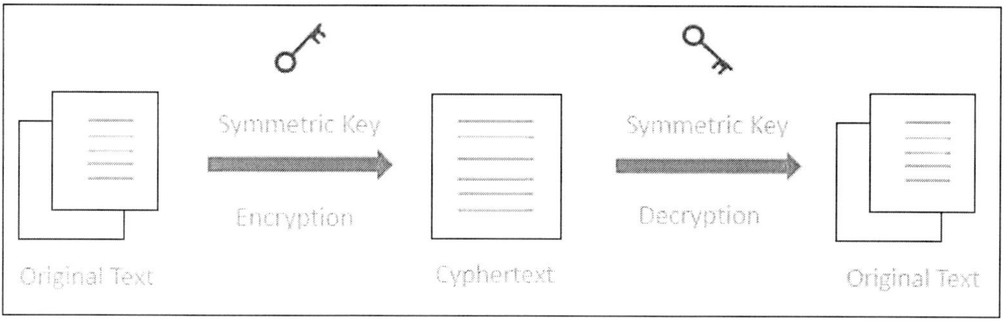

Fig.4.9

- **Encryption:** In this step, the plaintext (this is the original message to be sent over the network) is converted to some bogus, unintelligible text called the ciphertext using the shared secret key and some algorithm.

- **Transfer of CipherText:** In this step the ciphertext is transferred over the network, since we have encrypted the original message even if this ciphertext is intercepted it will be unintelligible to the interceptor unless and until our shared secret key and algorithm is also compromised.

- **Decryption:** This is the last step where the receiver uses the reverse encryption algorithm and the shared secret key to convert the ciphertext back to the plaintext this is called decryption.

2. Asymmetric Key Encryption: Some cryptography methods employ one key for data encryption and another key for data decryption. As a result, anyone who has access to such a public communication will be unable to decode or read it. This type of cryptography, known as "public-key" encryption, is used in the majority of internet security protocols. The term "asymmetric encryption" is used to describe this type of encryption.

In asymmetric encryption, the sender uses the recipient's public key to encrypt the data. The recipient then uses their private key to decrypt the data. This approach allows for secure communication between two parties without the need for both parties to have the same secret key. Asymmetric encryption has several advantages over symmetric encryption, which uses the same key for both encryption and decryption. One of the main advantages is that it eliminates the need to exchange secret keys, which can be a challenging process, especially when communicating with multiple parties. Additionally, asymmetric encryption allows for the creation of digital signatures, which can be used to verify the authenticity of data. Asymmetric encryption is commonly used in various applications, including secure online communication, digital signatures, and secure data transfer. Examples of asymmetric encryption algorithms include RSA, Diffie-Hellman, and Elliptic Curve Cryptography (ECC).

Asymmetric encryption, commonly known as public-key cryptography, employs two distinct keys for encryption and decoding. The private key is a separate key from the public key that is kept private by the owner of the public key while the public key is made available to everyone. Anyone can encrypt a message using the public key, but only the holder of the private key can unlock it. With no chance of the communication being intercepted and read by a third party, anyone can send a secure message to the public key's owner. Asymmetric encryption is frequently used for secure Internet communication, including email encryption, e-commerce, and online banking. Digital signatures, which are used to confirm the legitimacy of digital documents and messages, are another application for it.

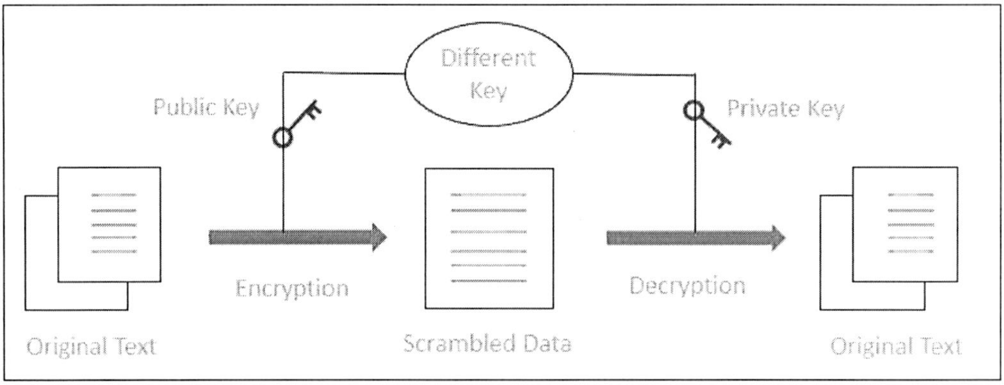

Fig.4.10

Differences Between Symmetric and Asymmetric Encryption: The differences between symmetric and asymmetric are listed in table 4.2.

Table 4.2

S.No.	Feature	Symmetric Encryption	Asymmetric Encryption
1	Key Type	Uses a single key for both encryption and decryption.	Uses two keys i.e., a public key for encryption and a private key for decryption.
2	Key Distribution	Key must be securely shared between sender and receiver.	Public key can be shared openly; private key remains confidential.
3	Speed	Generally faster as it uses simpler algorithms.	Slower due to more complex mathematical operations.
4	Security	Security relies on keeping the shared key secret.	Security relies on the complexity of public-private key pairs.
5	Use Case	Typically used for encrypting large amounts of data (e.g., file encryption).	Often used for securing communication channels (e.g., SSL/TLS, email encryption).
6	Example Algorithms	AES, DES, RC4, Blowfish.	RSA, ECC (Elliptic Curve Cryptography), DSA.
7	Performance Impact	Minimal impact on system performance due to its efficiency.	Higher system performance impact due to computational complexity.
8	Scalability	Less scalable, as each pair of users requires a unique key.	More scalable, as public keys can be shared with many users without compromising security.

******

10

Performance Optimization and Scalability

Performance optimization and scalability are critical aspects of system design that ensure efficiency and growth. Performance optimization involves fine-tuning systems to maximize speed, responsiveness, and resource utilization. Techniques include reducing computational complexity, optimizing algorithms, minimizing memory usage, and improving data processing throughput. On the other hand, scalability refers to a system's ability to handle increased loads or growth in demand without sacrificing performance. This can be achieved through vertical scaling (upgrading hardware) or horizontal scaling (distributing the load across multiple servers or resources). Both concepts are interrelated: optimized performance helps systems scale more effectively by ensuring that each resource is used efficiently, while scalability ensures that systems can handle higher loads as they grow. A well-optimized and scalable system can adapt to changing demands and provide a seamless user experience even under high stress or large-scale usage.

Performance Optimization: Performance optimization refers to the process of improving the efficiency and responsiveness of software applications, ensuring they use minimal resources (CPU, memory, disk, network bandwidth) while delivering fast and reliable results. The goal is to improve both the speed and scalability of the software without compromising functionality. Key strategies for performance optimization in software engineering include:

1. **Profiling and Benchmarking**: Identifying performance bottlenecks using profiling tools and benchmarks to measure which parts of the code consume the most resources.

2. **Code Refactoring**: Refactoring inefficient or redundant code to make it more efficient, which could involve simplifying logic, removing unnecessary operations, or optimizing data structures.

3. **Algorithm Optimization**: Improving the efficiency of algorithms, reducing time and space complexity. For example, replacing an O(n^2) algorithm with an O(n log n) one can dramatically improve performance in larger datasets.

4. **Memory Management**: Efficiently managing memory allocation and garbage collection, avoiding memory leaks, and using memory efficiently (e.g., using stack memory instead of heap memory where possible).

5. **Concurrency and Parallelism**: Leveraging multi-core processors by making the application capable of running multiple tasks in parallel, using threads, asynchronous programming, or distributed computing to split workloads.

6. **Database Optimization**: Writing efficient queries, indexing frequently queried fields, and minimizing database round trips. Also, using connection pooling to reduce the overhead of establishing database connections.

7. **Caching**: Storing frequently used data in memory (e.g., using Redis, Memcached) to avoid redundant calculations or repetitive database lookups.

8. **Load Balancing and Distributed Systems**: In larger applications, using load balancing to distribute workloads across multiple servers can ensure that no single server is overwhelmed and that the system can scale to handle increasing user demands.

9. **Reducing I/O Operations**: Minimizing file or network input/output operations by batching requests or utilizing faster data transfer protocols can reduce latency and improve performance.

10. **Code Optimization for Specific Platforms**: Tailoring code to the hardware architecture or specific environment, ensuring that it runs optimally across different devices or servers.

Common Areas of Optimization in Software Engineering: Performance optimization is a vital part of software engineering aimed at improving the efficiency, speed, and scalability of applications. Various system components contribute to performance, and optimization focuses on refining these key areas to ensure the software runs smoothly under different loads and conditions.

1. **Algorithm and Code Optimization:** At the core of any application lies its logic and structure. Algorithmic efficiency plays a significant role in performance. A poorly chosen algorithm can make even powerful systems sluggish. For example, using a bubble sort ($O(n^2)$) on a large dataset instead of a more efficient quicksort ($O(n \log n)$) can lead to performance bottlenecks. Optimizing code also includes eliminating redundant operations, reducing function calls in loops, and selecting efficient data structures. Clean, well-structured code not only runs faster but is easier to maintain and debug.

2. **Memory Optimization:** Efficient memory management is crucial, especially in high-performance or resource-constrained systems. Poor memory use can lead to increased garbage collection time, memory leaks, or application crashes. Developers should minimize memory allocations in critical paths and reuse objects where possible. In languages like C or C++, manual memory management must be handled carefully to avoid fragmentation and leaks. In managed languages, understanding garbage collection behavior can significantly help in optimizing memory usage.

3. **I/O Optimization:** Input/output operations including file access, disk writes, and network communications are often much slower than in-memory operations. To optimize I/O, developers can use buffering, batch operations, and caching. For example, instead of writing to a file one line at a time, writing data in chunks reduces overhead. Asynchronous I/O is also useful for improving responsiveness in applications that perform heavy data transfer or rely on user input.

4. **Database Optimization:** Databases are frequently the performance bottleneck in modern applications. Efficient database interaction involves writing optimized SQL queries, using proper indexing, and choosing the right database schema design (normalized or denormalized) based on the use case. Caching frequently accessed data and avoiding expensive operations like full table scans can significantly enhance application speed. Tools like query analysers help in identifying slow queries and indexing opportunities.

5. **Concurrency and Parallelism:** Utilizing multi-core processors through parallelism is essential for scaling modern applications. Multithreading, asynchronous programming, and distributed processing allow applications to

handle more tasks simultaneously, improving throughput. However, concurrency introduces complexity, including race conditions and deadlocks. Safe handling through thread synchronization mechanisms and careful resource sharing is key to effective optimization in this area.

6. **Frontend Optimization:** In web and mobile applications, the client-side experience is crucial. Frontend optimization involves reducing page load times by minifying CSS and JavaScript files, using lazy loading for images, and minimizing HTTP requests. Tools like Google Lighthouse and Chrome DevTools help analyze frontend performance and suggest improvements.

Scalability: Scalability in software engineering refers to a system's ability to handle increased load whether in terms of users, data volume, or transaction rates without sacrificing performance, reliability, or usability. A scalable system can grow efficiently in capacity and performance as demand increases, making scalability a fundamental aspect of software design for modern, high-traffic applications. There are 2 types of scalabilities which are as under:

1. **Vertical Scalability (Scaling Up):** Vertical scaling involves enhancing the capacity of a single machine by adding more CPU, RAM, or storage. This is often simpler but has physical and economic limits. For example, upgrading a server from 16 GB to 64 GB of RAM can improve performance, but only up to the hardware's maximum capacity.

   Vertical scalability, also known as scaling up, refers to enhancing the capacity of a single system or server to handle increased workload by upgrading its hardware resources—such as adding more CPU power, increasing RAM, or using faster storage. This approach is often the first step in improving performance because it's straightforward to implement: the application remains on the same machine, so there's no need to modify the software architecture or manage multiple nodes. Vertical scaling is commonly used in databases and monolithic applications where distributing tasks across multiple machines would be complex or unnecessary. However, while vertical scalability can deliver significant performance boosts in the short term, it has inherent limitations. There's only so much hardware that can be added to a single machine before physical or cost boundaries are reached. Additionally, scaling up typically requires downtime to perform hardware upgrades, which can disrupt service availability. It may also lead to a single point of failure, as the entire system depends on one machine. Despite these drawbacks, vertical scalability remains useful in scenarios where simplicity is favored, or when the application's demands do not yet justify the complexity of horizontal scaling. In modern cloud environments, vertical scaling can also be automated to a degree, allowing for dynamic resource allocation. Overall, while not as flexible or fault-tolerant as horizontal scalability, vertical scaling is a practical and often cost-effective solution for moderate performance improvements, especially in the early stages of application growth or when workloads are predictable and manageable.

2. **Horizontal Scalability (Scaling Out):** Horizontal scaling means adding more machines (nodes) to a system. This approach is more flexible and cost-effective at scale, especially in distributed systems and cloud environments. Web applications that use load balancers to distribute traffic across multiple servers are a common example of horizontal scalability.

   Horizontal scalability, also known as scaling out, refers to the process of increasing a system's capacity by adding more machines or servers to work in parallel, rather than upgrading a single machine's hardware. This approach is essential in distributed systems, cloud-native applications, and high-traffic platforms, where workloads can be distributed across multiple nodes to improve performance, availability, and fault tolerance. Unlike vertical scaling, horizontal scalability does not have the same physical hardware limitations, making it more suitable for large-scale, dynamic environments. A common example is a web application that uses a load balancer to route incoming requests across several web servers, ensuring no single server becomes a bottleneck. Horizontal scaling allows organizations to respond more flexibly to spikes in traffic by automatically adding or removing instances as needed, especially in cloud platforms like AWS, Azure, or Google Cloud. It also enhances system reliability, since the failure of one node doesn't bring down the entire application. However, horizontal scalability introduces added complexity in terms of architecture, deployment, and data management. Applications must be designed to be stateless or use shared storage, and maintaining data consistency across multiple instances becomes more challenging, especially for databases. Despite these challenges, horizontal scaling is crucial for systems requiring high availability, global distribution, and real-time responsiveness. It provides long-term growth potential and supports continuous service delivery under variable load conditions, making it a foundational strategy in modern software engineering practices.

Importance of Scalability in Software Engineering: Scalability is one of the most critical non-functional requirements in software engineering. It determines whether an application or system can handle increasing loads, users, and data without compromising performance, reliability, or cost-efficiency. As technology adoption grows and systems are expected to support dynamic usage patterns, scalability becomes essential for long-term sustainability and success.

1. **Ensures System Performance Under Load:** Scalable systems maintain high performance even as traffic grows. This is especially important for applications with variable or unpredictable demand, such as e-commerce platforms during peak shopping seasons or social media apps during viral events.
2. **Supports Business Growth:** As a business expands, its software systems must support more users, larger datasets, and increased transactions. Scalable software allows the business to grow without needing a complete system overhaul.
3. **Improves Cost Efficiency:** Properly scaled systems use resources more effectively. Horizontal scaling (adding more machines) and cloud auto-scaling enable applications to allocate computing power dynamically, reducing waste and operating costs.
4. **Enhances User Experience:** Slow response times or downtime during traffic surges frustrate users and can lead to lost customers. Scalability ensures a consistent, smooth user experience regardless of load.
5. **Facilitates High Availability and Reliability:** Scalable systems are often built with redundancy and fault tolerance in mind. Distributing workloads across multiple nodes reduces the risk of single points of failure, improving system uptime.
6. **Enables Global Reach:** Modern applications often serve users across different regions. Scalable architectures, supported by content delivery networks (CDNs) and distributed systems, allow applications to perform well globally.
7. **Supports Future-proofing:** Scalability ensures that systems can evolve with technological advancements and user demands without needing complete rewrites. It lays the foundation for continuous improvement and innovation.

Performance Bottlenecks and Profiling

Performance bottlenecks refer to parts of a system that limit its overall efficiency or speed, causing delays or sluggishness in performance. These bottlenecks can occur in various system layers, including the CPU, memory, disk I/O, network, or database. Identifying these bottlenecks is crucial to optimizing system performance, and this is where profiling comes into play. Profiling is the process of analyzing the execution of an application to pinpoint performance issues. It involves measuring various metrics such as CPU usage, memory consumption, response time, and throughput. Tools like gprof, JProfiler, or VisualVM can provide insights into which functions, methods, or queries consume excessive resources. Once bottlenecks are identified, developers can optimize the problematic areas whether by improving algorithms, minimizing database queries, optimizing memory management, or utilizing caching. Profiling and resolving performance bottlenecks are essential for ensuring applications remain responsive and scalable as they grow.

Performance Bottlenecks: Performance bottlenecks refer to specific parts of a system that limit its overall speed, efficiency, or throughput, causing delays or reduced responsiveness. Bottlenecks can appear in various components of a software system, from the hardware level to the application logic. Identifying and addressing these bottlenecks is critical to improving system performance, ensuring smooth user experiences, and scaling applications to meet growing demands.

Types of Performance Bottlenecks

1. **CPU Bottlenecks CPU Bottlenecks:** This occur when the processor is unable to handle the volume of instructions being processed. This may happen if the system is executing complex algorithms, performing intensive calculations, or handling too many concurrent processes. Such issues can result in high CPU utilization, leading to slowdowns. Common solutions include optimizing algorithms to reduce computational complexity or offloading heavy computations to more powerful servers or parallelizing tasks across multiple cores or machines.

2. **Memory Bottlenecks Memory bottlenecks:** This occur when there isn't enough available RAM to handle the active processes and data being used by the system. This can cause applications to slow down significantly, as the system resorts to swapping data between memory and disk storage, which is much slower. These issues are often found in applications dealing with large datasets or performing memory-intensive operations. Memory optimizations, such as reducing memory allocations, using efficient data structures, and optimizing garbage collection in languages like Java, can mitigate memory-related bottlenecks.

3. **Disk I/O Bottlenecks Disk I/O Bottlenecks:** This happen when the system is unable to read from or write to storage devices fast enough. This issue is

especially common in applications that rely heavily on database interactions, file systems, or large-scale data storage. Disk I/O bottlenecks can slow down performance significantly, particularly when frequent access to large files or databases is involved. Solutions include optimizing disk access patterns, using faster storage devices like SSDs instead of HDDs, or implementing caching mechanisms to reduce disk read/write frequency.

4. **Network Bottlenecks Network Bottlenecks:** This arise when the bandwidth or latency of the network connection becomes insufficient to handle the volume of data being transferred. In distributed systems or web applications, slow or unreliable network connections can cause delays, especially when data is being transferred between servers, databases, or clients. Network-related bottlenecks can be alleviated by reducing the volume of data being transferred (e.g., by using data compression), optimizing communication protocols, or deploying content delivery networks (CDNs) to speed up access to data from geographically distant users.

5. **Database Bottlenecks:** Database bottlenecks are one of the most common types of performance issues, particularly in applications with large amounts of data and frequent queries. Slow query execution, lack of proper indexing, and poor database design can lead to delays in data retrieval or storage. Optimizing database performance often involves indexing frequently queried columns, optimizing SQL queries, normalizing or denormalizing database tables appropriately, and using caching mechanisms to store frequently accessed data temporarily.

6. **Application Logic Bottlenecks:** Application logic bottlenecks are related to the design and implementation of the software itself. Inefficient algorithms, redundant computations, or poorly structured code can cause significant slowdowns. Profiling and optimizing application code, improving algorithm efficiency, reducing unnecessary computations, and eliminating redundant operations can address these bottlenecks.

Tips and Best Practices: There are valuable tips and best practices for performance bottleneck:

1. **Set Clear Performance Goals:** Define clear performance goals, such as response times, throughput, and error rates. Clear goals provide direction and help prioritize your efforts.

2. **Load Testing and Stress Testing:** Regularly perform load testing and stress testing to understand how your system behaves under various levels of load. This helps identify breaking points and weak areas.

3. **Code Reviews:** Use profiling tools to analyze code execution and identify resource-intensive sections. Regular code reviews with a focus can uncover potential bottlenecks.

4. **Optimize Database Access:** Database performance is critical. Optimize queries, use indexes effectively, and consider database caching strategies to reduce database load.

5. **Efficient Resource Usage:** Ensure efficient use of resources like memory, CPU, and network. Resource leaks or inefficient algorithms can lead to bottlenecks.

6. **Implement Browser Caching:** Leverage browser caching by setting appropriate cache headers. This reduces the need for repeated requests for static assets.

7. **Keep Dependencies Up to Date:** Regularly update libraries and dependencies to leverage testing improvements and security updates.

8. **Plan for Peaks and Surges:** Design your infrastructure to handle sudden traffic spikes, whether due to promotions, events, or viral content.

9. **Document and Share Learnings:** Document bottlenecks you've identified and how you addressed them. Share these learnings with your team to build a collective understanding.

10. **Continuous Performance Testing:** Integrate performance testing into your continuous integration/continuous deployment (CI/CD) pipeline. This ensures that performance regressions are caught early.

Profiling: Profiling in software engineering refers to the process of analyzing a program's runtime behavior in order to identify performance bottlenecks, inefficiencies, and areas for improvement. Profiling provides detailed insights into how an application uses system resources such as CPU, memory, disk I/O, and network bandwidth. This analysis helps developers optimize the application's performance by pinpointing resource-heavy functions, inefficient algorithms, or other performance issues that may not be evident from just reading the code. Profiling is an essential practice in software engineering, especially for applications expected to scale or handle large user loads. Profiling can be divided into various categories based on the resource being monitored or the type of information being collected. The key types of profiling include:

1. **CPU Profiling:** CPU profiling tracks how much CPU time is consumed by different functions or code paths in a program. It helps developers understand which parts of the code are computationally expensive or inefficient. CPU profiling is especially useful when diagnosing performance issues like high latency, slow computations, or poor responsiveness. Profiling tools often provide information about function call counts and execution times, helping identify hotspots in the application.

2. **Memory Profiling:** Memory profiling focuses on how an application uses memory, including heap and stack memory allocations. It tracks memory consumption, potential memory leaks, and objects that consume an excessive amount of memory. Memory profiling helps developers optimize memory usage, prevent memory overflows, and manage garbage collection more effectively. This type of profiling is critical in applications dealing with large datasets or those running on resource-constrained environments like mobile devices.

3. **I/O Profiling:** I/O profiling involves tracking the program's interactions with the disk, database, or network. It measures the time spent on reading and writing data, as well as network latency in the case of distributed applications. I/O bottlenecks can significantly slow down an application, especially in systems dealing with large files or database queries. Profiling helps identify excessive disk reads, inefficient database queries, or network congestion.

4. **Database Profiling:** Database profiling focuses on monitoring database performance, such as query execution time, the number of queries, and their complexity. Poorly optimized SQL queries or inefficient database structures can severely affect application performance. By profiling database interactions, developers can optimize queries, add proper indexes, and redesign schemas to improve performance.

Working of Profiling: Profiling typically works by collecting performance data during the execution of the application. This can be done in two main ways:

1. **Instrumentation** In this approach, additional code is inserted into the application to record performance metrics. The profiling tool injects tracking calls into functions or methods to record how long they take to execute, how often they are called, and what resources they consume. While this method provides

accurate and detailed data, it can introduce some performance overhead, making the profiling results slightly less representative of real-world performance.

2. **Sampling** Sampling involves periodically checking the state of the application while it runs. Instead of instrumenting every function, sampling tools take snapshots of the program's state at fixed intervals (e.g., every few milliseconds). This allows the profiler to determine where the program spends the most time without significantly impacting performance. Sampling is less intrusive and can be used in production environments, though it might provide less granular data than instrumentation.

Popular Profiling Tools: There are various profiling tools available depending on the programming language and the type of profiling required:

1. **gprof**: A GNU profiler that provides CPU profiling for C/C++ programs.
2. **JProfiler** and **VisualVM**: Popular tools for profiling Java applications, offering insights into memory, CPU, and thread usage.
3. **Valgrind**: A tool for memory profiling, including memory leak detection, for C/C++ applications.
4. **Xdebug**: A debugging and profiling tool for PHP applications, providing detailed call graphs and execution time analysis.
5. **New Relic** and **AppDynamics**: APM (Application Performance Management) tools that offer comprehensive profiling for web applications, including real-time monitoring of CPU, memory, database queries, and I/O.

Benefits of Profiling

1. **Identifying Performance Bottlenecks**: Profiling helps developers identify the sections of code that consume disproportionate amounts of resources, such as CPU time or memory. These bottlenecks can then be optimized for better performance.
2. **Optimizing Resource Usage**: By understanding how an application uses system resources, developers can optimize memory management, reduce CPU consumption, and avoid unnecessary I/O operations.
3. **Improving Scalability**: Profiling ensures that applications scale efficiently under increased load by identifying and addressing resource-heavy operations early in the development process.

4. **Enhancing Code Quality**: Profiling can highlight inefficient algorithms, redundant operations, and other coding issues that affect performance. Addressing these issues improves the overall quality of the code.

5. **Guiding System Design**: Profiling results can inform decisions about system architecture. For example, if profiling reveals that an application's database queries are a bottleneck, it may prompt the adoption of database sharding, caching, or the use of a more suitable database system.

Challenges in Profiling

While profiling is incredibly valuable, it also comes with challenges. Intrusiveness is one such issue; the act of profiling itself can introduce performance overhead, making it hard to capture an accurate picture of how the application performs in a production-like environment. Additionally, profiling may not always catch problems that occur under extreme loads or edge cases, so it's important to complement profiling with load testing and other performance testing techniques. Furthermore, interpreting profiling data requires expertise, as it's easy to misinterpret metrics or focus on the wrong areas.

Profiling is an essential tool in software engineering for identifying and resolving performance issues. By providing insights into how a program utilizes system resources, profiling enables developers to optimize their applications for better performance, reduced resource consumption, and improved scalability. Whether it's CPU, memory, I/O, or database profiling, these tools allow developers to fine-tune their code and build more efficient and reliable systems. Despite its challenges, the value of profiling in delivering high-performance software cannot be overstated, especially for applications that need to handle large-scale user demands or data processing tasks.

Load Balancing and Caching Strategies

Load Balancing and Caching are essential strategies in software engineering for optimizing performance, scalability, and reliability.

Load balancing involves distributing incoming network traffic across multiple servers or resources to ensure no single server becomes overwhelmed, thereby improving responsiveness and uptime. It helps handle high volumes of requests, prevents server overload, and ensures high availability. Techniques like Round Robin, Least Connections, and IP Hashing are commonly used for load distribution.

Caching is the process of storing frequently accessed data in a fast-access storage layer, such as memory, to reduce the load on backend systems and improve data retrieval times. Caching can be implemented at various levels, including client-side, server-side, and database caching. Popular tools for caching include Redis and Memcached. Caching strategies like Time-to-Live (TTL), Write-through, and Lazy Loading help maintain data consistency and ensure that users experience minimal delays.

Together, load balancing and caching ensure efficient resource utilization and improve the overall performance of systems under high traffic conditions.

Load Balancing: Load balancing is a critical technique in software engineering used to distribute incoming network traffic or workloads across multiple servers, services, or resources to ensure efficient resource utilization, prevent server overloads, and maintain high availability. In large-scale systems and applications, where millions of user's access services concurrently, load balancing plays a vital role in improving performance, scalability, and fault tolerance. By ensuring that traffic is evenly distributed, it helps maintain optimal response times and prevent any single resource from becoming a bottleneck. As applications grow and handle more traffic, relying on a single server can quickly become inefficient or unreliable. A single server has a finite capacity, and as the load increases—whether from more users, more data requests, or more complex transactions—it can become overwhelmed, leading to slow response times, crashes, or system downtime. Load balancing solves this problem by distributing the workload across multiple servers, ensuring no individual server bears the full brunt of the traffic. Additionally, load balancing helps ensure high availability by rerouting traffic to healthy servers in case one or more servers fail. Furthermore, load balancing allows horizontal scaling, where organizations can add more servers to the system without requiring major changes to the architecture, offering an efficient way to scale as demand increases. This flexibility is especially crucial for cloud environments, where resource allocation can be automated to match fluctuating workloads.

Types of Load Balancing: There are several types of load balancing techniques, each suited to different use cases and deployment scenarios. Broadly, these techniques can be classified into hardware load balancing and software load balancing, with both utilizing algorithms to decide how traffic should be routed.

1. **DNS Load Balancing:** DNS load balancing is a simple form of load balancing where multiple IP addresses are associated with a single domain name in the DNS records. When a client makes a request to the domain, the DNS server responds with one of the available IP addresses based on the load balancing algorithm. This method is inexpensive and simple but doesn't provide advanced features like health checks or dynamic traffic distribution.

2. **Layer 4 Load Balancing (Transport Layer):** Layer 4 load balancing works at the **transport layer (Layer 4)** of the OSI model. It uses IP addresses and TCP/UDP protocols to forward client requests to the appropriate backend servers. The load balancer is unaware of the application-level data being transmitted. It simply distributes the traffic based on TCP/IP information, such as the client's IP address, port number, and the server's health status. Common algorithms used in Layer 4 load balancing include:

    - **Round Robin**: Distributes requests sequentially to each server.
    - **Least Connections**: Directs traffic to the server with the fewest active connections, ensuring no server becomes overloaded.
    - **IP Hashing**: Uses the client's IP address to determine which server will handle the request.

3. **Layer 7 Load Balancing (Application Layer):** Layer 7 load balancing, also known as application load balancing, operates at the application layer (Layer 7) of the OSI model. Unlike Layer 4, it examines the content of the traffic, such as HTTP headers, cookies, or URL paths. This allows for more sophisticated load balancing, where traffic can be routed based on specific content or user behavior, such as routing requests for different microservices or specific geolocations. Common features of Layer 7 load balancing include:

    - **SSL Termination**: Offloading the SSL handshake to the load balancer to reduce the computational load on backend servers.
    - **Content-Based Routing**: Directing requests based on URL paths or hostnames, such as sending traffic for an API to one server and static content to another.
    - **Session Persistence (Sticky Sessions)**: Ensuring that a user's requests are consistently directed to the same server, preserving session states, often used in e-commerce platforms.

4. **Global Load Balancing:** Global load balancing, sometimes called geographic load balancing, directs traffic based on the location of the user. This technique routes requests to the closest data center or server, reducing latency and improving response times. It is particularly useful in globally distributed systems or services that require low-latency access, like streaming platforms or content delivery networks (CDNs). DNS-based load balancing can also be a part of

this approach, where DNS records are updated to point to the closest available server based on the user's geographic location.

Load Balancing Algorithms: Different load balancing algorithms are used to distribute the incoming traffic or workload efficiently across the servers. Some of the most common algorithms include:

1. **Round Robin**: This is one of the simplest and most widely used algorithms. Each incoming request is sent to the next server in the list, in a circular manner. This algorithm is effective when all servers are of equal capacity, and there are no significant differences in processing requirements between requests.

2. **Least Connections**: This algorithm sends traffic to the server with the fewest active connections. It's more effective in situations where requests vary in size or resource consumption, as it helps prevent overloading any particular server.

3. **Weighted Round Robin**: This variation of Round Robin assigns a weight to each server based on its capacity. Servers with higher weights receive more traffic, while those with lower weights get less, ensuring that more powerful servers are used proportionally.

4. **IP Hash**: In IP Hashing, the client's IP address is hashed, and the resulting value is used to determine which server handles the request. This ensures that the same client IP address is always directed to the same server, which is useful for maintaining session consistency.

5. **Random**: Traffic is directed randomly to one of the available servers. While not as efficient as other algorithms, it can be used in scenarios where no significant differences between servers exist or when the system is in a steady state.

Benefits of Load Balancing: The benefits of load balancing are as under:

1. **Improved Performance**: By distributing traffic evenly across multiple servers, load balancing prevents any one server from becoming a bottleneck, which enhances system responsiveness and throughput.

2. **High Availability and Reliability**: Load balancers constantly monitor the health of servers. If one server fails, the load balancer automatically redirects traffic to healthy servers, ensuring continuous service availability and minimizing downtime.

3. **Scalability**: Load balancing enables horizontal scaling, allowing businesses to easily add more servers to meet growing traffic demands without disrupting the existing infrastructure.

4. **Cost Efficiency**: Instead of relying on expensive, high-performance hardware to handle all traffic, load balancing allows the use of multiple smaller, less expensive servers that can be scaled as needed, optimizing costs.

5. **Redundancy and Fault Tolerance**: With load balancing, systems become more fault-tolerant. Even if one or more servers fail, the load balancer ensures that the traffic is rerouted to healthy servers, providing redundancy and minimizing the risk of service disruptions.

Caching Strategies: Caching is a fundamental technique used in software engineering to enhance performance by storing frequently accessed data in fast-access storage. This reduces the need to fetch the same data repeatedly from slower backend systems such as databases, disk storage, or external APIs. By temporarily storing data in a cache, applications can dramatically reduce latency, improve response times, and reduce the load on primary data sources. The key challenge, however, is to manage the cache efficiently to balance performance with data consistency. Caching is crucial for applications that handle high traffic, large datasets, or complex computations. Whether it's a web application, an API service, or a large-scale database system, caching helps ensure that commonly requested data can be served instantly rather than requiring repeated, time-consuming operations. For instance, when a user requests a web page, the server may first check the cache to see if the page is available. If it is, the server serves it from memory rather than recomputing or querying the database. Caching reduces system resource consumption, minimizes load on databases, and improves the scalability and availability of applications. However, caching strategies must be implemented carefully to avoid issues like stale data or cache pollution.

The types of caching are as follows:

1. **Client-Side Caching:** Client-side caching refers to the practice of storing data directly on the user's device, such as within a web browser, mobile app, or local storage. The goal is to minimize the need for repeated requests to the server for the same data, improving the speed and efficiency of the application. For web applications, client-side caching often involves storing static resources like images, stylesheets, JavaScript files, and even entire HTML documents in the browser cache. This allows the browser to serve these assets directly from local storage on subsequent requests, thus reducing page load times and server load.

In a mobile application, client-side caching can involve saving data locally, either in the device's memory or persistent storage, to avoid making network requests for the same information each time. This technique enhances the user experience by making apps feel faster, particularly when network conditions are poor or intermittent. Popular technologies for client-side caching include localStorage, sessionStorage, and IndexedDB for web apps, and SQLite or Room for mobile apps.

Advantages:

- Reduces server load by avoiding unnecessary requests for frequently accessed data.
- Improves response time, particularly for static assets.
- Enhances user experience in cases of poor network connectivity.

Challenges:

- Requires cache invalidation strategies to prevent users from seeing outdated or stale data.
- Can increase complexity in managing data consistency between the client cache and the server.

2. **Server-Side Caching:** Server-side caching involves storing data on the server, typically in memory, to prevent repeated and resource-heavy operations like database queries or complex computations. By caching results of expensive database queries, API responses, or computations, server-side caching reduces the load on databases and back-end systems, speeding up response times for end-users. Common tools for server-side caching include Redis, Memcached, and in-memory caches in programming languages such as Java's EHCache.

   In a typical server-side cache, the cache stores data like query results, objects, or computation results. When a request is made for the same data, the server checks the cache first. If the data is found in the cache (a "cache hit"), it's returned immediately, without having to access the original data source. If the data isn't found (a "cache miss"), it's fetched from the backend, cached for future use, and then returned.

Advantages:

- Significantly reduces database load and improves application performance.
- Helps in handling high traffic by providing a quick, in-memory lookup for frequently used data.
- Easier to manage consistency than with client-side caching.

Challenges:

- Memory limitations on the server can restrict the size of the cache.
- Cache invalidation can become complex, especially in scenarios involving real-time data updates.
- Requires a mechanism for synchronization if using a distributed cache across multiple servers.

3. **Distributed Caching:** Distributed caching involves caching data across multiple servers or nodes, ensuring that cached data is available even if a single server fails. In a distributed caching system, cached data is shared and synchronized between different servers in a network. This is typically done to handle larger datasets, improve fault tolerance, and scale the application horizontally. Tools like Redis Cluster, Amazon ElastiCache, and Memcached are commonly used for distributed caching.

   Distributed caching offers a high level of redundancy, meaning that even if one cache node fails, the data is still accessible from other nodes, reducing the risk of downtime or service interruption. It is particularly useful in systems that need to scale out to accommodate growing traffic and large amounts of data. Distributed caches can operate in various modes, including replication (where data is mirrored across multiple nodes) and partitioning (where data is split across nodes to balance the load).

Advantages:

- Provides high availability and fault tolerance by distributing data across multiple servers.
- Scales horizontally by adding more cache nodes to handle increasing demand.

- Reduces the impact of individual cache node failures.

Challenges:

- More complex to set up and manage than local server-side caches.
- Network latency and data synchronization between nodes can impact performance.
- Cache consistency is harder to maintain, especially in the event of node failures or network partitioning.

4. **Content Delivery Network (CDN) Caching:** CDN caching is a specialized form of caching that stores static content, such as images, videos, stylesheets, and scripts, at multiple locations around the world. A Content Delivery Network (CDN) consists of a network of geographically distributed servers designed to cache and deliver content to users based on their geographic location. This reduces latency by serving content from the closest server to the user, which speeds up load times and improves the overall user experience.

   For example, when a user requests an image hosted on a CDN, the request is routed to the nearest edge server in the CDN network, reducing the distance and time required to retrieve the asset. CDNs like Cloudflare, Akamai, and Amazon CloudFront are widely used to handle large amounts of static content and offload traffic from the origin server.

Advantages:

- Reduces latency by serving cached content from the nearest server to the user.
- Relieves the origin server of traffic, leading to improved performance and reduced server load.
- Scalable solution to handle large traffic spikes, especially for static resources.

Challenges:

- Dynamic or personalized content cannot be cached easily, limiting the use of CDNs for certain types of data.
- Cache invalidation can be more complex since cached content may need to be purged or updated across multiple edge servers.

- Relies on a third-party service, which may incur additional costs.

5. **Database Caching:** Database caching focuses on caching the results of database queries or frequently accessed data to reduce the load on the database and improve performance. Database caching is usually implemented using in-memory caches like Redis or Memcached, or through integrated database caching systems such as Oracle's Result Cache or MySQL Query Cache.

   When a query is executed, the system first checks the cache to see if the result is already stored. If the data is found in the cache, it is returned immediately (a cache hit), avoiding the need to query the database again. If the data is not in the cache (a cache miss), it is retrieved from the database, stored in the cache for future use, and then returned to the user. This is particularly effective for read-heavy applications, where the same queries are repeatedly executed.

Advantages:

- Reduces the number of database queries, leading to improved performance and reduced load on the database.
- Helps with the scalability of database systems by reducing the time taken to fetch data.
- Can be applied to both the query results and frequently accessed tables or objects.

Challenges:

- Maintaining cache consistency with the database can be challenging, especially with rapidly changing data.
- Large caches may require significant memory, and incorrect cache invalidation can lead to serving stale data.
- In complex systems, ensuring that the cache is updated when the underlying data changes requires careful management.

Strategies of Caching: Caching is a vital performance optimization technique in software engineering, aimed at reducing data retrieval times, minimizing server load, and enhancing the responsiveness of applications. By storing frequently accessed or computationally expensive data in a faster storage medium often memory caching ensures that repeated requests can be served more efficiently. However, caching must be carefully managed to maintain accuracy and consistency. This is where effective caching strategies come into play, helping developers control how, when, and what to cache.

1. **Cache-Aside (Lazy Loading):** The cache-aside strategy is one of the most commonly used approaches. In this model, the application code is responsible for reading and writing from the cache. When a request is made, the cache is checked first. If the data is not found (a cache miss), it is retrieved from the primary data store (e.g., a database), stored in the cache, and then returned. This approach ensures that only frequently accessed data is cached, reducing unnecessary memory usage. However, it requires explicit cache invalidation or updates when the underlying data changes.

2. **Write-Through Caching:** In the write-through strategy, every time data is written to the main database, it is simultaneously written to the cache. This ensures that the cache always contains up-to-date data. While this method helps maintain consistency between the cache and the database, it can introduce additional write latency because data must be saved in two locations at once. Write-through caching is suitable for systems where data consistency is a priority.

3. **Write-Behind (Write-Back) Caching:** With write-behind caching, updates are written to the cache immediately but deferred when writing to the underlying data store. These writes are queued and periodically flushed to the database in batches. This reduces the latency of write operations and improves throughput in write-heavy applications. However, there is a risk of data loss in case of cache failure before the data is persisted to the database.

4. **Time-to-Live (TTL) and Expiration:** Time-based expiration is a straightforward yet effective strategy for cache management. Each cached item is assigned a Time-to-Live (TTL), after which it is automatically removed. TTL helps avoid serving outdated or stale data and is useful for data that changes infrequently or on a schedule, such as news headlines or daily statistics. However, choosing appropriate TTL values is crucial too short may lead to frequent cache misses; too long could serve stale data.

5. **Least Recently Used (LRU) Eviction:** When the cache reaches its memory limit, older data must be evicted to make room for new entries. The Least Recently Used (LRU) strategy evicts the data that hasn't been accessed for the longest time. This approach assumes that recently accessed data is more likely to be reused. It's widely supported by in-memory caching tools like Redis and Memcached.

Effective caching strategies are essential for building high-performance, scalable, and responsive systems. Choosing the right strategy depends on the application's read/write patterns, consistency requirements, and data volatility. A well-implemented caching layer can drastically improve application efficiency, reduce backend strain, and provide a smoother user experience.

Horizontal vs. Vertical Scaling

Horizontal scaling and vertical scaling are two primary strategies used to improve a system's capacity and performance. Horizontal scaling, also known as scaling out, involves adding more machines or servers to a system, such as distributing the load across multiple instances or nodes in a cluster. This approach enhances fault tolerance, allows for greater redundancy, and can handle increasing user demand effectively by spreading the load across many resources. It is ideal for cloud-based and distributed systems where elasticity and availability are critical. In contrast, vertical scaling, or scaling up, involves increasing the resources (CPU, RAM, storage) of a single server or machine to handle more load. This method can be simpler to implement as it doesn't require changes in the application architecture, but it has hardware limits and can become costly. While vertical scaling is effective for short-term growth or legacy systems, it presents a single point of failure and less flexibility in distributed environments. Ultimately, horizontal scaling offers better long-term scalability and resilience, whereas vertical scaling provides a quick and often cheaper way to improve performance—at least up to the hardware's capacity limits. Most modern systems use a combination of both to achieve optimal performance and availability.

Horizontal Scaling: Horizontal scaling, also known as scaling out, is the process of increasing system capacity by adding more machines or nodes to the existing infrastructure. Instead of upgrading the hardware of a single server, horizontal scaling distributes the load across multiple machines, often working together as part of a cluster. This method is commonly used in distributed computing environments, cloud-based applications, and systems requiring high availability and fault tolerance. A key advantage of horizontal scaling is elasticity. Systems can scale dynamically, adding or removing nodes based on demand. This is particularly beneficial in cloud platforms like AWS, Azure, or Google Cloud, where resources can be allocated on-the-fly. For example, during peak traffic periods, more web servers can be spun up behind a load balancer to handle the increased number of requests.

Horizontal scaling also improves fault tolerance and reliability. If one node fails, others can take over its workload, ensuring continuous system operation. In contrast to vertical scaling, which creates a single point of failure, horizontal scaling spreads risk across multiple nodes.

Implementing horizontal scaling requires stateless architecture and efficient load balancing. Applications must be designed so that requests can be served by any server without dependency on session state. Technologies like Docker, Kubernetes, and microservices architecture support horizontal scaling by making it easy to deploy and manage containers across many machines.

However, horizontal scaling is not without challenges. It introduces complexity in system design, especially around data consistency, synchronization, and distributed computing. Maintaining a shared state, synchronizing databases, and handling concurrency in a distributed environment can be complex and may require additional tools like distributed caches or message queues.

In summary, horizontal scaling offers better long-term flexibility, scalability, and reliability. It is ideal for modern, cloud-native applications where workloads can be distributed, and services are designed to operate independently. While it requires more architectural planning and coordination, it provides robust performance for systems that need to handle large volumes of users or data.

Vertical Scaling: Vertical scaling, or scaling up, is the process of increasing the capacity of a single server or machine by adding more resources such as CPU, RAM, or storage. Instead of distributing the workload across multiple systems, vertical scaling aims to make one system more powerful so it can handle more tasks or data.

This approach is often simpler to implement because it doesn't require changes to the application's architecture. For example, if a database is experiencing performance issues due to limited memory, upgrading the machine to include more RAM can provide immediate benefits. Vertical scaling is common in traditional monolithic applications, legacy systems, or environments where applications are not designed to run on multiple nodes.

The primary advantage of vertical scaling is ease of use. System administrators can upgrade hardware with minimal disruption and without reconfiguring the application to handle multiple nodes. It also maintains data consistency more easily since all operations happen within a single system.

However, vertical scaling has limitations. There is a physical cap to how much a single machine can be upgraded. As hardware becomes more powerful, it also becomes more expensive. Moreover, the server becomes a single point of failure if it crashes, the entire system goes down. This lack of redundancy can be a major risk in high-availability systems.

Vertical scaling also doesn't provide the resilience or elasticity of horizontal scaling. It's not ideal for systems that experience highly variable workloads or need to serve millions of concurrent users. Cloud environments do offer vertical scaling options, such as resizing virtual machines, but the changes often require downtime or reboots. Despite these drawbacks, vertical scaling is still useful in specific scenarios. For example, in systems where data consistency and low-latency access are critical such as transactional databases it might be more efficient to scale vertically rather than introduce the complexity of distribution.

In conclusion, vertical scaling is a quick and sometimes cost-effective way to improve system performance, particularly for single-node applications or legacy systems. However, it lacks the flexibility and fault tolerance of horizontal scaling and can become a bottleneck as demand continues to grow. Many modern systems begin with vertical scaling for simplicity and later evolve into horizontally scaled architectures for better scalability and resilience.

Table 4.2

S.No.	Aspect	Horizontal Scaling (Scaling Out)	Vertical Scaling (Scaling Up)
1	Definition	Adding more machines or nodes to a system	Increasing the capacity of a single machine
2	Approach	Scale by distributing workload across multiple systems	Scale by upgrading the existing system's hardware
3	Architecture Dependency	Requires distributed or stateless architecture	Suitable for monolithic or legacy systems
4	Fault Tolerance	High – failure of one node doesn't affect the whole system	Low – single point of failure
5	Scalability	High – can scale almost indefinitely with additional nodes	Limited – constrained by hardware maximums
6	Implementation Complexity	More complex – needs load balancing, distributed data management	Simpler – usually involves upgrading hardware
7	Cost Structure	Cost grows with the number of nodes and infrastructure complexity	Cost increases steeply with high-end hardware upgrades
8,	Elasticity	Highly elastic – resources can be added/removed easily (especially in cloud)	Less elastic – hardware upgrades may require downtime
9,	Examples	Web farms, microservices, Kubernetes clusters	Upgrading a database server's CPU and RAM
10	Ideal Use Case	Cloud-native, large-scale, high-availability systems	Legacy apps, small-scale systems, or when redesign is not feasible

Cloud-native Application Development

In the world of modern software development, cloud-native applications have become a pivotal approach to building scalable, resilient, and agile systems. As businesses and organizations increasingly move towards the cloud, understanding the principles and best practices of cloud-native application development is crucial. A cloud-native application is an application designed and built to fully leverage the benefits of cloud computing. Unlike traditional monolithic applications that are typically hosted on physical servers or virtual machines, cloud-native applications are built to take advantage of the cloud's flexibility, scalability, and distributed nature. These applications are designed to run efficiently in cloud environments like Amazon Web Services (AWS), Microsoft Azure, Google Cloud Platform (GCP), and others.

Cloud-native applications are typically composed of microservices, which are small, independent components that work together to form a complete system. These services are often deployed in containers and managed with orchestration tools like Kubernetes.

Cloud-native development is a modern approach to creating and managing applications using tools from cloud computing. It's not just about technology; it involves changing how teams work together and adopting new ways of building software. The goal is to make it easier to handle complex tasks and speed up the development of software.

When organizations use cloud-native development, they can quickly bring new ideas to the market and respond faster to customers' needs. This method relies on technologies like containers and Kubernetes, which help build and run applications efficiently. Cloud-native development includes important practices like DevOps, continuous integration, and continuous delivery (CI/CD). It embraces modern application design methods, such as microservices and serverless architecture.

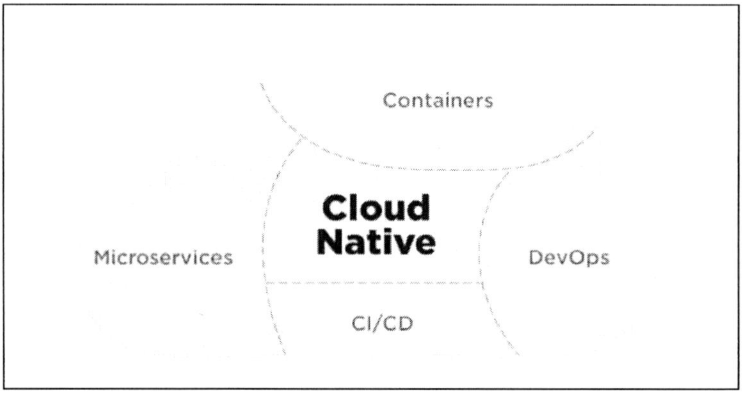

Fig.4.11

Whether an application is deployed on-premises, in the public cloud, or in a mix of different environments, the focus is on having flexible computing power and access to the latest tools for data and applications. This flexibility ensures success in the ever-evolving world of modern development.

Core technologies involved in cloud-native development are as under:

1. **Containers**: Containers are a cornerstone of cloud-native development. Docker is the most widely used containerization technology, providing developers with a way to package applications and all their dependencies into a portable container. Containers are designed to run anywhere, which is a key advantage in cloud-native architectures.

   Containers are a foundational element of cloud-native development, enabling software applications to be packaged with all their dependencies, including libraries, runtime environments, and configurations. This packaging allows applications to be consistently deployed across any environment, whether it's a developer's local machine, a testing server, or a production cloud infrastructure. Docker is the most popular containerization platform, offering a lightweight solution for running applications in isolated environments.

   Containers help solve the problem of "it works on my machine," which is common in traditional software development, by ensuring that the application behaves the same way across various environments. They encapsulate the entire runtime environment, including the application and its dependencies, which results in faster deployment times and reduced risk of compatibility issues.

   The main advantage of containers in cloud-native development is portability. A containerized application can be deployed on any platform that supports Docker, including cloud platforms like AWS, Google Cloud, and Azure, or even on-premises environments. Containers also support scalability, allowing multiple instances of a service to run on-demand without impacting performance. Containers work well in a distributed architecture, where microservices can be independently scaled and managed.

   Additionally, containers contribute to resource efficiency. Since they are lightweight and share the host system's kernel, they use fewer resources compared to traditional virtual machines, making them ideal for running applications in cloud environments where scalability and cost-efficiency are important.

2. **Kubernetes**: Kubernetes is the de facto standard for container orchestration. It automates the deployment, scaling, and management of containerized applications. Kubernetes helps manage the complexity of maintaining large-scale cloud-native applications by offering features like automatic load balancing, self-healing, and rolling updates.

   Kubernetes is an open-source container orchestration platform that automates the deployment, scaling, and management of containerized applications. It has become the industry standard for managing large-scale, cloud-native applications, especially in environments with complex and dynamic workloads.

   Kubernetes simplifies the operational complexity associated with managing microservices-based architectures. It automates key tasks such as load balancing, self-healing, scaling, and rolling updates. For instance, if a container fails or a service becomes unresponsive, Kubernetes can automatically restart the container or redistribute the workload, ensuring high availability and resilience. This helps cloud-native applications remain operational even in the face of failures.

   Kubernetes enables declarative configuration and automation, meaning that developers can define the desired state of their application infrastructure and Kubernetes will ensure that it is maintained. Kubernetes also facilitates auto-scaling, where resources are dynamically allocated based on demand, and horizontal scaling, where more instances of containers are added to handle increased load.

   One of the key features of Kubernetes is its support for multi-cloud and hybrid cloud environments, allowing developers to deploy applications across different cloud providers or on-premises infrastructures. This flexibility is crucial for organizations that want to avoid vendor lock-in or need to comply with specific data residency requirements.

3. **Service Mesh**: A service mesh is a dedicated infrastructure layer for managing service-to-service communication in microservices architectures. It provides observability, traffic management, and security for microservices. Istio is a popular service mesh that works with Kubernetes to simplify the management of complex microservices networks.

   A service mesh is an infrastructure layer designed to manage and monitor communication between microservices in a distributed architecture. It abstracts the complexities of service-to-service communication and offers critical features like traffic management, security, observability, and reliability. One of the most widely adopted service mesh solutions is Istio, which integrates seamlessly with Kubernetes and provides a unified way to manage communication between microservices.

Service meshes are particularly important in cloud-native development because they help engineers avoid the complexity of manually managing individual service interactions. With Istio, developers can configure fine-grained traffic routing, implement retries or circuit breakers for fault tolerance, and enforce security policies such as mutual TLS (mTLS) to ensure encrypted communication between services. Istio also provides extensive observability features, such as tracing, monitoring, and logging, allowing teams to gain deep insights into how microservices are performing and to identify potential bottlenecks or issues.

In terms of security, Istio simplifies the process of managing authentication and authorization policies across services. It can enforce rules on who can communicate with which services and how, reducing the complexity of securing microservices in a dynamic, cloud-native environment.

Overall, a service mesh like Istio helps software engineers ensure that communication between microservices is reliable, secure, and efficient, without having to manually code these capabilities into each service.

4. **Cloud Platforms (AWS, Azure, GCP)**: Cloud-native applications rely heavily on cloud infrastructure services provided by major cloud platforms. These platforms offer tools for compute (e.g., EC2, Kubernetes Engine), storage (e.g., S3, Blob Storage), networking (e.g., Virtual Private Cloud), and databases (e.g., RDS, Bigtable). They also provide serverless offerings (e.g., AWS Lambda, Google Cloud Functions) that are well-suited for event-driven architectures.

   Cloud-native applications rely heavily on cloud platforms such as Amazon Web Services (AWS), Microsoft Azure, and Google Cloud Platform (GCP) to provide the necessary infrastructure for hosting, scaling, and managing applications. These platforms offer a wide array of services that facilitate the development, deployment, and monitoring of cloud-native applications.

   Cloud providers offer compute services (e.g., EC2 on AWS, Virtual Machines on Azure), which allow developers to run their applications on virtual servers, and container orchestration services (e.g., EKS for AWS, AKS for Azure, GKE for Google Cloud) that integrate with Kubernetes to manage containerized workloads.

In addition to compute, cloud platforms provide managed storage services (e.g., S3 on AWS, Blob Storage on Azure), which can store vast amounts of unstructured data, and databases (e.g., RDS on AWS, Cloud SQL on GCP), which provide managed relational and NoSQL databases. They also offer serverless computing options, such as AWS Lambda, Azure Functions, and Google Cloud Functions, which allow developers to run code without worrying about server management. This serverless model fits perfectly with cloud-native development, enabling applications to scale automatically in response to traffic and only pay for what they use.

Cloud platforms are also key to achieving high availability and disaster recovery, as they provide services like load balancing, auto-scaling, and multi-region deployments. These capabilities ensure that cloud-native applications remain resilient, scalable, and performant, regardless of the amount of traffic or unexpected failures.

5. **CI/CD Tools**: CI/CD tools are essential in cloud-native development for automating the building, testing, and deployment of code. Jenkins, GitLab CI, CircleCI, and GitHub Actions are popular tools for continuous integration and continuous delivery. These tools enable rapid iteration and frequent deployments, which are key principles in cloud-native development.

   Continuous Integration (CI) and Continuous Delivery (CD) are practices that enable cloud-native development to be more agile, ensuring rapid and reliable software delivery. CI/CD tools automate the process of building, testing, and deploying applications, facilitating frequent and consistent updates to the application with minimal manual intervention.

   Popular CI/CD tools include Jenkins, GitLab CI, CircleCI, and GitHub Actions. These tools integrate with version control systems like Git to trigger builds and tests automatically when changes are made to the codebase. They can also integrate with containerization platforms like Docker and container orchestration systems like Kubernetes to deploy applications automatically to cloud environments.

   CI/CD pipelines automate various stages of the software lifecycle, such as code compilation, unit testing, integration testing, security checks, and deployment. For example, a typical pipeline might start with a commit to a version control system, which triggers an automatic build and test process. If tests pass, the code is automatically deployed to a staging environment for further testing and then to production. This ensures that software updates are delivered continuously and that code changes are always in a deployable state.

By implementing CI/CD practices, cloud-native teams can improve collaboration, reduce errors, and release software more frequently and reliably. This agility is essential in today's fast-paced software development environments, where rapid iteration and continuous improvement are key to staying competitive.

Core Principles of Cloud-Native Development

1. **Microservices Architecture:** At the heart of cloud-native application development lies the **microservices architecture**. Instead of building large, monolithic applications, developers decompose the system into smaller, loosely coupled services that focus on specific business functionalities. Each service is independently deployable, maintainable, and scalable. This architectural approach allows teams to develop, test, and deploy features more rapidly and efficiently, as each service can be developed and updated without affecting other services in the system. Microservices communicate with each other via lightweight protocols such as HTTP/REST, gRPC, or message queues.

   In cloud-native development, API-first design is essential, as it ensures that services can easily interact with one another, regardless of where they are hosted.

2. **Containers and Containerization:** Containers are a cornerstone of cloud-native development. A **container** is a lightweight, portable unit that encapsulates an application and all of its dependencies (such as libraries, configurations, and runtimes). Containers ensure that the application can run consistently across different environments, whether it's on a developer's laptop, a staging environment, or a cloud infrastructure. Docker is the most widely used containerization platform, allowing developers to create, deploy, and run applications in containers. Containers provide significant benefits in terms of portability, performance, and scalability, which are especially critical in cloud-native environments. Once applications are containerized, they are often orchestrated and managed using platforms like Kubernetes, which automates tasks such as deployment, scaling, load balancing, and monitoring. Kubernetes

ensures that containerized applications can run efficiently in large, distributed cloud environments.

3. **Continuous Delivery and DevOps Practices:** Cloud-native development is inherently aligned with DevOps principles, which emphasize collaboration between development and operations teams to streamline the development lifecycle. Continuous Integration (CI) and Continuous Delivery (CD) are central practices in DevOps that help ensure that software is always in a deployable state.

    - **Continuous Integration (CI)** refers to the practice of automatically building and testing software whenever new code is committed to a version control system. This ensures that defects are identified early and that the codebase remains stable.

    - **Continuous Delivery (CD)** extends CI by automating the release process. With CD, applications are continuously deployed to production in small, incremental updates, allowing for faster time-to-market and reduced risk of failure.

    In cloud-native development, CI/CD pipelines are essential for automating testing, deployment, and scaling of applications in real-time, thus ensuring faster, safer, and more reliable delivery of software.

4. **Automation and Infrastructure as Code:** In cloud-native application development, infrastructure as code (IaC) plays a critical role in managing infrastructure in a repeatable and automated manner. With IaC, developers can define cloud resources such as servers, networks, and storage using code (often YAML, JSON, or a domain-specific language like Terraform).

    This automation allows for more consistent environments, faster provisioning of resources, and easier scaling and maintenance of infrastructure. Common tools used in IaC include Terraform, CloudFormation, and Ansible. The ability to automate both infrastructure and application deployment is one of the key factors that enables cloud-native applications to scale and adapt quickly.

5. **Scalability and Resilience:** One of the primary advantages of cloud-native applications is their ability to scale and recover from failure with minimal human intervention. Cloud environments offer near-infinite resources that can be provisioned or decommissioned dynamically based on demand. Cloud-native

applications are designed to scale horizontally, meaning that new instances of a service can be added or removed in response to traffic or load.

6. **Resilience:** This is another important characteristic of cloud-native applications. Cloud-native architectures are designed to be fault-tolerant, meaning that the failure of one service will not cause the entire application to fail. This is made possible by the use of microservices, containers, and automated recovery mechanisms like auto-scaling, self-healing, and multi-region deployments.

******

11

Software Engineering for Emerging Technologies

Software engineering for emerging technologies focuses on the development, design, and implementation of software systems that incorporate cutting-edge innovations. As technologies such as artificial intelligence (AI), machine learning (ML), blockchain, the Internet of Things (IoT), augmented reality (AR), and quantum computing continue to evolve, they demand new approaches to software engineering. Unlike traditional software systems, which are primarily concerned with stability, performance, and security, software development for emerging technologies requires flexibility, adaptability, and a deep understanding of complex, often interdisciplinary, concepts. Engineers must integrate emerging tools and frameworks while addressing challenges like real-time data processing, massive scalability, and novel user interactions. For instance, in AI and ML, the software engineering process involves data preparation, model training, algorithm selection, and the continuous evaluation of model accuracy and efficiency. Similarly, IoT systems must be built to handle large amounts of sensor data, ensure seamless device interoperability, and address issues like latency and security at the edge.

The software engineering process for these emerging technologies is inherently iterative and experimental, requiring constant innovation. Teams need to embrace agile methodologies and DevOps practices to ensure rapid prototyping and continuous integration, which is essential when dealing with fast-changing fields. Moreover, software engineers working on these technologies must be comfortable with research and development, as the tools and standards for emerging fields are still maturing. For example, blockchain developers must understand decentralized systems, cryptographic protocols, and consensus mechanisms, while quantum computing engineers need to grasp principles like superposition and quantum entanglement. To support these technological advancements, software engineering practices are evolving to include specialized skills in data science, ethical AI, and distributed systems. The integration of these emerging technologies into everyday applications is poised to redefine industries, but it requires a collaborative approach among software engineers, domain experts, and stakeholders to create robust, scalable, and secure systems.

Evolving Role of Software Engineering: Software engineering has traditionally focused on creating software that is stable, efficient, and user-friendly. However, with the rise of emerging technologies, the role of software engineers is evolving rapidly. These technologies often require new approaches to system design, development, testing, and deployment due to their complexity, scalability requirements, and interdisciplinary nature. Emerging technologies like AI, blockchain, and IoT not only present novel technical challenges but also introduce new paradigms in how software interacts with users, data, and other systems.

In AI and machine learning, for example, software engineers must deal with vast datasets, train models, optimize algorithms, and ensure that systems can learn and adapt over time. This requires a deep understanding of both the underlying algorithms and the data used to train the models. Unlike traditional software development, which typically focuses on fixed logic, AI systems are dynamic, constantly evolving as they learn from new data. This introduces challenges in terms of model performance, bias, transparency, and interpretability.

Similarly, blockchain technology challenges traditional concepts of centralized systems. Blockchain systems, especially in the context of cryptocurrencies like Bitcoin and Ethereum, rely on decentralized networks of nodes to maintain the integrity and security of distributed ledgers. This calls for specialized skills in cryptographic protocols, consensus algorithms, and distributed systems. Software engineers working with blockchain must ensure that the systems are not only secure but also efficient and scalable, as blockchain applications often need to handle millions of transactions.

Key Practices in Software Engineering for Emerging Technologies

1. **Agile Development and Rapid Prototyping:** Emerging technologies are evolving at a breakneck pace, which makes traditional waterfall development approaches less effective. Agile methodologies, characterized by iterative

development, continuous feedback, and quick iterations, are better suited for these rapidly changing fields. Agile practices allow teams to continuously refine the software in response to emerging requirements, changing technologies, and user feedback. Rapid prototyping is particularly important in fields like AI and AR, where engineers often need to build working models and demonstrate proof of concepts quickly to evaluate feasibility, usability, and performance.

In AI and ML development, for instance, software engineers may build prototype models that are tested and refined through frequent iterations. These models evolve as new datasets are incorporated or as the requirements change, highlighting the importance of a flexible and adaptive approach. Similarly, in the context of IoT, prototyping allows for early testing of interconnected devices, ensuring that they operate efficiently and securely within a larger system.

2. **Data-Driven Development:** One of the defining characteristics of emerging technologies like AI, IoT, and blockchain is the massive volume of data they generate. Data is at the core of machine learning algorithms, IoT sensor networks, and decentralized applications. Software engineering for these technologies requires a deep integration of data science and data engineering practices. Engineers must not only focus on how the data is processed and stored but also on how to ensure that the data is clean, reliable, and representative of real-world conditions.

   In machine learning, for instance, data preprocessing is a critical step in ensuring that models are trained on high-quality data. The development process involves not only building algorithms but also acquiring, cleaning, and labeling data, which can be time-consuming and costly. Engineers working on AI and ML must be adept at managing large datasets, ensuring that they are properly stored, analyzed, and fed into algorithms for training. In IoT, the data generated by devices must be efficiently transmitted, stored, and processed. As the number of connected devices grows, so does the volume of data. Software engineers must design systems capable of handling this influx of real-time data, often processing it at the edge (on the device itself) or through cloud platforms to extract meaningful insights.

3. **Cloud Computing and Distributed Systems:** Emerging technologies like AI, blockchain, and IoT require scalable, distributed architectures to process and store the massive amounts of data they generate. Cloud computing has become a fundamental enabler of these technologies. Software engineering

for emerging technologies often involves building cloud-based solutions that can scale dynamically to meet the demand.

For AI and ML, cloud platforms like AWS, Google Cloud, and Microsoft Azure offer specialized services like machine learning APIs, GPU instances, and data lakes that allow engineers to run complex algorithms and store large datasets. Cloud computing resources enable the rapid provisioning of infrastructure needed to process data at scale, without the limitations of on-premises hardware.

Similarly, blockchain systems rely on a distributed network of nodes, where each node stores a copy of the ledger. These systems need to be optimized for performance and scalability, which is particularly challenging as blockchain applications grow in popularity. Engineers must ensure that the system can handle increasing numbers of transactions while maintaining its decentralized nature and high security.

4. **Security and Privacy:** Security is one of the most critical concerns when developing software for emerging technologies. Whether it's ensuring the confidentiality of personal data in AI systems, securing blockchain transactions, or protecting IoT devices from cyberattacks, software engineers must adopt a security-first mindset. Emerging technologies often introduce new attack vectors that traditional security models are not equipped to handle. In AI, for example, one of the major concerns is the security of models and data. Adversarial attacks on machine learning models where malicious actors manipulate the input data to mislead the model can have severe consequences. Ensuring that AI systems are robust against these attacks while also safeguarding user data is a critical challenge. In blockchain, the decentralized nature of the system makes it inherently resistant to certain types of attacks, but it still faces challenges related to 51% attacks, smart contract vulnerabilities, and private key management. Blockchain developers must ensure that cryptographic protocols are robust and that the systems can resist tampering and fraud. IoT systems are often vulnerable to cyberattacks due to the sheer number of connected devices and their inherent lack of centralized control. Software engineers working in IoT must design systems that include strong encryption, access control mechanisms, and regular updates to ensure that devices are secure from intrusion.

5. **Ethics and Responsible Development:** Emerging technologies raise new ethical challenges that software engineers must address. AI, for example, can

perpetuate or even amplify bias in decision-making if not carefully designed. Engineers must ensure that AI models are transparent, explainable, and fair. In blockchain, ethical issues may arise around the environmental impact of cryptocurrency mining or the potential for misuse in illicit activities. In IoT, privacy concerns are paramount as devices collect vast amounts of personal data. Software engineers must collaborate with ethicists, legal experts, and other stakeholders to ensure that emerging technologies are developed responsibly and in ways that respect privacy, fairness, and accountability. The emphasis on responsible development is not only about adhering to laws but also about considering the broader social and ethical implications of these technologies.

Software engineering for emerging technologies is a dynamic and multifaceted field that requires a unique blend of technical expertise, adaptability, and forward-thinking. Engineers must be prepared to address complex challenges related to data processing, security, scalability, and ethical concerns while leveraging the latest advancements in cloud computing, AI, and distributed systems. As these technologies continue to evolve, so too must the practices and methodologies used by software engineers. By embracing agile development, focusing on data-driven approaches, and ensuring security and ethical responsibility, software engineers can help unlock the full potential of emerging technologies, driving innovation and shaping the future of our digital world.

Key Emerging Technologies and Their Impact on Software Engineering

1. **Artificial Intelligence and Machine Learning:** Artificial intelligence and machine learning are perhaps the most transformative technologies impacting software engineering today. AI systems are designed to simulate human-like intelligence, enabling software to "learn" from data and make decisions autonomously. Machine learning, a subset of AI, specifically focuses on algorithms that allow systems to improve from experience without being explicitly programmed.

   For software engineers, the challenge lies in creating robust and scalable AI systems. Unlike traditional software development, where the logic is typically defined in advance by the developer, AI and ML systems often rely on data to "train" the system and adapt over time. This introduces new challenges related to data collection, data preprocessing, model selection, algorithm optimization, and evaluation. Engineers must ensure that their AI models are not only accurate but also explainable, accountable, and free from biases.

Key challenges include:

- **Data management**: AI and ML require large volumes of high-quality data, which must be curated, cleaned, and labeled. This involves new workflows and tools, such as data pipelines and feature engineering.
- **Model training and tuning**: Selecting the right machine learning model (e.g., supervised, unsupervised, deep learning) and tuning hyperparameters are crucial for performance. This requires specialized knowledge of algorithms and computational power.
- **Scalability and deployment**: AI systems must be able to handle large amounts of data and make predictions in real time. Efficient deployment practices, such as model versioning, containerization (e.g., Docker), and orchestration (e.g., Kubernetes), are critical.
- **Ethics and fairness**: AI systems must be designed to avoid biases, ensure fairness, and be transparent in their decision-making. Engineers need to be trained in the ethical implications of AI and ML.

2. **Blockchain Technology:** Blockchain technology, originally developed as the foundation for cryptocurrencies like Bitcoin, is now being applied across various industries, from finance to supply chain management. Blockchain provides a decentralized ledger system where transactions or data entries are stored across multiple nodes in a secure and transparent manner, ensuring immutability and eliminating the need for intermediaries.

   For software engineers, building blockchain applications involves deep knowledge of cryptographic techniques, consensus algorithms, and distributed systems. Unlike traditional databases, blockchain systems require engineers to ensure data integrity and security across a decentralized network.

Key challenges include:

- **Security and privacy**: Blockchain's decentralized nature requires strong cryptographic protocols to ensure that data cannot be tampered with. Engineers need to ensure that keys are securely managed, and that the network is resistant to attacks.
- **Consensus mechanisms**: Different blockchain platforms (e.g., Bitcoin, Ethereum) use different consensus algorithms (e.g., Proof of Work, Proof

of Stake) to validate transactions. Engineers must understand and select the right consensus model for each use case.

- **Scalability**: Blockchain networks can face performance bottlenecks as they grow. Engineers need to design systems that scale effectively, especially for applications with high transaction volumes.

- **Interoperability**: Blockchain networks often need to communicate with other systems, including traditional databases, APIs, or other blockchain networks. Ensuring interoperability and standardization is crucial.

3. **Internet of Things (IoT):** The **Internet of Things (IoT)** refers to the growing network of interconnected devices, ranging from smart home appliances to industrial sensors and wearables. IoT systems rely on sensors, devices, and communication networks to collect and share data in real time, enabling automation, monitoring, and optimization.

   For software engineers, the main challenge lies in designing systems that can efficiently handle vast amounts of data generated by IoT devices. These systems must support real-time data processing, device interoperability, and low-latency communication, often in environments with constrained resources (e.g., limited power or bandwidth).

Key challenges include:

- **Device and network management**: IoT devices are diverse and often have varying capabilities. Engineers must design systems that can handle these differences and ensure reliable communication across devices, networks, and cloud platforms.

- **Data management**: IoT systems generate enormous volumes of data that need to be processed and analyzed in real time. This requires robust data management strategies and integration with edge computing or cloud infrastructure.

- **Security**: IoT devices are often vulnerable to cyber-attacks. Engineers must implement strong security measures, such as device authentication, encryption, and secure data transmission, to protect against vulnerabilities.

- **Scalability**: As the number of connected devices grows, the IoT ecosystem must be able to scale efficiently. Engineers must design systems that can handle a large number of devices without sacrificing performance or reliability.

4. **Augmented Reality (AR) and Virtual Reality (VR):** Augmented Reality (AR) and Virtual Reality (VR) are immersive technologies that blend digital and physical worlds. AR overlays digital content onto the physical environment (e.g., through mobile apps or smart glasses), while VR creates a completely digital environment that users can interact with via headsets.

   Software engineers working with AR and VR must consider the unique constraints and requirements of these technologies, including real-time rendering, low-latency performance, user experience design, and hardware compatibility.

Key challenges include:

- **Real-time rendering**: AR and VR applications require high-quality, real-time graphics rendering, often with complex 3D models and animations. This demands powerful computing resources and optimized code for smooth performance.
- **User interaction and experience**: Designing intuitive and engaging user interfaces for AR and VR is a challenge. Engineers must think beyond traditional input methods (e.g., keyboard, mouse) and design for motion tracking, gestures, and haptic feedback.
- **Hardware constraints**: AR and VR systems rely on specialized hardware, such as headsets, motion sensors, and cameras. Engineers need to ensure their software integrates seamlessly with this hardware and provides a smooth, immersive experience.
- **Data synchronization**: AR and VR systems often require real-time data synchronization across multiple devices and sensors. Ensuring that the physical and digital worlds remain in sync is essential for a convincing experience.

5. **Quantum Computing:** Quantum computing represents a fundamental shift in computing capabilities. Unlike classical computers that process data as binary values (0 or 1), quantum computers use quantum bits (qubits) that can exist in multiple states simultaneously. This enables quantum computers to solve certain types of problems much faster than classical computers, such as optimization problems, cryptography, and complex simulations.

For software engineers, working with quantum computing introduces new concepts, algorithms, and tools. Since quantum computers are still in their infancy, developing quantum software often involves combining classical and quantum computing principles, requiring interdisciplinary knowledge.

Key challenges include:

- **Quantum algorithms**: Developing algorithms that leverage quantum principles, such as superposition and entanglement, requires deep understanding of quantum mechanics and quantum gates.
- **Hybrid computing**: Most practical quantum applications today rely on hybrid systems that combine classical and quantum computing. Engineers must design systems that efficiently integrate these two types of computing paradigms.
- **Error correction**: Quantum computers are prone to errors due to quantum decoherence. Engineers need to implement error-correcting codes and techniques to ensure the reliability of quantum computations.
- **Toolchain and platform maturity**: The quantum computing ecosystem is still evolving, with several quantum computing platforms and languages emerging (e.g., Qiskit, Microsoft Quantum). Engineers must stay up-to-date with these developments and understand how to use them effectively.

Artificial Intelligence and Machine Learning in Software Development

Artificial Intelligence (AI) and Machine Learning (ML) are revolutionizing software development by enabling systems to learn from data and improve over time without explicit programming. AI techniques such as natural language processing, computer vision, and predictive analytics are being integrated into applications to enhance user experiences, automate tasks, and improve decision-making. ML algorithms enable systems to identify patterns and make predictions based on data, optimizing processes like recommendation systems, anomaly detection, and personalized services. These technologies require specialized knowledge in data science, algorithm development, and model training, reshaping how software is built, deployed, and maintained.

Artificial Intelligence: Artificial Intelligence (AI) is reshaping the landscape of software development by enabling applications to simulate human-like intelligence, allowing systems to make decisions, recognize patterns, and learn from data autonomously. In software development, AI is primarily used to enhance user experiences, automate processes, and improve system efficiency. For instance, AI-driven features like voice assistants (e.g., Amazon Alexa, Apple Siri) use natural language processing (NLP) to understand and respond to user queries. In addition, AI can optimize decision-making in various applications, from healthcare diagnostics to financial trading, by analyzing vast datasets far quicker and more accurately than human counterparts. AI algorithms are integrated into software systems to automate mundane tasks like code generation, bug detection, and testing, making development cycles faster and more efficient.

Moreover, AI tools in development are increasingly being used for predictive analytics and intelligent automation. Machine learning models, a subset of AI, analyze historical data to predict future outcomes, thus improving decision-making. For example, AI can automate testing and bug fixing by analyzing code and identifying patterns or potential flaws that developers may miss. Additionally, AI can assist in creating self-healing applications that automatically identify and fix problems in real-time, reducing downtime and improving the reliability of software systems. As AI technologies continue to evolve, the role of software engineers is also changing, with more emphasis placed on data collection, model training, and system integration to fully harness AI's potential.

Machine Learning: Machine Learning (ML), a subfield of AI, is fundamentally changing how software is built by enabling systems to learn from data and improve automatically over time. In ML, algorithms are trained using data sets to recognize patterns, make decisions, and predict future outcomes without explicit programming for each scenario. In the context of software development, ML is widely used for creating intelligent applications such as recommendation systems, fraud detection systems, and personalized content delivery. For example, Netflix's recommendation algorithm and Amazon's product suggestions rely heavily on ML techniques that analyze user behavior to predict preferences and provide customized experiences. ML's ability to process vast amounts of data quickly and find underlying patterns is a game-changer, offering solutions that would be impractical using traditional programming methods.

Machine learning also plays a significant role in automating tasks that were previously manual and time-consuming. For instance, ML models can automatically classify images, detect anomalies in data, and optimize user interactions through predictive algorithms. Additionally, in the realm of software development itself, ML is used for code generation, refactoring, and even in identifying software vulnerabilities. The ability of ML to improve continuously by learning from new data makes it an invaluable tool in environments where data is abundant, and speed is critical. As the complexity of applications increases and the demand for intelligent software grows, machine learning provides developers with powerful tools to build more efficient, scalable, and autonomous systems, paving the way for a new era of software engineering.

Differences Between Artificial Intelligence and Machine Learning: Table 4.3 shows the basics differences between artificial intelligence and machine learning.

Table 4.3

S.No.	Aspect	Artificial Intelligence (AI)	Machine Learning (ML)
1	Definition	Artificial Intelligence (AI) is a broader concept that refers to the simulation of human intelligence in machines, enabling them to perform tasks that typically require human cognitive processes, such as problem-solving, decision-making, and understanding language.	Machine Learning (ML) is a subset of AI that specifically focuses on the use of algorithms and statistical models to allow machines to learn from data and improve their performance over time without being explicitly programmed for each task.
2	Scope	AI covers a wide range of techniques, including machine learning, natural language processing, computer vision, robotics, and expert systems. Its goal is to enable machines to perform tasks that require general intelligence or human-like capabilities.	ML, on the other hand, is specifically concerned with teaching machines to learn from data. It is more focused on data-driven decision-making and pattern recognition, often through techniques like supervised, unsupervised, and reinforcement learning.
3	Objective	The goal of AI is to create systems that can perform tasks intelligently, mimicking human behavior. AI systems can involve reasoning, planning, learning, and decision-making, often combining multiple techniques to create "smart" systems.	The goal of ML is to develop algorithms that enable machines to recognize patterns in data and make predictions or decisions without being programmed for every scenario. The machine improves its performance based on past data or experiences.
4	Approach	AI generally involves rule-based systems or expert systems where predefined rules and logic are used to make decisions. AI systems may also involve heuristic problem-solving methods or search algorithms.	ML relies on data-driven methods, where algorithms are trained on data sets to identify patterns and correlations. ML models learn from this data to make predictions or decisions without following a specific rule set.
5	Dependence on Data	AI does not necessarily depend on data as much as ML. While AI may use data, it also incorporates human logic, reasoning, and other non-data-driven techniques for decision-making and problem-solving.	ML is inherently data-dependent. It requires large volumes of data to train models, make predictions, and improve over time. The accuracy and effectiveness of machine learning models depend heavily on the quality and quantity of the data they are trained on.

Blockchain and Smart Contracts

Blockchain is a decentralized, distributed digital ledger that records transactions across multiple computers in a secure, transparent, and tamper-proof manner. Each block contains a list of transactions, and once added to the chain, data cannot be altered without changing all subsequent blocks, making it highly secure. Smart contracts are self-executing programs stored on a blockchain that automatically enforce and execute the terms of an agreement when predefined conditions are met. These contracts eliminate the need for intermediaries, reduce transaction costs, and increase trust between parties. Smart contracts are commonly used in finance, supply chains, real estate, and legal processes, enhancing efficiency and transparency. By combining blockchain's immutability with smart contracts' automation, businesses and individuals can create more reliable and streamlined systems for managing digital interactions. This transformative technology continues to reshape industries by promoting decentralization, security, and trust in digital transactions.

Blockchain: Blockchain technology, originally developed as the foundation for cryptocurrencies like Bitcoin, has significantly evolved and now influences various industries, including software engineering. At its core, blockchain is a decentralized, distributed ledger that records transactions in a secure, transparent, and immutable way. This innovative approach to data management and validation presents new opportunities and challenges in software development. In software engineering, blockchain is reshaping traditional design models, security paradigms, and data handling strategies, offering novel solutions for problems like trust, data integrity, and distributed collaboration. Before delving into its application in software engineering, it's essential to understand how blockchain works. A blockchain is a chain of blocks, each containing a list of transactions, a timestamp, and a cryptographic hash of the previous block. This design ensures that once data is recorded, it cannot be altered retroactively without changing all subsequent blocks a process considered practically infeasible due to the consensus mechanisms employed by the network.

Blockchains can be categorized into public, private, and consortium (or permissioned) types. Public blockchains, like Ethereum and Bitcoin, are open to anyone, while private and consortium blockchains restrict access to certain users or organizations. This flexibility in design allows software engineers to tailor blockchain solutions based on the specific needs of their projects.

Blockchain in the Software Development Lifecycle: The software development lifecycle (SDLC) includes stages such as planning, analysis, design, implementation, testing, deployment, and maintenance. Blockchain can enhance or transform several of these stages.

1. **Requirements Analysis and Planning:** Blockchain introduces new architectural considerations during the planning phase. Developers must determine whether a blockchain is necessary and, if so, which type suits the project. For instance, applications requiring decentralized trust, such as voting systems or supply chain tracking, can benefit from blockchain. Key questions include transaction volume, privacy requirements, and scalability constraints.

2. **Design:** Designing a blockchain-based system involves decisions around consensus mechanisms (e.g., Proof of Work, Proof of Stake), smart contract logic, and data structure. Smart contracts are a critical component in decentralized applications (dApps), acting as the programmable logic layer of blockchain platforms. Engineers must carefully architect smart contracts to ensure security and performance, as errors are often irreversible once deployed.

3. **Implementation:** During implementation, software engineers write code for both off-chain components (e.g., web interfaces, APIs) and on-chain logic (smart contracts). Languages like Solidity (for Ethereum), Rust (for Solana), and Go (used in Hyperledger Fabric) are commonly used. This phase also includes integrating cryptographic functions for hashing, digital signatures, and key management.

4. **Testing:** Testing in blockchain projects is uniquely challenging. Since smart contracts are immutable, extensive testing is essential to catch bugs and vulnerabilities before deployment. Testnets—blockchain replicas like Ethereum's Goerli or Sepolia—allow developers to simulate network behavior without using real assets. Unit testing, integration testing, and fuzz testing are critical practices, as are audits by specialized security firms.

5. **Deployment and Maintenance:** Once deployed, smart contracts and blockchain systems are difficult to update. Unlike traditional software, developers cannot simply push patches to fix bugs. This makes pre-deployment validation crucial. For upgrades, mechanisms like proxy contracts or governance protocols may be used. Continuous monitoring tools help detect unusual activity and performance bottlenecks.

Blockchain Working: The transaction process in a blockchain can be summarized as follows:

1. **Facilitating a transaction:** A new transaction enters the blockchain network. All the information that needs to be transmitted is doubly encrypted using public and private keys.

2. **Verification of transaction:** The transaction is then transmitted to the network of peer-to-peer computers distributed across the world. All the nodes on the network will check for the validity of the transaction like if a sufficient balance is available for carrying out the transaction.

3. **Formation of a new block:** In a typical blockchain network there are many nodes and many transactions get verified at a time. Once the transaction is verified and declared a legitimate transaction, it will be added to the mempool. All the verified transactions at a particular node form a mempool and such multiple mempools form a block.

4. **Consensus Algorithm:** The nodes that form a block will try to add the block to the blockchain network to make it permanent. But if every node is allowed to add blocks in this manner, then it will disrupt the working of the blockchain network. To solve this problem, the nodes use a consensus mechanism to ensure that every new block that is added to the Blockchain is the only version of the truth that is agreed upon by all the nodes in the Blockchain, and only a valid block is securely attached to the blockchain. The node that is selected to add a block to the blockchain will get a reward and hence we call them "miners". The consensus algorithm creates a hash code for that block which is required to add the block to the blockchain.

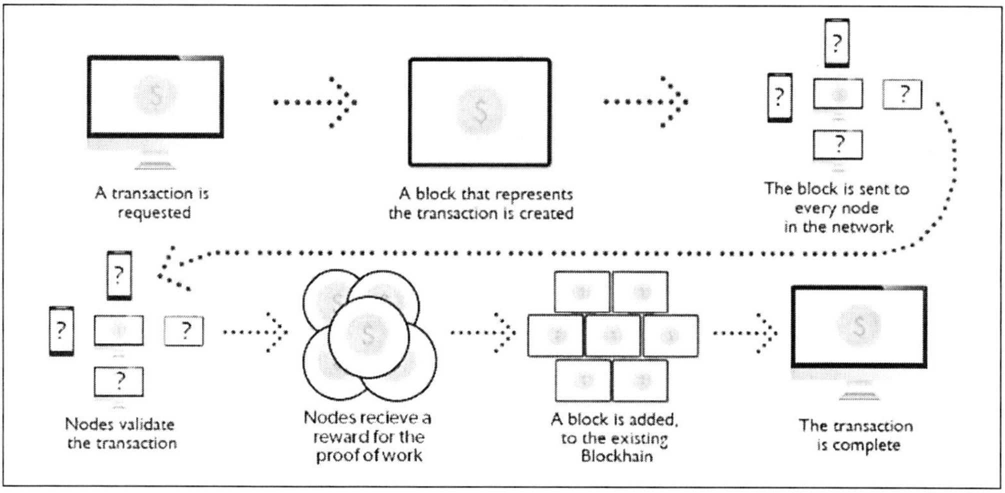

Fig.4.12

5. **Addition of the new block to the blockchain:** After the newly created block has got its hash value and is authenticated, now it is ready to be added to

the blockchain. In every block, there is a hash value of the previous block and that is how the blocks are cryptographically linked to each other to form a blockchain. A new block gets added to the open end of the blockchain.

6. **Transaction complete:** As soon as the block is added to the blockchain the transaction is completed and the details of this transaction are permanently stored in the blockchain. Anyone can fetch the details of the transaction and confirm the transaction.

Use Cases in Software Engineering: Blockchain is enabling new categories of software applications and improving existing systems across various domains:

1. **Decentralized Applications (dApps):** Blockchain has enabled the development of dApps, which run on decentralized networks rather than centralized servers. These apps operate transparently, often governed by communities, and rely heavily on smart contracts for automation. dApps are commonly found in finance (DeFi), gaming (GameFi), identity management, and digital collectibles (NFTs).

2. **Secure Software Distribution:** Software engineers can use blockchain to ensure the integrity and provenance of software packages. By recording version histories and cryptographic hashes on a blockchain, developers can verify the authenticity of distributed code and prevent tampering or malicious updates.

3. **Intellectual Property Management:** Blockchain allows for transparent tracking of code ownership and licensing. Smart contracts can automate licensing agreements, royalty payments, and copyright enforcement, which is particularly useful in open-source or collaborative software projects.

4. **Collaborative Development and Version Control:** While tools like Git are widely used for version control, blockchain offers a new paradigm where changes can be immutably recorded and verified across distributed teams. Decentralized version control systems built on blockchain ensure that contributions are traceable and tamper-proof.

5. **Identity and Access Management:** Blockchain-based identity solutions enable secure, decentralized authentication mechanisms. Instead of relying on centralized credentials, users can authenticate using cryptographic wallets. This approach improves user privacy and reduces the attack surface for hackers.

Benefits of Blockchain in Software Engineering

1. **Enhanced Security:** Blockchain's cryptographic foundations ensure high levels of data security. Data stored on a blockchain is tamper-resistant, and each transaction is independently verified and recorded across multiple nodes.

2. **Improved Transparency and Trust:** By decentralizing control and making data publicly verifiable, blockchain fosters trust between users and developers. This is especially valuable in systems where third-party verification would traditionally be required.

3. **Automation with Smart Contracts:** Smart contracts automate processes that would otherwise require manual intervention, reducing operational overhead and the potential for human error. This is particularly useful for recurring tasks like subscription billing, royalties, or compliance checks.

4. **Data Integrity:** Blockchain ensures that once data is recorded, it cannot be changed without detection. This immutability makes it ideal for audit logs, transaction histories, and provenance tracking in critical systems.

Challenges and Limitations: Despite its potential, blockchain also introduces certain challenges:

1. **Scalability:** Most blockchain platforms struggle with scalability. The time and resources required for consensus protocols can lead to high latency and low throughput, which are unsuitable for high-performance applications.

2. **Complexity:** Blockchain development requires a deep understanding of cryptography, distributed systems, and smart contract security. The learning curve is steep, and mistakes can be costly.

3. **Regulatory and Legal Concerns:** The legal status of blockchain-based applications is often unclear, particularly concerning data privacy (e.g., GDPR compliance) and smart contract enforceability. Engineers must work closely with legal experts to ensure compliance.

4. **Irreversibility:** Mistakes in smart contracts, once deployed, are difficult or impossible to fix. This immutability, while a strength in terms of security, is also a risk if bugs or vulnerabilities are discovered post-deployment.

Future of Blockchain in Software Engineering: As blockchain technology matures, it is likely to become a standard component in the software engineering toolkit. Developments in scalability (such as layer-2 solutions and sharding), interoperability (cross-chain communication), and privacy (zero-knowledge proofs, confidential computing) are addressing many current limitations.

Furthermore, the integration of blockchain with other emerging technologies like artificial intelligence, IoT, and edge computing is creating new development paradigms. For instance, blockchain can securely log sensor data from IoT devices or record AI model decisions for transparency and accountability.

Smart Contracts: Smart contracts, in the context of software engineering, are self-executing computer programs stored on a blockchain that automate the execution of agreements. They represent a new paradigm for software development, allowing for secure and transparent interactions between parties without the need for intermediaries. Smart contracts are typically developed using specialized programming languages like Solidity (for Ethereum) and are deployed on blockchain platforms.

Smart Contract Working: A smart contract is just a digital contract with the security coding of the blockchain.

1. **Identify Agreement:** Multiple parties identify the cooperative opportunity and desired outcomes and agreements could include business processes, asset swaps, etc.

2. **Set conditions:** Smart contracts could be initiated by parties themselves or when certain conditions are met like financial market indices, events like GPS locations, etc.

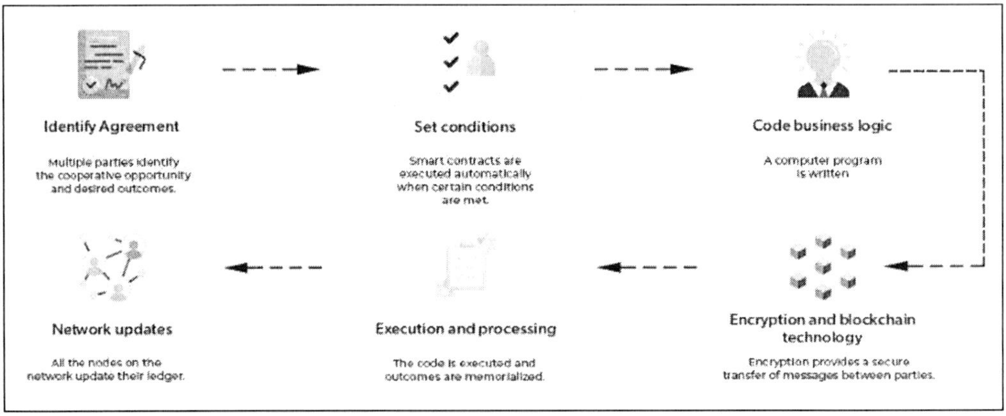

Fig.4.13

3. **Code business logic:** A computer program is written that will be executed automatically when the conditional parameters are met.

4. **Encryption and blockchain technology:** Encryption provides secure authentication and transfer of messages between parties relating to smart contracts.

5. **Execution and processing:** In blockchain iteration, whenever consensus is reached between the parties regarding authentication and verification then the code is executed and the outcomes are memorialized for compliance and verification.

6. **Network updates:** After smart contracts are executed, all the nodes on the network update their ledger to reflect the new state. Once the record is posted and verified on the blockchain network, it cannot be modified, it is in append mode only.

Types of Smart Contracts: The types of smart contracts are as:

1. **Smart Legal Contract:** There are legal guarantees for smart contracts. They follow the format seen in contracts: "If this occurs, then this will occur." Legal smart contracts provide more openness between contracting entities than traditional documents because they are stored on blockchain and cannot be altered. Contracts are executed by the parties using digital signatures. If certain conditions are met, such as paying a debt when a predetermined date is reached, smart legal contracts may operate on their own. If stakeholders don't comply, there may be serious legal ramifications.

2. **Decentralized Autonomous Organizations (DAOs):** DAOs are democratic organisations with voting powers granted by a smart contract. A decentralised autonomous organisation, or DAO, is a blockchain-based entity with a shared goal under collective governance. There is no such thing as an executive or president. Instead, the organization's operations and the distribution of assets are governed by blockchain-based principles that are incorporated into the contract's code. One example of this kind of smart contract is VitaDAO, which uses technology to power a community dedicated to scientific inquiry.

3. **Application Logic Contracts:** Application-based code that usually keeps up with multiple other blockchain contracts makes up application logic contracts, or ALCs. It permits device-to-device interactions such as blockchain integration and the Internet of Things. These are signed between computers and other

contracts rather than between people or organisations like other kinds of smart contracts.

Features of Smart Contracts: The following are some essential characteristics of a smart contract:

1. **Distributed:** Everyone on the network is guaranteed to have a copy of all the conditions of the smart contract and they cannot be changed by one of the parties. A smart contract is replicated and distributed by all the nodes connected to the network.

2. **Deterministic:** Smart contracts can only perform functions for which they are designed only when the required conditions are met. The final outcome will not vary, no matter who executes the smart contract.

3. **Immutable:** Once deployed smart contract cannot be changed, it can only be removed as long as the functionality is implemented previously.

4. **Autonomy:** There is no third party involved. The contract is made by you and shared between the parties. No intermediaries are involved which minimizes bullying and grants full authority to the dealing parties. Also, the smart contract is maintained and executed by all the nodes on the network, thus removing all the controlling power from any one party's hand.

5. **Customizable:** Smart contracts have the ability for modification or we can say customization before being launched to do what the user wants it to do.

6. **Transparent:** Smart contracts are always stored on a public distributed ledger called blockchain due to which the code is visible to everyone, whether or not they are participants in the smart contract.

7. **Trustless:** These are not required by third parties to verify the integrity of the process or to check whether the required conditions are met.

8. **Self-verifying:** These are self-verifying due to automated possibilities.

9. **Self-enforcing:** These are self-enforcing when the conditions and rules are met at all stages.

Internet of Things (IoT) Software Engineering

The Internet of Things (IoT) in software engineering refers to the development of software systems that enable communication, data processing, and control of interconnected physical devices over the internet. These devices ranging from sensors and wearables to smart home appliances and industrial machines collect and transmit data to provide intelligent services in real time.

In IoT software engineering, developers design systems across multiple layers: the device layer (embedded programming for sensors and microcontrollers), the network layer (communication protocols like MQTT, CoAP, or HTTP), and the application layer (cloud-based services and user interfaces). Popular programming languages include C/C++ for embedded devices and Python, Java, or JavaScript for server-side applications. Engineers also use IoT platforms like AWS IoT, Microsoft Azure IoT, or Google Cloud IoT for device management, analytics, and scalability.

A major challenge in IoT software engineering is ensuring security, as IoT devices often operate with limited resources and are vulnerable to cyberattacks. Techniques such as data encryption, device authentication, and secure firmware updates are essential.

Another critical aspect is real-time data processing. Many IoT applications, like health monitoring or industrial automation, require low-latency, reliable communication and quick decision-making, which often involves edge computing processing data close to the source.

In summary, IoT software engineering is a multidisciplinary field that combines embedded systems, cloud computing, networking, and cybersecurity. It plays a vital role in creating smart, responsive systems across industries such as healthcare, manufacturing, agriculture, and smart cities.

Key Components of IoT Software Engineering

1. **Embedded Systems and Firmware Development**: IoT devices are typically resource-constrained, necessitating efficient embedded software development. Engineers utilize languages like C, C++, and Python to program microcontrollers and sensors, ensuring optimal performance within limited memory and processing capabilities. Real-Time Operating Systems (RTOS) such as Zephyr provides the necessary infrastructure for managing hardware resources and scheduling tasks in time-sensitive applications.

2. **Communication Protocols**: Effective communication between IoT devices and backend systems is crucial. Common protocols include:

   - **MQTT (Message Queuing Telemetry Transport):** Lightweight and ideal for low-bandwidth, high-latency environments.

- **CoAP (Constrained Application Protocol):** Designed for simple devices and low-power sensors.
- **HTTP/HTTPS:** Standard protocols for web-based communication.
- **Bluetooth Low Energy (BLE), Zigbee, and LoRaWAN:** Suitable for short-range and long-range device communication, respectively.

Selecting the appropriate protocol depends on factors like power consumption, range, and data throughput requirements.

3. **Data Management and Cloud Integration:** IoT systems generate vast amounts of data that require efficient storage, processing, and analysis. Cloud platforms such as AWS IoT, Microsoft Azure IoT, and Google Cloud IoT provide scalable infrastructure to handle this data influx. These platforms offer services for device management, data analytics, and machine learning, enabling real-time insights and decision-making.
4. **Edge Computing**: To mitigate latency and bandwidth issues, edge computing processes data closer to the source on the device or nearby edge servers. This approach is particularly beneficial for applications requiring real-time responses, such as autonomous vehicles and industrial automation systems.
5. **Security and Privacy**: Given the pervasive nature of IoT devices, ensuring robust security is paramount. Key considerations include:
   - **Data Encryption:** Protecting data both at rest and in transit.
   - **Authentication and Authorization:** Ensuring only authorized devices and users can access the system.
   - **Regular Firmware Updates:** Addressing vulnerabilities and enhancing functionality.
   - **Compliance with Standards:** Adhering to regulations like GDPR and industry-specific standards to safeguard user privacy.

Tools like E4 provide open-source cryptographic solutions to enhance end-to-end encryption for IoT devices.

Architectural Models in IoT Software Engineering

1. **Perception Layer:** This is the first layer of IoT architecture. In the perception layer, a number of sensors and actuators are used to gather useful information

like temperature, moisture content, intruder detection, sounds, etc. The main function of this layer is to get information from surroundings and to pass data to another layer so that some actions can be done based on that information.

2. **Network Layer:** As the name suggests, it is the connecting layer between perception and middleware layer. It gets data from perception layer and passes data to middleware layer using networking technologies like 3G, 4G, UTMS, Wifi, infrared, etc. This is also called communication layer because it is responsible for communication between perception and middleware layer. All the transfer of data done securely keeping the obtained data confidential.

3. **Middleware Layer:** Middleware Layer has some advanced features like storage, computation, processing, action taking capabilities. It stores all data-set and based on the device address and name it gives appropriate data to that device. It can also take decisions based on calculations done on data-set obtained from sensors.

4. **Application Layer:** The application layer manages all application process based on information obtained from middleware layer. This application involves sending emails, activating alarm, security system, turn on or off a device, smartwatch, smart agriculture, etc.

5. **Business Layer:** The success of any device does not depend only on technologies used in it but also how it is being delivered to its consumers. Business layer does these tasks for the device. It involves making flowcharts, graphs, analysis of results, and how device can be improved, etc.

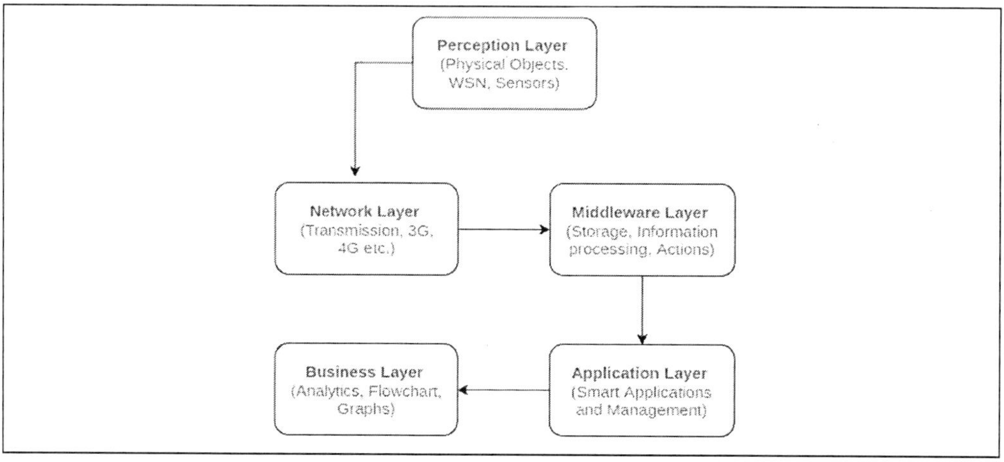

Fig.4.14

Quantum Computing and Future Trends

Quantum computing is a revolutionary technology that uses the principles of quantum mechanics to perform complex computations far faster than classical computers. Instead of binary bits, it uses qubits, which can exist in multiple states simultaneously due to superposition and interact through entanglement, enabling massive parallel processing. This makes quantum computers particularly powerful for tasks like cryptography, optimization, and molecular simulation.

Looking ahead, key trends include achieving quantum advantage, where quantum systems outperform classical ones in real-world tasks, and the rise of quantum-safe cryptography to protect against future threats. Companies like IBM, Google, and startups are pushing cloud-based quantum computing, expanding global access. Advancements in error correction and scalable hardware are also accelerating progress. Additionally, hybrid quantum-classical models and quantum machine learning are emerging as promising areas. Though still in early stages, quantum computing is poised to transform industries, from pharmaceuticals to finance, in the coming decades.

Quantum Computing: Quantum computing is reshaping the field of software engineering by introducing new paradigms for algorithm design, problem-solving, and system architecture. Unlike classical systems that use binary bits (0s and 1s), quantum computers use qubits, which can exist in multiple states simultaneously due to superposition, and be interlinked through entanglement. These properties enable quantum systems to solve complex problems exponentially faster than traditional computers in areas like optimization, cryptography, and data analysis.

In software engineering, quantum computing impacts the way algorithms are written and executed. Engineers must learn quantum programming languages like Qiskit (Python-based), Q# (by Microsoft), and Cirq (by Google) to develop applications for quantum hardware. Instead of traditional control flows, quantum software relies on quantum circuits, quantum gates, and probabilistic outcomes, requiring a fundamental shift in thinking.

Quantum computing is particularly relevant in fields like machine learning, cybersecurity, and complex simulations. For example, quantum algorithms can optimize machine learning models more efficiently or break encryption schemes used in software systems, prompting the need for quantum-safe cryptography.

While still in its early stages, quantum computing in software engineering is a rapidly growing field that encourages innovation in algorithm design, architecture modeling, and the development of hybrid classical-quantum systems.

Quantum computing can significantly enhance IoT software engineering by accelerating data processing, improving security, and optimizing resource allocation. Quantum algorithms can analyze large IoT datasets faster and more efficiently, leading to real-time insights and better predictive modeling. Additionally, quantum cryptography offers stronger encryption schemes like Quantum Key Distribution (QKD) to secure IoT communication channels. Benefits of Quantum computing are as under:

1. **Enhanced Data Processing:** Quantum computing can significantly enhance IoT software engineering by accelerating data processing, improving security, and optimizing resource allocation. Quantum algorithms can analyze large IoT datasets faster and more efficiently, leading to real-time insights and better predictive modeling. Additionally, quantum cryptography offers stronger encryption schemes like Quantum Key Distribution (QKD) to secure IoT communication channels.

    - **Faster and more efficient processing:** Quantum computers can process large volumes of data from IoT devices much faster than classical computers, enabling real-time analysis and decision-making.

    - **Complex algorithm execution:** Quantum algorithms like Grover's and Shor's can be used to analyze massive IoT data, optimize network performance, and enhance energy efficiency.

    - **Real-time insights:** Quantum computing can facilitate real-time decision-making, allowing IoT systems to adapt to changing conditions and optimize resource allocation.

2. **Improved Security:** Quantum computing enhances security through quantum cryptography, particularly Quantum Key Distribution (QKD), which enables ultra-secure communication by detecting any eavesdropping attempts. Unlike traditional encryption, which relies on mathematical complexity, QKD uses the laws of quantum physics, making it theoretically unbreakable. Additionally, quantum computing encourages the development of post-quantum cryptography new algorithms designed to resist attacks from future quantum systems. While quantum computers could potentially break current encryption standards, their advancement also drives innovations that strengthen digital security frameworks, offering a more robust defense against cyber threats and ensuring secure communication for governments, industries, and individuals.

- **Quantum Key Distribution (QKD):** QKD offers a highly secure method for exchanging encryption keys, ensuring that communication channels are protected from eavesdropping and tampering.
- **Stronger Encryption:** Quantum computing can potentially break existing cryptographic algorithms, necessitating the development of quantum-resistant encryption methods like QKD

Future Trends: Future trends in software engineering are being shaped by rapid technological advancements and evolving user demands. One of the most significant shifts is the integration of artificial intelligence (AI) and machine learning (ML) into the development lifecycle. Tools like GitHub Copilot and AI-based testing platforms are improving productivity and code quality. Low-code and no-code platforms are also gaining traction, enabling faster development by allowing non-technical users to create applications. Meanwhile, cloud-native technologies such as microservices, containers, and serverless architectures are making software more scalable and resilient.

Security and sustainability are becoming central concerns in modern software development. The rise of DevSecOps reflects the growing need to embed security from the earliest stages of development. Additionally, software supply chain security is now critical to prevent attacks on widely-used components and dependencies. Developers are also embracing sustainable engineering practices to reduce energy consumption and carbon footprints. Emerging technologies such as edge computing and quantum software development are expected to revolutionize industries by offering faster processing and solving complex problems. As user expectations rise, hyper-personalized software and ethical AI practices will be essential for creating trusted and adaptive digital experiences. These trends point to a future where software is smarter, safer, greener, and more inclusive.

Software engineering is evolving at a rapid pace, driven by technological innovation, increasing user expectations, and the need for more secure, scalable, and intelligent systems. As digital transformation reshapes every industry, software engineers must adapt to emerging paradigms and tools that redefine how software is designed, developed, deployed, and maintained. This essay explores the key future trends that are expected to shape the field of software engineering over the next decade.

1. **AI-Driven Software Development:** Artificial Intelligence (AI) and Machine Learning (ML) are revolutionizing software engineering. From code generation and debugging to testing and deployment, AI is increasingly being integrated into every phase of the software development lifecycle. Tools such as GitHub

Copilot, powered by OpenAI, can auto-complete code snippets, suggest improvements, and assist developers in writing efficient, error-free code.

AI-driven testing tools are also gaining traction, enabling automated test generation, bug detection, and performance monitoring. As these tools mature, they will significantly reduce the manual effort required for software development and enhance productivity. Moreover, AI can analyze large datasets to optimize user experiences, personalize interfaces, and automate decision-making in applications, making software more intelligent and user-centric.

2. **Low-Code and No-Code Development:** The demand for rapid application development has led to the rise of low-code and no-code platforms. These platforms enable developers and even non-technical users to build applications using graphical user interfaces and pre-built components rather than traditional programming. Tools like Mendix, OutSystems, and Microsoft Power Apps are enabling faster development cycles and democratizing software creation.

   This trend is particularly beneficial for startups, small businesses, and organizations with limited IT resources. It also supports agile methodologies by enabling faster iterations and deployments. However, while these platforms simplify development, they still require oversight from professional developers for complex integrations, security, and scalability.

3. **Cloud-Native and Serverless Architectures:** Cloud computing has already transformed software deployment, but the next phase is centered on cloud-native and serverless architectures. Cloud-native development leverages technologies such as containers (e.g., Docker), orchestration tools (e.g., Kubernetes), and microservices to build applications that are highly scalable, resilient, and portable across environments.

   Serverless computing, where cloud providers manage the server infrastructure and dynamically allocate resources, allows developers to focus solely on writing code. Services like AWS Lambda, Azure Functions, and Google Cloud Functions are gaining popularity for building event-driven, stateless applications. These models reduce operational complexity and cost, making them ideal for modern, scalable web and mobile applications.

4. **DevSecOps and Shift-Left Security:** Security is no longer an afterthought in software development. The DevSecOps approach integrates security practices into the DevOps pipeline, ensuring that vulnerabilities are identified

and mitigated early in the development process. This "shift-left" approach emphasizes proactive security measures, including code scanning, vulnerability assessments, and automated compliance checks.

With increasing cyber threats and stricter data protection regulations, secure coding practices are essential. Tools like Snyk, SonarQube, and Aqua Security are helping teams to embed security checks within CI/CD pipelines. As applications become more interconnected through APIs and third-party integrations, securing the software supply chain will also be a major focus moving forward.

5. **Edge Computing and Real-Time Processing:** Edge computing involves processing data closer to the source such as IoT devices, autonomous vehicles, or smart cameras — rather than relying solely on centralized cloud servers. This approach reduces latency, enhances real-time performance, and improves reliability for time-sensitive applications.

   In software engineering, this trend demands a shift in architecture and design patterns. Developers must optimize applications for constrained environments with limited bandwidth and computational power. As 5G and IoT adoption grow, edge-native development will become a critical skill set, particularly in industries like manufacturing, healthcare, and transportation.

6. **Sustainable Software Engineering:** As awareness of climate change and energy consumption grows, the software engineering community is paying closer attention to sustainability. Sustainable software engineering focuses on designing applications that consume less energy, use computational resources efficiently, and contribute to a smaller environmental footprint.

   Green software development may involve writing efficient algorithms, minimizing data storage, optimizing network usage, and choosing energy-efficient hosting providers. Companies are beginning to report on the carbon footprint of their digital operations, and software engineers are expected to consider sustainability as a key quality attribute alongside performance and security.

7. **Quantum Software Development:** Quantum computing, though still in its infancy, has the potential to revolutionize problem-solving in areas like cryptography, material science, and complex simulations. As quantum hardware matures, the demand for quantum software engineers will grow.

Quantum programming languages like Q#, Qiskit, and Cirq are being used to develop quantum algorithms and applications. While mainstream adoption is still years away, forward-thinking organizations are investing in quantum research and education to prepare for this disruptive shift. Software engineers who understand quantum principles will be at the forefront of this emerging frontier.

8. **Hyper-Personalized and Adaptive Applications:** Personalization is becoming a key driver of user satisfaction and engagement. With the help of AI, analytics, and behavioral data, software applications are becoming more adaptive offering content, features, and interfaces tailored to individual users.

   For example, e-commerce platforms personalize product recommendations, streaming services tailor content feeds, and learning management systems adapt courses based on learner behavior. The trend toward hyper-personalization requires software engineers to integrate real-time data pipelines, recommendation engines, and user modeling techniques while maintaining user privacy and consent.

9. **Software Supply Chain Security:** High-profile attacks like the SolarWinds and Log4Shell incidents have highlighted vulnerabilities in the software supply chain. As software projects increasingly rely on open-source components and third-party libraries, ensuring the security and integrity of these dependencies has become a top priority.

   Future trends in this area include the widespread adoption of Software Bills of Materials (SBOMs), digital signatures for software artifacts, and frameworks like SLSA (Supply-chain Levels for Software Artifacts). These initiatives aim to improve transparency, traceability, and trust in the software development ecosystem.

10. **Ethical and Responsible AI Development:** As AI becomes embedded in more applications, ethical considerations are moving to the forefront of software engineering. Developers must ensure that AI systems are transparent, explainable, unbiased, and accountable. This involves incorporating fairness metrics, conducting bias audits, and involving diverse stakeholders in system design. Ethical software engineering also includes data privacy, informed consent, and responsible data usage. Governments and organizations are introducing AI regulations, and engineers must comply with these frameworks while building systems that respect human values and societal norms.

SUMMARY OF ADVANCED TOPICS IN SOFTWARE ENGINEERING

Software engineering is a multifaceted field that continues to evolve, with new methodologies, technologies, and challenges emerging constantly. As the complexity of systems increases, engineers must understand advanced topics to design, develop, and maintain robust and scalable software. This summary covers key advanced topics in software engineering, including security practices, performance optimization, scalability, and the impact of emerging technologies like AI, blockchain, IoT, and quantum computing.

9. Security in Software Engineering

Security is a critical concern in software development, especially as the frequency and sophistication of cyberattacks continue to rise. Security practices must be integrated into every stage of software development to protect user data and ensure system integrity.

- **Secure Coding Practices:** Secure coding is essential to prevent vulnerabilities from being introduced into the software. Developers must follow secure coding guidelines to avoid common pitfalls, such as buffer overflows, SQL injection, and cross-site scripting (XSS). Secure coding practices include proper input validation, output encoding, and the use of secure libraries.

- **Common Vulnerabilities (OWASP Top 10):** The OWASP Top 10 outlines the most critical web application security risks, including injection flaws, broken authentication, sensitive data exposure, and security misconfigurations. These vulnerabilities are commonly exploited by attackers and can lead to severe security breaches. Developers must stay informed about these risks and implement mitigation strategies to protect their applications.

- **Authentication and Authorization:** Authentication ensures that only legitimate users can access a system, while authorization defines what actions an authenticated user can perform. Secure authentication methods, such as multi-factor authentication (MFA), and role-based access control (RBAC) for authorization, are essential to prevent unauthorized access and safeguard sensitive data.

- **Data Privacy and Encryption:** Protecting user data is a fundamental aspect of software security. Data encryption, both at rest and in transit, ensures that data cannot be read by unauthorized parties. Data privacy laws, such as GDPR, require developers to implement strict data protection measures and ensure that users' personal information is handled responsibly.

10. Performance Optimization and Scalability

Performance and scalability are critical factors in ensuring that software can handle increasing traffic, complex tasks, and large datasets. Software that performs poorly can frustrate users and lead to lost revenue, while scalability ensures that systems can handle growing demands over time.

- **Performance Bottlenecks and Profiling:** Performance bottlenecks occur when certain parts of a system become overwhelmed and prevent optimal performance. These bottlenecks can be identified through profiling, which analyzes the execution of an application to pinpoint slow or inefficient code. Common bottlenecks include inefficient algorithms, memory leaks, and slow database queries.

- To ensure high performance and availability, load balancing distributes incoming traffic across multiple servers. Caching strategies store frequently accessed data in a faster, temporary storage layer, reducing the need to fetch data from the database repeatedly. These techniques help in maintaining fast response times and improving overall system performance.

- **Horizontal vs. Vertical Scaling:** Scaling is the process of expanding a system's capacity to handle more users or data. Vertical scaling involves adding more resources (e.g., CPU, memory) to a single server, while horizontal scaling involves adding more servers to distribute the load. Horizontal scaling is often preferred for large-scale, cloud-based systems because it offers greater flexibility and fault tolerance.

- **Cloud-Native Application Development:** Cloud-native applications are designed to take full advantage of cloud computing environments. These applications are typically built using microservices architecture, where each component is loosely coupled and independently scalable. Cloud-native apps also leverage containerization (e.g., Docker) and orchestration tools (e.g., Kubernetes) to ensure easy deployment and scalability.

11. Software Engineering for Emerging Technologies

As technology evolves, new challenges and opportunities arise for software engineers. Emerging technologies like artificial intelligence (AI), blockchain, the Internet of Things (IoT), and quantum computing are rapidly changing the landscape of software development. Engineers must adapt their skills to harness the power of these technologies while addressing the unique challenges they bring.

- **Artificial Intelligence and Machine Learning in Software Development:** AI and machine learning (ML) are transforming software engineering by enabling systems to learn from data and make decisions without explicit programming. AI-driven software can automate tasks like code generation, testing, and bug detection, enhancing productivity and reducing human error. ML models can also be embedded in applications to offer intelligent features such as recommendations, anomaly detection, and natural language processing (NLP).

Incorporating AI and ML into software development requires specialized knowledge in data science, algorithms, and model deployment. Additionally, ethical considerations such as bias, fairness, and transparency must be carefully managed to ensure responsible AI development.

- **Blockchain and Smart Contracts:** Blockchain technology has revolutionized the way data is stored and shared. By using a decentralized, tamper-resistant ledger, blockchain provides enhanced security, transparency, and traceability. Smart contracts, which are self-executing contracts with predefined conditions, run on blockchain platforms like Ethereum and enable automated transactions without intermediaries.

  For software engineers, blockchain presents unique challenges such as managing distributed networks, ensuring security, and dealing with scalability issues. Smart contracts have applications in areas like finance, supply chain management, and healthcare, but they require careful implementation to avoid vulnerabilities like re-entrancy attacks.

- **Internet of Things (IoT) Software Engineering:** The Internet of Things (IoT) refers to the growing network of connected devices, such as sensors, wearables, and home automation systems. Developing software for IoT involves challenges related to real-time data processing, energy consumption, and security.

  IoT systems often require low-latency, high-throughput communication protocols (e.g., MQTT) and must be capable of processing data at the edge to reduce latency. Engineers need to design robust, scalable systems that can handle large volumes of data generated by connected devices while ensuring security and privacy.

- **Quantum Computing and Future Trends:** Quantum computing is an emerging field that uses quantum mechanics to solve problems that are computationally infeasible for classical computers. Quantum computers have the potential to revolutionize fields like cryptography, optimization, and complex simulations. For software engineers, quantum computing presents a new set of challenges and opportunities.

Quantum algorithms, such as Grover's and Shor's algorithms, offer the possibility of solving problems exponentially faster than traditional algorithms. However, quantum programming requires specialized knowledge in quantum mechanics and quantum algorithms. As quantum hardware becomes more accessible, software engineers will need to develop new tools and frameworks to leverage its power.

******

PART–5

SOFTWARE PROJECT MANAGEMENT AND CAREER DEVELOPMENT

Software Project Management (SPM) refers to the process of planning, executing, monitoring, and closing software projects. It encompasses a set of methodologies, tools, and practices aimed at ensuring software products are delivered on time, within budget, and according to specified quality standards. Career development in this domain involves the continuous growth of professionals in both technical and managerial roles, as they adapt to the evolving landscape of software engineering.

At the core of SPM are the fundamental project management processes: Initiation, Planning, Execution, Monitoring and Controlling, and Closure. During initiation, the project's feasibility is assessed, and goals are defined. Planning involves outlining the scope, timeline, resource allocation, budgeting, and risk management. Execution turns plans into action through coding, testing, and integration. Monitoring tracks progress and performance, often using metrics such as cost variance and schedule variance. Finally, closure involves project delivery, documentation, and evaluation.

Key methodologies in software project management include Agile, Scrum, Waterfall, and DevOps. Agile promotes iterative development and customer collaboration, while Waterfall follows a linear, sequential approach. Scrum, a subset of Agile, focuses on short development cycles called sprints. DevOps integrates development and operations to enhance automation and delivery speed. Choosing the right methodology depends on project requirements, team dynamics, and stakeholder expectations.

Critical roles in software project management include the Project Manager, Product Owner, Scrum Master, Developers, Testers, and Stakeholders. The project manager is responsible for overall coordination, risk mitigation, and stakeholder communication. Leadership, time management, and decision-making are vital skills in this role. Risk management is an essential aspect of SPM, involving the identification, analysis, and mitigation of potential issues that could affect project outcomes. Common risks include scope creep, technical challenges, resource constraints, and changing customer requirements. Mitigation strategies may involve contingency planning, buffer time, and continuous stakeholder engagement.

Effective communication, team collaboration, and stakeholder management are pivotal for project success. Tools like JIRA, Trello, MS Project, and Slack aid in tracking tasks, sharing updates, and maintaining team coordination. In terms of career development, professionals typically start as developers or testers and can progress to roles like team lead, project manager, program manager, or technical architect. Career growth requires not only technical proficiency but also the development of soft skills such as leadership, conflict resolution, and negotiation. Certifications such as PMP (Project Management Professional), Certified ScrumMaster (CSM), and PRINCE2 can enhance career prospects and validate expertise. Continuous learning through training, attending seminars, and participating in communities of practice helps professionals stay relevant in a rapidly evolving industry. Software project management blends technical expertise with managerial acumen to ensure successful software delivery. Career development in this field demands a proactive approach to skill-building, adaptability to new technologies and methodologies, and a commitment to lifelong learning. By mastering both the tools and the mindset of effective project management, professionals can drive innovation and growth in the software industry.

12

Software Project Management

Software Project Management (SPM) is the discipline of planning, organizing, leading, and controlling software projects to ensure successful delivery within defined constraints of time, cost, scope, and quality. It involves applying project management principles specifically to software development, using methodologies like Waterfall, Agile, Scrum, and DevOps, each suited to different project needs. The project lifecycle includes initiation, planning, execution, monitoring, and closure, with an emphasis on defining clear goals, estimating resources and timelines, managing risks, and maintaining effective communication among stakeholders. A software project manager is responsible for coordinating teams, resolving issues, tracking progress, and ensuring that deliverables meet client expectations. Tools such as JIRA, MS Project, and Trello are commonly used to manage tasks and track project performance. Risk management is a critical component, addressing potential threats such as changing requirements, technical challenges, and resource limitations. Success in software project management requires a combination of technical knowledge, leadership ability, time management, and problem-solving skills. In today's dynamic software industry, the ability to adapt to changing technologies and methodologies is essential. Certifications like PMP, PRINCE2, or Certified ScrumMaster (CSM) can further validate a professional's expertise and enhance their career trajectory. Overall, software project management is integral to delivering high-quality software products efficiently and plays a key role in the success of software development initiatives across various industries.

Project Planning and Estimation

Project Planning and Estimation is a crucial phase in software project management that involves defining the project scope, identifying tasks, allocating resources, setting timelines, and estimating costs to ensure successful project execution. Planning provides a roadmap that guides the development team, stakeholders, and managers throughout the project lifecycle. It begins with requirement gathering and scope definition, followed by work breakdown structure (WBS) creation to divide the project into manageable tasks. Resource planning ensures the right people, tools, and technologies are assigned to tasks, while scheduling determines start and end dates using techniques like Gantt charts or network diagrams. Estimation involves predicting the time, effort, and cost required to complete each task or the entire project. Common estimation techniques include expert judgment, analogy-based estimation, parametric models (like COCOMO), and planning poker in Agile. Accurate estimation is critical to avoid under or over-committing resources and to prevent delays or cost overruns. Risk assessment is also part of planning, identifying potential problems and developing mitigation strategies. A well-crafted project plan includes milestones, dependencies, budgets, quality standards, and communication plans. Regular reviews and updates to the plan are necessary to adapt to changes and ensure project alignment with goals. In summary, project planning and estimation lay the foundation for successful software delivery by setting clear expectations, improving predictability, and enabling informed decision-making throughout the development process.

Project planning and estimation in software engineering involve forecasting the time, effort, resources, and budget needed to complete a software project. It's a critical process for setting realistic deadlines, allocating resources efficiently, and managing expectations, ultimately contributing to project success.

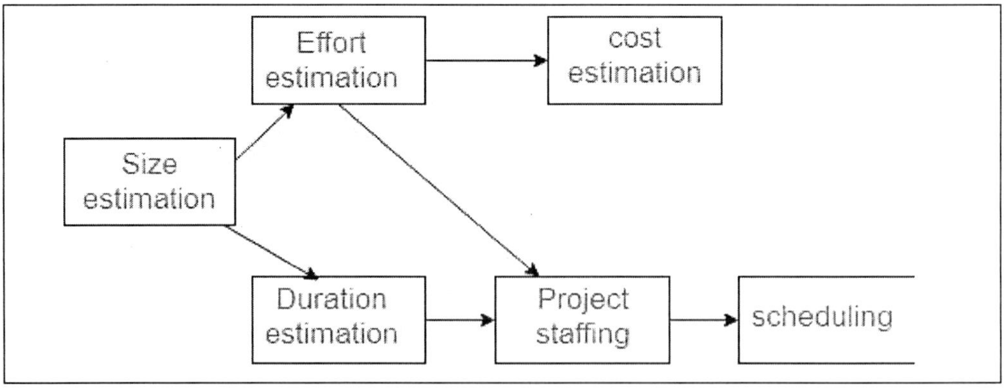

Fig.5.1

Key aspects of project planning and estimation are as under:

1. **Project Scope:** Defining what the project will deliver and the scope of work involved.

2. **Effort Estimation:** Predicting the amount of work (person-hours) required for different tasks.

3. **Cost Estimation:** Calculating the total cost of the project, including labor, tools, and materials.

4. **Timeline Estimation:** Determining the project duration and setting realistic deadlines.

5. **Resource Allocation:** Identifying and allocating the necessary resources (personnel, tools, etc.).

6. **Risk Management:** Identifying and assessing potential risks that could impact the project.

7. **Change Management:** Establishing procedures for handling changes to the project scope or requirements.

Project Planning and Estimation Techniques:

1. **Top-Down Estimating:** Top-down estimating is a project estimation technique that begins by determining the total project effort, duration, or cost at a high level and then breaking it down into smaller, more manageable components. This method is often used in the early stages of a project when detailed information may not be available. Senior managers or experienced stakeholders typically base top-down estimates on prior experience, similar projects, or strategic goals. After estimating the entire project, the effort is divided among phases, modules, or tasks to create a rough schedule and resource plan. Top-down estimating is quick and efficient, especially for projects with a tight timeline or limited scope. However, its accuracy heavily depends on the estimator's experience and the availability of comparable historical data. One key benefit is that it gives management a bird's-eye view and a fast estimation of costs and timelines, making it useful for early budgeting and feasibility studies. However, since this method doesn't consider granular details, it may overlook specific complexities or challenges in individual tasks, leading to potential underestimation. As a result, it is often supplemented later by more detailed techniques, such as bottom-up estimation. In summary, top-down estimating is

a useful starting point for project estimation that prioritizes speed and strategic alignment over precision, and it is best suited for high-level planning or when historical data provides a reliable reference.

2. **Bottom-Up Estimating:** Bottom-up estimating is a detailed and highly accurate project estimation technique that involves estimating the effort, cost, and duration of individual tasks or work packages and then aggregating them to determine the total project estimate. This method requires a clearly defined Work Breakdown Structure (WBS), where the entire project is broken down into smaller, manageable units. Each task is then individually assessed, often by the team members responsible for its execution, which increases the accuracy and reliability of the estimates. Once individual estimates are completed, they are summed up to form the overall project timeline and budget. Bottom-up estimating is ideal for projects where detailed requirements are available and where precision is critical. It supports resource planning, scheduling, and risk assessment at a granular level. However, this technique is time-consuming and labour-intensive, especially for large or complex projects. It may also lead to overly optimistic estimates if not managed carefully. Despite its resource demands, bottom-up estimation provides a clear understanding of project components and is particularly useful in Agile and iterative development environments where task-level detail is essential. It also facilitates accountability, as each team member is involved in the estimation process. In summary, bottom-up estimating delivers a high level of accuracy and control, making it suitable for projects where detailed planning is possible and necessary for successful execution.

3. **Planning Poker:** Planning poker is a consensus-based estimation technique commonly used in Agile project management, particularly during sprint planning sessions. It combines expert opinion, analogy, and relative sizing into a collaborative and engaging activity. The goal is to estimate the effort or complexity of individual user stories or tasks. In a planning poker session, each team member is given a deck of cards with numbers representing effort estimates, often following the Fibonacci sequence (e.g., 1, 2, 3, 5, 8, 13). The product owner or facilitator presents a user story, and team members independently choose a card that reflects their estimate of the effort required. Once all cards are revealed simultaneously, discrepancies are discussed, especially the highest and lowest estimates, allowing team members to explain their reasoning. The process is repeated until a consensus is reached. This

method encourages open communication, uncovers hidden assumptions, and promotes team alignment. Planning poker is highly effective for fostering shared understanding and improving estimation accuracy over time, especially for small to medium-sized tasks. Its collaborative nature ensures that all perspectives are considered, leading to more realistic and accepted estimates. However, it may be less suitable for very large teams or tasks that lack sufficient detail. In summary, planning poker is a lightweight, democratic estimation tool that enhances team collaboration, reduces estimation bias, and supports iterative development practices in Agile environments.

4. **Analogous Estimation:** Analogous estimation, also known as top-down or comparative estimation, is a technique where estimators use historical data from past, similar projects to predict the effort, cost, and duration of a current project. This method relies on the assumption that if two projects share key characteristics such as scope, complexity, and team structure then their resource needs will be comparable. Analogous estimation is typically performed at a high level and is faster and less resource-intensive than more detailed techniques like bottom-up estimating. It is particularly useful in the early stages of a project when limited information is available and when a quick, broad estimate is needed for feasibility studies or initial planning. Project managers often rely on organizational process assets, such as past project documentation, benchmarks, or expert judgment, to support this technique. The main advantage of analogous estimation is its speed and low cost, but its accuracy depends heavily on the quality and relevance of the historical data. If the reference projects differ significantly in terms of technology, team experience, or constraints, the estimates may be misleading. Therefore, it is often recommended to use this method as a preliminary estimation approach and refine it using more detailed methods later. In summary, analogous estimation is a pragmatic technique for generating early, high-level estimates by leveraging past experience, but it should be applied with caution and complemented by more detailed analysis as the project progresses.

5. **Empirical Models:** Empirical models use mathematical formulas and historical data to estimate software project effort, cost, and duration. One of the most well-known empirical models is COCOMO (Constructive Cost Model), developed by Barry Boehm. COCOMO estimates effort (measured in person-months) based on the size of the software, usually expressed in thousands of lines of code (KLOC), along with other factors such as project complexity,

team experience, and tools used. There are several versions of COCOMO Basic, Intermediate, and Detailed each offering increasing levels of precision by considering more variables. For example, COCOMO II, a modern adaptation, includes scale factors and cost drivers that adjust the raw estimates to reflect real-world conditions. These models are grounded in empirical data collected from past projects, making them statistically reliable when applied correctly. The advantages of empirical models include objectivity, consistency, and repeatability. They are particularly useful for large projects where data-driven insights are critical for managing risks and budgets. However, these models require accurate input data and are best suited for organizations with a history of similar projects. If input parameters are incorrect or not calibrated to the current environment, the output estimates may be flawed. Additionally, newer software practices like Agile may not align perfectly with models like COCOMO, which were designed for more traditional development environments. In summary, empirical models like COCOMO offer a systematic and quantifiable approach to project estimation, providing valuable guidance for planning and decision-making, especially in data-rich and structured development environments.

Risk Management in Software Development

Risk management in software development is the systematic process of identifying, analyzing, prioritizing, and mitigating potential issues that could negatively impact a software project's success. Risks in software development can stem from various sources, such as changing requirements, technical challenges, resource constraints, unrealistic timelines, security vulnerabilities, and external factors like market shifts or regulatory changes. The goal of risk management is not to eliminate all risks but to minimize their impact and improve project resilience.

The process typically begins with risk identification, where the project team brainstorms and documents possible threats. Next is risk analysis, which assesses the likelihood and potential impact of each risk using qualitative or quantitative methods. Risk prioritization follows, ranking risks based on severity to focus attention and resources on the most critical ones. Key aspects are as under:

Fig.5.2

1. **Risk Identification:** Risk identification refers to the systematic process of recognizing and evaluating potential threats or hazards that could negatively impact an organization, its operations, or its workforce. This involves identifying various types of risks, ranging from IT security threats like viruses and phishing attacks to unforeseen events such as equipment failures and extreme weather conditions.

2. **Risk Analysis:** Risk analysis is the process of evaluating and understanding the potential impact and likelihood of identified risks on an organization. It helps determine how serious a risk is and how to best manage or mitigate it. Risk Analysis involves evaluating each risk's probability and potential consequences to prioritize and manage them effectively.

3. **Risk Planning:** Risk planning involves developing strategies and actions to manage and mitigate identified risks effectively. It outlines how to respond to potential risks, including prevention, mitigation, and contingency measures, to protect the organization's objectives and assets.

4. **Risk Monitoring:** Risk monitoring involves continuously tracking and overseeing identified risks to assess their status, changes, and effectiveness of mitigation strategies. It ensures that risks are regularly reviewed and managed to maintain alignment with organizational objectives and adapt to new developments or challenges.

Understanding Risks in Software Projects: A computer code project may be laid low with an outsized sort of risk. To be ready to consistently establish the necessary risks that could affect a computer code project, it's necessary to group risks into completely different categories. The project manager will then examine the risks from every category square measure relevant to the project. There are mainly 3 classes of risks that may affect a computer code project:

1. **Project Risks:** Project risks concern various sorts of monetary funds, schedules, personnel, resources, and customer-related issues. A vital project risk is schedule slippage. Since computer code is intangible, it's tough to observe and manage a computer code project. It's tough to manage one thing that cannot be seen. For any producing project, like producing cars, the project manager will see the merchandise taking form. For example, see that the engine is fitted, at the moment the area of the door unit is fitted, the automotive is being painted, etc. so he will simply assess the progress of the work and manage it. The physical property of the merchandise being developed is a vital reason why several computer codes come to suffer from the danger of schedule slippage.

2. **Technical Risks:** Technical risks concern potential style, implementation, interfacing, testing, and maintenance issues. Technical risks conjointly embody ambiguous specifications, incomplete specifications, dynamic specifications, technical uncertainty, and technical degeneration. Most technical risks occur thanks to the event team's lean information concerning the project.

3. **Business Risks:** This type of risk embodies the risks of building a superb product that nobody needs, losing monetary funds or personal commitments, etc.

Risk management Standards and Frameworks: Risk management standards and frameworks give organizations guidelines on how to find, evaluate, and handle risks effectively. They provide a structured way to manage risks, making sure that everyone follows consistent and reliable practices. Here are some well-known risk management standards and frameworks:

1. **COSO ERM Framework: COSO ERM Framework was introduce in 2004 and updated in 2017. Its main purpose is to a**ddresses the growing complexity of Enterprise Risk Management (ERM). The COSO ERM Framework (Committee of Sponsoring Organizations of the Treadway Commission – Enterprise Risk Management) is a widely recognized model for managing organizational risk in a structured and integrated manner. Updated in 2017 as "Enterprise Risk Management – Integrating with Strategy and Performance," the framework emphasizes aligning risk management with strategic planning and performance measurement. The COSO ERM Framework consists of five interrelated components:

   - **Governance and Culture:** Establishes oversight, ethical values, and a risk-aware culture.
   - **Strategy and Objective-Setting:** Aligns risk appetite with strategic goals and sets objectives that consider risk.
   - **Performance:** Identifies and assesses risks that may impact performance and evaluates how well the risks are managed.
   - **Review and Revision:** Monitors changes, reviews performance, and revises the risk management approach as needed.
   - **Information, Communication, and Reporting:** Ensures relevant risk information flows across the organization and supports decision-making.

The COSO ERM framework helps organizations not just manage threats, but also recognize opportunities, improve resilience, and enhance value creation. It applies across industries and is particularly valuable in environments where regulatory compliance, financial integrity, and strategic alignment are critical. In software development, COSO ERM supports proactive risk identification and governance, improving project success and organizational performance.

Key Features:

- 20 principles grouped into five components: Governance and culture, Strategy and objective-setting, Performance, Review and revision, Information, communication, and reporting.
- It promotes integrating risk into business strategies and operations.

2. **ISO 31000**: ISO 31000 was introduced in 2009, revised in 2018. It provides principles and a framework for ERM. **ISO 31000** is an international standard for risk management, providing guidelines and principles that help organizations manage risk effectively across all activities and industries. First published in 2009 and updated in 2018, ISO 31000 offers a structured approach to integrating risk management into an organization's governance, strategy, planning, operations, and reporting processes. The framework is built on three key components:

    - **Principles**: Risk management should create value, be integrated, structured, and responsive to change. It must be customized, inclusive, and continuously improved.
    - **Framework**: Involves leadership commitment, integration into organizational processes, and continual improvement.
    - **Process**: Consists of risk identification, risk analysis, risk evaluation, and risk treatment, followed by monitoring, reviewing, and communication.

ISO 31000 does not prescribe a specific methodology but offers a universal foundation adaptable to any context. It promotes a proactive culture, encouraging organizations to understand uncertainty and take action before risks materialize. In software development, ISO 31000 helps teams address technical, operational, and strategic risks such as scope creep, system failures, or regulatory non-compliance by embedding risk thinking into decision-making and project planning. Overall, ISO 31000 enhances resilience, supports informed decisions, and enables consistent and measurable risk management across the organization.

Key Features:

- It offers guidance on applying risk management to operations.
- It focuses on identifying, evaluating, and mitigating risks.
- It promotes senior management's role and integrating risk management across the organization.

3. **BS 31100**: This framework is British Standard for Risk Management and latest version issued in 2001. It offers a structured approach to applying the principles outlined in ISO 31000:2018, covering tasks like identifying, evaluating, and addressing risks, followed by reporting and reviewing risk management efforts. BS 31100 provides a comprehensive framework for effective risk

management within organizations. Its components are designed to ensure that risk management is systematic, integrated, and aligned with strategic and operational objectives. The key components of BS 31100 include

- **Risk Management Policy:** Establishes the organization's commitment to risk management. Defines objectives, scope, and principles. Clarifies roles, responsibilities, and accountability.
- **Risk Governance and Leadership:** Ensures top-level involvement and oversight from the board and senior management. Aligns risk management with corporate governance. Encourages a risk-aware culture throughout the organization.
- **Risk Identification:** Systematically identifies internal and external risks that could impact objectives. Involves input from stakeholders and all relevant departments.
- **Risk Assessment:** Evaluates the likelihood and impact of identified risks. Uses qualitative and/or quantitative methods to prioritize risks.
- **Risk Treatment:** Defines actions to mitigate, transfer, accept, or avoid risks. Supports the implementation of control measures.

Key Features:

- It integrates risk management with an organization's overall governance and strategic planning.
- It emphasizes the importance of embedding risk awareness across the organization.

Agile Project Management Tools (JIRA, Trello, etc.)

Agile Project Management Tools like JIRA, Trello, and others play a crucial role in facilitating Agile practices by helping teams plan, track, and manage their work efficiently. These tools support iterative development, continuous feedback, and team collaboration core principles of Agile methodology. JIRA, developed by Atlassian, is widely used for managing Scrum and Kanban projects. It allows teams to create user stories, plan sprints, track bugs, and generate real-time reports such as burndown charts and velocity tracking. JIRA's robust customization and integration capabilities make it ideal for complex software development projects that require detailed workflow and performance tracking.

On the other hand, Trello is a more lightweight, visual tool based on the Kanban method. It uses boards, lists, and cards to help teams organize tasks, set priorities, and track progress in a simple and intuitive interface. Trello is especially popular among smaller teams and startups due to its ease of use and flexibility. Both tools promote transparency, real-time collaboration, and adaptability, making them effective in Agile environments where requirements and priorities evolve frequently. Other notable tools include Asana, ClickUp, and Monday.com, each offering different levels of complexity and features tailored to Agile workflows. These tools help teams stay aligned, focused, and responsive to change.

1. JIRA Agile Project Management Tool: JIRA is a powerful Agile project management tool developed by Atlassian, widely used by software development teams to plan, track, and manage Agile projects. It supports frameworks like Scrum, Kanban, and Scaled Agile Framework (SAFe), making it ideal for teams of all sizes from startups to large enterprises.

JIRA allows teams to break down large projects into manageable user stories, assign tasks, and track progress in real time. Its core components include projects, issues (tasks, bugs, stories), workflows, and boards. Scrum boards in JIRA are used to manage sprints, plan backlogs, and monitor sprint progress through burndown charts and velocity reports. Kanban boards visualize the continuous flow of work, ideal for teams focused on optimizing cycle time. One of JIRA's biggest strengths is its customization. Teams can create custom workflows, fields, permission schemes, and automation rules tailored to specific processes. JIRA also integrates seamlessly with a wide range of tools such as Confluence, Bitbucket, Slack, GitHub, and CI/CD pipelines, enabling end-to-end project visibility.

In Agile environments, where requirements and priorities shift frequently, JIRA provides dynamic backlog grooming, sprint planning, and retrospective tracking tools to adapt quickly. It supports epics, versions, and components, allowing teams to structure and scale projects easily. JIRA's reporting capabilities, such as control charts, cumulative flow diagrams, and sprint reports, help stakeholders make data-driven decisions.

However, due to its depth, JIRA can have a steep learning curve for new users. It's best suited for technical teams with defined processes that require detailed tracking and control. For non-technical users or smaller teams, JIRA may feel overly complex. JIRA is a feature-rich and scalable Agile tool ideal for software development teams seeking advanced functionality, detailed tracking, and robust reporting. Its versatility and integration capabilities make it a leading choice for managing Agile projects in complex and fast-paced environments.

The key features of JIRA:

- **Customizable Workflows:** JIRA allows teams to design custom workflows for issue tracking. This feature enables organizations to define how tasks, bugs, and other issues move through stages, such as To Do, In Progress, and Done. Workflows can be tailored for different teams and projects, ensuring alignment with business processes. Users can set up specific transitions and conditions, giving them full control over how work is tracked and managed.

- **Scrum and Kanban Boards:** JIRA offers Scrum and Kanban boards for visualizing and managing tasks. Scrum boards are designed for teams working in iterative sprints, helping manage the backlog and track progress. Kanban boards, on the other hand, help teams with continuous delivery workflows, visualizing work items and managing Work in Progress (WIP) limits. These boards provide real-time insights into task status and facilitate collaboration among team members.

- **Advanced Reporting and Analytics:** JIRA provides a wide array of Agile reports like burndown charts, velocity charts, cumulative flow diagrams, and sprint reports. These reports help teams track sprint progress, measure performance, and identify bottlenecks. Teams can use these insights to adjust their workflows, improve productivity, and make data-driven decisions for future sprints.

- **JIRA Query Language (JQL):** JQL (JIRA Query Language) is a powerful search tool that allows users to create custom queries to filter, sort, and analyze project data. With JQL, users can retrieve complex datasets, create custom reports, and track specific issues based on various criteria. This feature enhances flexibility and provides users with precise data for project tracking and decision-making.

- **Integration with Other Tools:** JIRA seamlessly integrates with other tools within the Atlassian suite (such as Confluence, Bitbucket, and Bamboo) and third-party applications like GitHub, Slack, and Jenkins. These integrations enable cross-team collaboration, ensure seamless communication, and streamline workflows by connecting development, testing, and project management activities in one unified environment.

2. Trello Agile Project Management Tool: Trello is a visual project management tool based on the Kanban methodology, designed to help individuals and teams organize and prioritize tasks efficiently. Developed by Atlassian, Trello uses a simple, intuitive board and card system to manage workflows. Each project is represented by a board, which contains lists (representing stages of work, e.g., To Do, In Progress, Done) and cards (representing individual tasks or work items).

The simplicity of Trello makes it an ideal tool for both technical and non-technical teams, as well as individuals managing personal projects. Users can create cards for specific tasks, add due dates, checklists, attachments, and labels, and assign team members to each card. The drag-and-drop interface allows users to move cards through lists, providing a visual representation of work progress.

Trello's collaboration features include comments, where team members can discuss tasks directly on the cards, and notifications, which keep everyone updated on task changes. Power-Ups (integrations) expand Trello's functionality, allowing users to integrate with tools like Google Drive, Slack, GitHub, and Trello's calendar view. While Trello lacks advanced reporting features like burndown charts or velocity reports, it's still powerful for managing simple workflows, team collaboration, and day-to-day task tracking. It's particularly effective for small teams or cross-functional teams working in fast-paced environments, providing a lightweight, easy-to-use alternative to more complex project management tools like JIRA.

The key features of Trello:

- **Boards, Lists, and Cards:** Trello organizes tasks using boards, lists, and cards. Each board represents a project, with lists representing stages of work (e.g., To Do, In Progress, Done). Cards represent individual tasks or work items that can be moved between lists as they progress through stages. This simple, visual setup helps teams quickly see the status of tasks at a glance.

- **Collaboration and Team Communication:** Trello enables seamless team collaboration by allowing members to comment on cards, tag colleagues, and provide real-time updates. Notifications keep users informed of changes, and team members can easily discuss tasks directly within the app, ensuring all communication stays centralized.

- **Checklists and Due Dates:** Each card can include checklists to break tasks down into smaller subtasks, making it easier to track progress. Due dates can also be set to ensure timely completion. Trello sends notifications as deadlines approach, helping teams stay on track and meet project timelines.

- Power-Ups (Integrations): Trello offers Power-Ups, which are integrations with third-party tools such as Slack, Google Drive, Zapier, GitHub, and Calendar.

These integrations extend Trello's functionality, enabling users to connect with other tools they already use and streamline workflows across platforms.

- **Drag-and-Drop Interface:** Trello features an intuitive drag-and-drop interface that makes it easy to move cards between lists, assign tasks, and organize work visually. This simplicity allows users to quickly adjust priorities and tasks without needing to go through complex menus, making it very user-friendly.

These features make Trello a versatile, user-friendly tool for managing both personal and team projects effectively.

3. Asana Agile Project Management Tool: Asana is a flexible and powerful project management tool designed to help teams plan, track, and manage work efficiently. It enables teams to organize tasks, set deadlines, and track progress in an intuitive interface. Key features of Asana include task creation and assignment, where users can create tasks, assign them to team members, set due dates, and add comments. Project timelines allow teams to visualize project schedules and track deadlines, ensuring that tasks are completed on time. Kanban boards offer a visual way to organize tasks, allowing users to move tasks through stages such as To-Do, In Progress, and Done. Task dependencies are another key feature, enabling teams to mark tasks as dependent on others, ensuring work is completed in the correct order. Asana also provides collaboration tools such as real-time comments, file sharing, and team discussions, making it easier for team members to communicate and stay updated. The platform integrates seamlessly with tools like Slack, Google Drive, and Microsoft Teams, enhancing productivity. With reporting features, teams can track performance, identify bottlenecks, and optimize workflows. Asana is highly customizable, making it suitable for various project management methodologies, including Agile and traditional project management.

The key features of Asana:

- **Task Management:** Asana allows users to create, assign, and organize tasks efficiently. Each task can include a due date, assignee, priority, subtasks, and attachments. Tasks are easily trackable, helping teams manage their workload and ensure timely completion.

- **Project Timelines:** Asana's timeline view helps visualize project schedules by displaying tasks and milestones on a linear timeline. This feature enables teams to track deadlines, manage dependencies, and adjust project plans in real time to keep projects on track.

- **Kanban Boards:** Asana offers Kanban-style boards that provide a visual representation of work in progress. Users can move tasks through customizable columns like To-Do, In Progress, and Done, allowing teams to manage workflows efficiently and track task status.

- **Task Dependencies:** Asana allows teams to set task dependencies, which helps track relationships between tasks. You can mark tasks as dependent on others, ensuring that work is completed in the correct order and preventing bottlenecks.

- **Team Collaboration Tools:** Asana promotes collaboration with features like real-time comments, file sharing, and team discussions. Team members can stay updated on task progress, provide feedback, and communicate directly within the platform, ensuring streamlined communication and coordination.

4. VersionOne Agile Project Management Tool: VersionOne is a robust Agile project management tool designed for enterprise-level teams to scale and manage Agile processes across multiple teams and projects. It supports Scrum, Kanban, and Scaled Agile Framework (SAFe), making it flexible for various Agile methodologies. Key features of VersionOne include backlog management, which allows teams to prioritize, plan, and organize user stories and tasks for better sprint planning. Sprint planning and tracking tools help teams define goals, track progress, and manage iterations effectively, while burndown charts and velocity tracking provide insight into team performance and project health. The release planning feature enables teams to plan and track the delivery of features and milestones across projects. VersionOne also supports collaboration through comments, notifications, and team updates to ensure communication is streamlined. With Agile reporting and real-time dashboards, teams can monitor performance and make data-driven decisions. VersionOne integrates seamlessly with other tools like JIRA, GitHub, and Jenkins, allowing for an efficient development workflow. Its enterprise-level capabilities and scalability make it ideal for larger organizations managing multiple Agile teams and projects simultaneously.

The key features of VersionOne:

- **Backlog Management:** VersionOne allows teams to efficiently manage and prioritize their product backlog. Teams can easily organize user stories, tasks, and bugs, assign them to sprints, and adjust priorities based on business needs, ensuring that work is aligned with the project's goals and deadlines.

- **Sprint Planning and Tracking:** VersionOne supports Agile sprint planning by helping teams break down large projects into manageable iterations (sprints).

It provides tools to assign work, track progress, and manage tasks during each sprint. Teams can monitor sprint health through burndown charts and velocity tracking, giving them insight into their capacity and delivery.

- **Release Planning:** VersionOne facilitates release planning by helping teams organize and track the delivery of features across multiple sprints. Teams can set up milestones, define release timelines, and align work across sprints to ensure timely and efficient delivery of product versions.
- **Agile Reporting and Dashboards:** VersionOne offers powerful reporting tools and customizable dashboards that provide real-time data on project health and team performance. Key reports include burndown charts, velocity charts, and cumulative flow diagrams, enabling teams to monitor their progress and make data-driven decisions.
- **Collaboration Tools:** VersionOne promotes collaboration with features like comments, notifications, and activity streams. Team members can engage in discussions directly within the tool, ensuring smooth communication, tracking of feedback, and real-time updates on tasks and project statuses.

5. Targetprocess Agile Project Management Tool: Targetprocess is an Agile project management tool specifically designed for enterprise-level organizations to manage large-scale projects with multiple teams. It is highly adaptable, supporting Agile frameworks such as Scrum, Kanban, SAFe (Scaled Agile Framework), and Lean. Targetprocess focuses on providing high-level portfolio management, helping organizations align their teams around strategic goals. With features like backlog management, users can create and prioritize user stories, epics, and tasks across teams. The tool offers powerful release planning functionality, ensuring teams remain aligned with business milestones and can track the delivery of features over multiple iterations. Its visualization tools, including Kanban boards and Gantt charts, provide users with a clear, visual representation of project progress, dependencies, and timelines, ensuring full transparency across the organization.

Moreover, Targetprocess includes advanced Agile reporting capabilities, allowing teams to monitor their progress and identify bottlenecks through burndown charts, velocity tracking, and other Agile metrics. These reports provide actionable insights into team performance and help in making data-driven decisions. The tool integrates seamlessly with other development and project management tools like JIRA, GitHub, and Jenkins, streamlining workflows and improving overall efficiency. Additionally, Targetprocess's customizable workflows ensure that organizations can tailor the system to their unique needs, making it a highly versatile solution for large-scale Agile adoption. Whether for managing large product portfolios or overseeing multiple teams, Targetprocess enables organizations to maintain control, ensure alignment, and improve Agile delivery across the enterprise.

The key features of Targetprocess:

- **Agile Portfolio Management:** Targetprocess is designed to handle large-scale portfolio management, allowing organizations to manage multiple projects, teams, and product lines simultaneously. It enables teams to align work with strategic goals, track progress across portfolios, and ensure that resources are allocated effectively across initiatives.

- **Backlog Management:** Targetprocess provides powerful backlog management features, allowing teams to create, prioritize, and manage user stories, epics, and tasks. Teams can organize work hierarchically, providing a clear view of project priorities and helping ensure alignment with the overall product roadmap.

- **Visual Project Tracking and Reporting:** Targetprocess offers robust visualization tools like Kanban boards, Gantt charts, and timeline views to help teams track progress, manage dependencies, and visualize project schedules. The tool also includes Agile reporting features like burndown charts and velocity tracking, providing real-time insights into team performance and project health.

- **Release Planning and Roadmaps:** Targetprocess helps with release planning by providing tools for managing product releases, timelines, and milestones. Teams can plan and track the delivery of features across multiple sprints or releases, ensuring that teams stay on target and aligned with the overall product vision.

- **Customization and Scalability:** Targetprocess offers a highly customizable workflow that allows organizations to tailor the tool to their specific needs. It supports various Agile methodologies (Scrum, Kanban, SAFe, Lean) and can be adjusted for different team sizes and project types. This flexibility makes it a great choice for scaling Agile practices in large enterprises.

6. Wrike Agile Project Management Tool: Wrike is a versatile project management and collaboration tool designed to help teams plan, track, and complete projects with efficiency and transparency. It offers a range of features that cater to Agile and traditional project management workflows, making it suitable for diverse team needs. One of Wrike's standout features is its task management system, which allows users to create, assign, and track tasks with detailed due dates, dependencies, priorities, and comments. The tool includes

Kanban boards and Gantt charts, providing visual representations of project timelines, task progress, and team workloads. Wrike also offers time tracking, enabling teams to log hours worked on individual tasks and monitor project progress against deadlines. Real-time collaboration is made possible through comments, file sharing, and notifications, ensuring that team members can stay connected and informed about task changes and project updates. Wrike's advanced reporting capabilities allow managers to generate customized reports and interactive dashboards for tracking key performance metrics, project health, and resource allocation. Additionally, Wrike supports seamless integration with tools like Slack, Google Drive, Microsoft Teams, and Salesforce, enhancing cross-platform collaboration. With its flexibility and scalability, Wrike is ideal for teams of any size, whether working on small tasks or large, complex projects, making it an effective solution for boosting productivity and improving project visibility.

The key features of Wrike:

- **Task and Project Management:** Wrike allows users to create and manage tasks and projects easily, assigning due dates, priorities, and team members. Tasks can be organized into projects with clear timelines, helping teams stay on track and meet deadlines. The platform also supports task dependencies, ensuring work is completed in the correct sequence.

- **Kanban Boards and Gantt Charts:** Wrike provides Kanban boards for visual task management, allowing teams to track progress by moving tasks between customizable columns such as To Do, In Progress, and Completed. Additionally, Gantt charts provide a timeline view of project milestones, task durations, and dependencies, offering a clear overview of project timelines.

- **Real-time Collaboration:** Wrike enhances team collaboration through real-time comments, file sharing, and notifications. Team members can discuss tasks, share feedback, and attach relevant files directly within the platform, ensuring that communication stays centralized and up-to-date.

- **Advanced Reporting and Dashboards:** Wrike's reporting features include customizable reports and interactive dashboards, allowing teams and managers to track project progress, performance metrics, resource allocation, and more. These insights help teams make data-driven decisions and ensure that projects stay on course.

- **Integrations:** Wrike integrates seamlessly with other popular tools such as Slack, Google Drive, Microsoft Teams, Salesforce, and more. These integrations enable smooth collaboration across platforms and ensure a cohesive workflow by centralizing all project-related information in one place.

Differences Between Agile Project Management Tool: The differences between agile project management tool are listed in table 5.1.

Table 5.1

Features	Wrike	JIRA	Trello	Asana	VersionOne	VersionOne
Primary Use Case	Versatile project & task management	Agile software development & issue tracking	Simple task & project tracking	Team collaboration & task management	Enterprise Agile planning	Scaled Agile portfolio/project management
Agile Support	Moderate (Kanban, Gantt, custom workflows)	Strong (Scrum, Kanban, SAFe)	Basic (Kanban only)	Moderate (Scrum/Kanban-style boards)	Strong (Scrum, Kanban, SAFe)	Strong (Scrum, Kanban, SAFe, Lean)
Complexity/Scalability	Medium to high (flexible, team-size adaptable)	High (complex, highly scalable)	Low (simple, best for small teams)	Medium (intuitive, scalable for teams)	High (built for large enterprises)	High (designed for large teams and scaling)
Customization	High (custom dashboards, automations)	Very high (workflows, fields, reports)	Limited (simple UI and structure)	Moderate (custom fields, templates)	High (custom reports, workflows, dashboards)	Very high (fully configurable for enterprise)
Reporting & Analytics	Advanced (real-time dashboards & analytics)	Advanced Agile reporting & charts	Minimal (Power-ups needed)	Moderate (task-based reporting)	Advanced (burn-down, velocity, dashboards)	Advanced (portfolio views, Agile metrics)

Team Collaboration and Communication

In today's dynamic work environment, effective team collaboration and communication are pivotal to achieving organizational goals. These elements not only enhance productivity but also foster innovation, employee satisfaction, and adaptability.

Team collaboration and communication are crucial in software engineering to foster efficient and effective teamwork, leading to better quality software and increased productivity. Effective communication ensures a shared understanding of project goals, reduces errors, and allows for quicker problem-solving.

Key aspects of team collaboration and communication in software engineering:

You've listed excellent points that represent key elements of effective team collaboration and communication in software engineering. Here's a refined and slightly expanded version that can serve as a more structured explanation or for use in a report or presentation:

Key Aspects of Team Collaboration and Communication in Software Engineering

1. **Open and Transparent Communication**: Clear, honest, and frequent communication ensures that all team members remain aligned throughout the development process. Real-time updates through stand-ups or messaging platforms prevent misunderstandings and help maintain momentum.

2. **Diverse Perspectives and Skills**: Cross-functional teams consisting of developers, testers, UX designers, and product managers bring varied experiences and expertise. This diversity leads to more innovative solutions and comprehensive problem-solving.

3. **Shared Goals and Role Clarity**: Defining shared objectives, project goals, and individual responsibilities ensures everyone understands their contributions to the bigger picture. Transparency in expectations boosts accountability and coordination.

4. **Conflict Management**: Differences in opinion are inevitable. Having a defined process for resolving conflicts whether through one-on-one discussions, team retrospectives, or mediation helps maintain a respectful and productive team culture.

5. **Employee Engagement**: Engaged team members are more motivated, collaborative, and productive. Involving them in decision-making, recognizing their efforts, and giving them autonomy can significantly increase job satisfaction and output.

6. **Collaboration Tools**: Tools such as JIRA, Slack, Confluence, GitHub, and Zoom enhance communication, task tracking, and documentation. These tools centralize information and streamline team interactions, especially in remote or distributed environments.

7. **Pair Programming**: This practice, where two developers work on the same code at the same time, promotes shared learning, immediate feedback, and early bug detection. It improves both code quality and team cohesion.

8. **Feedback and Iteration**: Regular feedback loops via code reviews, sprint reviews, or retrospectives—allow teams to refine their processes and product incrementally. Iterative development supports continuous improvement and adaptability to change.

These aspects, when applied effectively, contribute to higher quality software, reduced rework, and better team dynamics, all of which are essential in a fast-paced, complex field like software engineering. By prioritizing team collaboration and communication, software engineering teams can create a more efficient, productive, and enjoyable work environment, ultimately leading to better software and increased success.

Best Practices for Enhancing Team Collaboration and Communication: To cultivate a collaborative and communicative team environment:

1. **Define Clear Roles and Responsibilities**: Ensure each team member understands their duties and how they contribute to the team's objectives.

2. **Establish Regular Check-Ins**: Schedule consistent meetings to discuss progress, challenges, and feedback.

3. **Promote Open Feedback**: Encourage a culture where feedback is constructive and aimed at growth.

4. **Leverage Collaborative Tools**: Utilize platforms that facilitate document sharing, real-time communication, and project tracking.

5. **Foster Trust and Psychological Safety**: Create an environment where team members feel safe to express ideas and concerns without fear of judgment.

******

13

Ethics and Professionalism in Software Engineering

Ethics and professionalism are crucial in software engineering, guiding decision-making to ensure software development aligns with societal values and user trust. This includes adhering to professional codes, navigating ethical dilemmas, and being mindful of both intended and unintended consequences of software. The Importance of Ethics and Professionalism:

1. **Public Trust:** Ethical and professional conduct builds trust in the software engineering profession.

2. **Societal Benefit:** Software engineering that adheres to ethical principles can contribute to a more just and equitable society.

3. **Professional Reputation:** Software engineers who uphold ethical standards enhance their own professional reputation and the reputation of their field.

Key aspects of ethics and professionalism in software engineering:

1. **Code of Ethics:** Software engineers are expected to adhere to established codes of ethics, such as those provided by professional organizations like the ACM and IEEE. These codes outline principles like public interest, avoiding harm, honesty, and integrity.

Software engineers are guided by established codes of ethics, such as those from the ACM (Association for Computing Machinery) and IEEE (Institute of Electrical and Electronics Engineers). These codes outline essential principles that engineers must follow in their professional conduct. Key values include prioritizing the public interest, avoiding harm, maintaining honesty, and demonstrating integrity. By adhering to these standards, engineers help build trust with clients, users, and society. The codes also emphasize respecting privacy, intellectual property, and ensuring that software does not discriminate or cause unintended damage. For example, developers must ensure that algorithms do not reinforce racial or gender biases. Following a code of ethics also provides a framework for making difficult decisions—such as whether to disclose a security vulnerability or challenge unethical business demands. It transforms engineering from purely technical work into a socially responsible profession. Understanding and applying these principles helps ensure that software is not only functional but also fair, safe, and aligned with broader human values.

2. **Professional Conduct:** Software engineers demonstrate professionalism by upholding ethical standards, completing thorough documentation, and following best practices.

   Professional conduct in software engineering refers to behaving responsibly, ethically, and with technical competence in every aspect of the job. This means more than just writing quality code it includes documenting work thoroughly, following industry best practices, and communicating clearly with team members and stakeholders. Professional engineers meet deadlines, respect client confidentiality, and are honest about project limitations. They also take responsibility for their mistakes and work diligently to correct them. Upholding a professional demeanor helps build credibility and trust within teams and with clients. It also minimizes risks such as project failure, security flaws, or user dissatisfaction. Professional conduct extends to respectful behavior in the workplace, including collaboration, mentorship, and conflict resolution. A professional software engineer considers the long-term consequences of their work and avoids shortcuts that could result in technical debt or ethical lapses. Ultimately, professionalism reinforces the role of the engineer as a trusted and responsible contributor to society's technological advancement.

3. **Ethical Considerations:** Software engineers must consider the ethical implications of their work, including the potential for misuse of software, algorithmic bias, and the impact on users.

Ethical considerations in software engineering involve evaluating the impact of software on users, society, and the environment. Engineers must think beyond functionality to address how their work could be misused, whether it could cause harm, or whether it contains inherent bias. For instance, software used in hiring or lending should be assessed for algorithmic fairness to avoid reinforcing discrimination. Similarly, surveillance technologies must balance security with individual privacy rights. Software engineers must also consider the transparency of their systems can users understand how decisions are made? Will they have control over their data? Another ethical issue involves the potential for unintended consequences, such as a self-driving car making life-or-death decisions, or a healthcare algorithm misdiagnosing a patient. Engineers should involve diverse stakeholders, conduct thorough testing, and anticipate edge cases. Ethical considerations also require engineers to speak up when something feels wrong, even at personal or professional risk. They must be aware of how their tools may be used or abused, and strive to design with safety, equity, and accountability in mind. Ethics in software isn't optional it's a core responsibility that affects millions of lives.

4. **Accountability:** Developing software with a focus on responsibility, transparency, and ethical considerations is essential. Accountability in software engineering means taking ownership of one's work, being transparent about decisions, and accepting responsibility for outcomes positive or negative. A responsible engineer doesn't shift blame but instead ensures that their code is robust, secure, and ethically sound. Accountability also involves communicating openly about the limitations of the software, known bugs, or risks that may affect users. If an error or security flaw is discovered, ethical engineers act promptly to inform stakeholders, fix the issue, and prevent future occurrences. Transparency in design and documentation also supports accountability, allowing others to audit, understand, and improve the system. In a team or enterprise environment, accountability extends to collaborating effectively, meeting deadlines, and delivering work that meets agreed-upon standards. With increasing reliance on software in sectors like finance, healthcare, and public services, the consequences of software failure can be severe ranging from privacy breaches to physical harm. Therefore, accountability is not just a personal trait it is a professional obligation. By embedding accountability into their work culture, software engineers help build safer, more trustworthy, and more socially responsible technologies.

5. **Public Interest:** Software engineers should prioritize the public good in their work, ensuring that their creations benefit society. Serving the public interest is a core ethical obligation for software engineers. This means developing software that contributes positively to society while avoiding harm, bias, or disruption. Engineers should prioritize the health, safety, and well-being of users and broader communities. In practice, this might involve designing accessible applications for people with disabilities, ensuring systems are secure against cyber threats, or building platforms that promote democratic discourse rather than misinformation. Public interest also includes respecting user privacy, avoiding exploitative monetization models, and advocating for transparency in algorithms. For example, an engineer working on facial recognition software must consider how it could be misused for surveillance or discrimination. Upholding the public good may also require speaking out against unethical company policies or refusing to work on technologies that could cause widespread harm. While client demands and business goals are important, they should not override societal well-being. By anchoring their decisions in the public interest, software engineers uphold the true purpose of the profession: to build tools that empower, protect, and enhance human lives.

6. **Continuous Learning:** Staying up-to-date on ethical guidelines, industry standards, and legal requirements is crucial for maintaining ethical conduct. Software engineering is a rapidly evolving field, with constant advancements in technology, security practices, legal regulations, and ethical expectations. Engineers must commit to lifelong learning to stay current not only with technical skills but also with emerging ethical challenges. For example, understanding the ethical implications of artificial intelligence, data analytics, or blockchain requires ongoing education. Laws such as GDPR (for data protection) or ADA (for accessibility) also evolve, and staying updated ensures compliance and responsible design. Continuous learning can involve attending workshops, earning certifications, reading industry publications, or participating in professional communities like ACM or IEEE. It also includes developing soft skills such as communication, teamwork, and cultural competence. As software engineers increasingly influence society through their work, ignorance of current standards ethical or legal is no longer acceptable. Continuous learning supports informed decision-making, enhances professional reputation, and ensures that engineers are equipped to design software that is secure, inclusive, and beneficial to users. In essence, ethical conduct in software development is inseparable from the pursuit of knowledge.

Specific Ethical Issues in Software Engineering:

1. **User Privacy and Security:** Protecting user data and ensuring the security of software are paramount ethical considerations.

2. **Fairness and Bias:** Software engineers must strive to create unbiased algorithms and avoid perpetuating discrimination.

3. **Transparency and Openness:** Software development should be transparent, with users and stakeholders informed about the capabilities and limitations of the software.

4. **Intellectual Property:** Software engineers must respect copyright and other intellectual property rights.

5. **Conflict of Interest:** Recognizing and managing potential conflicts of interest is essential for maintaining ethical conduct.

By prioritizing ethics and professionalism, software engineers can ensure that their work is not only technically sound but also aligned with societal values and principles.

Ethical Dilemmas in Software Development

In the field of software development, ethical dilemmas often arise when the interests of users, developers, businesses, and society come into conflict. One common dilemma involves user privacy versus business goals. For example, developers may be asked to design features that collect extensive user data to support targeted advertising. While this data can increase company revenue, it may infringe on user privacy and violate data protection laws. Similarly, ethical challenges arise when companies pressure engineers to release unfinished or untested software to meet market deadlines. Doing so can lead to security vulnerabilities, system failures, or even harm users particularly in sensitive sectors like healthcare or transportation. Engineers must often choose between complying with management directives and adhering to their professional duty to avoid harm. Another dilemma occurs with intellectual property, where developers may be asked to reuse code from open-source projects without proper attribution, breaching licensing agreements and professional ethics.

A more complex ethical dilemma involves algorithmic bias and fairness. As software increasingly influences hiring, lending, policing, and healthcare, biased algorithms can unintentionally reinforce systemic discrimination. Developers working on such systems must decide how to address these issues—especially if their employer prioritizes speed or profit over fairness. Ethical tensions also exist in the development of controversial technologies, such as surveillance tools or autonomous weapons. Some engineers may be asked to work on systems that conflict with their personal or professional values. In such cases, they must weigh the consequences of speaking out, resigning, or trying to influence ethical decision-making internally. These dilemmas underscore the importance of strong ethical foundations, supportive workplace cultures, and adherence to professional codes of conduct like those from ACM or IEEE. By recognizing and addressing ethical dilemmas proactively, software engineers can help ensure that their work benefits society and aligns with their moral responsibilities. Key aspects of ethical dilemmas in software development:

1. **Privacy and Data Protection:** Developers often handle sensitive user data. Ethical dilemmas arise when companies push to collect, store, or share this data without proper consent, putting user privacy at risk. Engineers must balance business goals with compliance to laws like GDPR and users' rights to privacy.

2. **Algorithmic Bias and Fairness:** Machine learning models can unintentionally perpetuate discrimination if trained on biased data. Ethical issues emerge when these models are used in hiring, lending, or policing. Engineers must ensure fairness, transparency, and regular auditing of algorithms.

3. **Security vs. Usability:** Sometimes developers are forced to choose between strong security features and user convenience. Simplifying user access may weaken security, while enforcing complex measures may hinder usability creating ethical tension between protecting users and providing accessibility.

4. **Responsibility and Accountability:** Engineers face dilemmas when their software causes harm due to bugs, design flaws, or oversight. Questions arise over who is accountable: the developer, manager, or organization? Ethical practice demands ownership, transparency, and corrective action.

5. **Workplace Pressure and Deadlines:** Developers may be pressured to release unfinished or untested software to meet deadlines, risking user harm. Ethical responsibility requires pushing back against unrealistic demands to uphold quality and safety standards.

6. **Dual-use and Misuse of Software:** Software created for positive purposes can be repurposed for harm (e.g., surveillance tools, facial recognition). Engineers must consider potential misuse and decide whether to participate in such projects.

Importance of Ethical Dilemmas in Software Development: The importance of ethical dilemmas in software development lies in their profound impact on individuals, organizations, and society at large. As software becomes increasingly embedded in critical areas such as healthcare, finance, education, and public safety the decisions software engineers make can have far-reaching consequences.

1. **Protecting Public Trust and Safety:** Ethical dilemmas often center around user safety, privacy, and well-being. Addressing them ensures that technology does not cause harm, whether through data breaches, biased algorithms, or faulty systems. Public trust in digital products depends on how ethically they are designed and maintained.

2. **Ensuring Fairness and Non-Discrimination:** Software systems can unintentionally embed and amplify societal biases. By confronting ethical dilemmas, developers can promote equity and inclusion, ensuring their systems treat all users fairly, regardless of background, race, or gender.

3. **Preventing Misuse and Harm:** Understanding ethical dilemmas helps engineers anticipate how software might be misused intentionally or unintentionally. This foresight can prevent harmful applications of technology, such as in surveillance, misinformation, or exploitation.

4. **Encouraging Accountability and Integrity:** Recognizing and addressing ethical issues reinforces professional responsibility. It empowers engineers to speak up, follow best practices, and hold themselves and their organizations accountable.

5. **Aligning Technology with Social Good:** Ethical decision-making ensures that software development contributes positively to society rather than prioritizing profits at the expense of human rights or environmental impact.

Open-source and Intellectual Property

Open-source software has become a cornerstone of modern software development, enabling collaboration, transparency, and innovation across the global tech community. Open source refers to software whose source code is made publicly available, allowing anyone to view, use, modify, and distribute it, typically under licenses like MIT, Apache, or GNU General Public License (GPL). These licenses set the legal terms for how the software can be used and redistributed. Open-source promotes faster development, peer review, and community-driven improvements, often leading to more secure and reliable software. Major platforms like Linux, Kubernetes, and Python are examples of successful open-source projects. Developers and companies alike benefit from reduced costs, access to proven solutions, and the ability to customize software for their needs. However, open source also requires responsible management maintainers must ensure code quality, security patches, and clear contribution guidelines to maintain the integrity of the project.

Despite the collaborative nature of open source, intellectual property (IP) remains a critical concern. IP laws protect creators' rights over their inventions, including software code, designs, and trademarks. While open-source licenses grant broad usage rights, they still function within the legal framework of copyright law. Misunderstandings often arise when proprietary and open-source code are combined without respecting license conditions, potentially resulting in legal disputes. For example, using GPL-licensed code in a commercial application may require disclosing the source code of the entire application, which some businesses may wish to avoid. Therefore, developers must be familiar with open-source licenses and ensure compatibility with their project's goals and legal requirements. Additionally, companies must establish clear policies for contributing to and using open-source software to prevent unintentional IP infringement. Balancing the openness of open source with the protections of intellectual property rights is essential to fostering ethical, legal, and sustainable software innovation.

Open-source: Open-source refers to a development model where the source code of software is made freely available to the public under a license that permits use, modification, and distribution. This model fosters transparency, collaboration, and rapid innovation, and it has become a foundational element in modern software development practices. Open-source software (OSS) plays a critical role in both academic and commercial software engineering. Engineers can leverage existing open-source libraries and frameworks to build applications faster and more cost-effectively. This approach reduces duplication of effort and encourages reuse of proven solutions. Popular tools such as Git, Linux, Apache, and Docker are open source and widely used in software engineering workflows. Moreover, open source promotes peer review and community-driven testing, which often leads to improved reliability, performance, and security over time.

However, incorporating open source in software engineering also requires careful consideration of licensing terms (such as MIT, GPL, or Apache licenses), intellectual property rights, and project governance. Software engineers must ensure compliance with license requirements, especially when integrating open-source code into proprietary systems. In professional practice, this often involves using Software Bill of Materials (SBOMs) and open-source compliance tools. Ultimately, open source in software engineering is not just about free code it's about fostering a culture of ethical development, shared responsibility, and global collaboration. Benefits of Open-source software

1. **Cost Efficiency**: One of the most compelling advantages of OSS is its cost-effectiveness. Since the software is typically free to use, organizations can

significantly reduce licensing fees associated with proprietary software. This is particularly beneficial for startups and small businesses with limited budgets.

2. **Customization and Flexibility**: OSS allows developers to modify the source code to tailor the software to specific needs. This level of customization is often not possible with proprietary software, which may have limitations in terms of features and adaptability.

3. **Community Support and Collaboration**: Open-source projects often have vibrant communities of developers who contribute to the software's improvement. This collaborative environment leads to rapid identification and resolution of bugs, continuous feature enhancements, and a wealth of shared knowledge and resources.

4. **Transparency and Security**: The open nature of OSS means that anyone can inspect the code for vulnerabilities. This transparency often leads to more secure software, as security flaws can be identified and addressed promptly by the community.

5. **Innovation and Rapid Development**: The collaborative model of OSS accelerates innovation. Developers from diverse backgrounds contribute unique perspectives, leading to the rapid development of new features and solutions.

Challenges of Open-source Software

1. **Support and Maintenance**: While community support is valuable, it may not always be sufficient for organizations that require dedicated, professional support. Additionally, some open-source projects may lack regular updates or active maintainers, leading to potential security risks.

2. **Integration and Compatibility**: Integrating OSS with existing proprietary systems can pose challenges. Compatibility issues may arise, requiring additional development effort to ensure seamless operation within the organization's infrastructure.

3. **Legal and Licensing Concerns**: OSS comes with various licenses, each with its own set of rules and requirements. Organizations must ensure compliance with these licenses to avoid legal complications. For instance, some licenses may require modifications to be shared with the community, while others may impose restrictions on commercial use.

4. **Security Risks**: While the open nature of OSS can enhance security, it also exposes the software to potential threats. Malicious actors can scrutinize the code for vulnerabilities to exploit. Therefore, organizations must actively monitor and patch any security issues.

5. **Sustainability and Long-Term Viability**: Many open-source projects rely on volunteer contributions, which can be inconsistent. The long-term viability of a project depends on continued community involvement and adequate funding, which may not always be guaranteed.

Best Practices for Engaging with Open-source

1. **Adopt a Clear Licensing Strategy**: Organizations should establish clear policies regarding the use and contribution to open-source projects. This includes selecting appropriate licenses that align with the organization's goals and ensuring compliance with those licenses.

2. **Contribute Back to the Community**: Engaging with the open-source community by contributing code, documentation, or financial support helps sustain projects and fosters goodwill. This collaboration benefits both the organization and the broader community.

3. **Implement Robust Security Practices**: Organizations should actively monitor the security of the open-source software they use. This includes regularly updating software, applying patches, and conducting security audits to identify and mitigate potential vulnerabilities.

4. **Provide Adequate Training and Resources**: To maximize the benefits of OSS, organizations should invest in training their developers and IT staff. Understanding the intricacies of open-source tools and best practices ensures effective utilization and reduces the risk of errors.

5. **Evaluate Project Health and Activity**: Before adopting an open-source project, organizations should assess its health and activity level. Indicators such as recent commits, active maintainers, and a vibrant community can signal a project's viability and long-term support.

Open-source software has revolutionized the field of software engineering by promoting collaboration, innovation, and transparency. While it offers numerous benefits, including cost savings, flexibility, and community support, it also presents challenges related to support, integration, and security. By adopting best practices and actively engaging with the open-source community, organizations can harness the full potential of OSS, driving innovation and achieving their software development goals.

Intellectual Property (IP): Intellectual property rights are the legal rights that cover the privileges given to individuals who are the owners and inventors of a work, and have created something with their intellectual creativity. Individuals related to areas such as literature, music, invention, etc., can be granted such rights, which can then be used in the business practices by them.

The creator/inventor gets exclusive rights against any misuse or use of work without his/her prior information. However, the rights are granted for a limited period of time to maintain equilibrium.

The following list of activities which are covered by the intellectual property rights are laid down by the World Intellectual Property Organization (WIPO). Intellectual Property Rights can be further classified into the following categories:

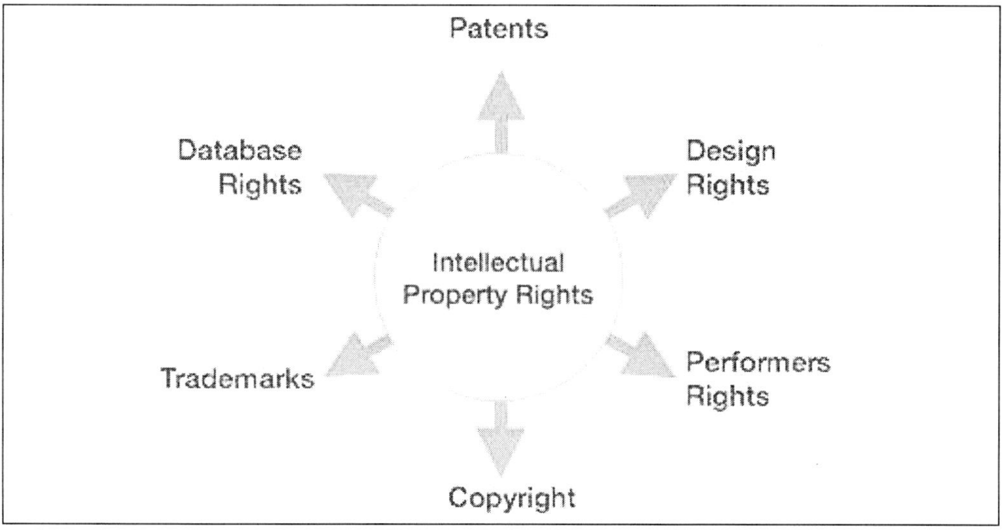

Fig.5.3

1. Copyright: Copyright protects original works of authorship including literature, music, art, films, architecture, and software. It arises automatically when a work is created and fixed in a tangible medium, without needing formal registration in many countries. Copyright grants creators' exclusive rights to reproduce, distribute, perform, display, and adapt their work. It also includes moral rights, such as the right to be identified as the author and to object to derogatory treatment.

Copyright typically lasts for the author's lifetime plus 70 years in most jurisdictions. For corporate or anonymous works, it may last 70 to 95 years from publication or creation. There are exceptions like "fair use" or "fair dealing," which allow limited use for criticism, news reporting, teaching, or research. Copyright is essential for the creative industries, ensuring authors and creators receive financial and reputational benefit from their work. However, enforcement in the digital age is challenging due to widespread online infringement. Governments and platforms use technologies like content ID systems to help monitor and enforce rights. In sum, copyright encourages creativity by protecting the expression of ideas, though not the ideas themselves.

2. Patents: Patents are legal protections granted to inventors for new, useful, and non-obvious inventions, covering processes, machines, compositions of matter, or improvements thereof. A patent gives the inventor exclusive rights to make, use, sell, and license the invention for a set period typically 20 years from the filing date for utility patents.

To obtain a patent, inventors must publicly disclose how the invention works in sufficient detail, allowing others to replicate it after the protection expires. This promotes scientific and technological advancement by encouraging innovation while sharing knowledge. There are three main types: utility patents (covering new inventions), design patents (protecting ornamental aspects), and plant patents (for new plant varieties). The application process is often complex and may require legal or technical expertise. Patents are crucial in sectors like pharmaceuticals, biotech, and engineering, where significant investment is needed in R&D. However, they are territorial protection must be sought in each country where rights are desired. Patent rights can be sold, licensed, or used as collateral. While patents incentivize innovation, critics argue they can stifle competition, especially when broad patents are granted or used aggressively. Balancing innovation incentives and public access remains a key policy concern.

3. Trademarks: Trademarks protect distinctive signs used by businesses to identify their goods or services. These can include brand names, logos, slogans, packaging, shapes, and even sounds or colors in some cases. The primary purpose of a trademark is to prevent consumer confusion by ensuring they can distinguish between different market players. Unlike copyrights or patents, trademarks can last indefinitely if they are actively used and periodically renewed (usually every 10 years). Registration is not always required in many countries; trademark rights arise through actual use. However, registered trademarks typically enjoy stronger legal protection and enforcement. Trademarks are vital business assets. A strong brand can build customer loyalty, enhance reputation, and command premium pricing. Trademark law prevents competitors from using confusingly similar signs that could dilute brand value or mislead consumers. Trademark infringement can lead to legal action, including injunctions and damages. Many countries participate in the Madrid Protocol, allowing for international registration through a single application. Trademark law must strike a balance between brand protection and fair competition. Generic terms, descriptive words, and misleading marks are usually not eligible for protection. With globalization and digital commerce, managing trademarks across borders has become a complex but critical task for businesses.

4. Database Rights: Database rights protect the contents and structure of databases where significant investment has been made in obtaining, verifying, or presenting data. These rights are most prominently recognized in the European Union through the EU Database Directive, although similar protections exist in some other jurisdictions.

Database rights are distinct from copyright. While copyright can protect the structure or arrangement of data (if sufficiently creative), database rights protect the effort and resources invested in compiling the database, even if there is no creative input. The right exists for 15 years from the date of completion or public availability. If substantial changes are made (e.g., new data is added), the 15-year period may restart. The owner of the database can prevent extraction or reuse of a substantial part of its content.

This form of protection is particularly important in data-heavy industries like finance, sports, research, and publishing. For example, sports leagues may claim database rights over match statistics or schedules. Unlike copyright, which arises automatically with creation, proving and enforcing database rights requires demonstrating investment and unauthorized use. In the age of big data and AI, the scope and enforceability of database rights are under increasing scrutiny, especially as automated scraping becomes common.

5. Design Rights: Design rights protect the visual appearance or aesthetics of a product — its shape, configuration, pattern, or ornamentation. This includes consumer products, furniture, clothing, electronics, and packaging. Unlike patents, which protect functional features, design rights cover non-functional aspects that appeal to the eye. There are two main forms:

- **Registered design rights**, which require application and examination (e.g., EU or UK registered designs, lasting up to 25 years with renewals every 5 years).
- **Unregistered design rights**, which arise automatically and offer limited protection (e.g., 3 years in the EU; 10–15 years in the UK).

To qualify, a design must be new and have individual character. It should not be dictated solely by the product's technical function.

Design rights enable businesses to differentiate products in the market and protect against copying by competitors. They are especially important in industries like fashion, consumer electronics, and automotive manufacturing. Enforcement can be complex, as proving infringement involves assessing whether the accused design creates the same overall impression. Design rights may overlap with other IP rights like trademarks and copyright, offering layered protection. As product aesthetics become key to brand identity and consumer appeal, design rights offer strategic value in commercial and legal planning.

6. Performance Rights: Performance rights protect the rights of performers such as actors, musicians, dancers, and singers in their live or recorded performances. These rights ensure performers are compensated when their performances are broadcast, streamed, or publicly played. Performance rights are often divided into two categories:

- **Performers' rights**, which give individuals control over how their recorded or live performances are used.
- **Neighbouring rights**, which extend protection to those involved in the performance's dissemination such as producers and broadcasters.

In most countries, performers have moral and economic rights. Moral rights include being credited and objecting to derogatory treatment. Economic rights allow performers to authorize or prohibit the recording, reproduction, and distribution of their performances.

Performance rights typically last 50 to 70 years after the performance date, depending on jurisdiction and whether the performance was recorded. Performers can license their rights individually or through collective management organizations (CMOs), which collect royalties on their behalf when performances are used commercially for example, on radio, television, or in public venues like restaurants and gyms.

These rights are crucial for ensuring fair remuneration in the entertainment and music industries, especially in the digital era where performances can be streamed or shared globally with ease.

Diversity and Inclusion in Tech

Diversity and inclusion (D&I) in the tech industry refer to efforts that ensure individuals from varied backgrounds such as different races, genders, sexual orientations, abilities, socio-economic statuses, and cultures are not only present but also valued, respected, and given equal opportunities to succeed. Despite being at the forefront of innovation, the tech sector has historically struggled with representation, particularly among women, ethnic minorities, and people with disabilities. This lack of diversity limits the perspectives brought to problem-solving and product design, often resulting in technologies that unintentionally exclude or disadvantage certain groups. For example, facial recognition software has been shown to perform less accurately on darker skin tones, revealing the consequences of homogenous development teams. Increasing diversity isn't just a moral or social imperative it's a business necessity. Research shows that diverse teams perform better, innovate more, and are more profitable.

Inclusion goes beyond hiring it means creating an environment where everyone feels safe, supported, and empowered to contribute. This includes addressing biases in hiring, fostering equitable career advancement, ensuring accessibility, and cultivating inclusive leadership. Tech companies are increasingly investing in employee resource groups, unconscious bias training, and transparent diversity metrics to drive change. However, progress remains slow and uneven across the industry. Real impact requires sustained commitment, structural changes, and accountability at all levels. Ultimately, building a diverse and inclusive tech industry is essential not only for fairness but also for creating technologies that truly serve and represent the global population.

Diversity: Diversity in software engineering is a crucial and multifaceted topic that encompasses various dimensions such as gender, race, ethnicity, socioeconomic background, sexual orientation, neurodiversity, and more. It's important because it leads to more innovative, creative, and effective solutions in the tech industry. Some key reasons why diversity matters in software engineering:

1. **Improved Problem Solving and Innovation:** Diverse teams bring different perspectives, experiences, and ways of thinking. This can lead to more creative solutions and innovative approaches to complex problems. When people with varied backgrounds collaborate, they challenge each other's ideas, which can result in more robust and thoughtful outcomes.

2. **Better Representation of Users:** The products we build often impact people from various walks of life. Having a diverse engineering team helps ensure that software is created with a broad range of users in mind, which can help avoid unintentional biases in design and functionality. For example, features that are useful or accessible to one group might not be for another, and a diverse team can recognize these gaps early.

3. **Improved Company Performance:** Studies have shown that companies with diverse teams tend to perform better. They are more adaptable and innovative, which can lead to increased profitability, better decision-making, and stronger team cohesion. In tech, where the industry is rapidly evolving, having diverse perspectives is key to staying ahead.

4. **Attracting Top Talent:** A diverse, inclusive workplace is more attractive to a wide range of candidates. It signals that a company values different voices, which is important to millennials and Gen Z employees who place high value on inclusivity. Companies that prioritize diversity can access a larger talent pool, increasing the likelihood of finding top talent.

5. **Improved Workplace Culture:** Diverse teams contribute to healthier work environments. By engaging with people from different backgrounds, team members learn to appreciate various perspectives, which can lead to increased empathy, respect, and collaboration. A positive and inclusive workplace culture can increase employee satisfaction and retention.

6. **Challenges in Achieving Diversity:** Despite the clear benefits of diversity, the tech industry still faces significant challenges when it comes to achieving it. Gender and racial disparities are often noticeable in engineering teams, and there can be biases in hiring practices. Underrepresentation of certain groups, such as women, Black, Latinx, and Native American individuals, persists in many tech companies, especially in leadership roles.

7. **Initiatives for Promoting Diversity:** Many companies and organizations are now focused on increasing diversity in software engineering through various initiatives:

   - **Mentorship and sponsorship programs** for underrepresented groups in tech.
   - **Diversity training and unconscious bias workshops** to help eliminate biases during hiring and in the workplace.
   - **Internships and outreach programs** that specifically aim to encourage diverse candidates to pursue careers in tech.
   - **Partnerships with universities and coding bootcamps** to provide underrepresented groups with the skills and opportunities needed to succeed in software engineering.

8. **Fostering Neurodiversity in Tech:** Beyond visible forms of diversity, neurodiversity (which includes conditions like autism, ADHD, and dyslexia) is also gaining attention in the software engineering field. Neurodivergent individuals can bring unique strengths, such as exceptional attention to detail, the ability to focus deeply, and different problem-solving approaches. Creating

an inclusive environment that supports neurodiversity can open doors to this untapped talent pool.

9. **Challenges in Building Diverse Teams:** This includes as:
   - **Bias in Hiring:** There's a tendency to favor candidates who "fit the mold" or who have similar experiences. Combatting unconscious bias in the recruitment process is essential.
   - **Lack of Support:** Once hired, diverse employees may face challenges in adjusting to workplace culture or may feel isolated or unsupported.
   - **Retention:** Keeping diverse talent is as important as hiring them. Without proper mentorship, career development opportunities, and inclusion efforts, diverse employees may leave, leading to high turnover rates.
10. **Key Resources for Promoting Diversity:** This includes as:
    - **Organizations and conferences** focused on diversity in tech, like AnitaB.org, Black Girls Code, or Women Who Code.
    - **Online communities** that support marginalized groups in tech, such as GitHub's LGBTQ+ community or the Women in Tech Slack group.
    - **Books and blogs** that discuss the intersection of diversity and technology, like "Bias in the Machine" or "Brotopia."

Building diversity in software engineering isn't just about meeting quotas or being politically correct it's about improving outcomes, fostering a more inclusive and productive workplace, and creating software that better serves the world. Progress is being made, but there's still a long way to go, and it requires intentional effort from individuals, companies, and the industry as a whole.

Inclusion: Inclusion is a critical concept in software engineering that goes hand in hand with diversity. While diversity focuses on the composition of a team ensuring representation from various backgrounds, genders, races, and identities inclusion is about creating an environment where all team members feel valued, respected, and empowered to contribute their unique perspectives and ideas. An inclusive environment is one where differences are embraced and where everyone has an equal opportunity to thrive.

The software industry is built on innovation, problem-solving, and collaboration. To generate the most innovative solutions, teams need to bring a wide range of perspectives, insights, and experiences to the table. Inclusion ensures that all voices are heard, not just the dominant or majority ones. This fosters creativity, enhances decision-making, and ultimately leads to better products and services.

Inclusion also has a direct impact on team dynamics. When team members feel included, they are more likely to engage, share ideas, and collaborate effectively. They feel a sense of belonging, which boosts morale and leads to increased productivity. On the other hand, exclusion can result in feelings of alienation, reduced motivation, and a lack of trust within the team, all of which can negatively affect performance and creativity. Key elements of inclusion are as:

1. **Respect for Diverse Perspectives:** In an inclusive environment, individuals are encouraged to share their ideas and viewpoints, and these contributions are treated with respect. Diverse perspectives should not only be heard but also considered when making decisions. When team members know their input matters, they are more likely to participate actively.

2. **Equitable Access to Opportunities:** Inclusion involves ensuring that all employees have equal access to opportunities for growth, development, and career advancement. This means that there should be no barriers to entry based on gender, race, socioeconomic status, or other factors. In an inclusive environment, everyone is given the tools and resources they need to succeed, regardless of their background.

3. **Psychological Safety:** Psychological safety is a fundamental aspect of inclusion. It refers to the ability of team members to speak up, share ideas, and take risks without fear of negative consequences such as judgment or retaliation. In a psychologically safe and inclusive workplace, employees feel secure in their ability to be authentic and contribute openly.

4. **Inclusive Leadership:** Leaders play a crucial role in fostering an inclusive environment. Inclusive leaders actively promote diversity and create spaces where all voices are heard. They set the tone for inclusive behavior, model empathy, and are committed to addressing any form of exclusion or discrimination. These leaders also support their team members in navigating challenges and growing in their careers.

5. **Inclusive Design and Product Development:** In software engineering, inclusion goes beyond the team to the products being developed. Inclusive design means creating software and technology that is accessible to people of

all abilities, backgrounds, and circumstances. It involves considering factors such as accessibility features for users with disabilities, ensuring the software meets the needs of diverse populations, and avoiding biases in algorithms.

Challenges in Achieving Inclusion: Achieving true inclusion can be challenging. Implicit biases, microaggressions, and exclusionary behaviors can undermine efforts to create an inclusive environment. Overcoming these obstacles requires ongoing education, self-awareness, and a commitment to change at both individual and organizational levels. Additionally, diversity alone does not guarantee inclusion; it requires intentional efforts to make sure all individuals feel welcome and valued.

Inclusion is not just a buzzword it's essential for fostering innovation, creativity, and a positive work environment in software engineering. By prioritizing inclusion, organizations create spaces where all employees can thrive, share their ideas, and contribute to building better products. When inclusion is actively cultivated, it enhances team dynamics, improves the overall work culture, and leads to more successful outcomes. To achieve lasting change, organizations must continue to prioritize both diversity and inclusion, creating environments that empower every individual to succeed.

******

14

Building a Successful Career in Software Engineering

Software engineering is an exciting and dynamic field that offers countless opportunities for growth, innovation, and impact. Whether you're just starting out or looking to advance your career, there are several key strategies and principles to keep in mind to build a successful and fulfilling career in software engineering.

1. **Master the Fundamentals:** A solid understanding of the core concepts in software engineering is essential. This includes knowledge of algorithms, data structures, programming languages, and software development methodologies. Mastering these basics will not only help you write efficient and maintainable code but also allow you to tackle complex problems with confidence. Key areas to focus on:

    - **Algorithms & Data Structures:** Understanding how to optimize performance and choose the right data structures is critical for solving complex problems efficiently.

    - **Programming Languages:** While it's useful to be proficient in several languages, having deep expertise in a few key languages (such as Python, Java, or C++) will make you more effective as a developer.

- **Software Development Methodologies:** Familiarity with Agile, DevOps, and other methodologies will help you work efficiently in teams and adapt to industry best practices.

2. **Continuous Learning and Adaptability:** The tech industry is evolving rapidly, with new tools, languages, and frameworks emerging regularly. To stay relevant, software engineers must embrace continuous learning and adaptability.

   - **Stay Updated:** Follow blogs, podcasts, and industry news to stay informed about trends and new technologies.

   - **Learn New Skills:** Take online courses or attend workshops to deepen your knowledge in areas such as machine learning, cloud computing, or cybersecurity.

   - **Experiment with New Technologies:** Building personal projects, contributing to open-source software, or exploring new programming languages can expand your skill set.

3. **Work on Real Projects:** Hands-on experience is crucial for becoming a proficient software engineer. While formal education and tutorials provide a foundation, real-world projects will hone your problem-solving skills and prepare you for the challenges of professional work.

   - **Contribute to Open-source:** Contributing to open-source projects allows you to work with other developers, receive feedback, and showcase your skills to potential employers.

   - **Build Personal Projects:** Developing your own software solutions gives you a chance to experiment and learn new concepts while also building a portfolio to show prospective employers.

   - **Freelancing or Internships:** Gaining practical experience in the industry through internships or freelance work can provide insight into how companies operate and help you apply your skills in real-world scenarios.

4. **Cultivate Strong Communication Skills:** While technical expertise is important, effective communication is just as critical in software engineering. You will often need to explain complex technical concepts to non-technical stakeholders, work in teams, and collaborate across different departments.

- **Be Clear and Concise:** Practice explaining your ideas in simple terms, whether in writing or during meetings.
- **Collaborate with Teams:** Software engineering is rarely a solitary activity. You'll work with product managers, designers, and other developers, so being able to communicate clearly and collaboratively is key.
- **Provide Constructive Feedback:** As a team member, you'll need to give and receive feedback regularly. Learn how to give feedback that is helpful, respectful, and focused on improving the work.

5. **Network and Build Relationships:** Building relationships within the tech community is essential for career growth. Networking can help you discover new job opportunities, learn from others, and stay inspired.
   - **Attend Meetups and Conferences:** Participating in events allows you to meet like-minded professionals, learn from industry leaders, and get exposed to new ideas.
   - **Join Online Communities:** Platforms like GitHub, Stack Overflow, and Twitter offer opportunities to interact with other software engineers and contribute to the broader tech ecosystem.
   - **Find Mentors:** Seek out experienced professionals who can provide guidance, share their experiences, and offer valuable insights into navigating your career.
6. **Develop Problem-Solving Skills:** Software engineering is all about solving problems. Strong problem-solving abilities are fundamental to building effective software.
   - **Break Down Problems:** Start by breaking complex problems into smaller, manageable components. This helps you focus on one step at a time and avoids feeling overwhelmed.
   - **Think Algorithmically:** Developing an algorithmic mindset will help you optimize solutions and write efficient code.
   - **Practice Coding Challenges:** Platforms like LeetCode, HackerRank, and Codewars offer coding challenges that improve your problem-solving skills and prepare you for technical interviews.

7. **Embrace Collaboration and Teamwork:** No matter how skilled you are as an individual developer; you will likely be part of a larger team. The ability to collaborate effectively is crucial for success.

   - **Work Well with Others:** Understand that software engineering often involves collaboration with product managers, designers, and other stakeholders. Develop the ability to listen, compromise, and work towards a common goal.

   - **Participate in Code Reviews:** Code reviews not only improve the quality of your code but also provide an opportunity for you to learn from others and share your knowledge.

8. Focus on Quality and Best Practices: Writing clean, maintainable code is essential for long-term success. While speed is important, quality should never be compromised.

   - **Follow Coding Standards:** Stick to industry best practices, such as using meaningful variable names, writing modular code, and ensuring your code is well-documented.

   - **Write Tests:** Ensure your code works as expected by writing unit tests, integration tests, and using tools like Test-Driven Development (TDD) to minimize bugs.

   - **Refactor Regularly:** Don't be afraid to revisit and improve your code. Refactoring keeps your codebase clean and maintainable.

9. **Seek Feedback and Improve:** Receiving and acting on feedback is a cornerstone of growth in software engineering.

   - **Ask for Constructive Criticism:** Seek feedback from peers, mentors, and managers to understand areas where you can improve.

   - **Self-Reflect:** Regularly assess your progress, identify strengths and weaknesses, and make a plan for ongoing improvement.

10. **Balance Work and Life:** A successful career doesn't only mean career advancement it also includes maintaining a healthy work-life balance. Burnout is common in high-pressure environments, so it's important to manage your time wisely and prioritize well-being.

- **Set Boundaries:** Establish clear boundaries between work and personal life to prevent burnout.
- **Stay Healthy:** Regular exercise, a balanced diet, and sufficient rest are important for maintaining focus and energy levels.
- **Pursue Hobbies and Interests:** Engaging in activities outside of work can help you relax, recharge, and stay motivated.

Building a successful career in software engineering requires a mix of technical skills, problem-solving abilities, communication, collaboration, and continuous learning. By mastering the fundamentals, seeking hands-on experience, networking, and embracing personal growth, you can pave the way for a rewarding and impactful career in this ever-evolving field.

Resume Building and Technical Interviews

Resume building and technical interview preparation are critical for success in software engineering careers. A strong resume should highlight technical skills (e.g., programming languages, frameworks, tools), relevant projects with measurable impact, and work or internship experience using the STAR method (Situation, Task, Action, Result). Include links to GitHub or personal websites to showcase your code. Tailor each resume to the specific job by aligning skills with the job description. For technical interviews, focus on mastering data structures and algorithms, especially arrays, linked lists, trees, graphs, dynamic programming, and sorting techniques. Practice coding problems regularly on platforms like LeetCode and HackerRank. For system design interviews, study concepts like scalability, load balancing, and distributed systems using resources like the System Design Primer. Behavioral interviews require strong storytelling; use the STAR technique to discuss past challenges and achievements. Mock interviews with peers or platforms such as Pramp and Interviewing.io can boost confidence and readiness. Overall, consistent practice, clear communication, and a results-focused resume are key to standing out in competitive software engineering roles.

In the competitive field of software engineering, two key components determine your ability to land top roles: a well-structured resume and strong performance in technical interviews. Whether you're a student, a new graduate, or an experienced engineer, understanding how to effectively present your skills on paper and confidently solve problems in interviews is essential for advancing your career.

Part 1: Resume Building for Software Engineering: A resume is often the first impression a recruiter or hiring manager has of you. It needs to be clear, concise, and tailored to the job you're applying for. Here's how to build a resume that stands out:

1. **Keep It to One Page (For most candidates):** Unless you have over 10 years of experience or are in a specialized role, your resume should be one page. Recruiters typically spend less than 10 seconds scanning a resume make every line count.

2. **Structure and Key Sections:** A typical software engineering resume should include:

   - **Contact Information:** Name, Phone number, Professional email address, LinkedIn profile and GitHub or portfolio link.

   - **Summary (Optional):** A short summary (2–3 lines) is optional but useful if you want to highlight your area of specialization or major achievements quickly.

   - **Technical Skills:** This is a quick-reference section listing your:

     - Programming Languages: For example, Python, Java, C++
     - Frameworks/Libraries: For example, React, Node.js, Django
     - Tools/Technologies: For example, Git, Docker, AWS
     - Databases: For example, MySQL, MongoDB

   List skills relevant to the job and rank them roughly by proficiency.

   - **Projects:** Include 2–3 substantial projects:

     - Title and tools used
     - 2–3 bullet points describing what you built, your role, and the impact
     - Use metrics when possible (e.g., "Reduced API response time by 40%")
     - Projects are especially important for students or those without much work experience.

- **Work Experience:** List jobs and internships in reverse chronological order. Use the STAR format:

  - Situation: Brief context
  - Task: What was your responsibility?

- Action: What steps did you take?
- Result: What impact did it have?

Quantify your results wherever possible (e.g., "improved efficiency by 25%").

- **Education:** Include Degree, University name, Graduation date and GPA (optional, include if 3.5+ or required by employer).
- **Additional Sections (Optional):** Certifications (e.g., AWS Certified Developer), Open-source contributions, Hackathons and coding competitions and technical blog posts or speaking engagements.

3. **Tailor for the Job:** Don't send a generic resume everywhere. Customize the skills, keywords, and even project descriptions based on the job description.
4. **Clean, Readable Design:** Use consistent fonts, bullet points, and spacing. Avoid large blocks of text. Use tools like Overleaf, Canva, or simple Google Docs resume templates to maintain a clean format.

Part 2: Technical Interview Preparation: Once your resume gets you in the door, the real test begins. Technical interviews are designed to assess your problem-solving skills, coding abilities, system design knowledge, and communication.

1. **Types of Technical Interviews:** You will typically encounter:

- **Coding Interviews:** Focus on data structures and algorithms
  - Common topics: arrays, strings, trees, graphs, hash tables, dynamic programming, recursion
  - Usually conducted on platforms like CoderPad, HackerRank, or Google Docs
  - Questions range from basic (e.g., reversing a string) to complex (e.g., finding shortest path in a graph)
- **System Design Interviews:** Focus on designing scalable, robust systems. For example: "Design a URL shortener" or "Design a ride-sharing service". Interviewers evaluate your understanding of API design, Scalability, Databases, Load balancing and Consistency vs availability (CAP theorem).
- **Behavioral Interviews:** Test your soft skills, communication, teamwork, and leadership Typical questions like "Tell me about a time you resolved a

conflict". "Describe a difficult bug you fixed and how you approached it". Use the STAR method here as well

- **Take-Home Assignments / Online Assessments:** These may involve building a small project or solving multiple-choice questions. Aim to write clean, well-documented, and tested code

2. **How to Prepare Effectively:** You will typically encounter:

- **Master DSA (Data Structures and Algorithms):** This is non-negotiable for most tech roles.

    - Recommended topics: Arrays & Strings, Hash Maps & Sets, Trees & Graphs (DFS, BFS), Recursion & Backtracking, Dynamic Programming and Sorting & Searching

    - Practice platforms: This includes LeetCode for company-specific questions, HackerRank for timed tests, Codeforces for competitive practice and Exercism, Codewars for additional challenges.

Create a schedule (e.g., 1–2 problems per day) and track your progress.

- **System Design Preparation:** For junior roles, a basic understanding is enough. For senior or backend-focused roles, deeper preparation is needed.

    - Key concepts: Horizontal vs vertical scaling, Microservices architecture, SQL vs NoSQL databases and Message queues (Kafka, RabbitMQ)

    - Study resources: System Design Primer on GitHub, Designing Data-Intensive and Applications by Martin Kleppmann

- **Behavioral Preparation:** Interviewers want to know if you're a good teammate and problem-solver.

    - **Prepare 4–5 stories from your past experience involving**: Conflict resolution, Team collaboration, Learning from failure and Leadership or initiative

    - Keep responses structured and concise

- **Mock Interviews:** Practice simulating real interview pressure. Tools to use:

- Pramp: free peer-to-peer mock interviews
- Interviewing.io: anonymous mock interviews with engineers
- Friends or mentors in the industry

3. **Interview Day Tips:** Clarify the question. Don't jump to coding. Ask questions and confirm edge cases. Think aloud. This shows your problem-solving approach and keeps the interviewer engaged. Write clean code. Use good naming, proper indentation, and explain your choices. Test your solution. Walk through with test cases before saying you're done. Be honest. If you get stuck, share your thoughts or ask for a hint rather than going silent.

4. **Post-Interview Etiquette:** Send a thank-you email within 24 hours to express appreciation and reiterate your interest. Reflect on what went well and what you could improve. Even if rejected, consider asking for feedback.

Resume building and technical interview preparation are core components of your success in the software engineering job market. A well-crafted resume that highlights your technical skills, projects, and experience can open doors. However, it's your problem-solving skills, clarity of thought, and ability to perform under pressure during interviews that will determine whether you land the offer. Be consistent with practice, stay updated with industry trends, and focus on clear communication. With preparation, confidence, and the right strategy, you'll greatly increase your chances of securing your next software engineering role.

Contributing to Open-source Projects

Contributing to open-source projects is one of the most rewarding and effective ways for software engineers to gain practical experience, build a public portfolio, and become part of a global community of developers. Whether you're a student just starting out, a self-taught coder, or a professional seeking to sharpen your skills, open-source contribution helps you grow technically and professionally. It's also a way to give back to the community that powers much of the software infrastructure the world relies on today.

Why Contribute to Open-source

1. **Gain Real-World Experience:** Open-source projects operate like professional software development environments. You get hands-on experience with real codebases, version control systems (like Git), code reviews, CI/CD workflows,

testing frameworks, and project management tools.

2. **Enhance Technical Skills:** When you contribute, you learn to read other people's code, understand architecture, debug issues, write clean code, and document your work. You'll also be exposed to best practices in software engineering.

3. **Build a Public Portfolio:** Your contributions are visible on platforms like GitHub. A well-maintained profile showing consistent contributions is a powerful addition to your resume and often more impressive than personal projects.

4. **Improve Soft Skills:** Communication is key in open source. You learn to discuss issues respectfully, ask good questions, explain your ideas clearly, and give and receive feedback all essential for working in any team environment.

5. **Network and Get Recognized:** You'll interact with developers from all over the world, including maintainers and contributors who may be industry veterans. This can open doors to mentorships, recommendations, internships, or even job offers.

6. **Make an Impact:** The code you write could be used by thousands or millions of users. Your small contribution might fix a critical bug, add a key feature, or improve the lives of developers worldwide.

How to Get Started with Open-source: Getting started might feel intimidating at first, but with the right approach, anyone can begin contributing, even without extensive experience.

1. **Set Up Your Tools:** Before contributing, make sure you're comfortable with:

    - **Git and GitHub:** Learn how to clone a repo, create branches, make commits, and open pull requests.

    - **Basic Terminal Commands:** Useful for navigating and managing code.

    - **Text Editor or IDE:** VS Code is a popular choice.

    If user is not familiar with these, free resources like freeCodeCamp, Codecademy, or GitHub Learning Lab can help.

2. **Find a Project:** Look for beginner-friendly projects or those that welcome new contributors. Use platforms like, GitHub Explore, Good First Issue, Up

For Grabs, First Timers Only and CodeTriage

Search GitHub issues labeled good first issue, help wanted, or beginner Focus on projects that align with your interests or tech stack (e.g., JavaScript, Python, machine learning, etc.).

3. **Understand the Project:** Once you find a potential project:
   - Read the **README.md** file to understand its purpose and usage.
   - Check the **CONTRIBUTING.md** file, which outlines how to contribute.
   - Look through **open issues** to see what kind of help is needed.
   - Try running the project locally and exploring how it works.

4. **Start Small:** You don't need to dive into complex bug fixes or feature development right away. Start with:
   - Fixing typos or grammar in documentation
   - Adding examples to the README
   - Writing or improving unit tests
   - Reproducing and documenting bugs
   - Refactoring simple code

   These tasks help you get familiar with the project and build trust with maintainers.

5. **Communicate with the Community:** Once you pick an issue:
   - Comment on it to indicate your interest
   - Ask questions if anything is unclear, but do your research first
   - Join the project's chat (Discord, Slack, Gitter, etc.) if available

     Good communication helps you get support and ensures you don't duplicate work.

6. **Make Your Contribution:** After making your changes:
   - Test your code thoroughly
   - Follow the project's code style and commit message conventions

- Write a clear Pull Request (PR) title and description
- Link it to the relevant issue (e.g., "Closes #42")

Be open to feedback. Maintainers may ask for changes this is part of the learning process.

Best Practices for Open-source Contributions:

Contributing to open-source projects is an enriching and rewarding experience that allows software developers to enhance their skills, collaborate with others, and give back to the community. However, like any collaborative endeavor, there are best practices that help ensure that your contributions are effective, professional, and beneficial for both you and the community. Below are best practices for contributing to open-source projects, organized into three main categories:

1. Preparation: Before contributing to any open-source project, invest time in preparation to set yourself up for a successful experience. Start by selecting a project that aligns with your interests, goals, and skill level. Platforms like GitHub and GitLab make it easy to explore projects; look for repositories with recent activity, clear documentation, and a welcoming tone.

Once you've identified a project, thoroughly read the documentation, especially the README, CONTRIBUTING guidelines, and CODE OF CONDUCT. These documents explain how the project is organized, what the maintainers expect from contributors, and how to behave within the community.

Set up the development environment on your local machine according to the project's setup instructions. Make sure you can build and run the code successfully, and don't skip the step of running existing tests—it's a crucial check that your setup is correct.

A smart strategy for beginners is to start small. Look for issues labeled as "good first issue" or "help wanted." These are often scoped to help new contributors get familiar with the codebase. Even small contributions like fixing typos, improving documentation, or updating dependencies are highly valuable. This early involvement helps you build confidence and familiarity, paving the way for more substantial contributions down the line.

Before diving in, set yourself up for success:

- **Choose the Right Project:** Look for projects that match your interests and skill level. Check for signs of project activity: recent commits, active issues, and responsive maintainers.

- **Understand the Project:** Read the README, CONTRIBUTING guide, and CODE OF CONDUCT. Explore the issue tracker to see common problems and developer discussions. Review the codebase structure and style.
- **Set Up Your Environment:** Fork and clone the repository. Follow setup instructions carefully to run the project locally. Run tests to ensure your environment is working properly.
- **Start Small:** Begin with documentation fixes, typo corrections, or minor bugs. Look for issues labeled "good first issue" or "help wanted."

2. Contribution Process: Once you're familiar with the project, it's time to start contributing. Always begin by creating a new branch from the main development branch (often main or develop). This isolates your changes and makes collaboration smoother.

Follow the project's coding standards and conventions closely. Consistency is key to maintainable software. Write clean, readable code, and include comments where necessary. Make sure your commit messages are clear and descriptive think of them as the history of your contribution. A good format often includes what was changed and why, such as "Fix: Handle edge case in date parser for leap years."

Test your changes thoroughly. This includes both automated tests and manual validation when applicable. If the project includes a test suite, run it and make sure all tests pass. If your changes add functionality or fix a bug, consider writing or updating relevant tests to cover the change.

When you're ready, open a pull request (PR). A well-crafted PR is focused and concise. Avoid bundling unrelated changes in the same PR. In your PR description, summarize the purpose of the change, link to any related issues, and explain the reasoning behind your approach.

After submission, be prepared to receive feedback. Maintainers may suggest improvements or request changes this is part of the collaborative process. Make revisions as needed and thank reviewers for their input. A well-handled PR not only improves the project but also builds your reputation as a thoughtful contributor.

Once you're ready to contribute, follow these steps:

- **Create a Branch:** Never work on the main branch; create a feature or fix-specific branch.

- **Write Clean, Maintainable Code:** Follow the project's coding standards. Write clear, concise commits with meaningful messages. Add or update unit tests where appropriate.

- **Test Thoroughly:** Ensure your changes don't break existing functionality. Run the full test suite and fix any issues.

- **Submit a Pull Request (PR):** Make sure your PR is focused one issue or feature per PR. Describe what you've done and why. Reference related issues (e.g., "Closes #123").

3. Communication: Strong communication is essential in open-source communities. Unlike workplace teams, contributors may be spread across the globe and work asynchronously. Clear, respectful communication helps foster collaboration and ensures your contributions are well-received.

Always follow the project's Code of Conduct, which sets the tone for acceptable behavior. Respect different perspectives and maintain a professional tone, especially during disagreements. Open-source thrives on diversity of thought and contribution, so inclusivity and empathy go a long way.

When you need help, do your homework first. Search through existing issues, discussion threads, and documentation before asking a question. When you do reach out, be concise and specific. Include details such as the steps you've taken, any error messages, and what you've already tried. This makes it easier for maintainers and other contributors to help you effectively.

During pull requests, respond promptly and positively to feedback. View reviews as opportunities to learn, not criticism. If you disagree with feedback, explain your perspective respectfully and be open to compromise. Beyond code, you can contribute by reviewing others' PRs, improving documentation, triaging issues, or mentoring new contributors. These non-code contributions are just as valuable and build trust in the community. Finally, stay engaged. Follow up on your contributions, thank reviewers, and continue participating where you can. Long-term contributors often become maintainers or community leaders. Effective communication not only improves your experience but also strengthens the entire project.

Effective communication builds trust and fosters collaboration:

- **Engage Respectfully:** Follow the project's Code of Conduct. Be respectful and constructive in all interactions.

- **Ask Smart Questions:** Before asking, search the issue tracker and documentation. Be specific: include error messages, what you've tried, and relevant context.
- **Respond to Feedback:** Be open to suggestions and ready to revise your PR. Respond promptly and professionally.
- **Stay Involved:** After your PR is merged, continue contributing. Help others by reviewing PRs or answering questions.

Freelancing vs. Full-Time Jobs

Freelancing and full-time employment offer distinct career paths, each with its own benefits and challenges. Freelancing provides flexibility and independence you choose your clients, set your own schedule, and often work remotely. It can be financially rewarding if you have a strong client base and in-demand skills. However, it comes with uncertainties: inconsistent income, no employer-provided benefits (like health insurance or paid leave), and the need to manage taxes, contracts, and self-promotion.

In contrast, full-time jobs offer stability, structured work hours, and employee benefits such as insurance, retirement plans, and paid time off. Your part of a team with clear responsibilities and often have access to training, mentorship, and career advancement opportunities. The trade-off is less autonomy; you work under supervision and may have less flexibility in choosing your projects or schedule.

Choosing between freelancing and full-time work depends on your personal goals, risk tolerance, financial situation, and preferred work style. Many professionals start in one and transition to the other as their priorities shift. Some even blend both by freelancing on the side. Ultimately, the "better" option varies by individual it's about finding the fit that aligns with your lifestyle and career aspirations.

Freelancing: Freelancing jobs in software engineering involve working independently on short-term or long-term projects for clients, rather than being employed full-time by a single company. These roles allow engineers to work on a wide range of projects, often remotely, and provide more control over work schedule, project selection, and income potential. Freelancing jobs offer developers the flexibility to work independently on a wide range of projects without being tied to a single employer. These roles can vary from short-term assignments like fixing bugs or building a website to long-term contracts involving full product development. Common freelance jobs include web and mobile app development, API integration, DevOps, cloud infrastructure setup, and data analytics. Developers often use languages and frameworks such as JavaScript, Python, React, Flutter, or Node.js, depending on the client's needs. The rise of remote work and the gig economy has made freelancing more accessible, with platforms like Upwork, Toptal, and Freelancer connecting engineers to clients worldwide. Freelancers can also find jobs through networking, personal websites, and open-source contributions.

While freelancing provides autonomy, it comes with challenges like inconsistent income, lack of benefits, and the need to manage all aspects of the business, including contracts, billing, and marketing. Success in freelance software engineering requires more than just technical skills—it also demands strong communication, time management, and problem-solving abilities. Building a strong portfolio, maintaining a professional online presence (e.g., GitHub and LinkedIn), and collecting client testimonials can significantly improve credibility and help secure high-quality gigs. Despite the challenges, many software engineers choose freelancing for the freedom it offers, the diversity of work, and the potential to earn more than in traditional roles. With the right mindset and preparation, freelancing can be a highly rewarding career path in software engineering.

Types of Freelance Software Engineering Jobs

1. **Web Development:** Web development involves building websites and web applications using front-end technologies like HTML, CSS, and JavaScript frameworks (e.g., React, Angular, Vue), along with back-end technologies such as Node.js, Django, Ruby on Rails, or PHP. Full-stack developers handle both. Web developers may work on everything from static landing pages to complex, interactive platforms like e-commerce sites or social networks. Freelancers in this space must understand responsive design, cross-browser compatibility, performance optimization, and accessibility standards. Many web developers also work with CMS platforms like WordPress or headless CMS solutions. Version control systems (like Git), deployment tools, and collaboration platforms are also essential. Web development is a high-demand area in freelancing due to the continuous need for businesses to maintain, build, or modernize their digital presence. Projects can range from quick updates to long-term development contracts, offering freelancers flexibility and opportunities to specialize or diversify their skills.

    - Front-end (HTML, CSS, JavaScript, React, Vue)
    - Back-end (Node.js, Django, Ruby on Rails, PHP)
    - Full-stack development

- E-commerce platforms (Shopify, WooCommerce)

2. **Mobile App Development:** Mobile app development focuses on creating software for smartphones and tablets, primarily for Android and iOS platforms. Developers may specialize in native app development using Swift (iOS) or Kotlin (Android), or they may use cross-platform tools like React Native, Flutter, or Xamarin to build apps that run on both systems from a single codebase. Freelance mobile developers work on a variety of projects, from simple utilities to full-featured consumer or enterprise apps. Key skills include UI/UX design, RESTful APIs integration, offline data handling, and app store deployment. Testing and performance optimization are critical to ensure apps run smoothly across devices and OS versions. As mobile usage continues to grow, businesses increasingly seek freelance developers to build new apps or maintain existing ones. Freelancers in this field benefit from staying current with platform updates, mobile security practices, and emerging trends such as wearable tech and mobile payments.

    - Android (Kotlin, Java)
    - iOS (Swift, Objective-C)
    - Cross-platform (React Native, Flutter)

3. **DevOps and Cloud Engineering:** DevOps and cloud engineering combine software development and IT operations to streamline the development lifecycle, automate workflows, and manage cloud infrastructure. Freelancers in this field often work with tools like Docker, Kubernetes, Jenkins, Terraform, and GitHub Actions, enabling continuous integration and deployment (CI/CD). They also manage cloud services on AWS, Google Cloud, or Azure, configuring scalable, secure, and cost-effective environments. Key responsibilities may include setting up CI pipelines, infrastructure as code, system monitoring, and performance tuning. Freelancers may be hired for migrations, automating deployment processes, or improving operational efficiency. Strong scripting skills (e.g., Bash, Python), security knowledge, and experience with version control are essential. DevOps is a rapidly growing area in freelancing due to the increasing demand for automation and cloud-native applications. Freelancers who excel in bridging development and infrastructure roles can find consistent opportunities across startups, mid-size businesses, and large enterprises transitioning to cloud-based architectures.

- CI/CD pipelines
- AWS, Azure, Google Cloud setup
- Infrastructure as code (Terraform, Ansible)

4. **Data and Machine Learning:** Freelancing in data and machine learning involves working with data to extract insights, build predictive models, and develop intelligent systems. Freelancers in this field may handle data preprocessing, visualization, statistical analysis, and machine learning model development using tools like Python, Pandas, NumPy, scikit-learn, TensorFlow, and PyTorch. Projects can include recommendation systems, sentiment analysis, fraud detection, or automation with AI. Freelancers are often hired to clean and analyze datasets, design dashboards, or develop prototypes for AI-powered features. Familiarity with databases (SQL, NoSQL), cloud platforms (e.g., AWS Sagemaker, Google AI), and data pipelines (e.g., Airflow) is important. Communication skills are also crucial, as clients often rely on freelancers to interpret technical results into business insights. With data becoming central to decision-making across industries, skilled freelance data scientists and ML engineers are in high demand for both short-term analysis and long-term AI product development.

   - Data analysis and visualization (Python, Pandas, Tableau)
   - Machine learning models (scikit-learn, TensorFlow, PyTorch)
   - Data engineering (ETL pipelines, big data)

5. **Custom Software and API Development:** Custom software and API development involve building tailored solutions to meet specific business needs, often when off-the-shelf software doesn't suffice. Freelancers in this space design and develop applications, internal tools, or integrations that align with a client's workflow and infrastructure. APIs (Application Programming Interfaces) are a major focus, allowing different systems to communicate; developers create RESTful or GraphQL APIs using technologies like Node.js, Express, Flask, or .NET. Custom software development may span desktop apps, backend services, or SaaS platforms, requiring expertise in architecture design, authentication, database management, and testing. Freelancers must also ensure scalability, performance, and security. Clients may seek help with legacy system modernization, business automation, or building MVPs for

startups. Because every business has unique processes, demand for custom solutions is constant. Successful freelancers in this field are those who combine strong technical execution with a clear understanding of the client's domain and goals.

- Building SaaS products
- Developing APIs and integrations
- Software modernization and refactoring

6. **Game Development:** Game development as a freelance role involves designing and building interactive games for platforms like PC, mobile, or web using engines such as Unity or Unreal Engine. Freelancers may be responsible for game logic, level design, 2D/3D asset integration, animation, physics, and user interface development. Programming is typically done in C# (for Unity) or C++ (for Unreal), and many also use scripting tools and custom engines. Freelance game developers might work on indie games, educational apps, advergames, or simulations. Some projects require collaboration with artists, sound designers, or writers, making communication and teamwork essential. Experience with version control, performance optimization, and cross-platform publishing is also valuable. Game development is a highly creative and technically demanding field, with fluctuating project lengths and budgets. For freelancers with both technical skills and a passion for storytelling or interactive media, this industry offers unique opportunities for creative expression and technical innovation.

   - Unity, Unreal Engine
   - 2D/3D game prototyping

Where to Find Freelance Jobs

1. **Freelance Platforms**: Upwork, Freelancer, Toptal, PeoplePerHour
2. **Developer Marketplaces**: Gun.io, Arc.dev, Lemon.io
3. **Job Boards**: We Work Remotely, Remote OK, Stack Overflow Jobs
4. **Direct Outreach**: Personal websites, LinkedIn, GitHub networking
5. **Open Source**: Contributing to OSS can lead to freelance offers

Full-Time Jobs: Full-time jobs in software engineering refer to permanent positions where software engineers work for an employer on a regular, ongoing basis, typically with set working hours (usually 40 hours a week). These positions involve designing, developing, and maintaining software applications, systems, or platforms across various industries such as tech, healthcare, finance, and entertainment.

In a full-time software engineering role, professionals are expected to contribute to the entire software development lifecycle, which includes tasks such as writing code, debugging, testing, and deploying applications. They may specialize in areas like web development, mobile app development, cloud computing, DevOps, data engineering, or game development. Full-time positions often provide a structured work environment with additional benefits like health insurance, paid time off, retirement plans, and professional development opportunities.

In contrast to freelance or contract work, full-time roles offer more job stability, regular income, and long-term career growth, making them ideal for those looking for job security and a more predictable work-life balance.

Below are some of the common full-time positions in software engineering:

1. **Software Developer / Engineer**: Software developers design, build, and maintain software applications. They write code, debug, test, and deploy software solutions in a variety of programming languages such as Java, Python, C++, and JavaScript. Developers can specialize in front-end, back-end, or full-stack development depending on their skills.

2. **Web Developer**: A web developer builds websites and web applications, handling both the front-end (client-side) and back-end (server-side) of a project. They often work with HTML, CSS, JavaScript, and frameworks like React, Angular, or Vue, alongside back-end technologies like Node.js, Ruby on Rails, or Django.

3. **Mobile App Developer**: Mobile app developers specialize in building applications for mobile devices such as smartphones and tablets. They create apps for iOS or Android using languages and frameworks like Swift, Kotlin, React Native, or Flutter.

4. **DevOps Engineer**: A DevOps engineer focuses on the development, deployment, and operational maintenance of software, often involving continuous integration (CI), continuous delivery (CD), and cloud infrastructure management. They work with tools like Docker, Kubernetes, Jenkins, and cloud platforms like AWS or Azure.

5. **Data Scientist / Engineer**: Data scientists analyze large datasets to extract insights and develop machine learning models. They work with statistical tools and programming languages such as Python, R, and SQL. Data engineers focus on building and maintaining the infrastructure for collecting, storing, and analyzing data at scale.

6. **Quality Assurance (QA) Engineer**: QA engineers ensure that software products meet high-quality standards before they are released. They develop and execute test plans, write automated tests, and report bugs to developers. Automation tools like Selenium, Appium, and TestNG are commonly used in this role.

7. **Systems Engineer**: Systems engineers work with hardware and software systems to ensure they function properly and meet organizational needs. This role often involves setting up and maintaining server environments, managing networking infrastructure, and overseeing system security.

8. **Cloud Engineer**: Cloud engineers focus on designing, developing, and maintaining cloud-based infrastructure and services. They work with cloud platforms like AWS, Google Cloud, or Microsoft Azure to create scalable, secure, and cost-effective solutions for businesses.

9. **Game Developer**: Game developers specialize in creating video games. They use game engines like Unity or Unreal Engine, programming languages like C# or C++, and tools for game design, animation, and interactivity. Full-time game developers often work for game studios on both mobile and console games.

10. **Software Architect**: Software architects design high-level structures for software systems. They determine the overall design, technology stack, and frameworks used in the application. They ensure that the software architecture aligns with business needs, scalability requirements, and best practices.

Table 5.2

S.No.	Aspect	Freelancing Jobs	Full-Time Jobs
1	Job Stability	Less stable, income can fluctuate month-to-month	More stable, consistent paycheck
2	Work Schedule	Flexible, choose your hours and workload	Fixed hours (typically 40 hours/week)
3	Benefits	No employer-provided benefits (e.g., health insurance, paid leave)	Employer-provided benefits (health insurance, paid time off, retirement plans)
4	Independence	High independence, choose clients and projects	Less independence, assigned tasks and projects
5	Career Growth	Limited formal career advancement, must manage your own growth	Clear career path with opportunities for promotions and professional development
6	Work Environment	Usually remote, can work from anywhere	Typically, office-based, though remote options exist
7	Financial Management	Responsible for taxes, invoices, and setting rates	Employer handles taxes and payroll
8	Security	No job security, contracts can end at any time	More job security with long-term employment
9	Skill Development	Can choose projects to enhance specific skills	Exposure to a variety of skills through company projects
10	Client Interaction	Direct communication with clients, managing relationships	Communication typically through managers or teams

Continuous Learning and Staying Updated

In the fast-paced world of software engineering, continuous learning is essential to stay relevant and competitive. New programming languages, frameworks, tools, and methodologies emerge regularly, making it crucial for engineers to keep up. Technologies like AI, cloud computing, and blockchain are transforming the industry, and professionals who stay updated are better positioned to innovate and solve modern problems effectively.

To stay current, developers can read tech blogs, subscribe to newsletters, follow GitHub repositories, and take online courses from platforms like Coursera, Udemy, or freeCodeCamp. Engaging in coding challenges on sites like LeetCode or HackerRank and contributing to open-source projects also help sharpen skills. Attending tech conferences, webinars, and local meetups provides exposure to real-world use cases and networking opportunities.

Continuous learning isn't just about picking up new skills it's also about unlearning outdated practices and improving problem-solving abilities. Setting clear goals and regularly practicing what you learn ensures steady progress. In a field where change is constant, embracing a growth mindset and prioritizing learning is what keeps software engineers both effective and future-ready.

Continuous Learning: Continuous learning in software engineering is not just a career advantage it's a necessity. Technology evolves rapidly, and what is cutting-edge today might be outdated tomorrow. Software engineers must stay current with emerging tools, languages, frameworks, and best practices to remain effective and competitive in the field. Adopting a mindset of lifelong learning is essential for professional growth, adaptability, and job satisfaction.

One of the key drivers behind the need for continuous learning is the fast pace of technological change. New programming languages like Rust or Go, evolving frameworks such as React and Next.js, and paradigm shifts like serverless architecture or containerization require engineers to constantly update their knowledge. The rise of artificial intelligence, machine learning, blockchain, and cloud-native development further accelerates the demand for new skills.

To keep up, software engineers must proactively seek learning opportunities. Online learning platforms such as Coursera, Udemy, edX, and Pluralsight offer structured courses on almost every technology stack. Free resources like freeCodeCamp, YouTube tutorials, and documentation sites are also valuable. These platforms allow engineers to learn at their own pace, explore specialized topics, and deepen their expertise in high-demand areas.

Practice-based learning is equally important. Working on side projects, contributing to open-source, or building clones of real-world applications helps solidify knowledge and improve problem-solving skills. Websites like GitHub, CodePen, and Dev.to are great places to share work, get feedback, and learn from others. Additionally, coding challenge platforms such as LeetCode, HackerRank, and Codewars help sharpen algorithmic thinking, which is critical for interviews and technical excellence.

Staying engaged with the tech community also plays a crucial role. Forums like Stack Overflow, Reddit's r/learnprogramming, and Discord developer communities offer support, insights, and real-world discussions. Attending meetups, webinars, and conferences—whether local or online—can expose engineers to emerging trends, new tools, and innovative approaches from industry leaders. Networking with peers and mentors can also inspire new learning paths and provide guidance.

Another aspect of continuous learning is unlearning outdated practices and being open to change. Software engineers must be willing to let go of legacy approaches when better solutions emerge. For example, moving from traditional monoliths to microservices or adopting modern DevOps practices may require rethinking long-held coding or deployment habits.

To make continuous learning sustainable, it's important to set clear goals and track progress. Engineers can create personal learning roadmaps, maintain reading lists, or keep a journal of what they've learned. Using tools like Notion, Trello, or simple notebooks can help organize resources and monitor achievements.

In conclusion, continuous learning in software engineering is the key to long-term success. It ensures that engineers remain adaptable, valuable, and prepared for the challenges of an ever-evolving industry. Whether it's through formal education, self-driven exploration, or collaborative learning, staying curious and committed to growth is what separates thriving engineers from stagnant ones. The most successful professionals aren't necessarily those who know everything but those who are always learning.

Key reasons why continuous learning is so important:

1. **Keeping Skills Up to Date**: Technology becomes obsolete quickly. Continuous learning helps engineers stay current with the latest developments, ensuring their skills match industry needs.

2. **Career Growth and Opportunities**: Learning new tools or specializations (like cloud computing, AI, or cybersecurity) opens doors to higher-paying jobs, leadership roles, and innovative projects.

3. **Improved Problem-Solving**: Exposure to new techniques and best practices enhances critical thinking and enables more efficient, scalable, and secure software solutions.

4. **Adaptability to Change**: Companies constantly adopt new tech. Engineers who continuously learn adapt quickly to new environments and tools, making them more valuable to employers.

5. **Increased Confidence and Motivation**: Gaining new knowledge boosts confidence and keeps work engaging, preventing burnout and stagnation.

6. **Better Collaboration**: Staying updated helps developers communicate more effectively with peers, understand emerging tools, and contribute meaningfully to team discussions.

Staying Updated : In the dynamic and ever-evolving field of software engineering, staying updated is not a luxury it is a necessity. As new programming languages, frameworks, tools, and technologies are introduced frequently, software engineers must keep pace to remain relevant, effective, and competitive. Failing to stay current can lead to outdated practices, reduced job opportunities, and missed chances to innovate.

One of the most important reasons for staying updated is the fast-paced nature of technology. What was considered best practice a few years ago may now be obsolete or inefficient. For example, modern web development has moved from jQuery-based scripting to sophisticated frameworks like React, Vue, and Angular. Similarly, infrastructure management has shifted from manual server setups to cloud-based, automated DevOps pipelines. Engineers who fail to follow these changes risk falling behind and becoming less valuable in the job market.

To stay updated, software engineers should adopt a proactive approach to learning. Subscribing to newsletters such as JavaScript Weekly, Python Weekly, or The Pragmatic Engineer helps deliver curated content and news directly to your inbox. Reading industry blogs, GitHub discussions, and technology websites like Hacker News, Medium, and Stack Overflow provides insights into trends, best practices, and developer experiences.

Following thought leaders and open-source contributors on platforms like Twitter, LinkedIn, and GitHub can also help you spot trends early. These professionals often share what they're working on, new tools they're exploring, and insights about emerging technologies. Being part of these online conversations keeps you informed and connected.

Attending conferences, webinars, and tech meetups whether in-person or virtual is another valuable way to stay updated. Events like Google I/O, Microsoft Build, or AWS reinvent showcase the latest in tools and platforms, often with hands-on demonstrations. These gatherings also provide networking opportunities and exposure to real-world use cases from other professionals.

Online learning platforms like Coursera, edX, Udemy, and Pluralsight offer in-depth courses on newly released tools, frameworks, and technologies. Many courses are updated regularly to reflect the latest practices, making them ideal for engineers seeking to refresh or expand their knowledge. For more hands-on experience, websites like freeCodeCamp and Codecademy provide interactive lessons on a wide range of topics.

In addition, working on side projects or contributing to open-source software can help apply what you've learned and keep your skills sharp. These projects often require learning new libraries, adapting to changing APIs, or integrating the latest tech stacks real-world learning that no tutorial can fully replicate.

It's also important to stay updated within your own organization. Many companies adopt new technologies or frameworks, and being involved in these transitions can be a great learning opportunity. Participating in internal training, code reviews, or architecture discussions can help you stay in tune with current and upcoming tools.

In conclusion, staying updated in software engineering is essential for long-term success and adaptability. It ensures you're prepared to face new challenges, contribute meaningfully to projects, and continue growing in a fast-moving industry. By building habits around continuous learning and tech awareness, you'll remain not only relevant but also a valuable, forward-thinking professional.

Key reasons why staying updated is important:

1. **Relevance in the Job Market**: Employers look for candidates who are familiar with current technologies. Keeping up with trends ensures your skills remain marketable and in demand.

2. **Better Problem-Solving**: New tools and frameworks often offer more efficient, scalable, or secure ways to solve problems. Staying updated helps you deliver better solutions.

3. **Career Advancement**: Learning and applying modern tech give you an edge for promotions, raises, and leadership opportunities.

4. **Adaptability**: As companies shift to new stacks (e.g., cloud-native, microservices), engineers who stay current can adapt quickly and lead transitions.

5. **Innovation and Creativity**: Exposure to new technologies inspires innovation. Staying informed helps you build smarter, more advanced applications.

6. **Collaboration and Communication**: Being aware of current trends allows you to speak the same language as your peers and contribute more meaningfully to technical discussions.

SUMMARY OF SOFTWARE PROJECT MANAGEMENT AND CAREER DEVELOPMENT

Software Project Management and Career Development are critical components in a successful software engineering journey. Effective project management ensures that software is delivered on time, within budget, and meets quality standards. Key areas include project planning, risk management, and the use of Agile tools like JIRA and Trello to streamline tasks and enhance team collaboration. Strong communication and leadership are essential for team success.

On the career side, software engineers must uphold ethics and professionalism, handle intellectual property responsibly, and support diversity and inclusion in tech. Building a strong career involves creating impactful resumes, preparing for technical interviews, and contributing to open-source projects. Understanding the differences between freelancing and full-time jobs helps in making informed career choices. Most importantly, continuous learning and staying updated with evolving technologies are vital for long-term growth and relevance in the field. Together, these elements shape a capable, ethical, and future-ready software professional.

12. Software Project Management

Effective software project management is crucial for delivering high-quality software products on time and within budget. It involves organizing tasks, managing resources, and ensuring that technical and business goals align throughout the software development lifecycle.

- **Project Planning and Estimation:** Planning and estimation are the foundation of any successful project. This includes defining project scope, identifying stakeholders, creating a detailed timeline, allocating resources, and estimating time and cost accurately. Common estimation techniques include Use Case Points, Function Point Analysis, and Agile story points. Good planning ensures predictability, minimizes waste, and sets realistic expectations for delivery.

- **Risk Management in Software Development:** Risks in software projects can include scope creep, underestimation, technical failures, or poor communication. Risk management involves identifying potential issues early, assessing their impact and likelihood, and planning mitigation strategies. Creating a risk register and conducting regular reviews allows teams to address threats proactively. Effective risk management helps avoid costly surprises and keeps projects on track.

- **Agile Project Management Tools (JIRA, Trello, etc.):** Agile development relies on iterative cycles and adaptive planning. Tools like JIRA, Trello, Asana, and ClickUp help teams manage backlogs, sprints, and workflows efficiently. JIRA, commonly used for Scrum and Kanban teams, allows developers to track issues, assign tasks, and measure velocity. Trello, known for its simplicity, uses boards and cards to visually organize tasks. These tools promote transparency, streamline project tracking, and support continuous improvement through metrics and feedback loops.

- **Team Collaboration and Communication:** Software development is a collaborative process involving developers, testers, designers, and stakeholders. Effective communication is key to avoiding misunderstandings, delays, and rework. Tools like Slack, Microsoft Teams, and Zoom facilitate real-time collaboration, while documentation platforms like Confluence and Notion help centralize information. Agile ceremonies such as daily stand-ups, retrospectives, and sprint planning meetings foster communication and team alignment. A culture of open feedback and knowledge sharing strengthens team morale and project success.

13. Ethics and Professionalism in Software Engineering

As software becomes central to everyday life, software engineers face growing ethical and social responsibilities. Ethical decision-making and professional conduct are essential to building trustworthy, inclusive, and secure systems.

- **Ethical Dilemmas in Software Development:** Software engineers often face complex ethical dilemmas, such as handling user data responsibly, managing algorithmic bias, or deciding whether to report security flaws. Questions around privacy, automation impacts, and user manipulation must be addressed with integrity. Organizations should have clear ethical guidelines, but engineers must also rely on their personal values and principles. The ACM Code of Ethics and the IEEE Software Engineering Code of Ethics offer frameworks for ethical decision-making in the profession.

- **Open-source and Intellectual Property:** Open-source development fosters collaboration and innovation, but it also raises legal and ethical concerns regarding intellectual property (IP). Engineers must understand licensing models such as MIT, GPL, and Apache to respect usage rights and avoid legal violations. Using open-source responsibly means giving proper attribution, avoiding license conflicts, and contributing back when possible. Ethical engineers should also avoid plagiarism, code theft, and IP misuse, whether using others' code or safeguarding proprietary solutions.

- **Diversity and Inclusion in Tech:** A diverse and inclusive tech workforce leads to better innovation and fairer outcomes. However, systemic barriers such as bias in hiring, lack of representation, and toxic work cultures still exist. Engineers should actively support inclusive practices, such as writing accessible code, using gender-neutral language, and advocating for equitable hiring. Promoting mentorship, inclusive leadership, and open conversations about discrimination and bias helps foster a respectful and welcoming tech environment for everyone.

14. Building a Successful Career in Software Engineering

Career development in software engineering extends beyond technical skills. It includes building a personal brand, navigating different types of employment, and committing to lifelong learning.

- **Resume Building and Technical Interviews:** A strong resume highlights relevant experience, projects, education, and technical skills in a clear and concise format. Tailoring the resume to each job and quantifying achievements (e.g., "Reduced load time by 40%") can make a big impact. Technical interviews typically involve coding challenges, system design problems, and behavioral questions. Preparing through mock interviews, studying data structures and algorithms, and practicing on platforms like LeetCode, HackerRank, or Interviewing.io helps candidates succeed. Showcasing clear communication, problem-solving approaches, and coding efficiency is as important as getting the correct solution.

- **Contributing to Open-source Projects:** Open-source contributions are a great way to gain experience, build a portfolio, and collaborate with developers around the world. Beginners can start by fixing bugs, improving documentation, or writing tests. Platforms like GitHub and GitLab host thousands of open projects across various domains. Contributing teaches best practices like version control, code reviews, and issue tracking, while also helping engineers build a professional network and gain recognition in the community.

- **Freelancing vs. Full-Time Jobs:** Both freelancing and full-time employment offer unique pros and cons. **Freelancing** provides flexibility, the ability to choose projects, and often higher short-term earnings. However, it comes with income instability, no employee benefits, and the responsibility of managing contracts, taxes, and marketing. Full-time jobs offer job security, a steady income, benefits, and structured growth. Employees often receive mentorship, training, and a chance to work on large-scale systems. Choosing between the two depends on personal goals, lifestyle preferences, and risk tolerance.

- **Continuous Learning and Staying Updated:** In a field as dynamic as software engineering, continuous learning is essential. Engineers must keep up with new tools, frameworks, languages, and methodologies to stay competitive.

This can be achieved through online courses (Coursera, Udemy), reading blogs and documentation, attending conferences, and engaging with the developer community on platforms like Stack Overflow, Reddit, and Twitter. Working on personal projects, contributing to open-source, and setting learning goals all support lifelong development. Continuous learning not only sharpens technical skills but also improves problem-solving, adaptability, and career resilience in a fast-changing tech landscape.

******

Appendix

Case Studies of Successful Software Projects

Case Study 1: Spotify – Revolutionizing Music Streaming

Introduction

Spotify, launched in 2008 by Daniel Ek and Martin Lorentzon, transformed the music industry by introducing a streaming service that provided users with access to a vast library of music on demand. The company began in Sweden, offering a legal alternative to pirated music. Today, Spotify is one of the largest music streaming platforms globally, boasting over 400 million active users. The success of Spotify is a result of its ability to scale rapidly, adopt innovative technologies, and constantly enhance its user experience.

Key Success Factors

1. **Scalability and Infrastructure:** One of the main challenges Spotify faced in its early stages was building a platform that could handle an increasing number of users and vast amounts of data. Spotify achieved this by adopting a cloud-based architecture that could scale as the user base grew. It partnered with Google Cloud and Amazon Web Services (AWS) to store data, ensuring flexibility and reliability. The platform used a distributed architecture, allowing Spotify to serve millions of users simultaneously while maintaining fast load times and high availability.

   As Spotify expanded its reach, the engineering team focused on improving server infrastructure, database management, and network optimization. The platform leverages microservices to handle specific tasks like search, recommendations, and payment processing independently. This separation allows for easier scaling and faster deployment of new features.

2. **Data-driven Personalization:** Data is at the core of Spotify's success. The platform collects vast amounts of user data, including listening habits, song preferences, search history, and playlist creation. Spotify uses this data to power

its recommendation algorithms and create personalized playlists like "Discover Weekly" and "Release Radar". These playlists are generated based on a mix of user preferences, listening patterns, and machine learning models.

The recommendation engine, powered by collaborative filtering and natural language processing (NLP), plays a crucial role in keeping users engaged. The more a user listens to songs, the better the recommendations become. This data-driven approach ensures that users always have fresh content to explore, increasing user retention and engagement.

3. **Agile Development and Continuous Deployment:** Spotify adopted Agile methodologies to maintain flexibility in its development processes. The company uses Scrum and Kanban frameworks to manage its software development life cycle. Teams work in two-week sprints, releasing updates and improvements frequently. This approach enables the team to quickly iterate on user feedback and introduce new features to keep the platform competitive.

   Spotify also uses continuous integration and continuous deployment (CI/CD) pipelines, which allow new code to be integrated and deployed rapidly with minimal downtime. This focus on rapid iteration and short release cycles has helped the company stay ahead of its competitors.

4. **User-Centric Design and Experience:** Spotify places a strong emphasis on user experience (UX). The design team works closely with engineers to ensure that the platform is intuitive and easy to navigate. Features such as offline listening, playlist sharing, and social integration have been added to improve the overall experience. The user interface (UI) is consistent across multiple devices whether on a smartphone, desktop, or smart speaker ensuring that users can seamlessly switch between devices.

   The Spotify app is designed to reduce friction, with fast-loading pages, clear navigation, and an intuitive search function. Personalization is central to Spotify's UX, with a "home" page that highlights curated playlists, new releases, and recommended content based on the user's listening history.

5. **Innovative Business Model and Licensing:** Spotify's freemium business model has been a significant driver of its success. Users can choose between the free, ad-supported version or the premium subscription that removes ads and provides additional features. This model allows Spotify to attract a large user base, including those who prefer not to pay for music streaming. It also provides an ongoing revenue stream that supports the platform's growth.

On the back end, Spotify negotiated licensing deals with major music labels and independent artists, ensuring a wide selection of music available on the platform. Spotify has faced challenges with music royalties, but its focus on expanding its user base has led to substantial growth in its ability to negotiate better deals with content creators and music labels.

6. **Global Expansion and Market Penetration:** Spotify initially launched in Sweden but quickly expanded into other European markets, the United States, and eventually worldwide. The company's global expansion strategy involved localized content and region-specific partnerships. Spotify tailored its offerings to different regions, considering local music preferences and partnerships with local artists.

   One of the most significant challenges Spotify faced in its global expansion was adapting to local licensing laws and regulations. However, Spotify's ability to navigate these challenges and create partnerships in diverse markets has been one of the keys to its international success.

Outcome and Impact

Spotify has become a leader in the music streaming industry, surpassing traditional music distribution methods like CDs and downloads. It revolutionized the way people consume music by providing an affordable, convenient, and legal way to access millions of songs. Spotify's ability to build a scalable platform, leverage data for personalization, and continuously improve the user experience has made it a household name in the music industry. The company continues to innovate with features like Spotify for Artists, podcast integration, and AI-driven content creation, cementing its place as a pioneer in the world of streaming.

Case Study 2: Tesla – Revolutionizing the Automotive Industry with Software

Introduction

Tesla, founded in 2003 by Martin Eberhard and Marc Tarpenning and later led by Elon Musk, is renowned for revolutionizing the electric vehicle (EV) industry. However, Tesla is not only about hardware—its software innovations have played a key role in setting it apart from traditional automakers. From its Autopilot system to the over-the-air (OTA) software updates, Tesla's ability to innovate through software has been critical to its success.

Key Success Factors

1. **Autonomous Driving – Tesla Autopilot:** Tesla's Autopilot system is one of the most advanced and controversial software innovations in the automotive

industry. Autopilot utilizes a combination of camera sensors, radars, and machine learning algorithms to enable semi-autonomous driving. Tesla cars are equipped with hardware capable of full self-driving (FSD), with the software being continuously refined through OTA updates. Tesla's machine learning models are trained using data from the Tesla fleet on the road, which provides a continuous learning loop. This vast dataset allows Tesla to improve the algorithms and offer more reliable and safer features. Tesla FSD Beta, an advanced version of Autopilot, enables features like automated lane changes, automatic parking, and navigate on autopilot, which have been progressively improved through software updates.

2. **Over-the-Air (OTA) Software Updates:** Tesla's OTA updates have allowed the company to continuously improve its vehicles without requiring drivers to visit service centers. This has been a game-changer in the automotive industry, which traditionally relies on physical upgrades or recalls to address issues.

   Tesla has implemented numerous enhancements to its vehicles via OTA updates, such as better battery management, improved navigation, and upgraded Autopilot capabilities. These updates are seamless, and owners are notified automatically, with the car receiving the update in the background. This ability to continuously improve and enhance the car's performance without physical intervention has been one of Tesla's biggest differentiators.

3. **Software-Driven Car Experience:** Tesla's in-car infotainment system is a key part of the software-driven experience. The system, which is built on Linux, includes a large touchscreen interface that controls everything from navigation to media, climate control, and car settings. Tesla's software integrates all aspects of the driving experience into one system, and the user interface is regularly improved through OTA updates.

   The car's navigation system also uses real-time data, such as traffic information, to suggest routes and optimize energy consumption for the electric battery. This integration of hardware and software is central to Tesla's strategy, offering a unique driving experience that is continuously enhanced.

4. **Data Collection and Machine Learning:** Tesla collects vast amounts of data from its vehicles in real-time. This data includes driving patterns, sensor data, and usage information, which is sent back to Tesla's cloud servers. The company uses this data to improve software and hardware, test new features, and enhance the overall driving experience.

Tesla's focus on data-driven decision-making enables the company to fine-tune its algorithms and improve the performance of the vehicles over time. By leveraging real-world data, Tesla ensures that its software is not only cutting-edge but also relevant to the everyday needs of drivers.

5. **Integration with Energy Products:** Tesla's software strategy extends beyond just cars it also includes energy solutions. The Tesla Powerwall and Solar Roof products are also driven by sophisticated software systems that manage energy storage and optimize energy use. Tesla's energy software integrates with its cars to provide a holistic approach to sustainable living, where energy production, storage, and consumption are all controlled through a single system.

Outcome and Impact

Tesla has become a global leader in the electric vehicle market, with its software innovations being at the core of its success. The company's ability to continuously improve its vehicles through over-the-air updates, create autonomous driving technologies, and integrate software with hardware has set it apart from traditional car manufacturers. Tesla has not only disrupted the automotive industry but has also influenced the broader tech and energy sectors. The company's software-driven approach has redefined how cars are built, sold, and maintained, paving the way for the future of transportation.

******

Bibliography

ACM. (2022). *ACM Transactions on Software Engineering and Methodology (TOSEM)*. https://dl.acm.org/journal/tosem

ACM. (2022). *Communications of the ACM*. https://cacm.acm.org/

Ambler, S. W. (2012). *Disciplined Agile Delivery: A Practitioner's Guide to Agile Software Delivery in the Enterprise*. IBM Press.

Bass, L., Clements, P., & Kazman, R. (2012). *Software Architecture in Practice* (3rd ed.). Addison-Wesley.

Beck, K. (2002). *Test-Driven Development: By Example*. Addison-Wesley.

Bell, D. (2000). *Software Engineering: A Programming Approach*. Addison-Wesley.

Ben-Ari, M. (2006). *Principles of Concurrent and Distributed Programming* (2nd ed.). Addison-Wesley.

Booch, G., Rumbaugh, J., & Jacobson, I. (2005). *The Unified Modeling Language User Guide* (2nd ed.). Addison-Wesley.

Brooks, F. P. (1995). *The Mythical Man-Month: Essays on Software Engineering* (Anniversary ed.). Addison-Wesley.

Buschmann, F., Henney, K., & Schmidt, D. C. (2007). *Pattern-Oriented Software Architecture, Volume 5: On Patterns and Pattern Languages*. Wiley.

Cohn, M. (2004). *User Stories Applied: For Agile Software Development*. Addison-Wesley.

Cohn, M. (2009). *Succeeding with Agile: Software Development Using Scrum*. Addison-Wesley.

Davis, A. M. (2005). *Just Enough Requirements Management: Where Software Development Meets Marketing*. Dorset House.

DeMarco, T., & Lister, T. (2013). *Peopleware: Productive Projects and Teams* (3rd ed.). Addison-Wesley.

Dijkstra, E. W. (1976). *A Discipline of Programming*. Prentice Hall.

Dorr, B., & Sloane, A. (2021). *Software Engineering for Science*. CRC Press.

Eckel, B. (2006). *Thinking in Java* (4th ed.). Prentice Hall.

Elsevier. (2023). *Journal of Systems and Software*.

Fowler, M. (2003). *Patterns of Enterprise Application Architecture*. Addison-Wesley.

Fowler, M. (2010). *Refactoring: Improving the Design of Existing Code* (2nd ed.). Addison-Wesley.

Freeman, E., & Robson, E. (2020). *Head First Design Patterns* (2nd ed.). O'Reilly Media.

Gamma, E., Helm, R., Johnson, R., & Vlissides, J. (1994). *Design Patterns: Elements of Reusable Object-Oriented Software*. Addison-Wesley.

Glinz, M. (2020). *Requirements Engineering: Fundamentals, Principles, and Techniques*. Springer.

Goerzen, J. (2005). *Foundations of Agile Python Development*. Apress.

Hughes, B., & Cotterell, M. (2010). *Software Project Management* (5th ed.). McGraw-Hill Education.

Humphrey, W. S. (1995). *A Discipline for Software Engineering*. Addison-Wesley.

IEEE. (2014). *IEEE Guide to the Software Engineering Body of Knowledge (SWEBOK V3.0)*. IEEE Computer Society.

IEEE. (2020). *IEEE Transactions on Software Engineering*.

Jacobson, I., Booch, G., & Rumbaugh, J. (1999). *The Unified Software Development Process*. Addison-Wesley.

Jalote, P. (2005). *An Integrated Approach to Software Engineering* (3rd ed.). Springer.

Kan, S. H. (2002). *Metrics and Models in Software Quality Engineering* (2nd ed.). Addison-Wesley.

Kim, G., Behr, K., & Spafford, G. (2016). *The Phoenix Project: A Novel About IT, DevOps, and Helping Your Business Win*. IT Revolution.

Kim, G., Debois, P., Willis, J., & Humble, J. (2016). *The DevOps Handbook*. IT Revolution.

Kruchten, P. (2004). *The Rational Unified Process: An Introduction* (3rd ed.). Addison-Wesley.

Larman, C. (2004). *Agile and Iterative Development: A Manager's Guide*. Addison-Wesley.

Leach, L. P. (2005). *Critical Chain Project Management* (2nd ed.). Artech House.

MacCormack, A., Kemerer, C., Cusumano, M., & Crandall, B. (2003). *Exploring Quality in Open Source Software Projects: A Multiple-Case Study*. IEEE Software.

Martin, R. C. (2008). *Clean Code: A Handbook of Agile Software Craftsmanship*. Prentice Hall.

Martin, R. C. (2011). *The Clean Coder: A Code of Conduct for Professional Programmers*. Prentice Hall.

Martin, R. C. (2018). *Clean Architecture: A Craftsman's Guide to Software Structure and Design*. Prentice Hall.

McConnell, S. (1996). *Rapid Development: Taming Wild Software Schedules*. Microsoft Press.

McConnell, S. (2004). *Code Complete* (2nd ed.). Microsoft Press.

MDPI. (2023). *Information – Software Engineering Section*.

Meyer, B. (1997). *Object-Oriented Software Construction* (2nd ed.). Prentice Hall.

Newman, S. (2021). *Building Microservices* (2nd ed.). O'Reilly Media.

Nielsen, J. (1993). *Usability Engineering*. Morgan Kaufmann.

O'Reilly Media. (2022). *Software Engineering Daily*.

PLOS. (2023). *PLOS ONE – Software Engineering*.

Pressman, R. S. (2014). *Software Engineering: A Practitioner's Approach* (8th ed.). McGraw-Hill Education.

Royce, W. (1970). *Managing the Development of Large Software Systems*. IEEE WESCON.

Sommerville, I. (2016). *Software Engineering* (10th ed.). Pearson Education.

Sommerville, I. (2020). *Engineering Software Products: An Introduction to Modern Software Engineering*. Pearson.

Spinellis, D. (2006). *Code Reading: The Open Source Perspective*. Addison-Wesley.

Spinellis, D. (2012). *The Elements of Computing Systems*. MIT Press.

Springer. (2023). *Empirical Software Engineering*.

Springer. (2023). *Software and Systems Modeling*.

Stevens, R. (2001). *Systems Engineering: Coping with Complexity*. Prentice Hall.

Tanenbaum, A. S., & Van Steen, M. (2007). *Distributed Systems: Principles and Paradigms*. Prentice Hall.

Taylor & Francis. (2023). *Journal of Software: Evolution and Process*.

Taylor, R. N., Medvidovic, N., & Dashofy, E. M. (2009). *Software Architecture: Foundations, Theory, and Practice*. Wiley.

Thomas, D., & Hunt, A. (2019). *The Pragmatic Programmer* (20th Anniversary ed.). Addison-Wesley.

Tilley, S. R., & Huang, S. (2016). *Software Testing and Quality Assurance: Theory and Practice*. Wiley.

Tomayko, J. E. (1986). *Software Engineering: An Applied Approach*. Science Press.

van Vliet, H. (2008). *Software Engineering: Principles and Practice* (3rd ed.). Wiley.

Wazlawick, R. S. (2014). *Object-Oriented Analysis and Design for Information Systems: Modeling with UML, OCL, and IFML*. Morgan Kaufmann.

Wiegers, K., & Beatty, J. (2013). *Software Requirements* (3rd ed.). Microsoft Press.

Wiley. (2023). *Concurrency and Computation: Practice and Experience*.

Wolff, J. (2021). *Secure Coding: Principles and Practices*. Wiley.

Younas, M., & Awan, I. (2019). *Software Performance and Scalability*. Springer.

Zelkowitz, M. V. (2009). *Advances in Computers: Software Engineering and Development*. Academic Press.

Index

A

Actionable 77, 197, 204, 304
Adequately 213
Applicable 37, 98, 341
Automotive Industry 363
Automotive Industry 363
Availability
35, 48, 72, 122, 123, 153, 181, 196, 202, 223, 224, 225, 231, 232, 234, 235, 237, 241, 242, 246, 248, 282, 290, 322, 336, 361

C

Centralize Information 308, 356
Collaboration
5, 6, 9, 11, 13, 14, 27, 28, 30, 33, 36, 37, 39, 41, 42, 43, 44, 48, 54, 55, 56, 58, 59, 63, 74, 95, 97, 99, 100, 109, 111, 117, 132, 133, 136, 138, 139, 140, 144, 145, 148, 149, 150, 151, 153, 172, 177, 179, 180, 184, 188, 189, 191, 199, 249, 250, 264, 287, 292, 298, 299, 300, 301, 302, 303, 304, 305, 306, 307, 308, 309, 311, 316, 317, 318, 319, 320, 325, 327, 332, 333, 337, 341, 342, 343, 344, 347, 353, 355, 356, 372, 375
Collaborative
28, 30, 37, 39, 41, 43, 65, 71, 72, 74, 100, 107, 138, 143, 144,
145, 150, 153, 253, 267, 291, 292, 308, 309, 317, 318, 331, 340, 342, 352, 356, 361
Communication
6, 11, 13, 32, 33, 35, 36, 38, 39, 41, 55, 57, 58, 59, 65, 66, 70, 71, 74, 76, 79, 80, 84, 89, 94, 95, 97, 98, 99, 107, 109, 110, 111, 138, 144, 149, 160, 167, 169, 172, 177, 178, 199, 204, 211, 216, 217, 218, 222, 227, 246, 247, 258, 268, 271, 272, 273, 274, 276, 277, 283, 287, 288, 289, 292, 296, 297, 300, 301, 303, 304, 306, 307, 308, 309, 313, 331, 333, 335, 336, 337, 338, 340, 342, 343, 344, 346, 347, 355, 356, 357, 365, 375
Comprehensive
5, 25, 32, 46, 69, 70, 74, 76, 107, 150, 166, 182, 184, 197, 201, 204, 230, 298, 308, 371
Consumption
200, 226, 229, 230, 231, 234, 235, 273, 277, 279, 283
Corporate Governance 298

D

Deployment
4, 10, 14, 17, 23, 25, 27, 40, 41, 42, 43, 44, 45, 46, 47, 56, 57, 58, 59, 68, 72, 83, 84, 108, 111, 148, 149, 150, 151, 152, 153, 183, 193, 194, 200, 201, 204, 224, 228, 232, 245, 246, 247, 248, 249, 250, 251, 253, 257, 264, 265, 268, 277, 278, 282, 283, 344, 345, 346, 349, 352, 361, 373
Dissemination 323
Documentation
11, 12, 25, 31, 32, 33, 52, 57, 63, 70, 72, 74, 76, 77, 79, 80, 82, 99, 107, 111, 132, 134, 136, 138, 139, 140, 144, 148, 149, 150, 152, 165, 176, 180, 188, 199, 286, 292, 308, 311, 312, 319, 339, 340, 341, 342, 343, 351, 356, 357, 359, 372, 374

F

Feasible 71, 73, 264, 283
Flexibility
8, 9, 25, 27, 29, 32, 34, 36, 48, 49, 54, 56, 58, 59, 77, 82, 83, 84, 85, 89, 91, 92, 94, 103, 104, 109, 124, 128, 129, 130, 146, 151, 153, 177, 187, 191, 232, 241, 242, 243, 244, 245, 246, 252, 264, 282, 299, 300, 305, 306, 318, 320, 343, 344, 345, 359, 361
Fundamental
1, 7, 39, 55, 63, 76, 79, 80, 113, 185, 193, 198, 202, 211, 214, 223, 235, 255, 259, 261, 275, 289, 291, 333, 335, 337, 339, 366

G

Gathering Technique 69, 107, 373
Gathering Technique 69, 71

I

Implementation
17, 19, 20, 23, 25, 50, 52, 53, 54, 55, 58, 66, 67, 74, 79, 80, 81, 87, 89, 90, 92, 93, 100, 102, 117, 126, 177, 180, 181, 197, 198, 211, 214, 227, 252, 264, 265, 283, 295, 298
Inconsistent Income 343, 344
Infrastructure
7, 13, 36, 45, 85, 86, 87, 96, 97, 109, 124, 151, 152, 172, 201, 207, 215, 228, 235, 241, 245, 246, 247, 249, 250, 255, 258, 272, 273, 278, 319, 338, 344, 345, 346, 347, 349, 353, 360, 361

L

Lack of Benefits 344
Leadership
39, 122, 287, 288, 297, 298, 324, 325, 328, 336, 337, 352, 354, 355, 357
Low dependency 102

M

Modularization 110, 187, 188
Mutable Data 119, 120, 186

N

Necessary
6, 7, 15, 16, 20, 29, 31, 43, 50, 51, 53, 74, 97, 117, 134, 137, 139, 145, 161, 174, 177, 181, 188, 199, 201, 202, 203, 206, 207, 209, 211, 212, 214, 221, 223, 227, 230, 236, 240, 247, 264, 272, 289, 290, 291, 295, 341

O

Ornamentation 322
Ownership and Trust 72

P

Proprietary 317, 318, 357
Pseudonymization 211, 214

R

Representation
15, 22, 100, 301, 303, 304, 306, 324, 325, 327, 357
Responsibly
215, 256, 281, 311, 355, 356, 357

S

Sensitive Information
135, 138, 203, 206, 208, 211, 215
Simultaneously
52, 150, 215, 223, 240, 260, 275, 291, 303, 305, 361
Skilled Facilitation 72
Software Development
3, 4, 10, 15, 18, 48, 53, 54, 55, 56, 58, 125, 195, 212, 260, 264, 277, 279, 282, 293, 314, 316, 330, 355, 356, 365, 366, 371, 372, 373, 375
Sports leagues 322

T

Technology
5, 7, 10, 13, 24, 52, 64, 106, 129, 191, 225, 244, 245, 253, 257, 264, 268, 270, 275, 282, 283, 292, 313, 316, 326, 328, 350, 351, 352, 353
Traffic Information 363

U

Underestimation 290, 355

V

Visualization Tools 304, 305

W

Wide Range
127, 145, 201, 299, 325, 327, 344, 354